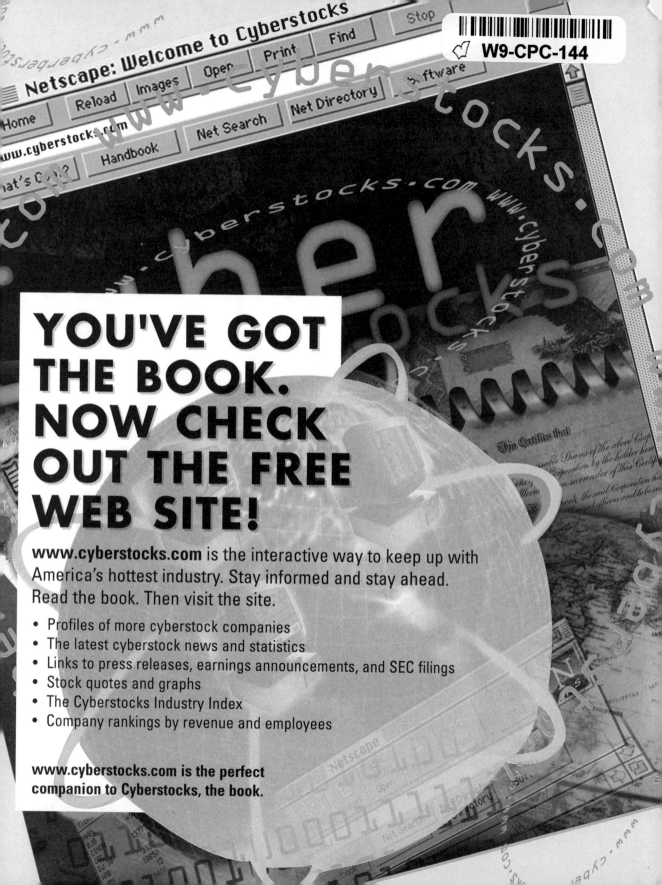

Cyberstocks

An Investor's Guide
to Internet Companies

EDITED BY ALAN CHAI

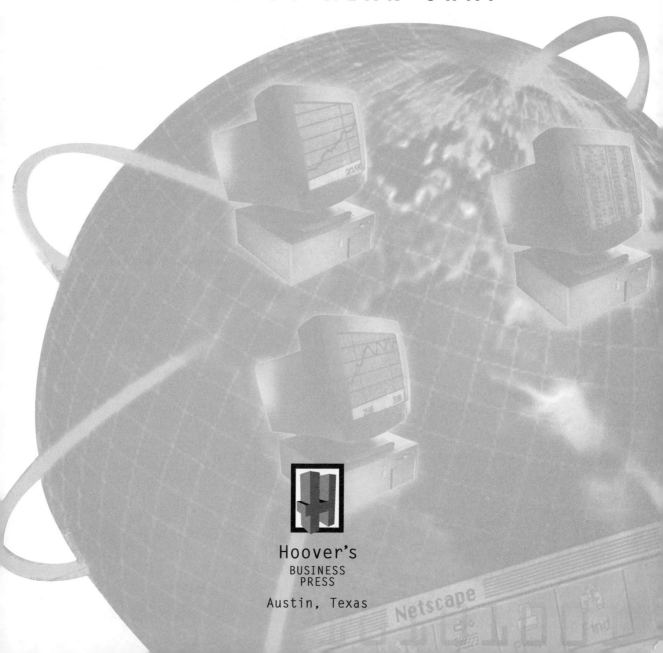

Hoover's
BUSINESS
PRESS

Austin, Texas

Cyberstocks: An Investor's Guide to Internet Companies is intended to provide its readers with accurate and authoritative information about the enterprises covered in it. Hoover's asked all companies and organizations profiled to provide information for the book. The information contained herein is as accurate as we could reasonably make it. In many cases we have relied on third-party material that we believe to be trustworthy, but were unable to independently verify. We do not warrant that the book is absolutely accurate or without error. Readers should not rely on any information contained herein in instances where such reliance might cause loss or damage. The publisher, the editors, and their data suppliers specifically disclaim all warranties, including the implied warranties of merchantability and fitness for a specific purpose. This book is sold with the understanding that neither the publisher, the editors, nor any content contributors are engaged in providing investment, financial, accounting, legal, or other professional advice.

The financial data in this book are from a variety of sources. Media General Financial Services, Inc., provided selected financial data for publicly traded companies. For historical information on public companies prior to their becoming public, we obtained information directly from the companies or from trade sources deemed to be reliable. Hoover's, Inc., is solely responsible for the presentation of all data.

Many of the names of products and services mentioned in this book are the trademarks or service marks of the companies manufacturing or selling them and are subject to protection under US law. Space has not permitted us to indicate which names are subject to such protection, and readers are advised to consult with the owners of such marks regarding their use. Hoover's is a trademark of Hoover's, Inc.

 Hoover's
BUSINESS PRESS

10 9 8 7 6 5 4 3 2 1

Company information and profiles from the *Hoover's* series of handbooks, guides, and directories are also available on America Online, Baseline, Bloomberg Financial Network, CompuServe, LEXIS-NEXIS, Microsoft Network, Reuters NewMedia, and on the Internet at Hoover's Online (www.hoovers.com), CNNfn (www.cnnfn.com), Farcast (www.farcast.com), IBM InfoMarket (www.infomkt.ibm.com), InfoSeek (www.infoseek.com), IBM Infosage (www.infosage.ibm.com), Pathfinder (www.pathfinder.com), PAWWS (www.pawws.com), Wall Street Journal Interactive (www.wsj.com), The Washington Post (www.washingtonpost.com), and others.

A catalog of Hoover's products is available on the World Wide Web (www.hoovers.com).

ISBN 1-57311-011-6

This book was produced by Hoover's Business Press using Claris Corporation's FileMaker Pro 3.0, Quark, Inc.'s Quark XPress 3.32, EM Software, Inc.'s Xdata 2.5, and fonts from Adobe's Stone Serif and Univers families. Cover design is by Design Island, Austin, Texas. Electronic prepress and printing were done by Custom Printing Company at its Frederick, Maryland plant. Text paper is 60# Postmark White.

US AND WORLD DIRECT SALES
Hoover's, Inc.
1033 La Posada Drive, Suite 250
Austin, TX 78752
Phone: 512-374-4500
Fax: 512-374-4501
email: info@hoovers.com

US BOOKSELLERS AND JOBBERS
Little Brown and Co.
200 West Street
Waltham, MA 02154
Phone: 800-759-0190
Fax: 617-890-0875

US WHOLESALER ORDERS
Warner Publisher Services
Book Division
9210 King Palm Drive
Tampa, FL 33619
Phone: 800-873-BOOK
Fax: 813-664-8193

EUROPE
William Snyder Publishing Associates
5, Five Mile Drive
Oxford OX2 8HT
England
Phone & fax: +44-186-551-3186

www·cyberstocks·com

HOOVER'S, INC.

Founder: Gary Hoover
Chairman, President, CEO, and Publisher: Patrick J. Spain

Senior Managing Editor — Production: George Sutton
Senior Managing Editor — Editorial: James R. Talbot
Senior Contributing Editor: Alan Chai
Senior Editor: Thomas Trotter
Editors: Chris Barton, Paul Mitchell, Anthony Shuga
Associate Editor: William Cargill
Editorial Coordinator: Ken Little
Assistant Editorial Coordinator: Melanie Lea Hall
Research Manager: Sherri M. Hale
Desktop Publishing Manager: Christina Thiele
Senior Researchers: Sarah Hallman, Jim Harris, Brian Pedder, David Ramirez
Researchers: Lynn Monnat, Patricia Pepin
Research Assistants: Leslie Navarro, Erica Taylor
Senior Writers: Joy Aiken, Stuart Hampton, Diane Lee, Barbara M. Spain, Jeffrey A. Twining
Financial Editor: Dennis L. Sutton
Copyeditors: Patrice Sarath, John Willis
Fact Checkers/Proofreaders: Michael G. Laster, Elizabeth Gagne Morgan, Marianne Tatom
Database Editors: Tweed Chouinard, Yvonne A. Cullinan, Karen Hill, Britton E. Jackson
Desktop Publishers: Trey Colvin, Michelle de Ybarrondo, Kevin Dodds, JoAnn Estrada, Gregory Gosdin, Elena Hernandez, Holly Hans Jackson, Louanne Jones
Database Entry: Eldridge N. Goins, Ismael Hernandez Jr., Danny Macaluso, Scott A. Smith

Director, Hoover's Online: Matt Manning
Senior Brand Manager: Leslie A. Wolke
Online Production Manager: Richard Finley
Online Content Editor: Martha DeGrasse
Online Editors: Kay Nichols, Perrin Patterson
Electronic Media Producers: Chuck Green, Rick Navarro

Senior Vice President, Sales and Marketing: Dana L. Smith
Vice President, Electronic Publishing: Tom Linehan
VP Finance and Administration and CFO (HR): Lynn Atchison
Director, Corporate Communications: Jani F. Spede
Controller: Deborah L. Dunlap
Systems Manager: Bill Crider
Fulfillment Manager: Beth DeVore
Office Manager: Tammy Fisher
Direct Marketing Manager: Marcia Harelik
Sales Manager: Shannon McGuire
Advertising Sales Manager: Joe McWilliams
Customer Service Manager: Rhonda T. Mitchell
Shipping Coordinator: Michael Febonio
Advertising Coordinator: Michelle Swann
Communications Coordinator: Angela Young
Customer Service Representatives: John T. Logan, Darla Wenzel
Publicity Assistant: Becky Hepinstall
Administrative Assistant: Margaux Bejarano

HOOVER'S, INC. MISSION STATEMENT

1. To produce business information products and services of the highest quality, accuracy, and readability.

2. To make that information available whenever, wherever, and however our customers want it through mass distribution at affordable prices.

3. To continually expand our range of products and services and our markets for those products and services.

4. To reward our employees, suppliers, and shareholders based on their contributions to the success of our enterprise.

5. To hold to the highest ethical busines standards, erring on the side of generosity when in doubt.

About This Book

We at Hoover's, Inc. have witnessed firsthand the explosive growth of the Internet. We have been fortunate to participate in its incredible birth and rapid growth by adopting it as a means of distributing our company profiles and other business information (See Hoover's Online at www.hoovers.com).

We have — and we're betting you have too — been confused by it. We've cursed at it. We've marveled. And, ultimately, we became convinced that it represents the communications future for our global society, probably in ways we have yet to imagine.

Our reputation at Hoover's is in large part based on our ability to describe the often complex and arcane ways of the business world in terms that are understandable. As we have watched the Internet grow, and realized the investment opportunity it represents, we came to believe we could provide a useful service by creating a guide for the average investor that explains in basic terms how the Internet works and what the companies that are contributing to its growth actually do.

A word about the book. One of the keys to success in investing in anything is to understand it. This is particularly difficult with the Internet because it brings with it a new vocabulary. Strange words like Ethernet and packets and even stranger acronyms like TCP/IP are important to understand. Throughout this book, we have italicized these words to call them to your attention, and we have tried to define them in layman's terms. In Chapter 1, we explain how we chose the 101 companies we profile. Read about these companies and learn: they are part of one of the most exciting market developments of a lifetime.

Alan Chai was one of the original employees of Hoover's, Inc. He has been involved in the high-tech industry since the late 1970s, and his ability to understand and explain the often complex technologies has been a great asset to this company. He has also shown a keen understanding of how to invest wisely in tech stocks. His counsel should point the way to many of the opportunities, as well as to the many risks involved, in the Internet.

Finally, by using the printed page to publish investment information about such a fast-growing industry, we knew that some of the most important data would soon be out of date. Fortunately, it is the very medium of electronic publishing that allows us to supply you with the latest information about cyberstocks, from stock quotes to quarterly earnings and changes in product or marketing strategies. Check out **www.cyberstocks.com**. You've bought Cyberstocks, the book. We hope you find Cyberstocks, the Web site, just as useful.

ABOUT THE NUMBERS

Most of the financial data in *Cyberstocks* have been provided by Media General Financial Services, Inc. Other company information, including number of employees, was compiled by Hoover's, Inc., which takes full responsibility for the content of this section.

The annual financial information contained is current at least through fiscal year-ends as late as May 1996. Our 6-year tables, with relevant annualized compound growth rates, cover:

- Fiscal year sales
- Fiscal year net income (before accounting changes)
- Fiscal year net income as a percent of sales
- Fiscal year earnings per share (EPS, fully diluted)
- Stock price high, low, and close (for the calendar year unless otherwise noted)
- High and low price/earnings ratio (P/E, for the calendar year unless otherwise noted)
- Fiscal year dividends per share
- Fiscal year-end book value (common shareholders' equity per share)
- Fiscal year-end or average number of employees

All revenue numbers are as reported by the company in its annual report. The year at the top of each column in The Numbers section is the year in which the company's fiscal year actually ends. Thus, data for a company with a January 31, 1996, year-end are shown in the 1996 column. Stock prices for companies with fiscal year-ends between January and April are for the prior calendar year and are so footnoted on the chart. Key year-end statistics in this section generally show the financial strength of the enterprise, including:

- Debt ratio (total debt as a percent of combined total debt and total shareholders' equity)
- Return on equity (net income divided by the average of beginning and ending common shareholders' equity)
- Cash, marketable securities, and short-term investments
- Current ratio (ratio of current assets to current liabilities)
- Total long-term debt, including capital lease obligations
- Number of shares of common stock outstanding (less treasury shares)
- Dividend yield (fiscal year dividends per share divided by the calendar year-end closing stock price)
- Dividend payout (fiscal year dividends divided by fiscal year EPS)
- Market value at calendar year-end (calendar year-end closing stock price multiplied by fiscal year-end number of shares outstanding)
- Research and development as a percent of sales

Per share data have been adjusted for stock splits and stock dividends.

Quarterly information is for the most recent quarter up to July 31 and for the year-to-date. It reports sales, net income (before accounting changes), EPS (fully dilluted), and shares outstanding.

The Editors
Hoovers, Inc.
September 1996

COMPANIES PROFILED

Cyberstocks

I. INVESTING IN CYBERSTOCKS

The Predicament of the Cyberstock Investor

For a while it seemed that Internet-related stocks could only go up. But in mid-1996, a market correction took place, one that attempted to separate cyberstocks into survivor and wanna-be categories. The easy-money days of Internet mania ended, and a new, more realistic period of cyberstock investing began.

For most individual investors, buying a cyberstock is more akin to gambling than investing. How many do-it-yourself investors really understand the technology and competitive positions of Internet-related companies? How many can truly understand their annual reports? How many have missed out on the opportunity to invest in one of the most exciting market developments of a lifetime because they are unable to evaluate the companies involved? Even more disturbing, how many have blindly invested in Internet plays anyway?

The purpose of this book is to open the world of intelligent cyberstock investing to the individual investor. We do not make any specific stock recommendations. Rather we provide a set of tools to enable investors to substitute knowledge for hype and make informed decisions for themselves. In addition, we have created **www.cyberstocks.com**, a free, companion World Wide Web service to enable investors to remain up-to-date on rapidly changing Internet technology, markets, and companies. Genius is not required to understand the technical and business issues of the Internet, but a willingness to think and learn is a necessity.

HOW THIS BOOK IS ORGANIZED

First of all, if you are ready to invest in cyberstocks but do not have Internet access, shame on you! You must gain firsthand experience with the Internet and World Wide Web if you are to grasp the opportunities and issues facing the industry. In most of the US, Internet access is available for $20 per month.

For an introduction to the Internet and a discussion of the magnitude of the business opportunity that the Internet represents, see Part II. The rest of the book is designed to help investors think through investment ideas — by company, by technology, or by industry. Part III contains discussions of the major Internet industry segments, including descriptions of important technologies and help with technical jargon, brief industry reviews that put companies in competitive context, and some food-for-investment-thought. Each review places Internet companies in context by analyzing the technologies, trends, and competitive factors affecting industry players. Wherever necessary, we further divide industries into smaller segments for more in-depth discussion. For easy reference, each discussion contains a list of profiled companies operating in the industry and a page number for each profile. The 7 industry groups and the products and services they provide are:

- **Infrastructure** — the networking hardware or "plumbing" required to create the Internet and intranets

- **Computers and modems** — the desktop hardware users need to experience the Internet

- **Application software** — the software that makes the Internet useful and entertaining

- **Specialized services** — new services made possible or necessary by the Internet

- **Content** — what you see and hear online

- **Internet access** — home and office connections to the Internet

- **Industry services** — help for businesses hoping to profit from the Internet

Each segment discussion is cross-referenced with profiles of 101 companies in Part V. The profiles include operational and product descriptions, financial and stock data, key competitor lists, contact information, and some pros and cons of

You must gain firsthand experience with the Internet and World Wide Web if you are to grasp the opportunities and issues.

investing in a company's stock. Profiles are cross-referenced to one or more industry segment discussions. Part IV contains some additional thoughts on trends and technical advances in the Internet industry. Current news and recent developments concerning the companies and industries covered in this book are available at **www.cyberstocks.com**.

We define cyberstocks as stocks of publicly traded or soon-to-be publicly traded companies with substantial proportions of their business influenced by Internet technology. Many large companies, including IBM, Intel, and Digital Equipment, have significant Internet-related operations but do not appear to be, as a whole, dependent on Internet growth for survival. They have been omitted in favor of smaller companies that are more nearly "pure plays." Many Internet-related companies filed to go public as this book was written, such as DEC's spin-off of Alta Vista. Although they could not be included in this book, profiles of several of these companies are available at **www.cyberstocks.com**.

The technology, industry, and company discussions in this book are intended to give nontechnical investors an introduction to cyberstock investment issues. As the discussions are not comprehensive in scope, we urge readers to further investigate industries and companies before investing. Readers who feel that cyberstock investors should be aware of additional or opposing points of view are encouraged to send their opinions and analyses by e-mail to achai@hoovers.com.

Uncertainty comes with the territory and is what makes cyberstock investing challenging, fun, risky, and, potentially, very profitable.

Many of the industry analyses refer to market forecasts made by highly reputable firms. While the analysts making these projections are almost certainly well-intentioned and knowledgeable, readers should be aware that most of the Internet industry is so new that such projections may be little more than educated guesses. Today, market researchers cannot even agree on how many people have access to the Internet. Current estimates of the number of North Americans with access range from about 10 million to about 40 million. Uncertainty of this nature comes with the territory and is what makes cyberstock investing challenging, fun, risky, and, potentially, very profitable.

Cyberstocks

II. INDUSTRY BACKGROUND

History of
the Internet

COLD WAR: AN UNEXPECTED BENEFIT

The beginnings of the Internet can be traced to a small satellite launched by the Soviet Union in 1957. Seeing the need to put the nation's research efforts into high gear after the Soviets sent Sputnik into orbit, President Eisenhower ordered the formation of the Advanced Research Projects Agency (ARPA) by the Department of Defense to keep the US on the cutting edge of new technology. ARPA's first task was to develop a satellite to compete with the Soviets, but others soon followed.

One of those projects was dreamed up by Bob Taylor, director of ARPA's Information Processing Techniques Office (IPTO). Taylor wanted to find a way to hook together the various computer science labs at college campuses on the East and West Coasts that were working on ARPA projects so they could share their (expensive) computer resources. He set up a team to begin looking into the problem in 1966.

The researchers came across the work of Paul Baran of the RAND Corporation, a military think tank that worked with ARPA. Baran had spent the early 1960s working out a way to protect the US government's communications system from destruction in case of nuclear war. The communication systems in use at the time were based on a system of hubs and spokes, so if the central switching point was destroyed, every station connected to it would be useless.

Baran's idea was to create a network like a spider's web or a fishnet with no central authority and no single route. A message that needed to get from Walt in Washington to Sandy in San Francisco would be addressed "Sandy in San Francisco," but it did not matter how it got there. It could wend its way on any available line on the network. Each point or node on the spider web would have the authority to route the message wherever it saw an opening. So in case half the nodes on the system were destroyed, and the sender of a message wasn't even sure which ones were working, the system itself was designed to figure out how to get the message to its destination.

Baran's *distributed network* included another feature. The message was broken into many pieces, later dubbed *packets*. Each packet contained the address to which it was destined but could get there however the system saw fit. Thus the entire message would not necessarily take the same route, the better to keep military information from enemy eyes or ears. Once the packets reached their destination, they would automatically reassemble into the original message.

What packets meant for ARPA researchers was not so much a protected network as an efficient one. Since short bursts of digital information could be sent along telecommunications lines in pieces, one computer would not have to keep one line to itself. Many computers could use the same line, their information packets finding an empty space among the stream of other packets coming down the line.

BIRTH OF A NET

ARPA's researchers built on Baran's basic idea to design their system. The Defense Department began its first test of such a distributed network in 1969, setting up what was called the ARPANET. A small *routing* computer, which sent incoming and outgoing packets to the next available node, was developed by computer consulting company Bolt, Beranek and Newman (now BBN). These routers were installed at university research centers at Stanford, UCLA, UC Santa Barbara, and the University of Utah, linking the 4 institutions' *host* computer systems. The hosts acted as repositories for information or computer applications that could be used by anyone on the system.

ARPANET was a hit with the scientists who used it. They could share their data and directly access and run applications off another point's computer. But the most popular application quickly became electronic mail, now known as e-mail.

More nodes were slowly added to the network, and in 1972 the ARPANET got its first public demonstration at the International Conference on Computer Communications at the Washington Hilton Hotel. By that time there were about 20 host computers at universities and research centers across the US. The demonstration was a huge success among the computer scientists gathered at the conference from around the world — much to the chagrin of the scientists from AT&T (or The Phone Company, as it was still known then) who doubted the system would ever work.

While the ARPANET was a success, problems loomed on the horizon. It took an immense amount of programming to get the computers at the various sites to work together. One solution would have been to use the same kind of computers at every site, but the higher-ups at ARPA knew they could never push such a request, for one large order to a single vendor, through the maze of Pentagon procurement procedures in any reasonable amount of time (it might still be sitting on an undersecretary's desk today). So they used a variety of computer systems and asked the researchers to come up with a single *network protocol* (a common language used by the computers connected to a network). The original protocol, called *Network Control Protocol* (NCP), proved inadequate, so another was developed.

The first version of what later became *TCP/IP* (Transmission Control Protocol/Internet Protocol) was introduced in 1973. TCP/IP worked with any type of computer and could be used to link sites within a network and link multiple networks together. Other networking protocols had been developed by commercial interests, but TCP/IP was public domain. Computer and telecommunications equipment makers, who couldn't agree on any one commercial protocol lest they give a competitor an advantage, agreed to use TCP/IP, and it became the standard network language for the Internet.

One of the features of the Net was its communal nature. Software was posted for free on the system and worked on collaboratively. In 1979 grad students at the

The first version of what later became TCP/IP was introduced in 1973.

NFSnet was
introduced in
1986 and was
the original
information
superhighway.

University of North Carolina and Duke University created Usenet, a bulletin-board system where users could post comments on topics of their choice, and in 1982 a file search and transfer system called *gopher* (a precursor to the World Wide Web) was introduced by the University of Minnesota. ARPANET remained small, however; by 1979 there were only about 60 hosts on the system. The 1980s would bring the beginning of explosive growth.

In the early 1980s Bill Joy, a programmer at California Berkeley who later founded Sun Microsystems, introduced a version of UNIX (a popular operating system originally introduced by Bell Labs in 1969) that included TCP/IP, giving the protocol a boost among computer scientists.

THE BACKBONE CONNECTS TO THE GROWTH BONE

Meanwhile, other organizations were getting into networking. Companies were setting up local area networks and some institutions were linking with private networks. What did most of these networks have in common? UNIX, which included TCP/IP. A movement was afoot to connect these computers that all spoke the same language.

Enter the National Science Foundation, which decided to set up a network like the ARPANET. It would serve members of the scientific community excluded by ARPA's system because they were not working on defense-related government research. NSF wanted to connect several supercomputer centers, allowing people to lease time on the powerful (and expensive) machines for research projects.

The new network, which the NFS built with the University of Michigan (which created a nonprofit corporation, Merit Networking, Inc., to manage the system), MCI (which provided very fast telecommunication lines), and IBM (which provided routers that directed traffic) was called NFSnet and was introduced in 1986. The NFSnet was the *backbone* of a system that linked the 5 supercomputers as well as several regional networks. The backbone used high-speed lines and advanced routers, and it linked the entire nation, making it the fastest (and preferred way) to move information around. It was the original information superhighway; there were other ways to transport data across the network, but the backbone was the biggest and the speediest.

The regional networks were allowed to hook up to the backbone for free, and the universities and research centers linked to their local regional network for a fee. NFSnet quickly began to grow, both because it was easier to access than directly hooking to ARPANET (although they were connected) and its high-speed system could handle more traffic and more sophisticated operations. The term Internet began to be used on a widespread basis to describe this collection of networks that included NFSnet, ARPANET, and others.

Through the late 1980s and early 1990s the NFS upgraded its backbone so it could carry more traffic, making it the *de facto* center of the Internet. More and more networks, both public and private, linked to it thanks to the widespread acceptance of TCP/IP. The burgeoning popularity of the system made the ARPANET unnecessary, and in 1989 it was shut down. A year later the Commercial Internet Exchange, a link to the NFSnet for commercial networks, was established, and the Net grew even faster. By the end of 1991 there were 4,500 networks interconnected via the NFSnet backbone and more than 300,000 host computers were linked to the system.

Tim Berners-Lee posted the code for the World Wide Web on the Net in 1991.

COMMERCIALIZATION

Perhaps one of the most important moments in the development of the Internet that moved it from a tool for academia to a new media sensation was the development of the *World Wide Web*. Tim Berners-Lee, a computer scientist at CERN, a European research center in Geneva, Switzerland, posted the code for the World Wide Web on the Net in 1991. It was designed to combine words, pictures, and sounds and also included a feature called *hypertext*. In hypertext, a user could click on a highlighted piece of text in one document to retrieve another document. Ironically, it was originally designed to allow academics to link a footnote or bibliographic entry from their research to another bit of research residing somewhere on the Internet, but young computer users, who grew up with a TV remote control in their hands, soon saw the potential for "surfing" this vast conglomeration of information for something more than a footnote to a monograph on the digestive systems of mollusks. One of those young, would-be surfers was Marc Andreessen, a student at the National Center for Supercomputing Applications (NCSA) at the University of Illinois. Andreessen, along with several other programmers, began work on a browser, which could retrieve data from a Web site and display it on a user's computer screen. In 1993 the NCSA released Mosaic, the first Web browser, for free on the Net, and surfing the Web was on its way to becoming a national pastime.

Meanwhile, the Internet was becoming more multimedia friendly. In 1992 audio and video were broadcast over a portion of the Internet called the *Mbone* for the first time. The Mbone (Multicast Backbone) is made up of a series of special multicast routers (mrouters) that can broadcast data such as moving pictures and music in uninterrupted streams to specific nodes on the network.

By 1994 the commercialization of the Web had begun to take off like a rocket. That year Jim Clark, former chairman of Silicon Graphics, founded Mosaic Communications with Marc Andreessen, to market the Mosaic browser that Andreessen had helped develop. The company would later change its name to Netscape and the name of the browser to Navigator.

Netscape's IPO in mid-1995 was one of the most successful in history.

More and more companies were beginning to see the huge potential the Internet offered. The 3 major consumer online services, America Online (AOL), CompuServe, and Prodigy, began offering Internet access.

In 1995, in a move that signaled the Internet's move from its scientific roots to its commercial future, the NFS began to withdraw its support of the backbone, handing over management to a group of commercial network service providers. Those service providers, which included AOL, Sprint, and MCI, would maintain their sections of the backbone (basically, sophisticated routers and high-speed phone lines) and would sell access to smaller service providers, corporations, and organizations.

The mainstream business world really began to take notice of the Internet in 1995. AT&T, which once scoffed at the engineers who created ARPANET, announced it would begin offering Internet access (in an alliance with BBN, which designed ARPANET's original routers). Netscape had gained a huge share of the market for browsers; its Navigator software became the basic system most new Internauts were using to "see" the World Wide Web. The company's IPO in mid-1995 was one of the most successful in history. Many were hailing Netscape as the "new" Microsoft.

The old Microsoft was still around, but it was having trouble keeping up with its rapidly changing world. As part of the launch of Windows 95, Microsoft introduced an online service, the Microsoft Network (MSN). While MSN included a lot of the content that Prodigy or AOL might include, it did not have Internet access. That quickly changed when the company saw it might be left behind as competitors, consumers, and advertisers were more interested in the Internet than another consumer online service. MSN was relaunched as an "Internet online service," and Microsoft altered its strategy to focus on the Internet.

Wall Street went wild for Internet stocks in the first half of 1996, looking for the 2nd coming of Netscape. It seemed any company dealing even remotely with the Internet could generate excitement for its IPO.

By mid-1996 the market for Internet stocks had begun to cool off a bit. The initial frenzy was over, and the serious investors began to take a hard look to see which companies were built to last. The Net had moved from a tool for cloistered academics to a utility accessed daily by millions of Americans. The market still remains relatively small, particularly overseas, where growth has been slow, but most analysts are predicting an increasingly important role for the Internet; some are even predicting it will be bigger than the telephone in a few years.

The Net had moved from a tool for cloistered academics to a utility accessed daily by millions of Americans.

NUMBER OF INTERNET HOSTS

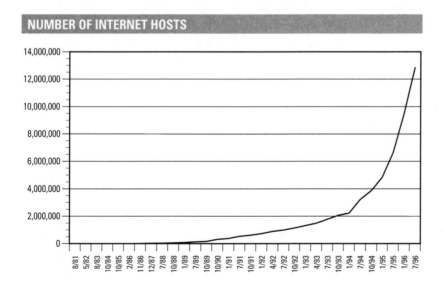

Source: Network Wizards (available on the Internet at www.nw.com)

THE BUSINESS OPPORTUNITY

Metcalfe's Law

Attributed to networking pioneer Bob Metcalfe, Metcalfe's Law suggests that a network's value equals the square of the number of users connected to the network. The Internet is the largest computer network the world has ever seen, and the rate of growth in connections appears to be more than 100% per year. So, if Mr. Metcalfe is correct, the Internet is becoming more valuable by leaps and bounds each day. To understand the reasoning behind Metcalfe's Law, consider the US telephone network. Is there any doubt that ubiquity of service contributes to the usefulness of the system? Like the telephone system, the Internet is a communications network that benefits from additional connections. Assuming that 30 million individuals have access to the Internet, the addition of one user creates 30 million more possible user-to-user connections.

A network's value equals the square of the number of users connected to the network.

The Mass Market Opportunity

Metcalfe's Law predicts gathering momentum in Internet growth, and most analysts agree that consumer adoption of the Internet is occurring at a rate that is at least as great as that of television, VCRs, or cable TV. That this is occurring despite the equipment expense involved ($2,000+ for a computer and modem), the level of difficulty in establishing an Internet connection (it's not like setting up your VCR), and the relatively primitive state of publishing and commerce on the Internet is an indicator of the power of the medium and its potential in the areas of entertainment and communications. If and when inexpensive, easy-to-use network computers arrive at mass-market outlets, the consumer Internet market could explode.

To understand the scale of the opportunity, consider that more than 95% of US households have televisions and telephones, and more than 85% have VCRs, according to the Electronic Industries Association. About one-third of US households own a PC and approximately 10% have a modem. So fewer than 10% of US households are currently connected to the Internet. Penetration is far lower outside the US, so the worldwide opportunity is massive.

RISING INTERNET USAGE

	August 1995	March 1996
Number of Internet users	23 million	37 million
Percent of US and Canadian population over 16 years old with Internet access	16%	24%
Used Internet in last 3 months	10%	—
Used Internet in last 6 months	—	17%
Used Web in last 3 months	8%	—
Used Web in last 6 months	—	13%

Source: CommerceNet/Neilsen Media Research

What Accounts for the Surging Use of the Internet?

The most heavily used service is e-mail. In the future, we may look back and see e-mail as the Trojan Horse of the World Wide Web. E-mail uses the same TCP/IP protocol as the Web, so installing it creates an environment that enables Web browsing. In addition, the development of graphical interfaces like Netscape's Navigator has given the Web a user-friendly feel. And a tremendous amount of venture capital, IPO cash, and corporate spending has created a proliferation of Web sites and services for users. Of course, the industry hype and "new," "fun," and "cool" aspects of surfing the Net have helped. How do people find time to use the Internet? According to a FIND/SVP survey, they spend less time watching TV, making long-distance telephone calls, and watching videos.

The Enterprise Market Opportunity

Better than 50% of the nation's Internet connections reside in businesses, where the emphasis is less on "new," "fun," and "cool" than on "standardized," "cheap," and "efficient." E-mail and promotional Web sites are two outwardly visible business applications but, because Internet technology is standardized and operates on all sorts of computers, corporations are increasingly using it to develop *intranets*, mini-Internets running on existing company computer networks. A recent survey of *FORTUNE* 1000 companies by Forrester Research found that 22% had already implemented an intranet and 40% were planning on or considering installing one.

For businesses, the decision to implement an intranet is the result of a cost/benefit analysis. The benefits come from simplified companywide access

People spend less time watching TV, making long-distance telephone calls, and watching videos.

History 2

to corporate information and workgroup collaboration, and the installation costs are enticingly low. In addition, corporate costs of Internet/intranet training are relatively modest, as many employees are already familiar with World Wide Web browsers and addicted to e-mail. By lowering the overall cost and expanding the benefits of networking, Internet technology encourages spending on networking equipment and software. Zona Research has forecast that, in 1998, intranet software sales alone will grow to $8 billion.

Cyberstocks

III. CURRENT INDUSTRY STRUCTURE

Infrastructure
Companies

Infrastructure

3

Infrastructure

"Build it and they will come." This line from *Field of Dreams* could well apply to the Internet. To the investor, it immediately raises the question "who sells the stuff to build it?" The short answer is computer networking and digital telecommunications equipment manufacturers. The leading companies in that group were already growing quickly before the Internet craze gripped the country, so the new demand for their products created by Internet expansion has kicked many companies into an era of hypergrowth.

To analyze the businesses involved in producing hardware for the Internet, an investor needs a basic understanding of networking. Gaining a working knowledge of networking requires a little work. In a recent advertisement placed in *FORTUNE* magazine, Cascade Communications CEO Daniel Smith boasted,

> "Our best-of-class multiservice switch platform
> provides a safe, cost-effective ATM migration
> path for enterprise network managers and
> service providers."

Was it the copyeditor's day off? A fair guess would be that Mr. Smith had lost 90% of the corporate executives, managers, and investors who subscribe to *FORTUNE* by the time they reached the word "platform." Perhaps he intended to communicate with only the other 10%. In any case, it is clear that the average investor faces a language barrier when researching networking hardware companies.

BASIC WORDS AND CONCEPTS

For our purposes, a network is a group of computers wired together so they can communicate with each other.

Networks come in 3 flavors, each with its own set of products. A *local-area network* (LAN) is the basic networking unit. Individual computers, also known as "workstations," are linked within workgroups, offices, and buildings to form LANs. At present, technological constraints limit LAN operations to a relatively small area, as the name implies. *Wide-area network* (WAN) technology, as you might imagine, enables long-distance networking. An *internetwork*, also known as an internet (lower-case "i"), is a collection of connected networks that function as a single network.

A word that one continually encounters in networking is *"bandwidth."* Substituting the word "capacity" for bandwidth usually works. So, a high-bandwidth circuit is one that can handle a lot of data flow. A "bandwidth hog" is a person or program that clogs a network by moving large volumes of data.

A "bandwidth hog" is a person or program that clogs the network by moving large volumes of data.

LOCAL AREA NETWORKS

How Do LANs Work?

Most of today's installed LANs employ a technology standard called *Ethernet*. Because Ethernet has been around for a while, the technology is stable and Ethernet hardware is cheap. *Fast Ethernet* is — you guessed it — faster than Ethernet. Because Fast Ethernet often can run on the same wiring as Ethernet, many organizations can upgrade to it without the trauma and expense of replacing existing cabling. Asynchronous Transfer Mode (*ATM*) is a very fast, very promising, but still somewhat experimental, technology that experts have all but declared the networking technology of the future. ATM also works as a WAN and internetworking technology, giving it additional appeal. Another networking technology to keep an eye on is *Gigabit Ethernet*, an ATM competitor.

ATTRIBUTES OF MAJOR LAN TECHNOLOGIES

	Ethernet	Fast Ethernet	ATM
Speed	to 10 Mpbs	to 100 Mpbs	to 2,500 Mpbs
Performance under high network traffic	Worst	Better	Best
Distance limitations?	Yes	Yes	No
Suitable for multimedia?	No	No	Probably
Fully standardized?	Yes	2 competing standards	No
Equipment cost	Low	Moderate	High
Cost to upgrade from Ethernet	—	Low/Moderate	High

LAN switches can speed up existing Ethernet and Fast Ethernet networks.

Each of the aforementioned LAN technologies requires different equipment, which discourages organizations from changing technologies. LAN hardware companies make network interface cards (*NICs*), *hubs*, and *switches*. NICs are installed in every computer on a network. A network cable is plugged into each one to establish a connection between the computer and the network. In their simplest form, hubs are boxes that accept several cables from workstations and connect them to each other and the rest of the network at a single point. Hubs are not absolutely necessary but are usually present in Ethernet networks. More sophisticated, "intelligent" hubs are required to manage data traffic in Fast Ethernet networks.

LAN switches can speed up existing Ethernet and Fast Ethernet networks by better managing data flows between specific points on a network. Switches are not cheap, but by limiting switching to portions of a LAN where heavy data flows create bottlenecks (the backbone, for example), a relatively modest expenditure can result in a dramatic increase in network performance. ATM switches have been installed in the backbones of some very large networks but are not yet in widespread use in LANs.

Industry

The market for LAN equipment has grown quite steadily and is expected to continue to expand at a rate of about 15% annually over the next few years. The Ethernet NIC market, dominated by 3Com with an estimated 40% market share, is probably among the slowest-growing segments. Sales of Fast Ethernet NICs have just begun, with Intel and 3Com vying for market leadership in the early going. Bay Networks leads in the expanding but highly competitive hub market. The market for Ethernet and Fast Ethernet LAN switches is already large and growing by as much as 50% annually, an attractive combination that has captured the attention of nearly every company in the networking hardware industry. Cisco Systems is #1 here. FORE Systems is the early leader in the brand-new ATM LAN market.

Investing

Perhaps the greatest appeal of the LAN hardware industry lies in its large installed base.

Buying stock in LAN hardware manufacturers gives an investor exposure to the growth of the Internet without depending on it. To the extent that the Internet proves useful as a business resource, it will drive companies to install or expand their networks. If the current trend toward intranetworking (using the Internet's open systems and technology within company networks) continues, it could drive down the overall cost of networks, encouraging businesses to build more. If and when Internet-based multimedia applications become necessary for businesses, a mass migration to ATM could occur. But the LAN market was healthy before the Internet became a household word and would probably be healthy if the Internet did not exist. Unlike many Internet-related industries, this one has a track record, profitable companies, and some degree of earnings visibility.

Perhaps the greatest appeal of the LAN hardware industry lies in its large installed base. At virtually every existing installation, users and managers are demanding better network performance. A slow network translates into low employee productivity, so the pressure to upgrade is enormous. Organizations running Ethernet LANs currently have 4 upgrade options: switching, Fast Ethernet, Fast Ethernet and switching, and ATM. Switching offers a compelling combination of relatively modest cost and a minimally disruptive installation and accommodates a one-step-at-a-time approach to deployment. Fast Ethernet upgrades give businesses better performance using a stable technology. Although it is attractive for new installations, current pricing makes Fast Ethernet upgrades somewhat expensive, but prices are always dropping. At the present, ATM is too expensive and too new to get serious consideration from most companies.

Today, investors should give careful consideration to leading companies, such as Cisco and 3Com, in the LAN switching and Fast Ethernet markets. Although they may be considered interim technologies waiting for ATM to be ready for prime-time, the interim period could be quite long, and ATM may never meet expectations in LAN applications. Being today's leader in ATM LAN technology may not mean much by the time ATM really catches on.

There is some near-term risk that the LAN switching market will attract too many competitors and the Fast Ethernet market become somewhat commoditized. And Intel has entered both markets, which may be a long-term worry to other industry players. Not only is Intel frighteningly large and successful, but the company has a habit of incorporating the functions of other companies' products into its chips, chipsets, and motherboards.

WIDE AREA NETWORKING

How Do WANs Work?

WAN equipment addresses the need of far-flung organizations to connect all of their offices to a single, enterprisewide network. Traditionally, corporate WANs have leased lines from telephone companies to wire their sites together and have employed a technology known as *time division multiplexing* (TDM) to allocate bandwidth to users. With TDM, the capacity of a typical leased line may be allocated to 24 separate telephone or data circuits under a time-sharing arrangement. The devices that manage the time sharing are often called *multiplexors*.

Because TDM reserves a fixed amount of bandwidth for each circuit, bandwidth is inevitably wasted when a circuit is idle. Also, the costs to an organization of leasing multiple lines for each remote location can add up quickly. *Frame relay* technology addresses these problems. Frame relay networks use a technique called *packet switching* to use all available bandwidth by breaking up data into packets and transmitting them, one-at-a-time, as bandwidth becomes available. The devices that break up transmit and reassemble the data packets are called *frame*

Intel has a habit of incorporating the functions of other companies' products into its chips, chipsets, and motherboards.

relay switches. Another, extremely important, advantage of frame relay is that the network connections are virtual — to the user they appear to be dedicated connections but, in fact, network facilities may be shared by everyone on the WAN. This has enabled telephone companies to offer public WAN services by building huge, shared frame relay networks. The cost to an organization of using a public frame relay service is often far less expensive than that of building a private network. The speed, efficiency, and cost savings of frame relay technology have made it extremely popular in Internet applications.

As good as frame relay is, there is a technology apparently waiting in the wings to overtake it. Enter our old friend ATM. Along with the advantages of frame relay, ATM offers high speed and, possibly, the ability to handle time-sensitive data, such as music and video. As you may have guessed, *ATM WAN switches* are used to implement ATM on WANs. The potential to unify LANs and WANs under a single technology is another attraction of ATM. Telephone companies, ISPs, and other companies requiring extremely high-speed WANs are beginning to deploy ATM technology today.

Industry

The WAN equipment market is growing at an astounding rate. Forecasts of the 1996 growth rate of the ATM WAN switch market generally exceed 100%. Frame relay market growth is forecast to run in the 30–40% range from a much larger base. Viewed by some customers as the first step toward implementation of ATM, frame relay sales may actually be helped by the hype surrounding the competing technology. Over the near term, frame relay sales may be more predictable than ATM sales. ATM equipment is still expensive and difficult to install, but the technology appears to have found a home in applications in which high speed is a requirement.

Although the WAN switch markets have attracted numerous new competitors, Cisco, Cascade, and Newbridge Networks remain the leaders. Cascade dominates in sales of frame relay backbone switches to ISPs and has a large installed base in RBOCs. The company was a pioneer in the development of multiservice switches (switches capable of simultaneously handling frame relay, ATM, ISDN, and other communications technologies) that provide a clear migration path to ATM. Cisco has a larger overall frame relay market share and a large piece of the ATM market.

It is trying to leverage its dominance in the router market to sell WAN switches in a soup-to-nuts pitch to ISPs. Newbridge's agreement to merge its ATM product line with that of Siemens will likely strengthen its already formidable position in the telephone company market. Newbridge is #1 in the TDM and ATM WAN switch markets.

A smaller but related market exists for equipment that enables LANs to communicate with WANs. This product category includes multiplexors. In a very interesting development, Premisys has begun selling integrated access equipment, devices capable of handling regular telephone lines, ISDN, frame relay, etc. The Premisys product replaces many separate components and offers telephone companies a very flexible building block for system expansion.

Investing

There is little question that the frame relay and ATM WAN switch businesses are going to grow rapidly over the next few years. Unfortunately, this prognosis has not been lost on Wall Street. On this book's publication date, Cisco and Cascade were expensive stocks. On a P/E basis, Newbridge was far cheaper, in part because a substantial proportion of its sales derives from the sale of TDM products and in part because of cloudy short-term prospects. Newbridge is positioned to profit from the growth in digital services of all kinds provided by telephone companies. With its acquisition of StrataCom, Cisco gained a particularly strong relationship with AT&T.

Because of its commanding share of the ISP market, Cascade's fortunes are inextricably bound with those of the Internet. Cascade investors should watch carefully to see if Cisco's all-in-one strategy enables the company to make significant inroads into the ISP market.

Reseller relationships are critical to access equipment manufacturers like Digital Link and Premisys. Investors need to be aware of new, important relationships and be on guard for termination of important reseller agreements.

There is little question that the frame relay and ATM WAN switch businesses are going to grow rapidly over the next few years.

INTERNETWORKING

What is Internetworking?

The notoriety of the Internet has made internetworking a high-profile business. The Internet consists of many tens of thousands of individual networks linked together, often using the WAN switches described above. One of the major challenges of internetworking is directing data packets from one network to another until they reach their final destination. Although switches can send a data packet from point to point within their own networks, they have no knowledge of what lies beyond. So the job of planning a data packet's itinerary falls to an appropriately named device called a *router*. Routers exist at all points at which one network connects with another. Unbelievably, routers actually continuously communicate with each other to determine the best route for data at any moment in time. And at each stop along the way, routers direct the data to the next network on the route. Routers are not particularly fast transmitters of data, so they are increasingly found working in tandem with switches.

The job of planning a data packet's itinerary falls to an appropriately named device called a router.

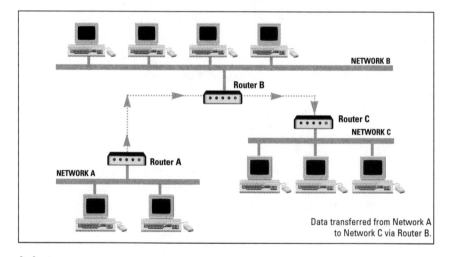

Data transferred from Network A to Network C via Router B.

Industry

Routers are losing ground to switches in LAN applications, but demand for routers in internets and WANs is more than making up the difference. The construction of the Internet and the integration of the huge existing base of SNA (IBM) networks into corporate networks represent large opportunities for router manufacturers. Cisco dominates the router market, enjoys a huge installed base, and is the clear favorite for capturing the lion's share of future orders. 3Com and Bay Networks are locked in a battle for the #2 spot.

The common wisdom in the networking industry holds that Cisco, by virtue of its routers' presence in the vast majority of large network installations, has a leg up on the competition in future sales. Another bit of common wisdom argues that, with network complexity increasing, customers will want to buy all of their networking hardware from a single vendor to be sure that it all works well together. While Cisco appears to be best positioned in this regard, 3Com and Bay have tried to keep pace by broadening their product lines through acquisitions. Ascend Communications recently acquired NetStar, thereby entering the router market. The purchase was motivated, in part, to counter the single-vendor, total solution sales strategies of competitors eyeing Ascend's network access equipment market.

Investing

There is no pure play in the router market, but Cisco is the king of routers. Its routers have been the building blocks of the Internet. The question a Cisco investor should continuously ask is, "Is the conventional wisdom still wise?"

REMOTE NETWORK ACCESS

What is Remote Network Access?

Network access equipment enables individuals, small offices, and traveling employees to connect to corporate networks and the Internet. ISPs use devices called *access switches* to connect their many telephone access lines to their networks. *Remote access servers* accommodate employees and small offices wishing to connect individual computers to corporate LANs. If a remote access server is installed in a corporate LAN, remote users can access the network in such a way that their computers appear to be directly connected to the LAN.

ISDN service is frequently used to connect a small LAN to a large one because ISDN is faster than regular telephone service and is relatively inexpensive. Typically, *remote access routers* are used to provide low-end WAN functionality in this environment.

Common wisdom argues that, with network complexity increasing, customers will want to buy all of their networking hardware from a single vendor.

Infrastructure 3

Industry

Demand for home Internet connections, telecommuting, the need to connect branch offices to corporate networks, and increasing reliance on such LAN applications as e-mail have created a large and rapidly growing network access market. Each of the network access industry segments has a clear leader. Ascend dominates the access switch market. Shiva is a well-established leader in the more fragmented remote access server market. Cisco is a strong leader in remote access routers. Each of these segments has attracted newcomers and each of the 3 leaders is selling products into at least one of the other segments. Shiva, Cisco, and Newbridge Networks have all mounted attacks on Ascend's enormous ISP market share, and 3Com and U.S. Robotics have been in the market for a while. Cisco's proposed purchase of Telebit indicates that it wants to invade Shiva's turf.

Investing

Ascend is clearly well positioned to benefit from the growth of the Internet, and its commanding position in the Internet access equipment arena has investors salivating. The stock's lofty valuation could be justified if the company manages to keep competitors in check. Shiva is in a similar position but is less Internet-dependent. Both companies are in enviable positions in markets with excellent prospects, but at their current valuations, they are highly vulnerable to a sudden loss in investor confidence as the result of a negative earning surprise or decrease in market share. Margins are likely to decline in all segments as new players vie for market share.

NETWORK SECURITY

How is data secured on networks?

The rapid rise of the Internet has created a new and potentially very lucrative market for security products. Any network attached to the Internet is vulnerable to invasion by unauthorized persons. Software products designed to keep out unauthorized users are called *firewalls*. Encryption software encodes messages to assure privacy even if they are intercepted. Today, most encryption software employs a technology known as *public-key cryptography*.

Until recently, the most common method of encryption had been a secret-key encryption technique, which used a single key to encrypt and decode a message.

The danger is that both the sender and receiver must first agree on the same key, which often makes keeping it a secret difficult. Public-key cryptography, on the other hand, uses a pair of keys, one public and one private. The public key encodes a message and the private key is used to decode it. So a sender can encrypt a message using the receiver's public key, which as its name implies, is available to everyone. The receiver can then decode that message with his or her private key. Since the private key is known only to its owner and never needs to be revealed, the system is significantly more secure than traditional, secret-key encryption schemes. If there is a flaw in this system, it is the reliance on the user to prevent unauthorized use of the private key. RSA Data Security holds patents protecting the most widely used versions of public-key cryptography.

The holy grail of the Internet security business is secure commercial transactions. Today, a combination of encryption and authentication enable such transactions, but smart card systems are too expensive for everyday commerce. Software-based *Digital IDs* were developed to address this issue. A Digital ID is meant to be an online passport, irrefutable proof of one's identity. A user registers with a trusted 3rd party, and receives a Digital ID containing his or her name and public key. The private key is held only by its owner. The Digital ID binds the keys with the user's personal information on file with the 3rd party. When employing a Digital ID, a user may be identified (with the information on file with the 3rd party) and the user's identity authenticated (by virtue of the use of the private key).

Remote (dial-up) access to networks may be secured (beyond standard password systems) with *authentication* techniques. Authentication schemes are designed to prove or disprove that the user requesting network access is, in fact, the person he or she claims to be. Lacking any reasonable way to use finger or voice prints, current means of authentication generally use a combination of password and a *token*, typically a *smart card* (similar to a credit card but with a built-in microprocessor). Smart cards may be programmed to change their passwords periodically according to a scheme known only to the host network.

Industry

The network security industry is relatively small and fragmented. A number of companies involved in securing government networks have recently jumped into the commercial world, hoping to cash in on what most analysts believe is a major

The holy grail of the Internet security business is secure commercial transactions.

opportunity. The firewall market, in particular, has become extremely crowded, and a shakeout and consolidation cannot be very far off. Bundling of firewalls with internetworking hardware is becoming more commonplace. While this trend will benefit some vendors with strong OEM partners, it will likely lead to declining margins throughout the industry.

The industry thrives on fear, and the periodic media storms over Internet security are generally positive for the network security vendors. The obvious exception would be a well-publicized failure of a widespread security technology. Such an event would shake up the industry and could potentially lead to turnover of industry leadership. Given the general fear that hackers will continue to become more sophisticated and the likelihood that, with the growth of the Internet, more spectacular security breaches will occur, the outlook for the industry is bright. If growth in the Internet firewall industry begins to slow, watch for vendors to attempt to heighten concerns over unauthorized employee access to information on corporate networks.

The industry thrives on fear, and the periodic media storms over Internet security are generally positive for the network security vendors.

Despite 1995 sales of only $34 million, Security Dynamics is a relative King Kong of network security. The company instantly became the industry leader in encryption technology with the acquisition of RSA Data Security and was already the leader in smart cards. Checkpoint was the firewall industry leader in 1995, but the situation remains fluid. Most other industry participants are sustaining operating losses.

Investing

With the security industry evolving so rapidly, it is extremely difficult to pick winners. Even Security Dynamics faces some difficult issues, including the expiration of key patents and potential competition to its lucrative smart card business from Digital IDs. The company is partially hedged against this possibility through its ownership of a small stake in Digital ID leader VeriSign (private). In the encryption arena, companies' international expansion has been slowed by US government restriction of the export of encryption products. The companies claim that if restrictions are not eased significantly, they will quickly lose the market to foreign rivals.

INTERACTIVE CABLE TELEVISION EQUIPMENT

Industry

Although the hype over 500-channel, interactive cable television service has been muted for some time now, efforts to develop such a service still exist. Delivery of high-bandwidth interactive services such as video to the home still requires a large investment on the part of a cable or telephone company. Both cable and telephone companies have wires that reach the home, but cable systems lack the necessary switching capability, and telephone cables lack the bandwidth required for such services. Although companies have slowed the deployment of this kind of service, they continue to experiment with new technology to find a financially feasible way to build out these systems. The potential rewards are enormous, which helps keep their interest up. Some are proceeding with interactive television and others have scaled back to high-speed Internet services.

Although building a new fiber-to-the-curb system is still expensive, new technology continues to bring down costs. Upgrading existing cable systems to be able to handle interactivity on a large scale is not cheap, and bandwidth remains an issue. In addition, satellite or wireless delivery may emerge as a serious competing delivery system in the future. Still, with telecommunications deregulation creating a slew of new potential service providers and with increasing demand for high-bandwidth home Internet connections, the industry is far from dead.

A full-blown rollout by one of BroadBand's RBOC customers would ignite the stock.

Investing

Investors seeking to gamble on fiber-to-the-curb might want to consider BroadBand Technologies, bearing in mind that the company is rapidly whittling away its cash hoard and that breakeven may be years away. BroadBand investors should keep their eyes peeled for news about the progress of trials of its systems by Bell Atlantic, SBC, and others. A full-blown rollout by one of BroadBand's RBOC customers would ignite the stock. More risk-averse investors may prefer Tellabs, a profitable, rapidly growing digital telecommunications equipment manufacturer. Part of Tellabs's business is to produce equipment enabling cable companies to offer telephone and online services using existing cabling.

Computer and Modem
Companies

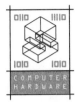

Computers and Modems

Among the most obvious beneficiaries of the adoption of online technologies are computer manufacturers. Users need computers to access any online network, and Internet publishers use computers to disseminate their information. Modem manufacturers, too, are thankful for the blossoming of the online services industries, particularly because the most commonly used modem technology requires modems at both ends of an online connection. We have paired the computer and modem businesses here because sales of modems increasingly accompany sales of computers to homes and small offices.

CLIENTS AND SERVERS

What are Clients and Servers?

A concept investors will frequently encounter is the *client/server model*. It is probably easiest to think of *client* computers as networked computers sitting on people's desks. Clients may share data and programs located on a more powerful networked computer sitting alone in a closet. That lonely computer, as well as any other piece of networked equipment performing a centralized function, is called a *server*. In client/server computing, users' computers take on a major data processing role.

*The role of
Internet server
has historically
fallen to
UNIX-based
hardware.*

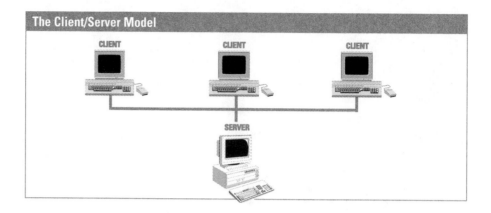

The Internet is a large-scale client/server computing environment with hundreds of thousands of servers. Internet servers receive and transmit data to millions of clients using the TCP/IP communications protocol. The Internet's TCP/IP standard is *platform-independent*, meaning that it works with any kind of computer and operating system. So any computer, if properly configured, could theoretically be used as either an Internet client or server. In practice, the role of Internet server has historically fallen to UNIX-based hardware. On the client side, Net surfers use whatever kind of computer and operating system they have — UNIX workstations; PCs running MS-DOS, Windows, Windows 95, and Windows NT; Macintoshes; etc.

Industry

All computer manufacturers could be considered client and/or server makers, and all stand to gain from the growth of the Internet and intranets. Even Intel, the dominant manufacturer of the chips that power PCs, has recognized the potential of the Internet to drive its customers' sales and has launched campaigns to promote Internet use. But some computer makers are more closely associated with the Internet than others, perhaps none more so than Sun Microsystems. The company rightly claims that it has been selling UNIX-based intranets for years and has relied on an internal TCP/IP-based e-mail system since its inception in 1982. Sun, Hewlett-Packard, and Silicon Graphics are among the leaders in sales of UNIX workstations.

Until recently, PCs have not been popular as Internet servers. This is, in part, because Microsoft's PC operating systems have been poorly suited to the task, and network operating system developer Novell for some time appeared to ignore the Internet/intranet market. With the release of Windows NT, Microsoft changed the competitive landscape and opened the Internet server market to PC makers. Compaq, IBM, and Packard Bell are the top PC sellers in the US.

Two years ago, Apple Macintosh computers seemed to be overrepresented on the Internet. The general decline in Apple's fortunes is now apparent on the Internet as well. Apple recently formulated a new strategy emphasizing the Internet to revive its business, principally by integrating Internet functions into its software and by taking advantage of the reputation of its Macintosh computers in authoring and multimedia to position them as tools for developing software for the World Wide Web.

Another platform to watch is the Internet appliance or Network Computer (NC) championed by Oracle. At first positioned as a diskless, low-cost home computer, it has recently generated more interest as an inexpensive client for corporate LANs. Conceptually, NCs would use the Internet or an intranet as its storage mechanism, eliminating the need for disk drives and centralizing applications on servers. Systems executives at large corporations are said to be interested in this approach because it would give them better ability to control and standardize applications used within their organizations.

Many consumer electronics companies, including Sony and Philips, have jumped on the bandwagon by announcing products connecting televisions to the Internet. Similarly, Apple's Pippin uses a simplified version of the Macintosh operating system to drive a video-game-style computer that attaches to a television and can be used to access the Internet. Taking a different approach, Gateway 2000 has introduced a large-screen computer/entertainment center capable of receiving television signals.

Investing

Most of the companies in this segment have businesses that will live or die for reasons unrelated to the Internet. We have included profiles of only 2, Sun and Apple, whose stakes in the growth of the Internet are greatest.

With the release of Windows NT, Microsoft opened the Internet server market to PC makers.

*How rotten
are the prospects
for Apple?*

Sun has been lifted by the Internet/intranet buzz because it is #1 in UNIX workstations, it is tops in Internet servers, and its Java programming language has captured the imagination of the Internet community. In addition, the company has, for the first time, mounted an attack on the lucrative high-end enterprise (big company) market. While it is extremely unlikely that Hewlett-Packard and others in this market will take Sun's initiative lying down, the mindshare that Sun has captured from its high-profile role in the growth of the Internet may give the company a significant boost in this and other new markets.

How rotten are the prospects for Apple? Bad enough for Microsoft to start acting charitably toward its onetime archrival. Microsoft recently gave its blessing to developers to create Internet software for the Apple only. In the past, Microsoft had insisted that, in exchange for Windows development help, independent programmers create for Windows any software they wrote for Apple computers. Microsoft's turnabout resulted from fears that the company would face antitrust problems should Apple go broke. The possibility of Apple's demise has resulted in worry among prospective computer buyers that the Macintosh could be a dead-end platform, creating a vicious cycle of lower sales and heightened fear. Given the prevailing perception that Apple is in critical condition, a revival will be very tricky to orchestrate, and recent strategic and management changes have done little to increase confidence in the company.

Although early excitement over NCs has abated, investors should try to stay up-to-date on new developments. If and when a capable home Internet product is offered at a consumer-electronics price point (less than $500), a large product category could be born, new players could rise to the top, and client computer makers could be adversely affected.

MODEMS

How do Modems Work?

Modems enable client computers to connect to networks via regular telephone, cable television, and ISDN lines as well as wireless services. The word "modem" derives from MOdulate/DEModulate, a reference to the original function of modems: translation between digital information used by computers and analog signals used by telephone lines. Today, the meaning of the word has expanded to include devices that do no such conversion but nonetheless act as an interface between client computers and some kind of communications circuit.

Analog modems, the kind used with regular telephone lines, have been around for a long time and are frequently augmented with fax and voice-mail capabilities. Today, a typical mass-market modem is capable of operating at a data transfer speed of 28.8 Kbps (kilobits per second). The fastest models can operate at 33.6 Kbps, a speed near the theoretical maximum for analog modems using typical telephone lines.

 "You can never be too rich, too thin, or have too much bandwidth" is an oft-repeated axiom on the Internet these days. The demand for higher bandwidth home and small-office connections has generated considerable interest in *ISDN* and cable modems. ISDN is a switched digital service used for both voice and data and is typically capable of a data speed of 128 Kbps. Cable modems boast theoretical speeds of 10 Mbps (10,000 Kbps), but the availability of cable Internet access has been limited, so far. Most cable systems were originally designed to send signals only downstream (to the home) and require upgrades to enable Internet access. Possible degradation of the shared service during peak usage periods remains a concern, and final agreement on standards is not expected until 1997.

RBOCs are currently working with a high-speed technology called *ADSL* (Asymmetric Digital Subscriber Line) which they hope to begin deploying in 1998. ADSL promises to deliver high-speed connections over existing copper wiring. If and when RBOCs begin offering ADSL service, ADSL modems will be needed to improve the quality of the telephone line connection.

Industry

Modem sales have soared, driven by demand from telecommuters, small and home offices, Net surfers, and online service subscribers. International markets have just begun to flourish. Today, analog modems rule the roost because they are inexpensive and telephone service is available everywhere. U.S. Robotics leads the pack with about a quarter of the highly competitive market. Because newer, faster modems command premium pricing for very short periods, keys to success in the

"You can never be too rich, too thin, or have too much bandwidth."

*U. S. Robotics
enjoyed nearly
double the gross
margin of the
group average.*

modem business are short product-development cycles, low manufacturing costs, and strong distribution, either retail or OEM. Unlike most of its competitors, U.S. Robotics maintains in-house manufacturing capability, enabling the company to usually be first to market with faster modems and enjoy low unit-production costs. Zoom has taken a low-price/high-volume approach to the modem market with some success.

All of the analog modem manufacturers are diversifying, or have already diversified, into other markets, perhaps out of concern over the current speed limitations of telephone lines. All have entered the nascent ISDN modem market, where they face competition from 3Com, Motorola, and others. If ISDN modems become commodities and are commonly sold through mass-market channels, the analog modem manufacturers, with their well-developed retail distribution systems, would have an advantage. But the market is still small, and its future is difficult to forecast. The cable modem business barely exists, although Motorola has lined up some big orders from cable companies. Although General Instrument, Hewlett-Packard, and many other companies have joined most of the analog modem makers in announcing cable modem products, Zoom appears to have opted out of the market. ADSL looms on the horizon, threatening to take away cable's edge in a couple of years.

Investing

Demand for remote connections and the low, continually decreasing cost of using analog modems should allow the market to keep growing quickly over the near term. International growth in online services should also help in the long run. However, the cutthroat nature of the analog modem business, coupled with the prospect of hitting a data speed ceiling, has manufacturers scrambling to diversify. Gross margins in the June 1996 quarter plunged for all analog modem makers except for U.S. Robotics, which enjoyed nearly double the gross margin of the group average. U.S. Robotics derives significant revenue from other, related businesses, and its broad and highly differentiated analog modem product line has shielded the company from some of the margin pressure facing its rivals. Its in-house manufacturing strategy helps keep unit costs down when demand is strong but could hurt the company if sales slacken and production facilities are underutilized. That Zoom could remain in the black despite a gross margin of only 17.7% speaks well of its ability to execute its high-volume/low-price strategy.

OEMs accounted for 64% of Boca's sales. Margins aside, the OEM business looks good because of the increasing proportion of home PCs that are sold bundled with modems. Prospects appear grim for Global Village, whose principal product lines address the shrinking Macintosh market.

It is far too early to forecast the ISDN and cable modem markets. They are both very crowded at the present despite relatively modest sales. The strength of existing distribution channels (retail, OEM, value-added reseller, direct to corporations) will probably be a major factor in a company's success in these markets. Investors should try to determine whether the mass-market channels will be viable for cable modems. If not, many of the familiar names in analog modems may become minor players in the cable modem market. Interestingly, Zoom appears to have opted out of the cable modem market, preferring to wait for ADSL deployment. Zoom's approach could turn out to be wise if, in 2 years, ADSL gains wide acceptance and cuts into the cable modem business.

The strength of existing distribution channels will probably be a major factor in a company's success.

Application Software
Companies

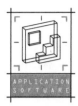

Application Software

What's Browser/Server/Plug-in Software?

When people talk about "surfing the Net," they are usually referring to the use of software to access and display information published on the World Wide Web. The display software that runs on a user's computer software is called a *Web browser*. On the publisher's computer, *Web server software* dishes out information over the Internet at the beck and call of the browser. Server software runs on server hardware.

Today, the World Wide Web is largely text-based, with most information displayed in a magazine-style format that includes text and graphics. Unlike magazines, Web pages employ hypertext that allows authors to link related documents. In order to add multimedia and other capabilities to Web browsers, 3rd-party software developers are creating companion applications known as *add-in software* or *plug-ins*. Typically, with one click of a mouse a user simultaneously launches a small program on his/her computer and instructs a Web server to send data to the program. For example, the plug-in could be an audio player and the data could contain a radio program broadcast earlier in the day.

Another way to add sound and motion to browsers is to employ *applets*, small programs transmitted by a server over the Internet and executed on a user's computer. Software technologies such as Sun's Java and Microsoft's ActiveX are used to create applets that run within browsers. Although the 2 technologies perform similar functions, each has advantages and disadvantages. ActiveX applets can be integrated into any Windows application but cannot run on non-Windows operating systems. A Java applet can run on any operating system and Java programming code is reusable, but it is difficult to program and is not yet fully developed. Java support is built into all popular browsers, including Microsoft's Explorer.

BROWSER/SERVER MARKET FORECAST ($ mil.)

	1995	1996	1997	1998	1999
Browsers	71	125	312	378	449
Server software	41	150	583	2,391	4,426

Source: Forrester Research

Microsoft had not simply set its sights on the browser market, but the whole enchilada.

COMPANIES AND MARKETS

Netscape vs. Microsoft

Before Microsoft stepped in, Netscape had been running away with the Web browser market. Netscape's giveaway of its popular Navigator browser had made it the industry standard, and the company had been making serious inroads into the lucrative corporate intranet market with its Web server and browser products. Microsoft's entry into the market with a free Explorer browser dashed any plans Netscape may have had to charge nonbusiness users for Navigator. Although early releases of Explorer were functionally inferior to Navigator, Microsoft rapidly caught up and, today, the companies are locked in a game of oneupmanship with respect to browser features.

Microsoft's focus on the Internet is relatively new. But once Microsoft CEO Bill Gates recognized what was at stake, he swiftly unveiled a strategy to "embrace and extend" the Internet. At that point it was clear that Microsoft had not simply set its sights on the browser market, but the whole enchilada — browsers, servers, development tools, and operating systems. The company elected to launch its war against Netscape by leveraging its stranglehold on desktop operating systems and giving away its Internet products for free. Microsoft announced that it would integrate its browser with its operating systems, eliminating the need of a Windows 95 user to procure another browser. Further, the company began including its Web server and Web development tool software with its Windows NT network operating system, a UNIX competitor, for free. Many of the tools used proprietary technology owned by Microsoft. The company inked deals with America Online, AT&T, CompuServe, and others that could turn millions of their subscribers into Explorer users. Most recently, Microsoft paid several content providers, including Dow Jones, ESPN, and MTV, to provide free subscriptions to their services to Explorer users.

Why, one might ask, are Netscape and Microsoft dueling over a market in which most of the products are given away for free? For Netscape, which charges business users for browsers, remaining the industry standard translates directly into dollars. Microsoft, which has begun integrating its browser into Windows 95, wants to own the browser market to strengthen its already vice-like grip on the operating systems market. In addition, the dominant browser software company gains leverage in other, related businesses. By controlling the technology used to view Web documents, a browser company would have a technical advantage in developing tools used to publish those documents. Similarly, a dominant browser company could begin using browser technology that worked optimally only with its server products, boosting its position in the server market. Controlling the window through which users see cyberspace also presents opportunities to charge advertisers and content providers for driving traffic to their Web sites. Netscape has already received $5 million each from several Internet search services for this.

Why, one might ask, are Netscape and Microsoft dueling over a market in which most of the products are given away for free?

Before the latest round of Microsoft initiatives, Dataquest estimated Netscape's browser market share to be more than 80%, so Microsoft has a long way to go to catch up. In the server market, Microsoft is at a disadvantage because its product will only run on its Windows NT operating system. In contrast, Netscape's server works with several operating systems, including UNIX, NT, and Macintosh. Although NT sales increased by 150% in the June quarter, its installed base in large corporations remains small. Of Web servers installed on the Internet, freeware products hold a share of 61%, Netscape 12%, and Microsoft 1%, according to a recent Webcrawler survey. Freeware products are unsupported in any traditional sense and, as a result, are generally thought to be less appealing to corporations with important applications. Around 83% of the servers surveyed by Webcrawler ran under UNIX.

Other Players

Some small companies in the browser and server businesses have departed rather than be caught in the Netscape/Microsoft crossfire. Spyglass licenses its Web technology to other companies, including Microsoft, which embed Web functions into their software. In this way, Spyglass avoids direct competition in the browser and server markets. Open Market is battling Netscape in the market for secure Web servers used for commercial transactions and seems to have gained a foothold. Oracle distributes specialized Web server software, mainly for the purpose of turning its database programs into Internet/intranet applications.

Plug-in product makers give away their proprietary "player" software to users in the hopes that publishers will buy their companion software tools to publish on the Web. Recently there has been a proliferation of plug-ins, so building consumer awareness for a new one is becoming a problem. Among companies profiled in this book, Adobe, Apple, and Macromedia have developed popular plug-ins, but it is not clear whether they are generating significant new sales of publishing software or simply satisfying existing customers. It remains to be seen if a serious business can be built using a plug-in strategy.

Recently there has been a proliferation of plug-ins, so building consumer awareness for a new one is becoming a problem.

Investment Considerations

Guessing who will win the battle of the Web browsers is a popular pastime in Internet circles. Many in the industry, particularly those fond of UNIX, openly root for Netscape or, perhaps more accurately, against Microsoft. To combat the software giant, Netscape needs such friends. One way Netscape has garnered support is by embracing open systems and attracting partners who develop software applications that work with Navigator. If Netscape's browser/server combination can become the centerpiece around which important Internet/intranet applications are built, the company may de-emphasize the importance of Windows in network computing. This is apparently what Netscape chairman Jim Clark meant when he said that his company was an operating system company.

To survive over the long run, Netscape needs to remain competitive in browsers and quickly make significant headway in the coveted intranet market. Netscape is in a race against time as Microsoft appears to be sparing no expense to overtake it. For this fiscal year, the software giant has budgeted $2 billion for R&D. Microsoft's

NT operating system is poised to take away Novell's market in small companies and is increasingly popular in large ones. The key indicators to watch are Microsoft's browser share and network operating system share. The faster NT penetrates the corporate market, the less time Netscape has to execute its strategy and become entrenched as a central fixture of the Internet. And if Netscape stumbles badly in the browser market, it could be over.

PUBLISHING TOOLS

What Are Publishing Tools?

To publish on the World Wide Web, authors must create documents using *HTML* (hypertext markup language), a standardized but evolving set of codes that tell the browser how to format elements of a document. For example, one set of codes tells the browser to display text in italics; another set tells it to display data in tabular format; yet another set tells the browser to display a link to a different document. To eliminate the need to memorize the codes and type them in by hand, many companies have created HTML editors which speed up and simplify the creation of Web documents.

The key indicators to watch are Microsoft's browser share and network operating system share.

Other publishing tools enable authors to present information in formats not made available by HTML, usually through the use of plug-ins. For example, multimedia presentations created with Macromedia's Director software may be displayed over the Internet by using the company's ShockWave plug-in player. Sun's Java programming language is another publishing tool.

Database programs are also used in the Web publishing process, though they are not, strictly speaking, publishing tools. Because most leading databases reside on servers and are accessed by clients, they are a natural means of information dissemination over the World Wide Web.

APPLICATION SOFTWARE MARKET FORECAST ($ mil.)					
	1995	1996	1997	1998	1999
Tools	15	90	330	769	1,236
Applets	—	3	41	192	629
Applications	0	14	107	581	1,760

Source: Forrester Research

The challenge

for Adobe and

Macromedia is

to transfer their

desktop dominance

to the Internet.

Companies and Markets

The market for HTML editors, though large, has become crowded and commoditized. Netscape has added editing features to its browser and Microsoft has distributed free code that turns its market-leading Word word processor into an HTML editor. In addition, several small, low-overhead companies are distributing reasonably capable editors over the Internet at low prices. Nevertheless, such companies as Adobe and SoftQuad continue to try to leverage their print media experience and technology to carve out a stake in HTML editing.

To date, most of the Web is dominated by print-media content that has been converted to HTML format by using editors and other translation tools, resulting in static pages. The industry is now rushing to bring out tools to convert other kinds of content, such as sound and video, to Web-friendly formats and to provide the means to create original, Web-specific material. Microsoft and Netscape are active in this market, as are Adobe, Macromedia, and a host of start-ups.

Oracle and Informix are the key database providers to the Internet/intranet industry. Oracle has developed software to integrate many of the features of its products with Web technology. Informix has a tight relationship with Netscape, which uses Informix products in several of its server applications.

Investment Considerations

No company could possibly create a large business based on simple HTML editors, which is bad news for SoftQuad. Many market participants are distributing HTML editors because they feel obligated to provide customers with all the tools necessary for Web publishing. Others, like Microsoft, Netscape, Apple, and Adobe, have grander designs, hoping to create integrated software suites capable of all sorts of multimedia Web publishing. Although it is too early to anoint any winners in this market, Microsoft and Netscape appear to have an edge by virtue of their position in the browser market. The challenge for Adobe and Macromedia is to transfer their desktop dominance to the Internet. They must provide a satisfactory migration path for their desktop customers to the Web or risk losing them to competitors. This task appears most formidable for Adobe, whose products have historically supported the static print media. All of the players have time to ready their multimedia products because current bandwidth limitations will discourage users from seeking out multimedia Web publications.

Database companies appear superbly positioned to profit from Internet/intranet growth. Oracle's transaction and business-oriented applications put the company in the middle of the booming intranet market. Informix, with its expertise in multimedia databases and relationship with Netscape, also seems a good bet.

BEYOND BROWSING

Many organizations and individuals would like to use the Internet for specific purposes not well served by browsers alone. A large number of companies are developing a variety of Web-based applications in the hopes of becoming major players in these emerging markets. To date, much of the development work has focused on information retrieval, commerce, and Internet telephony. No applications market is highly developed at this point, but many have the potential to be very large. When transacting over the Internet becomes practical, the market for Web-based business application software will likely mushroom, but, for now, the future for any individual company remains cloudy. We have profiled a diverse group of pioneering software companies whose products operate on the Web.

Database companies appear superbly positioned to profit from Internet/intranet growth.

OFF THE WEB

What Else Happens on the Internet?

The World Wide Web may have become the prime attraction of the Internet, but it is not the only one. The TCP/IP communications standard can be used for any kind of application. In fact, Web browser developers have incorporated older, non-Web-based Internet services into their software, allowing users to access many Internet services from a single program. These services include e-mail (electronic mail), Usenet (a collection of electronic message boards), and File Transfer Protocol or FTP (a system for transmitting and receiving data files). Software manages these and basic TCP/IP services on servers and clients.

When Microsoft announced that it would incorporate TCP/IP functionality into Windows 95, the outlook for the industry changed.

Companies and Markets

The market for providing software for basic TCP/IP connectivity and services has taken a leap forward with widespread corporate adoption of intranets. FTP, Novell, and NetManage, which generally sell their products in all-in-one suites, have benefited from the trend. But when Microsoft announced that it would incorporate TCP/IP functionality into Windows 95, the outlook for the industry changed. Confronted with encroachment on their TCP/IP market from the operating system side and incorporation of Internet services from the browser side, FTP and NetManage have elected to branch out into application software. In the e-mail market, Qualcomm's Eudora has emerged as an industry standard and is cutting into sales of proprietary network e-mail systems developed by Lotus, Novell, and Microsoft.

Investment Considerations

For the next year, the TCP/IP suite developers are probably safe. Microsoft's current TCP/IP implementation in Windows 95 is not strong enough to displace a full-featured software suite at corporate sites. But Microsoft is likely to add TCP/IP functionality to future versions of its operating systems, slowly dissolving the market for such products. Consequently, FTP and NetManage must successfully extend their product lines to continue to grow over the long run.

Although the possibilities for non-Web-based applications are limitless, most developers are setting their sights on the Web. The Web has taken most of the user mindshare and, more importantly, most of the user traffic. While this is unlikely to change any time soon, there is no technical reason why a new client/server application could not emerge, dethrone the Web, and turn the entire Internet industry upside down.

Specialized Services
Companies

SPECIALIZED
SERVICES

Specialized
Services

As Internet usage expands and technology improves, increasing numbers of companies are developing Web-based service businesses. At this stage, most of the activity has revolved around information search and retrieval services and transaction-related services.

SEARCH AND RETRIEVAL SERVICES

How do Internet Searches Work?

The Internet is, by its nature, a decentralized, disorganized amalgam of networks and information. Web-based Internet search sites attempt to bring order to the chaos. All such services employ *search engines,* software programs that sift through the search companies' catalogs of existing Internet sites in response to key words typed in by the user. The user is then presented with a list of sites, typically Web sites that the search engine has deemed relevant to the user's area of interest. While results returned from such searches are not always fully satisfactory, they are extremely useful in pointing users in the right direction. Such services are extremely popular and, for the foreseeable future, integral features of the Web.

Going one step further, information retrieval services scan a wide variety of electronic sources for information of interest (typically news) to the user and then deliver the information to the user's desktop, often via the Internet. The customized search is based on topics of interest indicated by the user.

While not considered search sites, stock quote services perform a similar function, retrieving quotations from company-controlled databases. Such services provide 15- or 20-minute-delayed quotes for free and charge fees for real-time quotes.

Companies and Segments

Among search sites, the current leaders in advertising revenue appear to be Yahoo! and Infoseek, with Lycos, America Online's Webcrawler, Excite and a host of others trailing. It is not clear how Digital Equipment's Alta Vista search service, which may be accessed on its own site or Yahoo!'s, will stack up when it begins selling advertising. All search sites are, or will soon be, free and advertising-supported, and their business models call for generating increasing levels of user traffic on their sites. Advertisers pay for user "impressions," so, in general, the more impressions a Web site can deliver, the higher the potential advertising revenue. Consequently, all of the services seek partners to establish inbound links from their sites to the search engines. Search companies sometimes pay for these links. Increasingly, these companies are adding content, such as news and feature articles, to enrich their sites.

All of the search services are attempting to build strong brand identities.

Differentiation of navigational services is difficult and technical barriers to entry appear to be relatively low at this stage, so all of the search services are attempting to build strong brand identities. Yahoo!'s early success appears to be related to its "attitude" and to its early adoption of a search method that combines hierarchical Web directory listings with keyword searching. Yahoo!, Lycos, Infoseek, Excite, and Alta Vista are all unprofitable.

Information retrieval companies such as Individual, Inc. and Desktop Data charge fees for their services. Their customers are generally business people and organizations with a need for timely news reports concerning their industries. Although these services did not originally deliver their information over the Internet or intranets, they are taking advantage of it now and have established Web-based services. UK-based M.A.I.D has put a different spin on the search and retrieval business by creating a fee-based online search service that focuses on business information. Like the information retrieval companies, M.A.I.D searches a large number of free and proprietary electronic databases, further differentiating it from Internet search services.

Quote services have rapidly expanded their presence on the Web. Demand for free stock quotes is high and rising. The Web business models of Data Broadcasting Corporation, PC Quote, Reuters, and CheckFree's PAAWS unit are similar to that of the search engine companies: bargain for lots of inbound links to generate traffic and sell advertising. A key difference is that the quote service companies also sell real-time quotes and other financial information, relatively tried-and-true businesses.

Investment Considerations

It seems unlikely that there will be a "Big Four" or "Big Five" in general search services over the long run. Through technological, organizational, or marketing innovation, one will likely rise to the top. The victor stands to gain a tremendous amount of user traffic as Internet usage grows. At the moment the best bet appears to be Yahoo!, but the battle has just begun, and many combatants have coffers filled with cash from recent IPOs. One potential long-term concern for the business is that browser companies could start rival services and build access to them directly into their browsers, cutting off traffic to rival search sites.

In quote services, DBC has more familiarity with delivering low-cost quotes to individuals, while PC Quote has more experience delivering financial information to large organizations. PC Quote faces large, well-heeled competition in its business, and its earnings have been volatile. Assuming that PC Quote's big rivals stay out of the less lucrative individual investor market, DBC appears to have smoother sailing ahead.

Demand for customized news delivered to the desktop appears to be quite strong, and both Individual, Inc. and Desktop Data are growing nicely. Internet technology greatly simplifies their data delivery process and has probably expanded their universe of prospective customers. The low end of the business may be threatened by new advertising-based services such as PointCast (private), which provide free customized news. At present, such services as PointCast cannot compete with Individual or Desktop on search capability or number of databases searched, and their presence may help heighten awareness of customized news. In the long run, however, PointCast and others could pose a problem.

In quote services, DBC has more familiarity with delivering low-cost quotes to individuals, while PC Quote has more experience delivering financial information to large organizations.

Yet another possible development, the use of electronic *"personal agents,"* could completely change the search and retrieval business. Companies like Verity and General Magic are set to release software that sends electronic agents into the Internet in search of information desired by the user. In the future, agents may gain the ability to pay for bits of information, greatly expanding the amount available to them. Widespread use of personal agents could negatively affect search and retrieval companies, but would not pose a big problem for stock quotation services.

TRANSACTION PROCESSING

How Does Transaction Processing Work on the Web?

In general, companies are concentrating on 3 kinds of Internet-based consumer transactions: home banking, online buying, and stock brokerage. For security reasons, critical elements of the transactions are performed on private networks. In the case of stock brokerage, the actual trades do not take place over the Internet; rather, only orders and account information are sent between the broker and trader. In home banking, account balances and related information are available over the Internet, but bill paying typically occurs electronically over private networks or physically with a financial intermediary actually sending a check to the seller. Schemes to enable online buying typically involve the use of credit cards because a large, developed, electronic infrastructure already exists to accommodate credit card transactions. Current systems use a "wallet" — data stored on the user's computer containing personal and credit card information as a kind of online credit card. To buy something from a Web-based merchant, the wallet information is encrypted and transmitted to the merchant's Web site, where information about the merchant is attached. The data is then transmitted to the transaction service company, which decrypts the data and processes the credit card transaction.

Companies and Segments

Growth in Web-based financial transactions has been hindered by security concerns, a glaring lack of standards, and operational problems. Because home-banking transactions have, so far, taken place off the Internet, they are more developed. CheckFree is the leader in consumer bill-paying. Intuit is trying to coax its base of 9 million Quicken (personal finance software) users to online banking. In the credit-card buying arena, CyberCash, CheckFree, and First USA Paymentech's First Virtual unit have set up shop, but each must persuade buyers and merchants to use their proprietary system. Perhaps the greatest problem facing these companies is the apparent lack of demand for commercial transactions. While consumer concerns over the security of Internet-based transaction accounts are partly to blame, the absence of compelling merchandising has also been a factor.

Stock brokerage seems to be a natural Web service. Communication takes place in real time, fully electronic communications reduce costs, brokerage services may be easily and naturally combined with other personal finance services, and the services are theoretically accessible anywhere. Lured by commissions of under $15 per trade, do-it-yourself investors have flocked to online brokers through the Internet and online services such as America Online and CompuServe. E*TRADE and Charles Schwab are among the leaders in the industry.

Investment Considerations

Everyone involved in Internet commerce is waiting for the industry to take off. Visa, MasterCard, and American Express are working to establish standards for Internet credit card transactions, which may help the online credit-card-related services. On the other hand, Electronic Data Systems and other large credit card processors pose a long-term threat to today's startups. A more immediate concern to companies like CyberCash is the imminent arrival of software from VeriFone that is promoted as an end-to-end solution enabling a merchant to use existing credit card clearing systems and eliminate 3rd-party clearing services.

A key to growth in electronic bill-paying is the development of systems to deliver bills electronically. Current systems are works in progress. A major challenge for companies in electronic banking is to change customer habits. Without very attractive pricing, customers will hesitate to do their banking online. Only by fully automating the payment process can companies in this business bring down costs enough to offer compelling pricing to the consumer.

Discount broker Charles Schwab burst onto the scene when the brokerage industry eliminated fixed commissions and has prospered ever since. While it is

A major challenge for companies in electronic banking is to change customer habits. Without very attractive pricing, customers will hesitate to do their banking online.

difficult to identify the next Schwab, it seems reasonable to expect similar success to shine on one or more online brokers. A major issue that all Internet-based brokers must deal with is reliability of service. On recent heavy trading days, some brokers have experienced problems handling the volume, angering customers. Other times, Internet connections have been unsatisfactory, an unacceptable condition for stock traders. With growth in Internet usage taxing the existing national network infrastructure, this problem may worsen. Although this is not within the control of the online brokers, it could severely dampen investor enthusiasm for their services.

WHAT'S HAPPENING IN ONLINE ENTERTAINMENT?

Many software developers dream of dynamic, interactive, multimedia entertainment delivered by the Internet into homes across the US. Unfortunately, bandwidth requirements for such activities simply cannot be met with the existing infrastructure. When bandwidth issues are resolved, most observers expect game software companies and film and video production companies to jump into the business. Many consider CD-ROM games to be an interim step toward online distribution of entertainment. Today several game makers are selling add-on software enabling users to play CD-ROM-based games against each other over telephone lines, LANs, and, to a lesser extent, the Internet. But, for now, there are a limited number of companies devoted to Internet-based entertainment beyond static, magazine-style Web pages. We have profiled 2 of them, trivia game producer NTN and online gambling startup Multimedia Games.

When bandwidth issues are resolved, most observers expect game software companies and film and video production companies to jump into the business.

Content

Companies

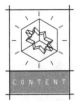

Content

Most of the hardware, networks, and software involved in the online world are designed to deliver *content* to the user's desktop. Content can take many forms, including text, pictures, sound, and video. Although the distinctions sometimes get blurry, the industry generally separates content-related companies into 2 groups: content aggregators and content providers.

WHAT IS A CONTENT AGGREGATOR?

Many companies organize information from various sources and publish it online. Such companies are known as *content aggregators*. Organizations and individuals who provide content to aggregators are called *content providers*. Online services, such as America Online, use proprietary software and networks to publish content, while Web-based content aggregators use standardized software and the Internet to make their information available.

Companies and Segments

The top online service providers, America Online and CompuServe, began service well before the Internet craze began. They have always organized and published a wide variety of content and provided services to individuals and organizations for hourly access fees. AOL toppled CompuServe and became the industry leader largely because of its easy-to-use interface and ability to facilitate the creation of online communities, groups of people sharing and discussing common interests online. Most other national online services failed as AOL and CompuServe continued to grow. But as the Web gained popularity and content, and as the cost of Internet access dropped, users began to wonder if online services were just expense mini-Webs. Recently AOL announced sluggish subscriber growth, and CompuServe admitted that its subscriber count dropped for the first time ever.

Industry analysts seem to feel that AOL and CompuServe are competing against the Web as a whole. Search services and Web-based aggregators, including Microsoft, AT&T, and thousands of others, have created sites that range in focus from general interest to the most obscure topics. Most of the content is available free, so the user pays only for Internet access. AOL and CompuServe have responded by providing Internet connectivity to their customers, but their prices make Internet access expensive. Online services have to pay for their networks, their software, their content, and their organizational effort, while ISPs need only pay network costs. Most search sites and Web publishers seem content to lose money for the time being, so an abundance of high-quality material (and even more low-quality material) is freely distributed over the Web.

The online service providers face significant challenges in retaining existing subscribers and attracting new ones.

Investment Considerations

Web content aggregation is a very new and seemingly unprofitable business. Most aggregators are experimenting with advertising-based business models but could eventually abandon them in favor of subscriptions or pay-per-view schemes. With the Internet growing as fast as it is, it seems clear that profitable businesses could emerge from the pack. But a shakeout could be a long way off because it is so inexpensive to publish on the Web.

Both AOL and CompuServe shares have plummeted in the recent past. Only subscriber growth will bring investors back to these stocks. The online service providers face significant challenges in retaining existing subscribers and attracting new ones. They must justify, and probably lower, their hourly rates. The key for both companies is to differentiate their services from the Web through ease of use, network speed and reliability, superior organization, quality of content, or, in AOL's case, sense of community. Advertising and online commerce have the potential to increase revenue for both companies significantly. And AOL's base of more than 6 million subscribers makes it a powerful presence in the online world. In contrast, NETCOM, the leading independent ISP, has just 500,000 subscribers.

CONTENT PROVIDERS

The growth and hype about the Internet has encouraged most publishers to find ways to recycle (the industry prefers "re-purpose") their content to generate revenues from the Web. This is typically accomplished by licensing content to an aggregator or creating a Web site and either selling information or generating advertising revenue from it.

Companies and Investment Considerations

The oft-repeated complaint that "nobody is making money on the Internet" usually comes from publishers. Many traditional publishers, lured by the siren song of no paper, printing, and binding costs, have tried to take their print products directly to the Web and have been disappointed with the results. Some, particularly those like Reuters, that provide time-sensitive information like news, and others who publish "need-to-know" reference information, have been more successful. No one knows the secret formula to success in Web publishing. What is clear is that the Internet, as a medium, rewards different kinds of content than that which most print publishers are accustomed to providing. A few obvious advantages of the Internet are that content can be disseminated extremely quickly, it can be accessed from any point on the globe, it can be linked to related information, and it is interactive. Investors should look for publishers employing these and other Internet-specific advantages to their benefit.

Today, many startup companies specialize in online publishing. Some, like Wired Ventures, c|net, and Mecklermedia, create content for multiple media. Wired's online business remains unprofitable, demonstrating that even intimate industry understanding is no guarantee of success.

Sites devoted to providing information useful to businesses may have the greatest chance for success over the near term. With the expansion of intranets giving increasing numbers of people Internet access from the workplace, the business audience is growing rapidly. If a publisher or service company creates and adequately promotes a Web site that will save businesses time or money, you can be sure that businesses will use it. Business publishers profiled in this book include Reuters and Telescan.

Many traditional publishers, lured by the siren song of no paper, printing, and binding costs, have tried to take their print products directly to the Web and have been disappointed with the results.

Content

7

Most Web publishers are trying out the advertising model of revenue generation, perhaps because the Internet community has traditionally held that information ought to be free. Web business models could change with the advent of personal agents, since these electronic servants would probably be programmed to ignore advertising when retrieving data. In all probability, a wide variety of viable business models will emerge, as they have in other media.

Internet Access
Companies

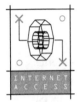

Internet Access

Although one might think that the RBOCs would be the first to provide basic Internet access, they seem to have been the last. Several start-up companies jumped into the vacuum in the Internet access marketplace and are now battling RBOCs and other giant telecommunications companies for consumer and business dollars.

What is an ISP?

Internet Service Providers (ISPs) offer dial-up and dedicated connections to their networks which are, in turn, connected to the Internet. National ISPs build hundreds of *points of presence* (POPs) around the country to provide local service to major population centers. Each POP is typically connected to the ISP's network through a regional hub, which is linked to the ISP's other hubs over very a fast, high-capacity portion of the network known as the *backbone*. The configuration is analogous to driveways, city streets, highways: the link between the consumer and the POP is the driveway, the connection between the POP and the hub is the city street, and the backbone is the highway. The ISP's backbone connects with other providers's backbones at various locations across the country, providing full Internet access. Backbones may be owned or leased from telecommunications carriers.

Companies and Segments

A few national ISPs, including NETCOM, BBN, MCI, and AT&T, operate as described above, but many others provide access at a regional or local level only. Some operate regionally under the same model as the national ISPs. Others lack sufficient connections to the Internet, so they arrange to link their networks with other national backbones owned by others. For example, PSINet sells access to its national backbone to Mindspring, Earthlink, and IDT.

NETCOM, with 500,000 subscribers, is the largest ISP. AT&T, despite operating only a few months, has rapidly assumed the #2 spot and is rising fast. America Online provides more than 6 million subscribers with Internet access but, because it is considered to be an online services company, it is not usually found in ISP rankings.

The consumer access segment has become extremely competitive since AT&T's entry into the business. Shortly after AT&T's announcement, UUNet sold out to MFS Communications and PSINet unloaded its consumer access business. Along with tough price competition, companies in the consumer segment face substantial customer turnover or "churn," high customer-service expense, and heavy customer acquisition costs. Capital spending requirements are high for all companies in the industry, particularly for those building out a national infrastructure.

Seeing growth in the business market and stiff price competition on the consumer side, many ISPs have redoubled their efforts to land corporate customers.

The corporate side of the access business is more profitable. Corporate accounts buy access and *hosting services*, maintenance of corporate Web servers by ISPs. Seeing growth in the business market and stiff price competition on the consumer side, many ISPs have redoubled their efforts to land corporate customers. AT&T, MCI, and the RBOCs constitute formidable competition in this market.

The high cost of wireless communications has discouraged its use for Internet access. To address the problem, a small company called Metricom has developed a system for using numerous, small, low-cost radio transmitters to provide wireless Internet connectivity at very low prices. The system has not yet been widely deployed.

Hambrecht & Quist estimates that the Internet access market will expand to 17 times its current size by the year 2000.

Investment Considerations

Consumer Internet access is a near-commodity service in which key differentiating factors are likely to remain network reliability, speed, and price. Independent ISPs now have their hands full combating the powerful AT&T and RBOC brand names and, at the same time, have to fund the expansion and upgrading of their systems. ISPs whose customer lists are heavily weighted toward the consumer market include NETCOM, Mindspring, Earthlink, and IDT. Any developments leading to price stratification within the consumer market (i.e., guaranteed bandwidth services, increased penetration of ISDN) would be favorable to the group.

Some investors like to evaluate ISPs on the basis of a value per subscriber, a method popular in the cable TV business. Using this methodology, the value of the franchise is determined by multiplying the number of subscribers by the value per subscriber. The recent sales price of PSINet's consumer subscriber base to Mindspring implies a current market value of about $230 per subscriber. Whether the cable TV valuation method is valid for ISPs is a matter of dispute because, unlike Internet access businesses, cable TV systems are generally operated as monopolies.

Corporate clients generate higher revenues, are less likely to switch ISPs, and are more likely to upgrade to faster, more expensive access than their consumer counterparts. Despite intensifying competition, the corporate market is likely to remain more profitable than the consumer business. BBN and PSINet have focused their access businesses on this segment, but their customer lists are not yet big enough to generate consistent profits. Teleport stock offers a different way to invest in the access business. Since the company offers telecommunications services, including WAN and LAN connectivity, to businesses in several metropolitan areas, it could be considered an intranet access play.

Corporate clients generate higher revenues, are less likely to switch ISPs, and are more likely to upgrade to faster, more expensive access than their consumer counterparts.

Industry Services Companies

Industry Services

A cottage industry of consultants has emerged to help companies take advantage of new business opportunities made possible by the rise of the Internet. Most companies offering such services are small and private or are units of much larger organizations. The usual suspects, such as Electronic Data Systems and Andersen Consulting, are ramping up their Internet services operations. The universe of publicly traded service companies with significant exposure to the Internet is quite small. Most of the companies we profile here specialize in marketing services.

HOW DOES WEB-BASED ADVERTISING WORK?

The Web is a new medium, and advertisers are still learning how to best use it for selling products and services. The way most companies go about advertising on the Web is to build a site promoting their products and then promote the site. Site promotion occurs in many forms, including advertising in traditional media, but the most effective way to draw traffic to a Web site is to promote it on the Web itself. Web site operators sell links to the promotional sites, usually in the form of "banner" ads along the top of a Web page that offer some sort of enticement to "click here." Clicking through to the site pulls users into the new frontier of interactive advertising. On the Web, the user controls the advertising experience. A motivated prospect could spend hours in an advertiser's site, digging deeper and deeper for more product information.

Using the Web, an advertiser can offer a lively, interactive catalog accessible by anyone, anywhere. To be successful, a company must advertise on Web sites used by prospective customers, lure prospects to its site, and promote its products in a manner that is engaging and useful to prospects.

Companies and the Web Advertising Industry

New-media advertising agencies have sprung up to help companies create and maintain promotional Web sites. CKS Group, founded in 1987, is the old-timer of publicly traded new-media advertising agencies. Another industry veteran, Poppe Tyson, filed for an initial public offering shortly before this book was published. The Leap Group is a newer entrant into the industry. All 3 companies specialize in using emerging technology as part of larger, cross-media advertising campaigns. All major agencies have established interactive or Web advertising groups, so CKS, Poppe Tyson, and Leap face significant, well-established competition.

The birth of the Web as a vehicle for advertising and commerce has created new opportunities for market researchers. Market research takes on special significance because the chaotic, decentralized nature of the Web makes estimates of market size and composition extremely difficult to determine. In addition, the technology enables advertisers to tailor their messages to the individual. Industry giant Nielsen and Find/SVP have entered the market, as has IntelliQuest, a small company profiled in this book.

Investment Considerations

The market for Web-based advertising appears to be strong and, as competition for customers increases, promotional Web sites are likely to get more elaborate. According to Jupiter Communications, the Web will become a $5 billion-per-year advertising medium by 2000. This is good news for Web advertising agencies. Although the new-media agencies must compete with enormous, international rivals, their focus on Web advertising may give them access to accounts that would ordinarily be out of their reach. Because they also work with traditional

According to Jupiter Communications, the Web will become a $5 billion-per-year advertising medium by 2000. This is good news for Web advertising agencies.

media and perform other traditional agency work, it is possible that they can leverage their Web expertise to sell additional services to clients. If they succeed in carving out a meaningful piece of the Web advertising pie, they could receive takeover offers. Investors should be aware that small advertising agencies are extremely dependent on key personnel, and one or two defections can have a devastating effect on business.

Cyberstocks

IV. INVESTING IN CHANGE

Change and the Cyberstock Investor

The key to successful cyberstock investing is coping with rapidly changing technologies, markets, and companies. Without a great deal of luck, a buy-and-hold strategy simply will not work. For example, about 15 years ago, as the microcomputer industry first caught the attention of the investors, the leading desktop operating system was CP/M, the #1 word processor was WordStar, and the top spreadsheet program was VisiCalc. The list of leading microcomputer makers included Kaypro and Osborne. All are distant memories now, companies made extinct by shifts in technical standards, competitive product innovations, and the rise of Microsoft.

No one knows for sure what kinds of events, trends, and technical advances will prove to be most important in shaping the future of the Internet. Many, including bandwidth expansion, are discussed earlier in the industry reviews in Part III. Also worth pondering are a few issues with implications for all Internet-related industries:

*If the experience
of the retail industry,
in which 4 of 5
startups fail, is any
guide, most online
merchants will be
unsuccessful.*

Network Overload — Metcalf's Law's Evil Twin

As additional users, services, and technologies increase the utility of the Internet, they generate ever-increasing levels of traffic. While at first this may seem to be uniformly positive for the industry and cyberstock investors, the rapid rise in traffic has taxed the infrastructure and, as any daytime Internet user knows, degraded network performance. A few experts, including Bob Metcalf, whose "law" was discussed in Chapter 2, have predicted an imminent breakdown of the Internet as a result of overloading the network. Should this occur, it could have devastating consequences for cyberstocks, particularly those of companies lacking intranet exposure. The market would seriously question the overall Internet investment thesis or, at a minimum, the near-term earnings prospects of Internet-based companies. And how attractive would high-speed cable or ADSL Internet access be if the Internet itself were abysmally slow?

Such events create opportunities for astute cyberstock investors, and not just because of lower stock prices. For example, adjusting the system of bandwidth allocation, perhaps by making users pay for guaranteed bandwidth, is a possible solution to the Internet gridlock problem outlined above. The ability to sell such premium Internet access services could significantly enhance the long-term earnings prospects of some national Internet service providers. Along these lines, MCI has already announced a private Internet service to circumvent the Internet's clogged public arteries.

Secure, Simple Transactions

When the kinks are worked out of Web-based transactions, the Internet may become an important commercial venue. Both business-to-business and consumer transactions could benefit from the efficiencies of digital commerce. The ability to conduct personalized sales pitches and the reduction in sales and order-processing costs would encourage merchants of all stripes to climb on the electronic commerce bandwagon. If the experience of the retail industry, in which 4 of 5 startups fail, is any guide, most online merchants will be unsuccessful. The Internet will probably turn out to be more friendly to some kinds of commerce than others.

So who is likely to succeed in online merchandising? Traditional retailing appears to be quite different from e-commerce. Mail-order companies seem to have the most experience relevant to online selling, but they have not had to deal with an interactive medium in which competitive price checking is fairly easy. A new breed of online merchants will probably emerge over the next few years, and some will go public as independent companies. Successful investing in this sector involves identifying the advantages of transacting online and buying stocks of companies whose merchandising reflects the unique capabilities of the medium. For example, a neighborhood store selling items wanted by a very small segment of the population might fail where a Web site selling the same goods to customers worldwide could succeed.

Internationalization

To date, most Internet activity has been confined to the US. Now rapid change is under way, and browsing the Internet is becoming an international experience. So far, most participants have been forced to communicate in English, giving a clear advantage to programmers and content developers located in English-speaking countries. Whether English will evolve into the international language of the Internet remains to be seen. If not, the Internet would probably cleave along language lines. Markets involving content would be segmented by language, with market size determined by language rather than geography or political boundaries. Companies based in English-speaking countries would have to adapt or accept a smaller piece of the Internet pie. Extremely long-term thinkers may want to consider that approximately 25% of the world's population is of Chinese descent.

Markets involving content would be segmented by language, with market size determined by language rather than geography or political boundaries.

Wireless Access

Whether by satellite, by Metricom's radio network, by Qualcomm's personal communication service system, or by some other means, fast, reasonably priced wireless Internet access will eventually become a reality. When it occurs, all Internet-based services will become portable. Combined with a light, portable, easy-to-read Internet computer, such a development could put an end to printed newspapers. The ability to deliver sound to automobile drivers could give a big boost to the audio-on-demand industry. Wireless Internet access has profound implications for telecommuters and mobile workers as well as consumers. What would you do if you could carry the Internet with you?

INVESTING IN CHANGE

The dizzying pace of change challenges the cyberstock investor to keep up with events and always to remain open-minded. It is the same challenge that confronts CEOs of Internet-related companies every day. While this book was being written, the boards of directors of several of those companies fired their CEOs and began looking for people who could look at their businesses from new perspectives. For these companies, last year's business model is out of date.

Investors in cyberstocks need to think like CEOs, only with less company loyalty. The first task is to understand a company's strategy and decide if it makes sense within the context of its industry. A good strategy is easily articulated and outlines how a company plans to create or maintain a unique advantage in the marketplace.

Investors in cyberstocks need to think like CEOs, only with less company loyalty.

Perhaps the most popular strategy among Internet-related companies today is the so-called "Trojan horse" strategy. This calls for a company to sell one, must-have component of a larger system to a rival's customer. Then, exploiting a foot in the door, the company sells the customer associated products until the rival's products have been eliminated from the customer site. The Trojan horse strategy generally is coupled with a "one-stop-shopping" pitch that argues for buying everything from a single vendor for simplicity's sake. For example, Cisco Systems has installed products called "routers" in a huge number of networks. After buying a large number of network equipment companies, Cisco can now use each of its routers as a Trojan horse to sell nearly an entire network installation, promising customers optimal interoperability between components and the advantages of dealing with a single vendor.

In many cases, evaluation of a corporate strategy will be hindered by the short history of the Internet industry in which the company operates. Occasionally an investor can gain some insight into the industry by simply browsing Web sites of the company and its competitors and trying out their products or services. A far less risky approach is to refrain from investing in these areas and instead focus on better-established segments such as infrastructure equipment manufacturing.

If a company's strategy seems solid, the next task is to establish a set of expectations to serve as a performance yardstick. A typical set of measures could include market share or position, sales, gross margin, earnings, earnings per share, and any other indicators of success or failure of the company's strategy, such as new product and technical developments. So armed, an investor can use **www.cyberstocks.com**, this book's companion Web site, to monitor the company's progress and review the validity of the investment thesis.

Timing a cyberstock purchase is a tricky business. One way to avoid the issue entirely is to dollar-cost average by phasing in stock purchases over several months. But most individual investors will opt for taking the plunge all at once, raising the vexing issue of valuation. At any moment in time, a stock's value may be in the eye of the beholder but, in the long run, its earnings dictate its value. Some cyberstock valuations are very high, with market capitalizations of several hundreds of millions of dollars despite very modest or nonexistent earnings. In cases such as these, the market has already priced a great deal of long-term success into the stocks. Investors should ask themselves what could go wrong and whether those risks have been adequately incorporated into stock prices. Technology shifts and delayed product releases regularly reverse the fortunes of high-tech companies.

Timing the sale of a cyberstock can be equally difficult. In general, a cyberstock should be sold when the original reasons for buying the stock are no longer true. As obvious as this seems, it is not always easy to determine if a company has simply had a bad quarter or faces grave strategic problems. Market share losses may be the best indication that the investment thesis should be challenged.

To sum up, there is no substitute for industry knowledge, current information, a little vision, and a lot of cold, hard logic when investing in cyberstocks. The only way to deal with a constantly changing industry is to remain alert for major shifts in technologies and markets. After spotting a change, individual investors can employ their key advantage over large financial institutions — they can react quickly.

Please be careful, good luck, and let us know how your cyberstock investments are doing.

Change

10

At any moment in time, a stock's value may be in the eye of the beholder but, in the long run, its earnings dictate its value.

Cyberstocks

V. COMPANY PROFILES

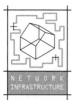 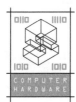

NETWORK INFRASTRUCTURE COMPUTER HARDWARE

3Com Corporation

San Francisco-based 3Com is looking to multiply the bang for its buck from the cyberspace explosion. The company designs and makes hubs (network control devices), routers (network linking devices), switches, remote access servers (for home or remote office), and network adapter cards (plug-in circuit boards that enable PCs to be linked to a network). CEO Eric Benhamou expects large businesses will need high-speed LAN and WAN connections to take full advantage of the Internet. 3Com has also introduced ISDN (high speed) remote-access products for the Internet and private intranets.

Engineer Robert Metcalfe, who invented Ethernet (a PC networking system that has become the industry standard), cofounded 3Com (for computer, communication, compatibility) in 1979 with Greg Shaw (who left in 1985) and others. In the early 1980s 3Com helped create the LAN market. It went public in 1984 and 3 years later acquired Bridge Communications (network hardware), giving 3Com its first direct sales force. The 2 companies never agreed on strategy, and 2 of Bridge's cofounders, William Carrico and Judith Estrin, left. In 1988, 3Com and Microsoft began a joint venture to develop a networking operating system that could compete with Novell's Netware (but failed 2 years later). Metcalfe (who described working with Microsoft as "mating with a black widow spider") again wanted to lead the company in 1990, but the job of turning 3Com around was given to Benhamou (a cofounder of Bridge), and Metcalfe left. In 1993 and 1994, 3Com bought Synernetics (LAN switches), Centrum Communications (remote access technology), and NiceCom (an ATM innovator), eventually

- Soup-to-nuts approach leverages client relationships
- #1 in Ethernet adapters
- Low-cost producer of Ethernet adapters
- Profiting from customer transition to Fast Ethernet networks
- Participating in growth of both Internet and intranet markets
- Penetrating new, hot, ATM, ISDN, and remote access markets

- Soup-to-nuts approach results in many battlefronts
- Ethernet adapter market is commodity-like and subject to margin pressures
- Network adapters account for nearly 50% of sales
- Intel has a foothold in the network adapter market
- Possible problems digesting recent acquisitions
- Facing entrenched competition (Cisco, Ascend) in new markets

3COM CORPORATION

HQ: 5400 Bayfront Plaza,
Santa Clara, CA 95052
Phone: 408-764-5000
Fax: 408-764-5001
Web site: www.3com.com

OFFICERS

Chairman, President, and CEO:
Eric A. Benhamou, age 39, $521,518 pay

EVP Network Systems Operations:
Robert J. Finocchio Jr., age 44, $373,758 pay

EVP Personal Connectivity Division:
Douglas C. Spreng, age 51, $344,592 pay

VP Channel Sales, Americas:
Ralph B. Godfrey, age 54, $332,239 pay

VP World Wide Customer Service:
Alan J. Kessler, age 37, $298,905 pay

VP Finance and CFO:
Christopher B. Paisley, age 42

VP and Chief Technical Officer:
John H. Hart, age 49

VP and Chief Information Officer:
Tom Thomas

VP Corporate Services:
Debra Engel, age 43

Director Human Resources: Susan Gellen
Auditors: Deloitte & Touche LLP

SELECTED PRODUCTS AND SERVICES

Adapters
3Com EtherLink III (Ethernet adapter)
Fast EtherLink 10/100 (Fast Ethernet adapter)
TokenLink III (Token Ring adapter)
TokenLink Velocity (PCI adapter)

Hubs
OfficeConnect Ethernet (hubs for small offices)
SuperStack Ethernet (flexible, fault-tolerant hubs)

Remote Access
AccessBuilder 4000 Remote Access Servers (multiprotocol servers)
AccessBuilder 8000 Integrated Remote Access System (for Internet providers)

Routers
LinkConverter II SNA-to-LAN Converters
NETBuilder Remote Office 32X Routers (multiprotocol routers)

Switches
Asynchronous Transfer Mode (ATM switches)
Multifunction
Stackable

KEY COMPETITORS

ADTRAN	IBM
Asante	Intel
Ascend Communications	Madge
Bay Networks	Newbridge Networks
Boca Research	Olicom
Cabletron	Optical Data Systems
Cisco Systems	Shiva
Digi International	Standard Microsystems
FORE Systems	U.S. Robotics
General Datacomm	Xylan

tipping into the red. The firm bought remote access systems maker Primary Access in 1995, greatly expanding its customer base, and rounded out its product line with its $775 million acquisition of rival Chipcom. 3Com acquired Axon Networks (remote monitoring software) in 1996 and spent $3.9 million to change San Francisco's famous Candlestick Park to "3Com Park."

3COM: THE NUMBERS

OTC symbol: COMS FYE: May 31	Annual Growth	1991	1992	1993	1994	1995	1996[1]
Sales ($ mil.)	42.3%	398.6	408.4	617.2	827.0	1,295.3	2,327.1
Net income ($ mil.)	—	(27.7)	4.2	38.6	(28.7)	125.7	177.9
Income as % of sales	—	—	1.0%	6.3%	—	9.7%	7.6%
Earnings per share ($)	—	(0.25)	0.04	0.30	(0.23)	0.86	1.00
Stock price – high ($)	—	3.16	7.50	12.13	26.63	53.63	52.00
Stock price – low ($)	—	1.38	2.41	4.91	10.06	22.19	35.75
Stock price – close ($)	74.7%	2.81	7.41	11.75	25.78	46.63	45.75
P/E – high	—		188	40	—	63	52
P/E – low	—		60	16	—	26	36
Dividends per share ($)	—	0.00	0.00	0.00	0.00	0.00	0.00
Book value per share ($)	27.1%	1.75	1.81	2.10	2.16	3.36	5.80
Employees	24.6%	1,731	1,963	1,971	2,306	3,072	5,190

[1] Stock prices are through June 30.

1996 YEAR-END

Debt ratio: 10.1%
Return on equity: 24.6%
Cash (mil.): $499.3
Current ratio: 2.99
Long-term debt (mil.): $110.0
No. of shares (mil.): 168.8
Dividends
  Yield: —
  Payout: —
Market value (mil.): $7,722.6
R&D as % of sales: 10.0%

QUARTER ENDED 5/31

	1996	1995
Sales ($ millions)	660.3	384.9
Net Income ($ millions)	29.5	47.6
Earnings Per Share ($)	0.17	0.32
No. of Shares (thou.)	168,800	138,462

12 MONTHS ENDED 5/31

	1996	1995
Sales ($ millions)	2,327.1	1,295.3
Net Income ($ millions)	177.9	125.7
Earnings Per Share ($)	1.00	0.86
No. of Shares (thou.)	168,800	138,462

STOCK PRICE HISTORY: High/Low/Close

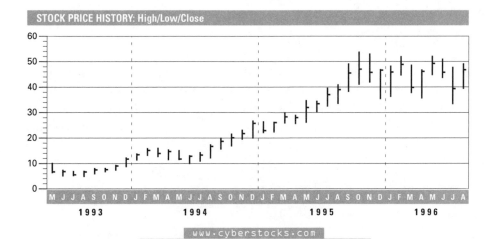

www.cyberstocks.com

- Unique product line positions company as beneficiary of internationalization of the Internet

- Has recently inked many OEM bundle deals

- Created new subsidiary to develop intelligent-agent technology

- First half fiscal 1996 sales up 92%

- Eventually, product features could be incorporated into standard browsers and servers

- Fixed royalty expenses are killing gross margins

- Marketing expenses exceed sales

- OEM revenue has been erratic

- Will need more cash to fund R&D, product marketing

- Losses are growing

- Market Cap $125 million (8/96) vs. first half 1996 sales of $4.1 million

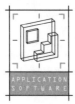

Accent Software

Accent is spending heavily to get the word out. The Jerusalem-based firm produces multilingual application software for PCs. Its Accent Professional word processing program enables users to write, check spelling, and translate individual words in over 30 languages. Its other major product, Internet with an Accent, includes multilingual e-mail, Web browser, and Web publishing software.

CEO Robert Rosenschein is intent on capturing as much of his company's market niche as possible — before a software heavy like Microsoft weighs in. To do that, Rosenschein has used much of the $18 million raised in public stock offerings to expand Accent's sales force. The company is also signing numerous marketing deals with computer hardware and software companies like Digital Equipment and Netscape. Investor Irwin Jacobs, through his IMR investment fund, owns 23.5% of Accent. Another investor, Elliot Broidy, owns about 10%. Rosenschein and his brother Jeffrey own about 11%.

Robert (an American expatriate and former software consultant) and Jeffrey (an artificial intelligence expert) formed Accent Software International (known in Israel as Kivun Computers) in 1988. The company initially focused on developing a Windows-based multilingual word processor but generated nearly all of its revenues from consulting services. (Accent helped

**ACCENT SOFTWARE
INTERNATIONAL**

HQ: 28 Pierre Koenig St.,
   Jerusalem, 93469, Israel
Phone: +972-2-793-723
Fax: +972-2-793-731
US HQ: 1401 Dove St., Ste. 470
   Newport Beach, CA 92660
US Phone: 1-800-535-5256
Web site: www.accentsoft.com

OFFICERS

President and CEO:
   Robert S. Rosenschein, age 43, $75,744 pay
EVP:
   Mitchell R. Joelson, age 44, $130,322 pay
SVP Engineering and Chief Scientist::
   Jeffrey Rosenschein, age 39
SVP Operations:
   Herbert Zlotogorski, age 44
VP; General Manager, Accent Software Europe:
   Paul Beard
Controller: Michael Sondhelm, age 33
Auditors: Andersen Worldwide

SELECTED PRODUCTS AND SERVICES

Internet
   Internet with an Accent (Internet tool suite that includes Accent Multilingual Mosaic, Accent Multilingual Web Publisher, and Accent Multilingual MailPad)

Word processing
   Accent Duo with Translation (includes bilingual Language Assistant from Globalink)
   Accent Professional (includes add-ins such as Bitstream fonts, Berlitz Interpreter, Delrina's WinFax Lite, and Lotus Organizer)
   Dagesh (sold primarily in Israel)

KEY COMPETITORS

Adobe Systems
Alis Technologies
Apple
CompuServe
Corel
Microsoft
NetManage
Netscape
Quarterdeck
SoftQuad
Spyglass

---

design the Arabic and Hebrew versions of Microsoft Windows in 1991.)

The company introduced Dagesh, its first multilingual word processor, in 1992. While it sold 5,000 copies in 6 months, the firm continued to lose money. Venture capitalist Irwin Jacobs stepped in with $3 million in 1994, and that year the company launched its Accent product line internationally.

The company introduced Accent 2.0 in 1995. It also shifted focus to the development of multilingual Internet software. Accent went public that year, and in late 1995 it released Internet with an Accent. The company formed subsidiary AgentSoft in 1996 to focus on developing automated search software for the Internet.

ACCENT SOFTWARE: THE NUMBERS

Nasdaq symbol (SC): ACNTF FYE: December 31	Annual Growth	1990	1991	1992	1993	1994	1995
Sales ($ mil.)	103.1%	—	0.3	0.3	1.2	1.9	5.1
Net income ($ mil.)	—	—	0.0	(0.3)	(0.7)	(3.1)	(7.8)
Income as % of sales	—	—	12.1%	—	—	—	—
Earnings per share ($)	—	—	—	—	(0.39)	(0.68)	(1.22)
Stock price – high ($)	—	—	—	—	—	—	21.00
Stock price – low ($)	—	—	—	—	—	—	7.33
Stock price – close ($)	—	—	—	—	—	—	15.67
P/E – high	—	—	—	—	—	—	—
P/E – low	—	—	—	—	—	—	—
Dividends per share ($)	—	—	—	—	—	—	0.00
Book value per share ($)	—	—	—	—	—	—	1.07
Employees	—	—	—	—	—	—	116

1995 YEAR-END

Debt ratio: 20.8%
Return on equity: —
Cash (mil.): $9.6
Current ratio: 3.08
Long-term debt (mil.): $2.3
No. of shares (mil.): 9.5
Dividends
　Yield: —
　Payment: —
Market value (mil.): $148.6

QUARTER ENDED 6/30

	1996	1995
Sales ($ millions)	1.3	1.5
Net Income ($ millions)	(6.1)	(1.1)
Earnings Per Share ($)	(0.63)	(0.20)
No. of Shares (thou.)	7,316	5,207

6 MONTHS ENDED 6/30

	1996	1995
Sales ($ millions)	4.1	2.2
Net Income ($ millions)	(10.0)	(2.9)
Earnings Per Share ($)	(1.05)	(0.61)
No. of Shares (thou.)	7,316	5,207

STOCK PRICE HISTORY: High/Low/Close

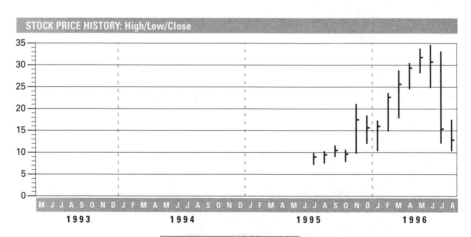

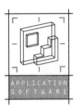

APPLICATION
SOFTWARE

Adobe Systems

Adobe is building its home in the Internet software industry. Based in Mountain View, California, the company is the #3 independent PC software vendor behind Microsoft and Novell. Its Adobe PageMill and Adobe SiteMill programs help users easily create pages for the World Wide Web by translating documents produced with a word-processing-like program into files the computer could use to construct the site. Adobe also makes PageMaker, Photoshop, Adobe Acrobat, and other desktop publishing software.

Charles Geschke and John Warnock left Xerox's Palo Alto Research Center (a place Warnock called "the world's greatest sandbox" for technology research), to start Adobe (named after a river near their homes in San Jose, California) in 1982. Their initial product was the PostScript printing command language. The company grew in the early 1990s by acquiring other software companies, including OCR Systems and Nonlinear Technologies (1992) and AH Software and Science & Art (1993). Also in 1993 the company began marketing Acrobat software, which enables users to create and distribute electronic documents over computer networks or online. The company acquired Aldus, whose PageMaker software had been instrumental in establishing the desktop-publishing market, in 1994.

Adobe teamed with Internet wunderfirm Netscape in 1995 to integrate Acrobat's viewing technology into Netscape's Internet software, including the Navigator browser. The next year Adobe and imaging software leader FileNet agreed to develop imaging standards that would enable different

- Leader in authoring software

- New features add Web publishing capability to desktop publishing products

- Acrobat and Internet publishing products have been well received

- Bravo graphics technology will be bundled with Sun's Java programming language

- Recently ended font war with Microsoft by agreeing to cross-licensing deal

- Faces considerable competition in Web authoring market

- Market transition to Web publishing provides rivals with chance to steal market share

- HP has announced plans to cut back on licensing of Adobe's PostScript technology

- So far, Framemaker acquisition has been a bust

- Most application software is sold for use on Apple computers

- Sales growth has slowed, earnings are declining

Adobe

ADOBE SYSTEMS INCORPORATED
HQ: 345 Park Ave.
San Jose, CA 95110-2704
Phone: 408-536-6000
Fax: 408-537-6000
Web site: www.adobe.com

OFFICERS

Chairman and CEO:
John E. Warnock, age 55, $668,322 pay

President and Acting CFO:
Charles M. Geschke, age 56, $668,322 pay

SVP and COO:
David B. Pratt, age 56, $439,282 pay

SVP and General Manager, Adobe Europe:
Derek J. Gray, age 46

VP, General Counsel, and Secretary:
Colleen M. Pouliot, age 37

Director Human Resources:
Rebecca Guerra

Auditors: KPMG Peat Marwick LLP

SELECTED PRODUCTS AND SERVICES

Acrobat (electronic document management software)

Adobe Acrobat (document formatting software)

Adobe Art Explorer (painting and drawing software for children)

Adobe Fetch (cataloging software)

Adobe Gallery Effects (special-effects software)

Adobe Illustrator (graphics software)

Adobe PageMill (Web-page creation software)

Adobe PhotoDeluxe (personalized photo software)

Adobe Photoshop (photographic image software)

Adobe Premiere (film and video editing software)

Adobe Persuasion (presentation software)

Adobe SiteMill (Internet link repair software)

FrameMaker (document authoring software)

PageMaker (page layout software)

PostScript (page description language and interpreter)

KEY COMPETITORS

America Online	Electronics for	Netscape
Apple	Imaging	Novell
Applix	IBM	Quark
Asymetrix	Interleaf	SoftKey
Avid Technology	Macromedia	Strata
Common Ground	Micrografx	
Corel	Microsoft	

image file formats to be shared more easily by different computer users. Also in 1996 Adobe unveiled its Bravo technology, which allows Internet publishers to use magazine-like graphics and typefaces on their Web sites. That year the company forecast that sales of its products for the Internet would grow at a rate of 100% per year and would be focused on business-to-business sites.

Adobe's stock price plummeted in early 1996 on fears that the acquisition of Frame Technology would hurt sales efforts and drag down revenues.

ADOBE SYSTEMS: THE NUMBERS

Nasdaq symbol: ADBE FYE: November 30	Annual Growth	1990	1991	1992	1993	1994	1995
Sales ($ mil.)	35.2%	168.7	229.7	265.9	313.5	597.8	762.3
Net income ($ mil.)	18.4%	40.1	51.6	43.6	57.0	6.3	93.5
Income as % of sales	—	23.8%	22.5%	16.4%	18.2%	1.1%	12.3%
Earnings per share ($)	6.5%	0.92	1.13	0.94	1.22	0.10	1.26
Stock price – high ($)	—	25.38	33.88	34.25	37.00	38.50	74.25
Stock price – low ($)	—	8.50	13.38	12.63	15.63	20.50	27.25
Stock price – close ($)	33.6%	14.56	32.75	15.75	22.25	29.75	62.00
P/E – high	—	28	30	36	30	385	59
P/E – low	—	9	12	13	13	205	22
Dividends per share ($)	10.8%	0.12	0.16	0.16	0.20	0.20	0.20
Book value per share ($)	30.1%	2.57	4.13	5.05	6.03	7.47	9.59
Employees	35.5%	508	701	887	1,000	1,584	2,319

1995 YEAR-END

Debt ratio: 0.0%
Return on equity: 16.2%
Cash (mil.): $516.0
Current ratio: 3.72
Long-term debt (mil.): $0.0
No. of shares (mil.): 72.8
Dividends
  Yield: 0.3%
  Payout: 15.9%
Market value (mil.): $4,515.5
R&D as % of sales: 18.2%

QUARTER ENDED 5/31

	1996	1995
Sales ($ millions)	204.3	168.0
Net Income ($ millions)	22.0	33.9
Earnings Per Share ($)	0.29	0.51
No. of Shares (thou.)	72,543	63,344

6 MONTHS ENDED 5/31

	1996	1995
Sales ($ millions)	398.0	336.6
Net Income ($ millions)	55.7	68.3
Earnings Per Share ($)	0.73	1.04
No. of Shares (thou.)	72,543	63,344

STOCK PRICE HISTORY: High/Low/Close

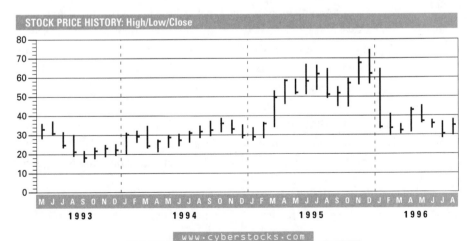

www.cyberstocks.com

- Focuses on high-growth market for local-loop digital-transmission products

- Dominates the market for BRITE cards, low-cost cards that extend ISDN service to new areas

- Leads in the market for ISDN terminal adapters that connect computers to ISDN lines

- Important new ADTRAN product promises to extend ISDN transmission range very inexpensively

- #2 in the rapidly growing HDSL market

- Company is a technology and manufacturing-cost leader

- More mature Digital Data Services business (est. 50% of sales) is not growing very quickly

- International presence is unimpressive

- PairGain invented and dominates the HDSL market

- P/E exceeds 70 (8/96)

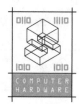

ADTRAN, Inc.

ADTRAN makes its pennies from copper. Based in Huntsville, Alabama, the company's products, including channel and data service units, dataports, and digital repeaters and extenders, are used to quickly transmit digital signals (used by modern phone equipment, computer networks, and video-on-demand) over existing copper wirelines. ADTRAN's products support 3 high-speed digital transmission formats that are vying for dominance: integrated services digital network (ISDN), digital data service (DDS), and high-bit-rate digital subscriber line (HDSL). The company's main customers are telephone companies: the RBOCs account for more than 55% of its sales, which are rising as ADTRAN moves into new markets. CEO Mark Smith and VP Lonnie McMillian own about 33% and 19%, respectively, of ADTRAN.

ADTRAN was founded in 1985 by Smith, McMillian, and John Jurenko to capitalize on the breakup of AT&T. Smith had founded Universal Data Systems, a modem maker, in 1970. He became a VP at Motorola when that company acquired Universal Data in 1979 (he left both to start ADTRAN). After 15 years at Universal Data, Smith chose the name ADTRAN (from "advanced transmission") to be near the top of alphabetical listings. ADTRAN introduced its HDSL products in 1993 and had 15% of that market by 1994, the year the company went public.

That year ADTRAN announced a 5-year, $50 million expansion of its research, engineering, and assembly facility in Huntsville, Alabama. In 1995 the company increased its foreign sales and focused on establishing foreign

ADTRAN, INC.

HQ: 901 Explorer Blvd.,
Huntsville, AL 35806-2807
Phone: 205-971-8000
Fax: 205-971-8699
Web site: www.adtran.com

OFFICERS

Chairman, President, and CEO:
Mark C. Smith, age 55, $216,408 pay

President and COO:
Howard A. Thrailkill, age 57, $205,000 pay
(prior to promotion)

VP Engineering, Secretary, and Treasurer:
Lonnie S. McMillian, age 67, $205,000 pay

VP Sales and Marketing:
John A. Jurenko, age 61, $188,000 pay

VP Finance and Administration, CFO (HR):
Irwin O. Goldstein, age 62, $136,750 pay

Auditors: Coopers & Lybrand L.L.P.

SELECTED PRODUCTS AND SERVICES

Extender and repeater products (devices that extend a digital signal's range)

Signal simulation and test equipment

Termination products (equipment that converts digital signals to voice, computer network, video, or PBX signals)

Transmission products (circuit assemblies that convert data communications into digital signals)

	1995 Sales	
	$ mil.	% of total
Telephone companies	105.4	58
OEMs	24.8	14
Customer premises equipment	51.3	28
Total	**181.5**	**100**

KEY COMPETITORS

3Com	Lucent
ADC Telecommunications	Motorola
Ascend Communications	PairGain
Brooktree	Telco
Digital Link	Tellabs
DSC Communications	Teltrend
General Instrument	U.S. Robotics
IBM	Westell Technologies

distribution agreements for its products. The following year ADTRAN entered the wireless communications market with the introduction of the TRACER Digital Spread Spectrum Radio, used to provide telephone service in areas not served by wirelines.

ADTRAN: THE NUMBERS

Nasdaq symbol: ADTN FYE: December 31	Annual Growth	1990	1991	1992	1993	1994	1995
Sales ($ mil.)	44.5%	28.8	42.6	57.0	72.4	123.4	181.5
Net income ($ mil.)	55.9%	3.2	6.5	8.7	8.5	18.6	29.5
Income as % of sales	—	11.2%	15.3%	15.2%	11.7%	15.1%	16.3%
Earnings per share ($)	51.2%	0.10	0.19	0.26	0.25	0.52	0.75
Stock price – high ($)	—	—	—	—	—	23.38	55.50
Stock price – low ($)	—	—	—	—	—	10.31	20.00
Stock price – close ($)	—	—	—	—	—	22.88	54.31
P/E – high	—	—	—	—	—	45	74
P/E – low	—	—	—	—	—	20	27
Dividends per share ($)	—	—	—	—	—	0.00	0.00
Book value per share ($)	—	—	—	—	—	2.36	3.49
Employees	30.6%	196	225	337	424	534	746

1995 YEAR-END

Debt ratio: 13.3%
Return on equity: 27.3%
Cash (mil.): $35.0
Current ratio: 9.68
Long-term debt (mil.): $20.0
No. of shares (mil.): 37.5
Dividends
 Yield: —
 Payout: —
Market value (mil.): $2,034.6

QUARTER ENDED 6/30

	1996	1995
Sales ($ millions)	63.3	45.5
Net Income ($ millions)	10.3	7.0
Earnings Per Share ($)	0.26	0.18
No. of Shares (thou.)	38,684	37,364

6 MONTHS ENDED 6/30

	1996	1995
Sales ($ millions)	117.8	83.6
Net Income ($ millions)	19.0	13.1
Earnings Per Share ($)	0.48	0.34
No. of Shares (thou.)	38,684	37,364

STOCK PRICE HISTORY: High/Low/Close

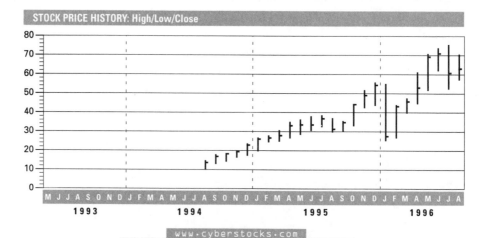

1993   1994   1995   1996

www.cyberstocks.com

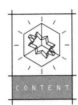
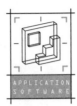
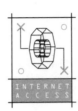

SPECIALIZED SERVICES

CONTENT

APPLICATION SOFTWARE

INTERNET ACCESS

America Online

For millions of consumers, life on the Internet begins when a free AOL starter kit arrives in the mail. Vienna, Virginia-based America Online (AOL) is the world's largest provider of online services. It offers members (more than 6 million) point-and-click access to conferences, e-mail, electronic magazines and newspapers, stock quotes, and the World Wide Web. The company hopes to duplicate its US success in Canada, Europe, and Japan.

The firm was founded by James Kimsey and Stephen Case in 1985 as Quantum Computer Services, which ran the Q-Link online service for Commodore computer users. In 1989 it launched a nationwide service called America Online and 2 years later Quantum adopted the name America Online. The company went public in 1992.

To boost its content (thus making its service more attractive), AOL signed deals with several media companies, including Knight-Ridder, Time Warner, and Turner Broadcasting. AOL began offering Internet access and a Windows version of its online software in 1993. By the end of the next year, AOL had more than one million subscribers.

AOL teamed with music and publishing empire Bertelsmann in 1995 to offer online services in Europe.

In 1996 AOL announced major alliances with Netscape Communications and Microsoft, allowing AOL members to use both companies' market-leading Web browsers – software for surfing the Internet. In addition Microsoft agreed to add AOL access to future versions of Windows 95. That year AOL

- #1 online service, with more than 6 million subscribers
- Easy-to-use interface to online service
- New business model emphasizes advertising and transaction revenue
- Moving to Web-based publishing tools
- ANS is #1 dial-up TCP/IP network
- Has launched European services

- Facing competition and pricing pressure from Web and ISPs
- Subscriber growth all but stopped in summer 1996
- Aggressive marketing is expensive, free trials are often followed by quick cancellations
- 3/31/96 balance sheet showed $280 million in deferred subscriber acquisition costs
- P/E over 100 (8/96)

AMERICA ONLINE, INC.

HQ: 8619 Westwood Center Dr.,
Vienna, VA 22182-2285
Phone: 703-448-8700
Fax: 703-883-1532
Web site: www.aol.com

OFFICERS

Chairman Emeritus:
James V. Kimsey, age 55

Chairman and CEO:
Stephen M. Case, age 36, $200,000 pay

SVP; President, AOL Technologies:
Michael M. Connors, age 53, $195,000 pay

SVP; President, AOL International:
John L. Davies, age 45, $195,000 pay

SVP, CFO, Treasurer, and CAO:
Lennert J. Leader, age 40, $188,333 pay

SVP; President, AOL Services:
Theodore J. Leonsis, age 39, $175,025 pay

SVP; President, AOL Enterprises:
David Cole, age 42

VP, General Counsel and Secretary:
Ellen M. Kirsh, age 47

VP Human Resources and Facilities:
Mark Stavish, age 40

VP Investor Relations: Richard Hanlon, age 47
Auditors: Ernst & Young LLP

AMERICA ONLINE CHANNELS

Computers & Software
Digital City
Entertainment
Games
Health & Fitness
The Hub
International
Internet Connection
Kids Only
Learning & Culture
Life, Styles & Interests
Marketplace
MusicSpace
Newsstand
Today's News
People Connection
Personal Finance
Reference Desk
Sports
Style Channel
Travel

KEY COMPETITORS

AT&T Corp.	Infoseek	Microsoft
BBN	International	Minspring
C|NET	Wireless	NETCOM
CompuServe	Lycos	PSINet
EarthLink	MCI	Time Warner
Excite	MFS	Yahoo!
IDT	Communications	

purchased Johnson-Grace, a developer of data compression technologies that make sound and pictures more accessible to lower-speed modems, and instituted a sharp cut in subscription prices. The online company also offered to give subscribers millions of free hours to settle class-action suits over billing practices that plaintiffs said included adding more than a minute to the time billed for many on-line sessions. The company began trading on the New York Stock Exchange in September, 1996 under the symbol AOL.

AMERICA ONLINE: THE NUMBERS

Nasdaq symbol: AMER FYE: June 30	Annual Growth	1990	1991	1992	1993	1994	1995
Sales ($ mil.)	78.1%	20.0	19.5	26.2	38.5	101.0	358.5
Net income ($ mil.)	—	0.0	0.9	2.2	3.1	6.2	(33.6)
Income as % of sales	—	0.0%	4.6%	8.4%	8.1%	6.1%	—
Earnings per share ($)	—	0.01	0.03	0.05	0.06	0.10	(0.50)
Stock price – high ($)	—	—	—	3.66	8.75	14.63	46.25
Stock price – low ($)	—	—	—	1.34	2.22	5.97	12.31
Stock price – close ($)	117.3%	—	—	3.66	7.31	14.00	37.50
P/E – high	—	—	—	73	146	146	—
P/E – low	—	—	—	27	37	60	—
Dividends per share ($)	—	—	—	0.00	0.01	0.00	0.00
Book value per share ($)	88.7%	—	—	0.43	0.50	1.71	2.90
Employees	115.1%	—	116	124	236	527	2,481

1995 YEAR-END

Debt ratio: 9.1%
Return on equity: —
Cash (mil.): $64.1
Current ratio: 1.00
Long-term debt (mil.): $19.5
No. of shares (mil.): 75.1
Dividends
  Yield: —
  Payout: —
Market value (mil.): $2,816.6
R&D as % of sales: 12.8%

QUARTER ENDED 6/30

	1996	1995
Sales ($ millions)	334.5	151.9
Net Income ($ millions)	16.1	6.2
Earnings Per Share ($)	0.14	0.07
No. of Shares (thou.)	112,031	75,110

12 MONTHS ENDED 6/30

	1996	1995
Sales ($ millions)	1,093.9	358.5
Net Income ($ millions)	29.8	(33.6)
Earnings Per Share ($)	0.28	(0.50)
No. of Shares (thou.)	112,031	75,110

STOCK PRICE HISTORY: High/Low/Close

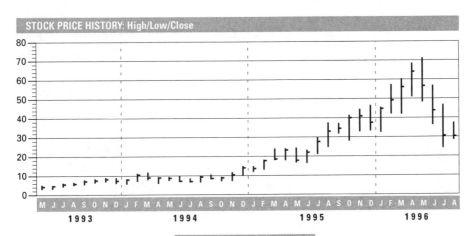

M J J A S O N D J F M A M J J A S O N D J F M A M J J A S O N D J F M A M J J A
1993   1994   1995   1996

- Still the leading hardware platform for desktop publishing

- Still enjoys a strong position in the education market

- New focus on high-end computers and Internet

- Clone makers sell to low-end, boost Macintosh Operating System use

- Has begun outsourcing manufacturing

- Appears to be planning Windows compatibility

- Possible breakup or takeover candidate

- Continues to lose market share

- New Microsoft operating systems have further closed the ease-of-use gap with Macintosh

- Still struggling to release a complete version of its new operating system

- Software companies are de-emphasizing development work for Macintosh computers

- How good a job did Amelio do at National Semiconductor?

- So far in 1996, P&L makes for grim reading

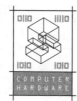

COMPUTER HARDWARE

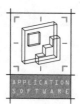

APPLICATION SOFTWARE

Apple Computer

Things have been looking a little wormy for Apple lately. The Cupertino, California-based company, which makes Macintosh computers as well as peripherals and software, has watched its market share dwindle (thanks to a policy of refusing to license clones until recently) because of aggressive pricing pressure from makers of Windows-based PCs.

College dropouts Steven Jobs and Stephen Wozniak founded Apple in 1976. Working in Jobs's garage, the 2 turned out Apple I microcomputers, selling them without keyboards, monitors, or casings. Wozniak, the machine's designer, soon added such features as keyboards, color monitors, and peripheral ports to the Apple II. With sales soaring, the company went public in 1980.

Wozniak left the company in 1983; Jobs was forced out in 1985. By then, the Mac had been released and revolutionized the personal computing industry with its user-friendly point and click options screen. The rest of the decade was fruitful for Apple. Then came Microsoft's Windows, which offered an easy point-and-click screen combined with the lower price of a PC. Management turmoil and downsizing followed, as the company consolidated its US and Canadian operations. As its market share evaporated, many software designers stopped designing products for the Mac.

In an effort to regain market share, in 1994 Apple began licensing its operating system to clone makers, including Power Computing, Pioneer Electric Corp., and Radius. It also attempted to enter the online service field with eWorld; but that failed in 1996. Apple is hoping the popularity of Apple

Apple Computer®

APPLE COMPUTER, INC.
HQ: One Infinite Loop,
Cupertino, CA 95014
Phone: 408-996-1010
Fax: 408-974-2113
Web site: www.apple.com

OFFICERS

Chairman and CEO: Gilbert F. Amelio, age 52
VC: Armas C."Mike" Markkula Jr., age 53
EVP and COO: Marco Landi, age 51
EVP and CFO: Fred D. Anderson Jr., age 51
EVP R & D, Chief Technical Officer:
Ellen Hancock, age 53
SVP Worldwide Operations:
G. Frederick Forsyth, age 51, $622,353 pay
SVP; President, Apple Americas:
James J. Buckley, age 45, $586,448 pay
SVP; President, Apple Pacific:
John Floisand, age 51
SVP Macintosh Systems: Howard F. Lee
SVP Marketing: Satjiv S. Chahil, age 45
SVP Human Resources:
Kevin J. Sullivan, age 54
Auditors: Ernst & Young LLP

SELECTED PRODUCTS AND SERVICES

Computers
Macintosh Performa
Macintosh PowerBook
Power Macintosh

Peripherals
CD-ROM drives   Printers
Monitors   Scanners

Networking and Connectivity Products
LAN connectivity products
Workgroup server systems

Personal Digital Assistant
Apple MessagePad

Software
Applications
Developer tools
Languages
System software
Utilities

KEY COMPETITORS

Acer	Machines Bull
AST	Microsoft
Compaq	NEC
Corel	Netscape
Dell	Novell
Gateway 200	Packard Bell
Hewlett-Packard	Power Computing
IBM	Radius
Intel	Sun Microsystems
LG Group	Toshiba

computers among Web page designers, graphic artists, and entertainment content providers will continue to bring in business as the Internet expands. In 1996 it announced plans to build information appliances that could be used with the World Wide Web, including a version of its personal digital assistant with a wireless connection to the Internet.

APPLE COMPUTER: THE NUMBERS

Nasdaq symbol: AAPL FYE: September 30	Annual Growth	1990	1991	1992	1993	1994	1995
Sales ($ mil.)	14.8%	5,558	6,309	7,087	7,977	9,189	11,062
Net income ($ mil.)	(2.2%)	475	310	530	87	310	424
Income as % of sales	—	8.5%	4.9%	7.5%	1.1%	3.4%	3.8%
Earnings per share ($)	(1.8%)	3.77	2.58	4.33	0.73	2.61	3.45
Stock price – high ($)	—	47.75	73.25	70.00	65.25	43.75	50.13
Stock price – low ($)	—	24.25	40.25	41.50	22.00	24.63	31.44
Stock price – close ($)	(5.8%)	43.00	56.38	59.75	29.25	39.00	31.88
P/E – high	—	13	28	16	89	17	15
P/E – low	—	6	16	10	30	9	9
Dividends per share ($)	1.8%	0.44	0.48	0.48	0.48	0.48	0.48
Book value per share ($)	13.5%	12.54	14.92	18.46	17.45	19.94	23.60
Employees	3.9%	14,528	14,432	14,798	14,938	14,592	17,615

1995 YEAR-END

Debt ratio: 20.8%
Return on equity: 16.0%
Cash (mil.): $952
Current ratio: 2.25
Long-term debt (mil.): $303
No. of shares (mil.): 123
Dividends
  Yield: 1.5%
  Payout: 13.9%
Market value (mil.): $3,918
R&D as % of sales: 5.6%

QUARTER ENDED 6/30

	1996	1995
Sales ($ millions)	2,179	2,575
Net Income ($ millions)	(32)	103
Earnings Per Share ($)	(0.26)	0.84
No. of Shares (thou.)	123,735	121,905

9 MONTHS ENDED 6/30

	1996	1995
Sales ($ millions)	7,512	8,059
Net Income ($ millions)	(841)	364
Earnings Per Share ($)	(6.81)	2.98
No. of Shares (thou.)	123,735	121,905

STOCK PRICE HISTORY: High/Low/Close

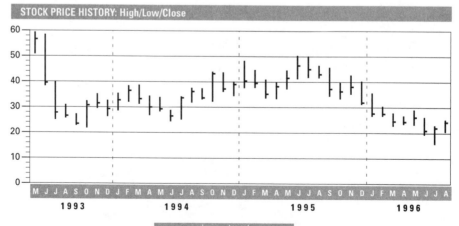

1993   1994   1995   1996

www·cyberstocks·com

NETWORK
INFRASTRUCTURE

Ascend Communications

Ascend hooked its rising star to workplace changes, but it's now going at warp speed as it rides the growth of the Internet, which now constitutes about 30% of its business. The Alameda, California-based firm makes remote networking access products that allow users to dial up a central computer from home, on the road, or in field offices. Its gadgetry — mainly network access equipment—works with existing digital and analog networks by adjusting the bandwidth, which controls information traffic, as needed. Ascend's rapid growth has come from providing products to Internet service providers, including UUNET and BBN, and telecommunications companies, including AT&T and MCI.

Ascend was founded in 1989 by Robert Ryan and 3 former employees of Hayes Microcomputer to build connecting devices for Integrated Service Digital Network phone lines. When companies were slow to embrace ISDN, Ryan redirected the company to create video conferencing products. The company launched Multiband (its first product line) in 1991, MAX in 1992, and the Pipeline series in 1993. Ascend went public in 1994, and the company shifted away from its focus on the videoconferencing access market toward remote and Internet access. Ryan stepped down as chairman and CEO for health reasons in 1995.

To bolster its top-selling MAX line, in 1995 the company purchased DaynaLINK remote access products and related technology from Dayna

- Appears well-positioned to grow in line with Internet usage
- Provides products and security for both ends of WAN connections
- A leader in"bandwidth-on-demand" ISDN technology
- MAX product line ("POP in a box") dominates ISP access server market
- NetStar's router gives Ascend a way to slow Cisco's advance in ISP market
- 1st half 1996 sales up 338%, earnings per share up 356%

- Heavily dependent on ISP market (25% of 1995 sales)
- New Shiva partnerships with Motorola and Nortel target Ascend
- With StrataCom purchase, rival Cisco can now sell entire solution to ISPs
- NetStar, acquired for $300 million, has never been profitable
- P/E over 80 (7/96)

ASCEND COMMUNICATIONS, INC.

HQ: 1275 Harbor Bay Pkwy.,
Alameda, CA 94502
Phone: 510-769-6001
Fax: 510-814-2300
Web site: www.ascend.com

OFFICERS

President and CEO:
Mory Ejabat, age 46, $463,103 pay

VP Finance and CFO:
Robert K. Dahl, age 55, $401,803 pay

**SVP International Sales and General
Manager International Operations:**
Curtis N. Sanford, age 37, $333,465 pay

SVP North American Sales:
Michael Hendren, age 49, $331,029 pay

VP Engineering and CTO:
Jeanette Symons, age 33, $283,000 pay

VP Marketing: Bernard Schneider, age 39

VP Manufacturing: Anthony Stagno

Controller and Chief Accounting Officer:
Michael J. Johnson, age 43

Assistant VP Strategic Marketing:
Jay Duncanson

**Manager, Human Resources and Investor
Relations:** Paula Cook

Auditors: Ernst & Young LLP

SELECTED PRODUCTS AND SERVICES

MAX (WAN access and integrated voice, video, and data access)

Pipeline products (telecommuting, remote office access, and Internet access)

Multiband products (videoconferencing networks)

	1995 Sales
	% of total
MAX products	63
Pipeline products	20
Multiband products	15
Other	2
Total	**100**

KEY COMPETITORS

3Com
ADTRAN
Bay Networks
Cabletron
Cisco Systems
Datapoint
Gandalf Technologies
General DataComm
Global Village
GTI
Motorola
Newbridge Networks
Northern Telecom
Shiva
U.S. Robotics
Zoom Telephonics

Communications. The next year Ascend announced 2 acquisitions: Morning Star Technologies, a provider of Internet security, and NetStar, a maker of high-speed computer switches. The company also teamed with rival Cisco Systems in 1996 to develop equipment to speed data flows between Ascend's dial access servers and Cisco's frame relay and ATM switches.

ASCEND: THE NUMBERS

Nasdaq symbol: ASND FYE: December 31	Annual Growth	1990	1991	1992	1993	1994	1995
Sales ($ mil.)	331.5%	0.1	3.2	7.2	16.2	39.3	149.6
Net income ($ mil.)	—	(3.1)	(2.4)	(3.8)	1.3	8.7	30.6
Income as % of sales	—	—	—	—	8.3%	22.1%	20.4%
Earnings per share ($)	274.2%	—	—	—	0.02	0.09	0.28
Stock price – high ($)	—	—	—	—	—	5.56	40.63
Stock price – low ($)	—	—	—	—	—	1.41	4.94
Stock price – close ($)	—	—	—	—	—	5.09	40.56
P/E – high	—	—	—	—	—	59	145
P/E – low	—	—	—	—	—	15	18
Dividends per share ($)	—	—	—	—	—	0.00	0.00
Book value per share ($)	—	—	—	—	—	0.46	2.69
Employees	86.9%	—	—	—	87	115	304

1995 YEAR-END

Debt ratio: 0.0%
Return on equity: 18.0%
Cash (mil.): $211.1
Current ratio: 6.98
Long-term debt (mil.): $0.0
No. of shares (mil.): 110.1
Dividends
  Yield: —
  Payout: —
Market value (mil.): $4,465.1
R&D as % of sales: 6.4%

QUARTER ENDED 6/30

	1996	1995
Sales ($ millions)	123.3	28.6
Net Income ($ millions)	29.8	5.3
Earnings Per Share ($)	0.24	0.06
No. of Shares (thou.)	122,581	96,732

6 MONTHS ENDED 6/30

	1996	1995
Sales ($ millions)	214.4	48.9
Net Income ($ millions)	50.7	8.8
Earnings Per Share ($)	0.41	0.09
No. of Shares (thou.)	122,581	96,732

STOCK PRICE HISTORY: High/Low/Close

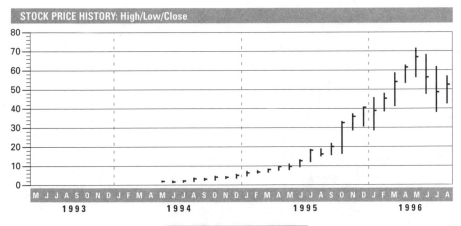

M J J A S O N D J F M A M J J A S O N D J F M A M J J A S O N D J F M A M J J A
1993   1994   1995   1996

www.cyberstocks.com

- Unparalleled global brand-name recognition in telecommunications

- Telecommunications deregulation opens up new markets

- Spinoffs make networking services even more important to earnings

- Should soon be able to provide "all-in-one" telecommuncations packages

- WorldNet Internet access service is poised to overtake leading ISP NETCOM

- Battling competitors on many fronts as a result of telecommuncations deregulation

- Until WorldNet, most online ventures had been failures

- Recently lost its president and COO, formerly considered heir apparent to current CEO

- Lackluster sales and earnings performance in 1st half of 1996

CONTENT

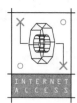

INTERNET ACCESS

AT&T Corp.

Brand recognition has its down side. When long-distance leviathan AT&T launched its WorldNet Internet access service, 600,000 subscribers wanted to sign up in the first 9 weeks, overwhelming the capacity of the new enterprise, which could only enlist 150,000 during that time. Despite the false start, AT&T plans to use its size (80 million residential phone subscribers) to squeeze smaller Internet access companies out of the market. New York City-based AT&T is also pumping funds into new areas like local phone service, wireless calling, credit cards, and satellite TV (AT&T will market DIRECTV's satellite television system to its long-distance customers).

Telephone inventor Alexander Graham Bell's backers founded Bell Telephone (1877) and New England Telephone (1878), which were consolidated as National Bell Telephone in 1879. The company became American Telephone and Telegraph in 1899. AT&T won control of Western Union in 1909. Bell Labs, the heralded R&D division, was formed in 1925.

FCC rulings stripped AT&T of its telephone equipment monopoly (1968) and allowed specialized carriers, such as MCI, to hook their microwave-based systems to the phone network (1969), injecting competition into the long-distance arena. A government suit led to the 1984 spinoff of the 7 regional Bells; AT&T kept long-distance services. Its acquisitions of Teradata and NCR in 1991 placed it 7th among the world's computer makers.

The company acquired McCaw Cellular, the nation's #1 cellular service, for $11.5 billion in 1994, and it also bought Interchange Network Company, an online service, from Ziff-Davis Publishing. The following year it agreed

AT&T CORP.
HQ: 32 Avenue of the Americas,
New York, NY 10013-2412
Phone: 212-387-5400
Fax: 212-841-4715
Web site: www.att.com

OFFICERS

Chairman and CEO:
Robert E. Allen, age 61, $2,677,400 pay

President, AT&T International:
Pier Carlo Falotti, age 53

SEVP Policy Development and Operations Support: John D. Zeglis, age 48

EVP; Chairman, Global Operations Team:
Victor A. Pelson, $1,270,600 pay

EVP and CFO:
Richard W. Miller, age 55, $1,061,200 pay

EVP Human Resources:
Harold W. Burlingame, age 55

Auditors: Coopers & Lybrand L.L.P.

SELECTED PRODUCTS AND SERVICES

Business Units
AT&T Solutions
Consulting
Systems integration

AT&T Universal Card Services Corp.

AT&T Wireless Services
Air-to-ground telephone services
Cellular services
Messaging services

Communication Services Group
Electronic mail
Long-distance services
Satellite transponder services
Toll-free and"800" services

KEY COMPETITORS

America Online	IDT	Pacific Telesis
Ameritech	International	PSINet
Bell Atlantic	Wireless	SBC
BellSouth	MCI	Communications
BT	MFS	Sprint
Cable & Wireless	Communications	Teleport
CompuServe	MindSpring	U S WEST
EarthLink	NETCOM	Communications
GTE	NYNEX	WorldCom

to pay $3.3 billion for the 48% of cellular communications company LIN Broadcasting it did not already own. That year the company split into 3 separate businesses: AT&T Corp., NCR Corp. (computers), and Lucent Technologies Inc. (telecommunications equipment). AT&T joined forces with BBN Planet, a division of networking products and services company BBN, to launch the WorldNet Internet access service in 1996.

AT&T CORP.: THE NUMBERS

NYSE symbol: T FYE: December 31	Annual Growth	1990	1991	1992	1993	1994	1995
Sales ($ mil.)	16.4%	37,285	63,089	64,904	67,156	75,094	79,609
Net income ($ mil.)	(44.9%)	2,735	522	3,807	3,974	4,710	139
Income as % of sales	—	7.3%	0.8%	5.9%	5.9%	6.3%	0.2%
Earnings per share ($)	(48.6%)	2.51	0.40	2.86	2.94	3.01	0.09
Stock price – high ($)	—	46.63	41.25	53.13	65.00	57.13	68.50
Stock price – low ($)	—	29.00	29.00	36.63	50.13	47.25	47.63
Stock price – close ($)	16.5%	30.13	39.13	51.00	52.50	50.25	64.75
P/E – high	—	19	103	19	22	19	—
P/E – low	—	12	73	13	17	16	—
Dividends per share ($)	0.5%	1.29	1.32	1.32	1.32	1.32	1.32
Book value per share ($)	(3.5%)	12.90	12.39	14.12	10.24	11.42	10.82
Employees	(1.8%)	328,900	317,100	312,700	308,700	304,500	300,000

1995 YEAR-END

Debt ratio: 62.0%
Return on equity: 0.8%
Cash (mil.): $908
Current ratio: 1.00
Long-term debt (mil.): $11,635
No. of shares (mil.): 1,596
Dividends
  Yield: 2.0%
  Payout: —
Market value (mil.): $103,341

QUARTER ENDED 6/30

	1995	1996
Sales ($ millions)	19,512.0	13,032.0
Net Income ($ millions)	1,335.0	1,491.0
Earnings Per Share ($)	0.85	0.94
No. of Shares (thou.)	1,585,385	1,610,361

6 MONTHS ENDED 6/30

	1995	1996
Sales ($ millions)	37,774.0	25,988.0
Net Income ($ millions)	2,553.0	2,853.0
Earnings Per Share ($)	1.61	1.77
No. of Shares (thou.)	1,585,385	1,610,361

STOCK PRICE HISTORY: High/Low/Close

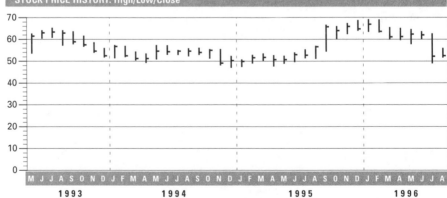

NETWORK
INFRASTRUCTURE

Bay Networks

Bay Networks directs the electronic traffic along the computer freeways. The Santa Clara, California-based company develops and manufactures intelligent hubs (the "switchboards" where a computer network's cables converge), multiprotocol routers (which allow different networks to interact), and other LAN and WAN products and services. Bay has struggled to keep pace with changes in technology in the networking market and is rumored to be a takeover target.

Bay Networks is the result of the $1 billion merger in 1994 of 2 networking pioneers, SynOptics Communications (headquartered near San Francisco Bay) and Wellfleet Communications (originally near Massachusetts Bay). SynOptics was founded by Andrew Ludwick and Ronald Schmidt, former colleagues at Xerox's Palo Alto Research Center. In 1984 IBM announced a LAN configuration based on a star-shaped cable layout, the token ring, that rivaled the linear Ethernet layout. With backing from Xerox, Ludwick and Schmidt opened SynOptics in 1985. Their first product, LattisNet, allowed Ethernet networks to use the star layout. SynOptics went public in 1988. By the mid-1990s competition had cut its lead, but the firm continued to develop products such as FDDI (a high-speed data transmission standard).

Wellfleet was formed in 1986 by Paul Severino and Bill Siefert. The company was a pioneer in enterprise networking, developing an expandable

- Very large customer base and direct and indirect sales networks
- Original merger combined industry leaders with complementary products
- Company is #1 in hubs, #2 in routers
- Alliance with Lucent gives Bay real-time switching, multimedia technology

- Merger resulted in culture clash
- Problems with merger of R&D departments has caused new product delays
- In the midst of a management shake-up
- Margins are under pressure as competition heats up in hub market
- Cisco/StrataCom merger creates a formidable competitor

Bay Networks

BAY NETWORKS, INC.

HQ: 4401 Great America Pkwy.,
Santa Clara, CA 95054
Phone: 408-988-2400
Fax: 408-988-5525
Web site: www.baynetworks.com

OFFICERS

Chairman:
Paul J. Severino, age 48, $429,207 pay

President and CEO:
Andrew K. Ludwich, age 49, $439,909 pay

EVP and Chief Technical Officer:
Ronald V. Schmidt, age 51, $434,919 pay

EVP and CFO:
William J. Ruehle, age 53, $382,493 pay

EVP Worldwide Field Operations and Marketing:
Gary J. Bowen, age 48, $366,258 pay

SVP Operations: Jeff Allen

SVP Hub Products Business Unit:
Dominic P. Orr, age 44

VP Human Resources: David M. Lietzke
Auditors: Ernst & Young LLP

SELECTED PRODUCTS AND SERVICES

Connectivity Products
Intelligent hubs and related host modules and transceivers

Internetworking Products
Backbone Node products
Local and remote bridges, local and remote routers, and switches

Network Management Products
Optivity network management systems

Switching Products
BaySIS (Bay Switched Internetworking Services, a networking architecture that combines switching technology with hub and router technology)

KEY COMPETITORS

3Com
Ascend Communications
Cabletron
Cascade
Cisco Systems
DEC
FORE Systems
Hewlett-Packard
IBM
Intel
Madge
Optical Data
U.S. Robotics
Xylan

system architecture. The company shipped its first products in 1988 and went public in 1991.

After the 1994 merger, Severino became chairman of Bay NetWorks, Ludwick president and CEO. The following year the company purchased Centillion Networks (token ring network products) for $140 million and agreed to acquire Xylogics (routers) for about $330 million. In 1996 Bay announced Ludwick would resign as CEO, although no timetable was given for his departure.

BAY NETWORKS: THE NUMBERS

NYSE: BAY FYE: June 30	Annual Growth	1991	1992	1993	1994[2]	1995	1996[3]
Sales ($ mil.)[1]	52.6%	248.3	338.8	704.5	1,086.0	1,342.3	2,056.6
Net income ($ mil.)	50.4%	26.8	42.4	75.9	120.9	131.0	206.3
Income as % of sales	—	10.8%	12.5%	10.8%	11.1%	9.8%	10.0%
Earnings per share ($)	—	0.44	0.66	1.09	0.71	0.73	1.04
Stock prices – high ($)	—	17.17	27.83	42.75	29.25	49.92	49.00
Stock prices – low ($)	—	4.75	6.25	20.25	12.42	18.33	24.63
Stock prices – close ($)	—	7.05	27.13	27.88	19.67	41.13	25.75
P/E - high	—	39	42	39	41	68	47
P/E - low	—	11	9	19	18	25	24
Dividends per share ($)	—	0.00	0.00	0.00	0.00	0.00	0.00
Book value per share ($)	—	2.37	3.39	5.19	3.43	4.32	5.81
Employees	43.1%	959	1,255	1,736	3,000	3,840	5,758

[1] 1991-1993 are for SynOptics only. [2] Proforma. [3] 1996 stock prices through June 30.

1996 YEAR-END

Debt ratio: 9.1%
Return on equity: 22.4%
Cash (mil.): $434.2
Current ratio: 3.70
Long-term debt (mil.): $110.1
No. of shares (mil.): 188.5
Dividends
  Yield: —
  Payout: —
Market value (mil.): $4,854.8
R&D as % of sales: 10.4%

QUARTER ENDED 6/30

	1996	1995
Sales ($ millions)	535.5	390.7
Net Income ($ millions)	55.1	54.4
Earnings Per Share ($)	0.28	0.28
No. of Shares (thou.)	198,013	172,315

12 MONTHS ENDED 6/30

	1996	1995
Sales ($ millions)	2,056.6	1,342.3
Net Income ($ millions)	206.3	131.0
Earnings Per Share ($)	1.04	0.73
No. of Shares (thou.)	198,013	172,315

STOCK PRICE HISTORY: High/Low/Close

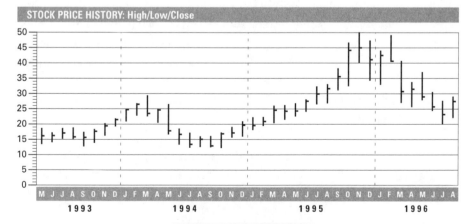

M J J A S O N D J F M A M J J A S O N D J F M A M J J A S O N D J F M A M J J A
1993   1994   1995   1996

- Recent reorganization emphasizes the Internet

- Internet services remain focused on lucrative corporate and institutional business

- AT&T resells BBN services to businesses under WorldNet brand name

- Internet revenue tripled in fiscal 1996

- New partnership with Andersen Consulting boosts systems consulting business

- Operating losses since 1992

- Heavy capital requirements for continued Internet backbone expansion

- Depends on government contracts for 50% of revenue

- Depends on America Online for 50% of Internet revenue

- Margins are declining in Internet services

- AT&T can begin winding down its reseller commitment in 2 years

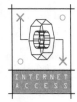 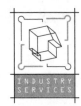

INTERNET ACCESS   INDUSTRY SERVICES

BBN Corporation

Adopting a ball as a new logo is great when things are bouncing along, but BBN's only upward kick in 3 years resulted from the 1995 sale of subsidiary LightStream, a maker of ATM network switches. Cambridge, Massachusetts-based BBN (formerly Bolt Beranek and Newman) is investing much of the $80 million in proceeds in its internetworking products and services. BBN also produces commercial speech recognition software and performs structural acoustic design consulting. CEO George Conrades implemented a major restructuring in 1996 to focus the company more intently upon Internet-related products and services. BBN Planet (Internet access services) is among the subsidiaries that have been merged into the parent.

The enterprise was founded in 1948 by MIT professors Richard Bolt and Leo Beranek, who were soon joined by Robert Newman, an MIT graduate student. Its first job was to help with the acoustic design of the UN General Assembly hall. The company expanded into military work, including communications and network software. In 1964 it introduced the first computer-based communication system, and in 1969 it created ARPANET, a government computer network that has evolved into the Internet. In the 1970s it introduced Telenet, the first packet-switching network (which can route e-mail). During the 1980s it invested heavily in a parallel supercomputer for the aerospace industry, but the project took a nosedive and was shelved in 1991.

With government budget-cutting hurting sales, the company hired Conrades (the former head of IBM's US sales) in 1994. His mandate was to pump up commercial sales. That year the company acquired SURAnet and

BBN CORPORATION

HQ: 150 Cambridge Park Dr.,
Cambridge, MA 02140
Phone: 617-873-2000
Fax: 617-873-5011
Web site: www.bbn.com

OFFICERS

Chairman, President, and CEO:
George H. Conrades, age 56, $400,000 pay
(prior to promotion)

SVP, CFO, and Treasurer:
Ralph A. Goldwasser, age 48, $207,500 pay

VP: John T. Kish Jr., age 39, $350,000 pay
**VP; General Manager and President, BBN
Planet:** Paul R. Gudonis
VP Human Resources: Steven P. Heinrich
Auditors: Coopers & Lybrand L.L.P.

SELECTED PRODUCTS AND SERVICES

Acoustic technologies
Development of ocean environmental acoustics
and sonar development, etc.

Collaborative systems
Distributed computing (artificial intelligence,
expert systems, etc.)
Language and speech processing (speech
recognition, spoken language systems)

Internet services
Access
Application development
Managed network security
World Wide Web server hosting

Internetworking
Development and operation of wide-area
communications network systems

KEY COMPETITORS

Advantis	Loral	SAIC
Bellcore	MCI	Sterling Software
Computer	MFS	Stratus Computer
Sciences	Communications	Sybase
Control Data	Microsoft	Titan Corp.
Systems	MindSpring	Unisys
EarthLink	Mitre	Voice Control
General Electric	Motorola	
IBM	NETCOM	
Kurzweil Applied	PSINet	
Intelligence	Raytheon	

BARRNET (Internet service providers). In 1995 it signed a deal with AT&T to provide the telecommunications giant's business customers Internet access through BBN Planet. Also in 1995 it signed an agreement to develop and support America Online's high-speed dial-up access service. Stephen Levy (a 30-year company veteran) retired as chairman in November, 1995, and Conrades assumed that position also. In 1996 BBN and Andersen Consulting formed a joint venture to help corporate customers conduct electronic commerce and other operations over the Internet.

BBN CORPORATION: THE NUMBERS

NYSE symbol: BBN FYE: June 30	Annual Growth	1990	1991	1992	1993	1994	1995
Sales ($ mil.)	(3.9%)	261.9	270.6	258.0	233.5	196.1	215.0
Net income ($ mil.)	—	(34.8)	9.1	4.2	(32.3)	(7.8)	64.8
Income as % of sales	—	—	3.4%	1.6%	—	—	30.2%
Earnings per share ($)	—	(1.91)	0.49	0.24	(2.05)	(0.48)	3.61
Stock price – high ($)	—	7.63	9.38	6.75	14.75	21.50	48.75
Stock price – low ($)	—	3.88	4.38	3.63	4.25	10.00	14.63
Stock price – close ($)	56.5%	4.38	5.38	4.75	12.00	14.88	41.13
P/E – high	—	—	19	28	—	—	14
P/E – low	—	—	9	15	—	—	4
Dividends per share ($)	(100.0%)	0.06	0.06	0.06	0.03	0.00	0.00
Book value per share ($)	15.1%	2.33	2.54	2.66	0.63	0.44	4.71
Employees	(3.3%)	2,367	2,284	2,086	1,663	1,694	2,000

1995 YEAR-END

Debt ratio: 47.1%
Return on equity: 144.4%
Cash (mil.): $110.8
Current ratio: 2.81
Long-term debt (mil.): $73.5
No. of shares (mil.): 17.5
Dividends
  Yield: —
  Payout: —
Market value (mil.): $720.7
R&D as % of sales: 11.8%

QUARTER ENDED 6/30

	1996	1995
Sales ($ millions)	68.7	60.2
Net Income ($ millions)	(11.0)	(5.9)
Earnings Per Share ($)	(0.60)	(0.34)
No. of Shares (thou.)	18,256	17,523

12 MONTHS ENDED 6/30

	1996	1995
Sales ($ millions)	234.3	215.0
Net Income ($ millions)	(56.6)	64.8
Earnings Per Share ($)	(3.18)	3.61
No. of Shares (thou.)	18,256	17,523

STOCK PRICE HISTORY: High/Low/Close

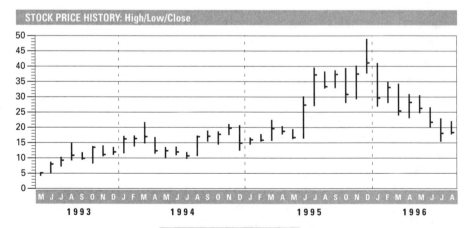

 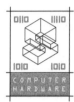

NETWORK INFRASTRUCTURE   COMPUTER HARDWARE

Boca Research

Boca Research is expanding communications way beyond word of mouth. Headquartered in Boca Raton, Florida, the company makes modems, ISDN phone line adapters, Ethernet adapters, sound and graphics cards, video accelerators, and other products used to enable or speed up the flow of information within and among computers. The popularity of the Internet and increased demand for high-tech communications equipment in small and home offices have driven up Boca's sales. In-house manufacturing allows it to control costs and respond quickly to changes in the marketplace.

With a few employees Timothy Farris started Boca Research in 1985 in a small office with a production room in the back. The next year the company launched the TophAT memory board, offering it at half the price of a similar model made by IBM. In 1987 Boca started selling its products in Europe, and through the late 1980s it expanded the memory board selection and added video graphics array (VGA) boards. In the early 1990s the company shifted away from memory boards and unveiled its first data communications product, a 2,400 bps modem (it now makes modems more than 10 times as fast). In 1993 Boca went public. That year it entered the networking market with Ethernet adapters and increased its retail presence with the purchase of telecommunications peripherals producer Complete PC for $2.6 million.

Director Roe Stamps succeeded Farris as chairman in 1995. The next year Boca formed a joint venture with a group of investors and Technology

- Consumer and small office demand for modems continues to surge
- Early entrant into market for equipment enabling videoconferencing over regular telephone lines
- Strong OEM distribution channel (64% of sales in 2nd quarter 1996)
- International sales are growing rapidly
- 1st half 1996 revenues up 51.5%
- P/E of 9 (8/96) is low for Internet-related stocks

- Most of its markets are brutally competitive
- Two OEM customers accounted for 38% of 2nd quarter 1996 revenue
- One big OEM account reported an overstock in Boca products (2nd quarter 1996)
- Gross margins are declining

BOCA RESEARCH, INC.
HQ: 1377 Clint Moore Rd.,
Boca Raton, FL 33487
Phone: 561-997-6227
Fax: 561-997-0918
Web site: www.bocaresearch.com

OFFICERS

Chairman: E. Roe Stamps IV, age 49
President and CEO:
Anthony F. Zalenski, age 52, $442,178 pay
COO:
Lawrence F. Steffann, age 43, $236,325 pay
SVP Finance and CFO:
R. Michael Brewer, age 53, $227,355 pay
SVP Manufacturing:
Michael A. Reale, age 56, $218,397 pay
SVP and General Manager International:
Charles R. Kenmore, age 46, $209,104 pay
VP Human Resources:
Martha A. Ritchason, age 56
Auditors: Deloitte & Touche LLP

SELECTED PRODUCTS AND SERVICES

Data communications
BBS modems
Fax/data modems
Video phones
Input/Output
Serial/parallel boards
IDE controllers
Multimedia
Sound cards
Graphic cards
Networking
Ethernet adapters
Ethernet hubs

KEY COMPETITORS

3Com	Intel
Asante	Motorola
Bay Networks	Number Nine Visual
DATA RACE	PairGain
Diamond Multimedia	STB Systems
Global Village	Trident Microsystems
GVC Technologies	U.S. Robotics
Hayes Microcomputer	Western Digital
IEC Electronics	Zoom Telephonics

Development Information Company, of India, to market products made by Boca and other suppliers in Africa and South Asia. In the same year Boca released a desktop videoconferencing product designed to operate with standard telephone lines.

BOCA RESEARCH: THE NUMBERS

Nasdaq symbol: BOCI FYE: December 31	Annual Growth	1990	1991	1992	1993	1994	1995
Sales ($ mil.)	49.8%	—	28.4	44.6	64.7	83.6	143.0
Net income ($ mil.)	18.0%	—	4.9	5.8	2.7	5.7	9.5
Income as % of sales	—	—	17.4%	13.1%	4.2%	6.9%	6.7%
Earnings per share ($)	21.9%	—	0.48	0.73	0.33	0.68	1.06
Stock price – high ($)	—	—	—	—	14.75	9.25	36.50
Stock price – low ($)	—	—	—	—	5.50	4.25	8.00
Stock price – close ($)	94.6%	—	—	—	7.00	9.00	26.50
P/E – high	—	—	—	—	45	14	34
P/E – low	—	—	—	—	17	6	8
Dividends per share ($)	—	—	—	—	0.00	0.00	0.00
Book value per share ($)	23.6%	—	—	—	3.58	4.28	5.47
Employees	—	—	—	—	—	—	386

1995 YEAR-END

Debt ratio: 0.0%
Return on equity: 23.1%
Cash (mil.): $0.5
Current ratio: 4.42
Long-term debt (mil.): $0.0
No. of shares (mil.): 8.5
Dividends
  Yield: —
  Payout: —
Market value (mil.): $225.9
R&D as % of sales: 1.9%

QUARTER ENDED 6/30

	1996	1995
Sales ($ millions)	46.7	33.2
Net Income ($ millions)	2.8	2.2
Earnings Per Share ($)	0.31	0.25
No. of Shares (thou.)	8,634	8,469

6 MONTHS ENDED 6/30

	1996	1995
Sales ($ millions)	91.6	60.5
Net Income ($ millions)	5.4	4.2
Earnings Per Share ($)	0.60	0.48
No. of Shares (thou.)	8,634	8,469

STOCK PRICE HISTORY: High/Low/Close

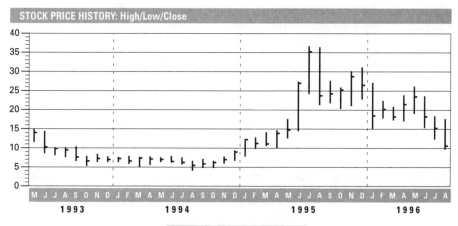

www.cyberstocks.com

- Telecommunications deregulation should spur customer activity in the US

- Products have home video, telephony, multimedia, and Internet applications

- Customers include Bell Atlantic, SBC, GTE, Samsung, France Telecom

- Company's products achieve high bandwidth with existing telephone cabling

- BroadBand partners include Lucent and Intel

- Remember the 500-channel "information superhighway"?

- Heavily dependent on Bell Atlantic

- RBOCs are proceeding slowly with new, nontelephonic digital services

- Rival technologies include ISDN, wireless, cable, ASDL, optical fiber

- BroadBand has never been profitable, is burning cash rapidly

- Market cap = $325 million (8/96), 1st half 1996 sales of $9.5 million

NETWORK INFRASTRUCTURE

BroadBand Technologies

Just as department stores offer clothes, electronics, and housewares under one roof, BroadBand provides data, voice communications, and television transmissions over a single network. Headquartered in Durham, North Carolina, BroadBand Technologies develops fiber loop access (FLX) systems, which send digital signals from telecommunications service providers to consumers' homes. These networks can be used to provide interactive TV, digital video, Internet access, and telephony. Bell Atlantic accounts for about 70% of the company's sales.

Heavy investments in R&D and high operating costs have kept the company from being profitable, though analysts predict BroadBand will be in the black in the late 1990's. Electronic connector maker AMP owns about 9% of the company. Three veterans of fiber optics supplier Siecor (a Siemens/Corning joint venture) — Salim Bhatia, John Hutchins, and Richard Jones — started BroadBand in 1988 to develop a system that could deliver multiple signals over the same network. By 1990 the company had developed the FLX system and had trials installed at 10 telephone companies in the US and abroad.

Broadband received its first volume purchase in 1993 when it agreed to supply Bell Atlantic with equipment costing about $44 million. That year BroadBand went public. It teamed with AT&T in 1994 to develop the SLC-2000 Access System, which uses FLX Switched Digital Video to transmit voice and other signals. Bell Atlantic received FCC approval that year for its

BROADBAND TECHNOLOGIES, INC.

HQ: 4024 Stirrup Creek Dr.,
Research Triangle Park, NC 27709
Phone: 919-544-0015
Fax: 919-544-3459
Web site: www.bbt.com

OFFICERS

Chairman: John R. Hutchins III, age 61
President and CEO:
Salim A. L. Bhatia, age 45, $223,220 pay
EVP Operations:
Richard L. Popp, age 57, $168,904 pay
EVP: J. Richard Jones, age 48, $159,500 pay
VP: Robert W. Henry, age 43, $178,714 pay
VP and CFO: Timothy K. Oakley
VP: Wayne C. Machon, age 50
VP: Salvatore Quattrocchi, age 48
Director Human Resources:
Loretta Woodall
Auditors: Ernst & Young LLP

SELECTED PRODUCTS AND SERVICES

FLX PC Adapter (Internet-access adapter card)
FLX-1100 System (telephony and video switcher)
FLX-2500 System (data and video switcher)

SELECTED CUSTOMERS AND PARTNERS

Bell Atlantic
Groupe Sagem
Samsung
SBC Communications

KEY COMPETITORS

ADC Telecommunications
Alcatel Alsthom
DSC Communications
Ericsson
Fujitsu
General Instrument
Lucent
Northern Telecom
PairGain
Reliance Comm/Tec
Scientific-Atlanta
Siemens
Westell Technologies

Video Dial Tone network, which uses BroadBand equipment to provide data and video services. Also in 1994 BroadBand's FLX system was selected for a project in Texas and another in Paris.

The Telecommunications Act of 1996 boosted the market for BroadBand's products by allowing telephone companies to offer a broader range of services and opening the door for other network operators to provide telecommunications services. The company unveiled its 2nd-generation FLX-2500 System, which facilitates the connection of a digital network to a consumer's home, in 1996.

BROADBAND: THE NUMBERS

Nasdaq symbol: BBTK FYE: December 31	Annual Growth	1990	1991	1992	1993	1994	1995
Sales ($ mil.)	77.2%	1.3	2.6	5.3	15.1	27.0	22.7
Net income ($ mil.)	—	(6.1)	(8.4)	(11.8)	(19.0)	(24.2)	(27.9)
Income as % of sales	—	—	—	—	—	—	—
Earnings per share ($)	—	(1.29)	(1.55)	(1.54)	(1.89)	(1.85)	(2.13)
Stock price – high ($)	—	—	—	—	52.25	33.50	31.75
Stock price – low ($)	—	—	—	—	25.00	11.00	15.75
Stock price – close ($)	(28.5%)	—	—	—	31.75	30.50	16.25
P/E – high	—	—	—	—	—	—	—
P/E – low	—	—	—	—	—	—	—
Dividends per share ($)	—	—	—	—	0.00	0.00	0.00
Book value per share ($)	(24.9%)	—	—	—	7.94	6.08	4.48
Employees	32.5%	—	100	162	225	284	308

1995 YEAR-END

Debt ratio: 0.5%
Return on equity: —
Cash (mil.): $65.4
Current ratio: 2.68
Long-term debt (mil.): $0.0
No. of shares (mil.): 13.2
Dividends
  Yield: —
  Payout: —
Market value (mil.): $213.7
R&D as % of sales: 85.6%

QUARTER ENDED 6/30

	1996	1995
Sales ($ millions)	5.5	5.5
Net Income ($ millions)	(6.5)	(6.5)
Earnings Per Share ($)	(0.49)	(0.50)
No. of Shares (thou.)	13,239	13,072

6 MONTHS ENDED 6/30

	1996	1995
Sales ($ millions)	9.5	8.7
Net Income ($ millions)	(14.1)	(14.5)
Earnings Per Share ($)	(1.07)	(1.11)
No. of Shares (thou.)	13,239	13,072

STOCK PRICE HISTORY: High/Low/Close

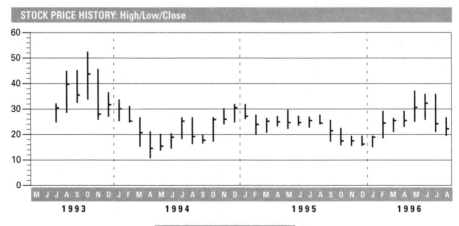

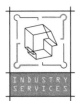
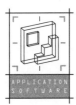

INDUSTRY SERVICES

APPLICATION SOFTWARE

BroadVision

Los Altos, California-based BroadVision has scanned the horizon of electronic commerce and sees a niche for its customized online marketing software. Its BroadVision One-To-One system enables a business to tailor Web sites to fit the needs and preferences of its customers, be they consumers or other companies. One-to-One allows users to manage online transactions involving ordering and payment, order fulfillment, billing, customer service, and other activities. It also lets users collect, track, and manage information about Web site visitors and use the resulting profiles to customize Web site content, such as product information, advertising, pricing, coupons, incentives, editorials, and promotions. BroadVision also provides consulting, education, and support services for users of its software. Its clients include Prodigy and Ameritech in the US, Olivetti in Italy, and Itochu and NTT in Japan.

New media veteran Pehong Chen sold his first company, GAIN Technology, a multimedia applications provider, to Sybase in 1992. He founded BroadVision the following year to develop interactive marketing and sales software. Rather than focusing on one or 2 aspects of electronic commerce, such as taking an order or selecting a method of payment, Chen sought to deliver a comprehensive marketing application with a strong emphasis on features that attract and retain consumers, i.e., personalized service. Between 1993 and 1995 BroadVision raised funding from

- Fully devoted to enabling companies to personalize Web marketing
- One-to-One is complete Web publishing tool that can link to existing transaction systems
- Prodigy and Olivetti are testing the system

- A One-to-One installation is expensive
- Successful implementation requires a new marketing mindset
- Sales may be limited until the public is comfortable with Web commerce
- Short sales history and very few customers
- Accelerating losses
- Stock is selling at about 50 times sales (8/96)

BROADVISION

BROADVISION, INC.
HQ: 333 Distel Circle,
Los Altos, CA 94022
Phone: 415-943-3600
Fax: 415-943-3699
Web site: www.broadvision.com

OFFICERS

Chairman, President, and CEO:
Pehong Chen, age 38, $106,664 pay

VP Business Development and General Manager, American Operations:
Mark D. Goros, age 45, $148,556 pay

VP Operations and CFO:
Randall C. Bolten, age 43

VP Engineering: Clark Catelain, age 48

VP Marketing: Robert Runge, age 41

VP and General Manager of Japan/Asia-Pacific Operations:
Giuseppe Kobayashi, age 40

VP and General Manager of European Operations:
Francois Stieger, age 47

Purchasing, Human Resources, and Facilities Coordinator: Judy Pace

Auditors: KPMG Peat Marwick LLP

SELECTED PRODUCTS AND SERVICES

BroadVision One-To-One (comprehensive online marketing and selling system)

Dynamic Command Center (Windows 95-based client application for operating Web sites in real-time)

Consulting, education, and support services for customers who want to design and set up online marketing and sales systems

KEY COMPETITORS
CKS
CONNECT
Leap Group
Microsoft
Netscape
Open Market
Oracle

Sutter Hill Ventures, the Mayfield Fund, Stanford University, Itochu, Olivetti, and Ameritech among others.

BroadVision went public in 1996. Chen owns 29% of the company. That year BroadVision signed a deal with Virgin Group of the UK to deliver personalized information and services on the Virgin Net online service.

BROADVISION: THE NUMBERS

Nasdaq symbol: BVSN FYE: December 31	Annual Growth	1990	1991	1992	1993	1994	1995
Sales ($ mil.)	—	—	—	—	0.0	0.0	0.5
Net income ($ mil.)	—	—	—	—	(0.1)	(1.7)	(4.3)
Income as % of sales	—	—	—	—	—	—	—
Employees	—	—	—	—	—	14	46

1995 YEAR-END

Debt ratio: 13.8%
Return on equity: —
Cash (mil.): $4.5
Current ratio: 4.88
Long-term debt (mil.): $0.5
No. of shares (mil.): —
Dividends
  Yield: —
  Payout: —
R&D as % of sales: 440.0%

QUARTER ENDED 6/30

	1996	1995
Sales ($ millions)	2.3	0.0
Net Income ($ millions)	(2.2)	(1.0)
Earnings Per Share ($)	(0.13)	(0.05)
No. of Shares (thou.)	17,699	18,888

6 MONTHS ENDED 6/30

	1996	1995
Sales ($ millions)	3.7	0.0
Net Income ($ millions)	(3.9)	(1.8)
Earnings Per Share ($)	(0.22)	(0.10)
No. of Shares (thou.)	17,699	18,888

STOCK PRICE HISTORY: High/Low/Close

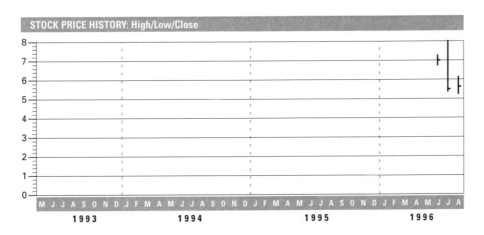

- A leader in high-end hubs and switches

- SMC purchase adds Fast Ethernet products, 3rd-party distribution

- Expanding its ATM and ISDN product lines

- ZeitNet acquisition gives in-house-manufactured ATM NICs

- A leader in next-generation LAN technology

- Beating Bay Networks to market with new products

- Most ATM products Cabletron sells are made by FORE Systems

- Must digest SMC's marginally profitable switch business

- A revival at Bay Networks could slow Cabletron's growth

NETWORK
INFRASTRUCTURE

Cabletron Systems

Cabletron is a LAN lover. The Rochester, New Hampshire-based company is a leading provider of such networking hardware as hubs and switches. Cabletron customers include such corporate end users as Audi and Microsoft and such OEMs as Lockheed and Bull Systems. Founders Robert Levine and Craig Benson each own about 13% of the company, a combined stake worth more than $1 billion.

Cabletron has climbed the networking products ladder by combining product innovations (it produced one of the first network hubs and now spends about 11% of revenues on R&D), an aggressive sales force that focuses on high-end corporate accounts, and a no-frills corporate culture (traveling employees must double up in hotel rooms). This combination has given Cabletron an 8-year earnings growth rate of nearly 40%. Although the company ranks 4th among networking products makers (behind Cisco Systems, 3Com, and Bay Networks), recent acquisitions have expanded its product lines and its customer list.

Cabletron got its start in 1983 when Levine, an independent wire and cable salesman, needed 1,000 feet of cable for a customer's computer network but could find only rolls of 10,000 feet. Craig Benson suggested they cut the cable and sell the shorter segments to business associates. The company's first-year revenues were $100,000. Cabletron soon began installing networks, then designing networking equipment. In 1988 the company intro-

CABLETRON SYSTEMS, INC.

HQ: 35 Industrial Way, PO Box 5005,
Rochester, NH 03866-5005
Phone: 603-332-9400
Fax: 603-337-2211
Web site: www.ctron.com

OFFICERS

Chairman, COO, and Treasurer:
Craig R. Benson, age 41, $52,000 pay

President and CEO:
S. Robert Levine, age 38, $52,200 pay

Director Engineering and Manufacturing:
Christopher J. Oliver, age 35, $275,000 pay

Director Finance and CFO:
David J. Kirkpatrick, age 44, $239,952 pay

Executive Director Sales, Worldwide:
Kenneth R. Levine, age 32

Secretary: Michael D. Myerow
Director Human Resources: Linda Pepin
Auditors: KPMG Peat Marwick LLP

SELECTED PRODUCTS AND SERVICES

Products

Coaxial cable, optical fiber, and twisted-pair wire

Network interconnection equipment

Network management software (SPECTRUM)

Network test equipment

Smart hubs and switches and related products

Services

Certification and documentation

Consulting, design, and configuration

Project management

KEY COMPETITORS

3Com	Network General
AMP	Newbridge Networks
Asante	Optical Data Systems
Bay Networks	Standard Microsystems
Belden	U.S. Robotics
Cisco Systems	Xylan
Corning	
DEC	
Digi International	
FORE Systems	
Hewlett-Packard	
IBM	
Intel	
Madge	

duced MMAC (Multi Media Access Center), an intelligent wiring hub used to simplify network installation, aid in troubleshooting, and facilitate modifications. Cabletron went public in 1989. In 1992 the company unveiled the first SCSI-to-Ethernet adapter, which allowed Macintosh users to connect to Ethernet LANs, and the industry's first bridge that linked Ethernet, token ring, and WANs.

In 1995 Cabletron purchased a unit of Standard Microsystems that makes high-speed LAN switches. The following year the company agreed to acquire network switch maker Network Express and networking connector maker ZietNet, paying more than $250 million for the pair.

CABLETRON: THE NUMBERS

NYSE symbol: CS FYE: February 28	Annual Growth	1991	1992	1993	1994	1995	1996
Sales ($ mil.)	42.7%	180.5	290.5	418.2	598.1	810.7	1,069.7
Net income ($ mil.)	35.4%	35.9	58.0	83.5	119.2	162.0	164.4
Income as % of sales	—	19.9%	20.0%	20.0%	19.9%	20.0%	15.4%
Earnings per share ($)	33.5%	0.54	0.83	1.19	1.68	2.27	2.29
Stock price – high ($)[1]	—	11.70	22.10	34.10	47.60	53.00	87.75
Stock price – low ($)[1]	—	2.75	10.20	16.85	29.80	33.05	37.37
Stock price – close ($)[1]	48.0%	11.40	21.50	33.60	45.00	46.50	81.00
P/E – high	—	22	27	29	28	23	38
P/E – low	—	5	12	14	18	15	16
Dividends per share ($)	—	0.00	0.00	0.00	0.00	0.00	0.00
Book value per share ($)	39.9%	2.01	2.90	4.09	5.94	8.22	10.77
Employees	24.1%	1,825	2,032	2,625	3,663	4,970	5,377

[1] Stock prices are for the prior calendar year.

1996 YEAR-END

Debt ratio: 0.0%
Return on equity: 24.1%
Cash (mil.): $253.5
Current ratio: 3.80
Long-term debt (mil.): $0.0
No. of shares (mil.): 72.2
Dividends
  Yield: —
  Payout: —
Market value (mil.): $5,851.0
R&D as % of sales: 10.8%

QUARTER ENDED 5/31

	1996	1995
Sales ($ millions)	315.1	240.8
Net Income ($ millions)	62.7	48.3
Earnings Per Share ($)	0.87	0.68
No. of Shares (thou.)	72,283	71,570

3 MONTHS ENDED 5/31

	1996	1995
Sales ($ millions)	315.1	240.8
Net Income ($ millions)	62.7	48.3
Earnings Per Share ($)	0.87	0.68
No. of Shares (thou.)	72,283	71,570

STOCK PRICE HISTORY: High/Low/Close

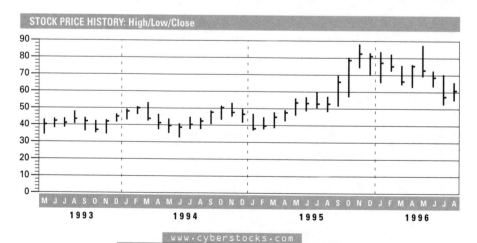

www·cyberstocks·com

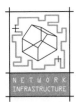

Cascade Communications

If Internet dominance is the bait, Cascade Communications has the switch. The company makes wide area network (WAN) switches based on high-speed broadband network technologies. It serves some of the world's largest commercial Internet service providers and estimates that up to 70% of Internet traffic passes through its switches. The switch vendor has become one of the world's fastest-growing data communications companies, largely owing to the deregulation of the phone industry, which caused nonvoice traffic to surge through newly deployed public carrier phone networks (85% of the company's customer base). Calling on Cascade's technology, Bell Atlantic and U S WEST ring up about 30% of the company's sales.

The Westford, Massachusetts-based company was founded in 1990 as Nexgencom by Gururaj "Desh" Deshpande, a founder of local area network (LAN) products maker Coral Network. Nexgencom became Cascade in 1991.

Backed by several venture capital firms, the company grew rapidly. In 1992 Daniel Smith, a former Proteon executive, was named president and CEO, succeeding Deshpande, who became EVP. The company went public in 1994 as one of the hottest-selling high-tech stocks of the year. Cascade's sales surged 169% in 1995, mainly attributed to the increased demand for broadband packet equipment. Favored by local exchange carriers and Internet service providers seeking cost-efficient datacom services, the com-

- Leads in sales of frame relay switches to RBOCs, ISPs
- Cascade's WAN switches lead industry in port density (lines/switch)
- Highest port density should yield lowest cost to buyer
- Tight focus on service provider (not private network) market
- Switches handle multiple services (ATM, frame relay, SDMS)
- 1st half 1996 sales up 160%, earnings per share up 180%

- Narrow product line
- Dependent on RBOC orders
- Now competes with Cisco
- P/E = 130 (8/96)

CASCADE

CASCADE COMMUNICATIONS CORP.
HQ: 5 Carlisle Rd., Westford, MA 01886
Phone: 508-692-2600
Fax: 508-692-9214
Web site: www.casc.com

OFFICERS
Chairperson: Victoria A. Brown, age 48
President and CEO:
Daniel E. Smith, age 46, $275,854 pay
EVP Marketing and Customer Service:
Gururaj Deshpande, age 45, $212,554 pay
VP Worldwide Sales:
Michael A. Champa, age 44, $278,981 pay
**VP Finance and Administration, CFO,
Treasurer, and Secretary:**
Paul E. Blondin, age 45, $164,139 pay
VP Operations:
John E. Dowling, age 42, $158,150 pay
VP Engineering: Hassan M. Ahmed, age 38
VP Marketing: Robert N. Machlin, age 38
Director Human Resources: Mary Cogan
Auditors: Coopers & Lybrand L.L.P.

SELECTED PRODUCTS AND SERVICES
B-STDX 8000/9000 Switch Family (high-performance multiservice WAN switches)
Cascade 500 ATM (high-capacity ATM switches)
CascadeView Network Management Systems (WAN/LAN network management applications)
STDX 6000 (multiservice WAN switches for smaller networks)

KEY COMPETITORS
Bay Networks
Cisco Systems
General DataComm
IBM
Newbridge Networks
Northern Telecom

pany's B-STDX line of higher-speed, greater-capacity switches accounted for more than 90% of 1995 sales.

Cascade entered partnerships with industry giants Motorola and IBM in 1996. Expanding its product line, that year Cascade paid $145.3 million for Arris Networks, a private developer of remote access technology. Networking leader Cisco Systems owns 6% of the company but plans to sell its stake following its 1996 purchase of WAN rival StrataCom.

CASCADE: THE NUMBERS

Nasdaq symbol: CSCC FYE: December 31	Annual Growth	1990	1991	1992	1993	1994	1995
Sales ($ mil.)	452.3%	—	—	0.8	7.0	50.1	134.8
Net income ($ mil.)	—	—	—	(3.1)	(2.6)	9.3	25.4
Income as % of sales	—	—	—	—	—	18.6%	18.8%
Earnings per share ($)	—	—	—	(0.15)	(0.12)	0.12	0.28
Stock price – high ($)	—	—	—	—	—	10.83	30.83
Stock price – low ($)	—	—	—	—	—	3.50	9.55
Stock price – close ($)	—	—	—	—	—	10.30	28.42
P/E – high	—	—	—	—	—	94	110
P/E – low	—	—	—	—	—	30	34
Dividends per share ($)	—	—	—	—	—	0.00	0.00
Book value per share ($)	—	—	—	—	—	0.64	1.03
Employees	144.3%	—	—	29	72	232	423

1995 YEAR-END

Debt ratio: 0.0%
Return on equity: 36.6%
Cash (mil.): $60.6
Current ratio: 3.71
Long-term debt (mil.): $0.0
No. of shares (mil.): 83.8
Dividends
  Yield: —
  Payout: —
Market value (mil.): $2,381.1
R&D as % of sales: 15.4%

QUARTER ENDED 6/30

	1996	1995
Sales ($ millions)	80.4	29.1
Net Income ($ millions)	16.7	5.3
Earnings Per Share ($)	0.17	0.06
No. of Shares (thou.)	88,901	90,558

6 MONTHS ENDED 6/30

	1996	1995
Sales ($ millions)	136.5	52.6
Net Income ($ millions)	27.1	9.5
Earnings Per Share ($)	0.28	0.10
No. of Shares (thou.)	88,901	90,558

STOCK PRICE HISTORY: High/Low/Close

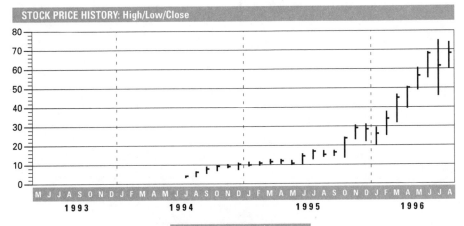

www.cyberstocks.com

- Growth in internetworking is fueling an explosion in demand for firewall products

- Unique "stateful inspection" technology is efficient and flexible

- Leads the firewall-software industry with a 40% share

- Aggressively cutting bundling deals with network equipment companies

- 1st half 1996 sales up 282%, earnings per share up 260%

- Secure Computing's purchase of Border Networks creates a strong #2 in firewalls

- Ascend has entered the firewall market via its acquisition of Morningstar

- The company is located in Israel, exposing investors to political, military risk

- OEM Sun Microsystems accounted for 58% of 1st quarter 1996 revenue

- P/E over 85 (8/96)

NETWORK
INFRASTRUCTURE

Check Point Software

The checkpoint at a country's border prevents illegal entries. So does Check Point Software Technologies. The company, based in Ramat Gan, a suburb of Tel Aviv, Israel, is the world's runaway firewall market leader (40%). A firewall enforces a boundary between networks, protecting computers against unauthorized users or viruses. Check Point's FireWall-1 supports more than 100 applications and is the only firewall product that can handle applications based on the TCP and UDP protocols (a common combination for Internet audio/video applications). The company sells its products through OEM partners and resellers worldwide. The Sun Microsystems SunSoft affiliate accounts for more than 50% of sales. Check Point went public in 1996. Israeli software firm BRM Technologies owns 26% of the company, and venture capitalists Venrock Associates and U.S. Venture Partners own another 17%. Founders Gil Shwed, Shlomo Kramer, and Marius Nacht each own 14%.

Shwed (a founder of software maker Metrogram), who dreamed of creating an easy-to-use but powerful and secure firewall product for the Internet, founded the company in 1993 with Kramer and Nacht. Check Point introduced the first version of FireWall-1 in 1994. The next year it introduced a newer version using encryption and key management technology licensed from RSA Data Security. (Cylink Corp. has sued RSA, now owned by Security Dynamics Technologies, for patent infringement; if RSA loses, Check Point may have to pay royalties to Cylink for the technology.) Also

CHECKPOINT
Software Technologies

CHECK POINT SOFTWARE TECH. LTD.

HQ: 35 Jabotinsky St.,
Ramat-Gan, 52511, Israel
Phone: +972-3-613-1833
Fax: + 972-3-575-9256
US HQ: 400 Seaport Court, Ste. 105
Redwood City, CA 94063
US Phone: 800-429-4391
US Fax: 415-562-0410
Web site: www.checkpoint.com

OFFICERS

Chairman: Nir Barkat
President and CEO: Gil Shwed
VP Product and Business Development:
Shlomo Kramer
VP International Operations: Marius Nacht
VP Finance and CFO: Hagi Schwartz
President and CEO, Check Point Software Technologies Inc.(US):
Deborah D. Triant
VP Worldwide Sales and Field Operations, Check Point Software Technologies Inc.(US):
John W. Cunningham
Auditors: Ernst & Young LLP

SELECTED PRODUCTS AND SERVICES

FireWall-1 Enterprise (enterprise, Internet, and intranet gateways with distributed management capabilities)

FireWall-1 Inspection Module (additional modules for multiple gateway implementation)

FireWall-1 Internet Gateway (Internet and intranet gateways for small to medium-sized businesses)

FireWall-1 Network Security Center (added router management capabilities)

FireWall-First! (Internet and intranet access control for entry level)

KEY COMPETITORS

America Online
Ascend Communications
Axent
Cheyenne Software
Cylink
DEC
Harris Corp.
IBM
Information Resource Engineering
Milkyway Networks
Network Systems
Raptor Systems
Secure
Sun Microsystems
Trusted Information System
Virtual Open Network Environment

in 1995, Check Point Software Technologies Inc., a US subsidiary for marketing and sales support, was formed.

The company has vigorously pursued alliances and partnerships with OEMs and resellers; more than a half dozen deals in 1996 include Hewlett-Packard, Computer Sciences Corp., and Vanstar. It went public that year and also opened an office in the UK, with plans to open offices in France and Germany.

CHECK POINT: THE NUMBERS

Nasdaq symbol: CHKPF FYE: December 31	Annual Growth	1990	1991	1992	1993	1994	1995
Sales ($ mil.)	—	—	—	—	0.0	0.8	9.5
Net income ($ mil.)	—	—	—	—	(0.1)	0.0	4.8
Income as % of sales	—	—	—	—	—	3.1%	50.8%
Employees	—	—	—	—	—	—	49

1995 YEAR-END

Debt ratio: 0.0%
Return on equity: 194.7%
Cash (mil.): $3.6
Current ratio: 3.20
Long-term debt (mil.): $0.0
No. of shares (mil.): —
Dividends
  Yield: —
  Payout: —
R&D as % of sales: 11.5%

QUARTER ENDED 6/30

	1996	1995
Sales ($ millions)	7.4	1.6
Net Income ($ millions)	3.2	0.8
Earnings Per Share ($)	0.10	0.02
No. of Shares (thou.)	33,900	33,812

6 MONTHS ENDED 6/30

	1996	1995
Sales ($ millions)	12.2	3.2
Net Income ($ millions)	6.0	1.7
Earnings Per Share ($)	0.18	0.05
No. of Shares (thou.)	33,900	33,812

STOCK PRICE HISTORY: High/Low/Close

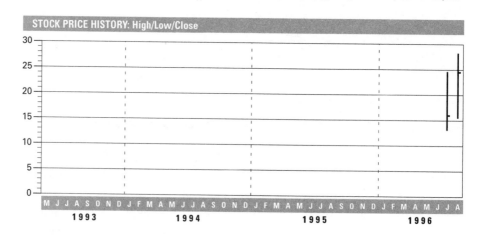

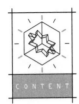

SPECIALIZED SERVICES

CONTENT

Checkfree Corporation

The paperless office of the future will be bill-free, invoice-free, and — hopes this Columbus, Ohio-based company — Checkfree. Checkfree offers electronic data interchange systems that handle all of these transactions, along with banking, payment, and securities trading functions. Founder Peter Kight owns about 17% of the company.

Kight dropped out of college and went to work managing a chain of health clubs. While there, he sought a less painful way for his customers to pony up their annual fees than making a lump sum payment. Taking a page from insurance companies, who routinely debited premiums from policyholder accounts, Kight sought and received backing from Banc One to devise a consumer bill payment system. His first customer was an apartment complex. The little service became viable, and in 1984 Columbus-based CompuServe began offering Checkfree's system to its subscribers During the 1980s and early 1990s, Checkfree's growth was powered by consumer business. The company offered its software both as an independent package and as part of other financial packages, including Managing your Money and Intuit's Quicken.

By 1995, when Checkfree went public, it was modestly profitable, and Quicken sales accounted for about 1/3 of revenues. Then Intuit announced

- Business opportunities in its markets are massive
- #1 in home banking services
- Security APL acquisition bolsters home banking service with investment portfolio services
- Handles electronic collections and payables for businesses, is near electronic bill presentment
- Key alliances with AT&T and ADP are part of aggressive expansion strategy
- Revenues for 6 months ended 6/96, rose 116%

- More than half of bill payments on behalf of customers are performed by issuing printed checks
- Software is not compatible with all versions of Intuit's Quicken personal finance program
- Former partner Intuit recently launched its own home banking service, replacing Checkfree
- Current strategy calls for market share growth, not profits
- CompuServe has an important marketing partner and is suffering from poor subscriber growth

CHECKFREE CORPORATION
HQ: 8275 N. High St.,
    Columbus, OH 43235-1497
Phone: 614-825-3000
Fax: 614-825-3307
Web site: www.checkfree.com

OFFICERS

Chairman, President, and CEO:
Peter J. Kight, age 40, $281,173 pay
EVP Retail Services:
Mark D. Phelan, age 41, $202,704 pay
EVP Business Development:
Mark A. Johnson, age 43, $192,711 pay
EVP Systems Support and Development:
Howard S. Baulch, age 42, $159,904 pay
EVP Corporate Services:
Kenneth J. Benvenuto, age 37
EVP Corporate Banking:
Lynn D. Busing, age 44
EVP Sales and Marketing:
James M. Garrett, age 38
Auditors: Deloitte & Touche LLP

SELECTED PRODUCTS AND SERVICES

Automated clearinghouse processing
Back-office automation
Electronic bill payment processing
Electronic billing, payment, cash management, and account reconciliation
Internet delivery development
Internet securities trading
Secure Internet transaction services

KEY COMPETITORS

CFI ProService	National City Bank
Concord EFS	National Data
Cybercash	PC Quote
Data Broadcasting	POS Systems
DigiCash	Reuters
First Data	Security First
First USA Paymentech	Sterling Commerce
GZS	Telescan
IBM	VeriFone
Intuit	

that it was becoming a competitor through its Intuit Services Corp. This forced Checkfree to scramble to replace this business.

Its solution was a new emphasis on banks. During 1995 the company steeply increased sales and research spending to develop new products and bring in clients (plunging the company into the red). The following year it targeted banks via several acquisitions and alliances. Purchases included Servantis Systems Holding (a back-office software company) and Security APL (whose PAWWS system offers securities portfolio accounting).

CHECKFREE: THE NUMBERS

Nasdaq symbol: CKFR FYE: June 30	Annual Growth	1990	1991	1992	1993	1994	1995
Sales ($ mil.)	17.7%	—	25.7	22.2	30.9	39.3	49.3
Net income ($ mil.)	—	—	2.5	(0.1)	1.0	0.5	(0.2)
Income as % of sales	—	—	9.7%	—	3.3%	1.2%	—
Earnings per share ($)	—	—	0.09	—	0.04	0.02	(0.01)
Stock price – high ($)	—	—	—	—	—	—	29.38
Stock price – low ($)	—	—	—	—	—	—	16.00
Stock price – close ($)	—	—	—	—	—	—	21.50
P/E – high	—	—	—	—	—	—	—
P/E – low	—	—	—	—	—	—	—
Dividends per share ($)	—	—	—	—	—	—	0.00
Book value per share ($)	—	—	—	—	—	—	3.02
Employees	—	—	—	—	—	—	442

1995 YEAR-END

Debt ratio: 7.8%
Return on equity: —
Cash (mil.): $84.9
Current ratio: 10.43
Long-term debt (mil.): $7.3
No. of shares (mil.): 32.9
Dividends
  Yield: —
  Payout: —
Market value (mil.): $706.6
R&D as % of sales: 14.2%

QUARTER ENDED 6/30

	1996	1995
Sales ($ millions)	29.4	12.6
Net Income ($ millions)	(41.1)	0.2
Earnings Per Share ($)	(1.02)	0.01
No. of Shares (thou.)	40,166	26,939

6 MONTHS ENDED 6/30

	1996	1995
Sales ($ millions)	51.0	23.6
Net Income ($ millions)	(138.2)	0.1
Earnings Per Share ($)	(3.69)	0.00
No. of Shares (thou.)	40,166	26,939

STOCK PRICE HISTORY: High/Low/Close

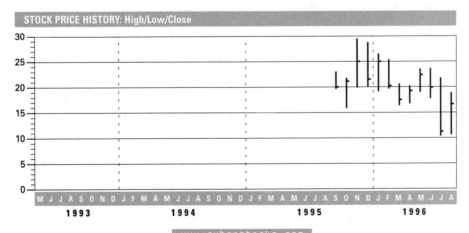

www.cyberstocks.com

- Broad product line covers LAN, WAN, and internetworking

- Company is dominant in routers, #1 in LAN and frame-relay WAN switches

- Cisco is well-positioned in network integration products and services

- Major opportunity in integration of SNA and client/server networks

- Huge router installed base = sales leverage in private network market

- Cisco has a great track record

- Market is shifting away from routers, favoring switching technologies

- StrataCom, bought for $4 billion, was a one-product company in 1995

- Rapid acquisition pace could cause operational problems

- LAN-switching market is getting crowded

- P/E of 40 (8/96) may be high for a big capital equipment company

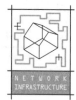

NETWORK INFRASTRUCTURE

Cisco Systems

Cisco's products allow spiders (computers) on one web (network) to communicate with spiders on another. The San Jose-based company is the world's #1 supplier of internetworking products that link LANs and WANs. Products include routers, switches, dial-up access servers, and Internetworking Operating System (Cisco IOS) network management software. The Internet's rapid growth has been a big boost to Cisco; it is the #1 supplier of routers for the Internet's backbone, and it continues to add products to maintain its place as a leading provider of Internet infrastructure.

Husband-and-wife team Leonard Bosack and Sandra Lerner started Cisco in 1984 after developing technology to interlink their departments' computer networks at Stanford University. They sold their first network router in 1986. As the market for network routers opened up in the late 1980s, Cisco, whose products had a proven track record with its customers at universities and other institutions, had a head start on competitors. Cisco's sales exploded, jumping from $1.5 million in 1987 to $28 million in 1989.

Cisco went public in 1990. In the early 1990s the company began to face increased competition from start-ups as well as computer giants IBM and DEC. It expanded its product offerings and beefed up overseas sales. The company addressed the lower end of the router market in 1993 by introducing the Cisco 2000. That year it made its first acquisition — Crescendo Communications — a Sunnyvale, California-based networking company.

The next year Cisco bought PC-operated router maker Newport Systems

CISCO SYSTEMS, INC.
HQ: 170 W. Tasman Dr.,
San Jose, CA 95134-1706
Phone: 408-526-4000
Fax: 408-526-4100
Web site: www.cisco.com

OFFICERS

Chairman:
John P. Morgridge, age 62, $294,799 pay
VC: Donald T. Valentine, age 63
President and CEO:
John T. Chambers, age 46, $394,274 pay
SVP Worldwide Sales:
Donald A. LeBeau, age 48, $345,723 pay
VP and General Manager, Core Business :
Frank J. Marshall, age 48, $321,459 pay
VP Business Development and CTO:
Edward R. Kozel, age 40, $274,508 pay
**VP Finance and Administration, CFO and
Secretary:** Larry R. Carter, age 52
Auditors:
Coopers & Lybrand L.L.P.

SELECTED PRODUCTS AND SERVICES

ATM switching products
Cisco IOS software
Ethernet switches
LAN switching products
Network integration
Routers
Vendor Partners
Alcatel
Cabletron Systems
Compaq
Fujitsu
Hitachi
LanOptics
NEC
Northern Telecom
Sun Microsystems
Toshiba

KEY COMPETITORS

3Com	IBM
Ascend	Newbridge Networks
Bay Networks	Northern Telecom
Cabletron	Optical Data Systems
Cascade Communications	Proteon
CrossCom	Shiva
DEC	U.S. Robotics
FORE Systems	Xylan
General DataComm	

Solutions and Kalpana, the leading maker of Ethernet switches.

Cisco pumped up its position in the asynchronous transfer mode (ATM) switching market in 1995 when it bought LightStream from networking products and services provider BBN. Cisco further increased its presence in the ATM market in 1996 with the $4 billion acquisition of StrataCom. Also in 1996 Cisco bought TGV Software, maker of MultiNet Internet access software, and Internet Junction, which makes software that connects Novell NetWare users with the Internet.

CISCO: THE NUMBERS

Nasdaq symbol: CSCO FYE: July 25	Annual Growth	1990	1991	1992	1993	1994	1995
Sales ($ mil.)	95.2%	69.8	183.2	339.5	649.0	1,243.0	1,978.9
Net income ($ mil.)	97.8%	13.9	43.2	84.4	172.0	314.9	421.0
Income as % of sales	—	19.9%	23.6%	24.9%	26.5%	25.3%	21.3%
Earnings per share ($)	90.9%	0.03	0.09	0.17	0.34	0.60	0.76
Stock prices – high ($)	—	1.42	4.27	10.09	16.44	20.38	44.69
Stock prices – low ($)	—	0.63	1.23	4.03	9.53	9.38	16.19
Stock prices – close ($)	92.6%	1.41	4.14	9.83	16.16	17.56	37.31
P/E – high	—	47	50	61	49	34	59
P/E – low	—	21	15	24	28	16	21
Dividends per share ($)	—	0.00	0.00	0.00	0.00	0.00	0.00
Book value per share ($)	73.4%	0.16	0.28	0.51	0.96	1.65	2.53
Employees	74.3%	254	505	882	1,451	2,443	4,086

1995 YEAR-END

Debt ratio: 0.0%
Return on equity: 37.8%
Cash (mil.): $439.5
Current ratio: 2.95
Long-term debt (mil.): $0.0
No. of shares (mil.): $544.5
Dividends
  Yield: —
  Payout: —
Market value (mil.): $20,316.4
R&D as % of sales: 8.5%

QUARTER ENDED 7/28

	1996	1995
Sales ($ millions)	1,292.2	621.2
Net Income ($ millions)	276.6	143.7
Earnings Per Share ($)	0.41	0.26
No. of Shares (thou.)	676,138	544,492

12 MONTHS ENDED 7/28

	1996	1995
Sales ($ millions)	4,096	1,978.9
Net Income ($ millions)	913.3	421.0
Earnings Per Share ($)	1.37	0.76
No. of Shares (thou.)	676,138	544,492

STOCK PRICE HISTORY: High/Low/Close

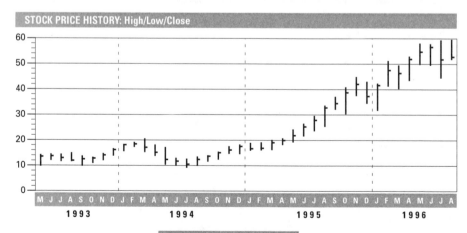

www·cyberstocks·com

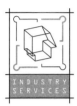

INDUSTRY
SERVICES

CKS Group, Inc.

Cyberspace is CKS's playground. The Cupertino, California-based company has created World Wide Web sites for "The Tonight Show" and insurance company TransAmerica. CKS designs and implements multimedia marketing programs for other companies' products and services, offering advertising, direct mail, media placement, and other brand promotion services. It offers new media marketing programs designed for the World Wide Web, online services, and other digital formats. Clients range from small communications and technology companies to corporate giants such as MCI (which accounted for 18% of CKS's 1995 sales). The company has 5 subsidiaries: CKS On-Site (marketing, production, and technology management), CKS Media (purchase of media space and time), CKS Partners (project design), CKS Interactive (web site development), and CKS Pictures (advanced video technology for programming).

Former Apple Computer employees Bill Cleary, Mark Kvamme, and Tom Suiter are the "C," the "K," and the "S" in the company's name. Cleary founded the company in 1987 as Cleary Communications, initially concentrating on the development and implementation of marketing plans and programs. The firm created its first interactive marketing program, for Apple, in 1988. Kvamme joined the group in 1989 and Suiter in 1991. In 1992 United Airlines hired CKS to revamp its logo and create a new look for its planes, printed materials, and ticket counters.

Rapid growth in new media has created a market niche for CKS. In 1994 it developed the strategy and implementation plan for MCI's online service, internetMCI. The following year the company created a 30-second televi-

- Specializes in new media advertising
- Has a head start over most competitors
- Can sell traditional agency work to new media clients
- Partnership with Interpublic should bring referrals
- Web advertising spending is growing rapidly
- Clients include MCI, Microsoft, Citibank
- First half 1996 revenues up 54%, EPS up 300%

- 5 clients accounted for 37% of 1st half 1996 revenue
- P/E over 100 (8/96)

CKS Group

CKS GROUP, INC.
HQ: 10441 Bandley Dr.,
Cupertino, CA 95014
Phone: 408-366-5100
Fax: 408-366-5120
Web site: www.cks.com

OFFICERS

Chairman, President, and CEO:
Mark D. Kvamme, age 34, $236,370 pay
Chief Creative Officer:
Thomas K. Suiter, age 41, $219,517 pay
Chief Marketing Officer:
William T. Cleary, age 48, $182,490 pay
EVP, COO, CFO, and Secretary:
Carlton H. Baab, age 38, $170,474 pay
President, CKS New Media: Lou Ryan
Manager Human Resources:
Sharon Fitzsimmons
Auditors: KPMG Peat Marwick LLP

SELECTED PRODUCTS AND SERVICES

Advertising
Collateral systems
Consumer promotions
Corporate identity and product branding
Direct mail
Media placement services
New media
Packaging
Strategic corporate and product positioning
Trade promotions

KEY COMPETITORS

ADVO
BroadVision
Bronner Slosberg
Cordiant
Dentsu
Eagle River Interactive
Harte-Hanks
Heritage Media
International Post
Interpublic Group
Leap Group
Modem Media
Omnicom Group
Onramp
Organic Online
Poppe Tyson
True North
WPP Group
Young & Rubicam
Ziff-Davis

---

sion ad for Wayne Gretzky's NHLPA All Stars video game for Time Warner Interactive. Also in 1995 CKS designed the user interface environments for Hewlett-Packard's Personal Page computer screens and went public.

In 1996 CKS acquired New York advertising and marketing firm Schell/Mullaney, Inc. Also that year it created a New Media division, containing both CKS Interactive and CKS Pictures and headed by Delrina (PC fax software) co-founder Lou Ryan.

CKS GROUP: THE NUMBERS

Nasdaq symbol: CKSG FYE: November 30	Annual Growth	1990	1991	1992	1993	1994	1995[1]
Sales ($ mil.)	60.8%	—	5.2	6.7	12.0	22.9	34.8
Net income ($ mil.)	93.4%	—	0.1	0.2	0.3	0.3	1.4
Income as % of sales	—	—	2.9%	2.2%	2.3%	1.3%	4.0%
Earnings per share ($)	59.7%	—	0.02	0.02	0.03	0.03	0.13
Stock price – high ($)	—	—	—	—	—	—	39.00
Stock price – low ($)	—	—	—	—	—	—	20.00
Stock price – close ($)	—	—	—	—	—	—	39.00
P/E – high	—	—	—	—	—	—	—
P/E – low	—	—	—	—	—	—	154
Dividends per share ($)	—	—	—	—	—	—	0.00
Book value per share ($)	—	—	—	—	—	—	0.45
Employees	149.7%	—	—	—	30	104	187

[1] 9-month fiscal year

1995 YEAR-END

Debt ratio: 14.6%
Return on equity: —
Cash (mil.): $1.5
Current ratio: 1.28
Long-term debt (mil.): $0.4
No. of shares (mil.): —
Dividends
  Yield: —
  Payout: —

QUARTER ENDED 5/31

	1996	1995
Sales ($ millions)	13.7	8.7
Net Income ($ millions)	1.3	0.3
Earnings Per Share ($)	0.10	0.03
No. of Shares (thou.)	12,714	10,750

6 MONTHS ENDED 5/31

	1996	1995
Sales ($ millions)	22.9	14.9
Net Income ($ millions)	2.0	0.4
Earnings Per Share ($)	0.16	0.04
No. of Shares (thou.)	12,714	10,750

STOCK PRICE HISTORY: High/Low/Close

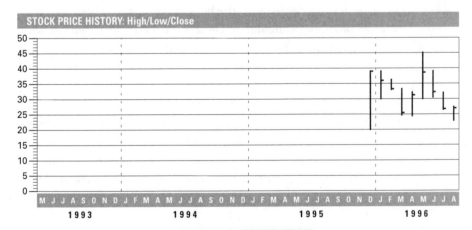

www.cyberstocks.com

- In part, a publicly traded Internet venture fund

- Holdings include Lycos, Ikonic, Black Sun, FreeMark

- Proposed Web-based Planet Direct service could build advertising revenue and a marketing database

- Planet Direct uses products and services of CMG's Internet portfolio companies

- 4/30/96 balance sheet showed more than $8 per share in cash and marketable securities

- Recent results for core direct-mail businesses have been weak

- Experiencing heavy start-up losses in Internet investments

- Lycos stock has declined substantially since its IPO

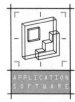

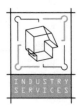

APPLICATION SOFTWARE

SPECIALIZED SERVICES

INDUSTRY SERVICES

CMG Information Services

It may look like a mailing list company, but CMG Information Services is behaving more and more like an Internet venture capital firm. A leading academic list marketer, CMG's core database products are the College List (featuring data on 700,000 members of the higher education community), the Information Buyers List (with 10 million names), and the Elementary/High School List (featuring 84,000 schools). But an increasing share of CMG's revenues comes from investments in Internet-related startup companies like search provider Lycos. Chairman and CEO David Wetherell owns about 25% of the company.

College Marketing Group (CMG) was founded in 1968 to provide sales representation for educational publishers. During its early years, it operated out of 2 bookmobiles that visited college campuses. The company began selling its mailing list in 1973. The business grew and in 1986 Wetherell, a software developer, bought it. As electronic database management became more sophisticated, the company developed search and manipulation software and expanded its business into client database management.

When the company went public in 1994, Wetherell spent about $1 million to start an Internet search company, Book Link, which he sold to America Online the same year for 1.4 million AOL shares. CMG formed CMG @Ventures, a limited partnership devoted to developing the commercial possibilities of the Internet, in 1995. That year, using funds derived from the AOL stock, @Ventures bought the rights to Carnegie Mellon Institute's

CMG INFORMATION SERVICES, INC.

HQ: 187 Ballardvale St., Ste. B110,
Wilmington, MA 01887-7000
Phone: 508-657-7000
Fax: 508-988-0046
Web site: www.cmgi.com

OFFICERS

Chairman, President, CEO, and Secretary:
David S. Wetherell, age 41, $355,250 pay

President and COO, SalesLink:
Richard F. Torre, age 44, $143,925

President and COO, CMG Direct Interactive:
Hemang Dave

CFO and Treasurer:
Andrew J. Hajducky III, age 41

SVP: John F. Hood, age 53, $116,243 pay
VP ListLine Brokerage: Rick Buck
VP ListLine Management: Mark Smith
Director Human Resources:
Susan Michelinie

Auditors: KPMG Peat Marwick LLP

SELECTED PRODUCTS AND SERVICES

CMG @Ventures (Internet product investment and development)

Black Sun Interactive, Inc. (3-D Internet interface)

FreeMark Communications, Inc. (40%, Internet e-mail advertising)

Ikonic Interactive, Inc. (20%, interactive television applications and interfaces)

Lycos, Inc. (59%, Internet search engine)

NetCarta Corp. (Web management, navigation, and design tools)

CMG Direct Interactive (database management services, list brokerage)

CMG List Division (direct marking lists for educational and business-to-business publishers)

SalesLink (mutual fund administration and fulfillment)

KEY COMPETITORS

Accel Partners	Institutional Venture
Acxiom	Partners
Advent International	Kleiner Perkins
American List	LCS Industries
Asset Management	Mayfield Fund
Austin Ventures	Menlo Ventures
Brentwood Associates	Paul Allen
Database America	R. R. Donnelley
Greylock Management	Sequoia Capital
Hambrecht & Quist	Sutter Hill Ventures
Hummer Winblad	Trinity Ventures
Inman & Bowman	Venrock Associates

Lycos Spider Technology (search engine). In 1996 Lycos, Inc., went public valued at $177 million.

The company has also bought interests in TeleT Communications (Internet telephony) and GeoCities (Internet advertising) and developed Black Sun (3D Internet software). In fiscal 1995, CMG derived vastly more income from its investments than from product marketing operations.

CMG INFORMATION: THE NUMBERS

Nasdaq symbol: CMGI FYE: July 31	Annual Growth	1990	1991	1992	1993	1994	1995
Sales ($ mil.)	(6.7%)	—	—	13.8	16.5	19.4	11.2
Net income ($ mil.)	313.1%	—	—	0.4	1.2	1.8	28.2
Income as % of sales	—	—	—	2.8%	7.3%	9.3%	251.8%
Earnings per share ($)	246.0%	—	—	0.07	0.19	0.23	2.90
Stock price – high ($)	—	—	—	—	—	7.75	50.25
Stock price – low ($)	—	—	—	—	—	2.08	5.50
Stock price – close ($)	—	—	—	—	—	7.75	46.44
P/E – high	—	—	—	—	—	34	17
P/E – low	—	—	—	—	—	9	2
Dividends per share ($)	—	—	—	—	—	0.00	0.00
Book value per share ($)	—	—	—	—	—	1.01	6.28
Employees	—	—	—	—	—	202	237

1995 YEAR-END

Debt ratio: 1.5%
Return on equity: 87.7%
Cash (mil.): $65.7
Current ratio: 3.12
Long-term debt (mil.): $0.5
No. of shares (mil.): 8.8
Dividends
  Yield: —
  Payout: —
Market value (mil.): $410.5

QUARTER ENDED 4/30

	1996	1995
Sales ($ millions)	7.5	6.0
Net Income ($ millions)	7.4	3.5
Earnings Per Share ($)	0.74	0.37
No. of Shares (thou.)	9,162	8,810

9 MONTHS ENDED 4/30

	1996	1995
Sales ($ millions)	19.4	17.2
Net Income ($ millions)	22.9	28.2
Earnings Per Share ($)	2.32	3.01
No. of Shares (thou.)	9,162	8,810

STOCK PRICE HISTORY: High/Low/Close

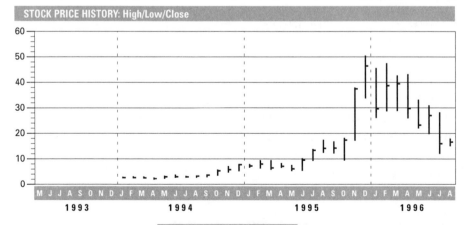

www.cyberstocks.com

C|NET, Inc.

C|NET can help you untangle the World Wide Web and computer technology. The San Francisco-based company provides Internet information via 3 Web sites and produces "c|net central," a television series covering computer, Internet, and technology topics (the program is carried on the USA Network, the Sci-Fi Channel, and San Francisco's CBS affiliate). C|NET also has several new TV series and Web sites in development, including a site it will launch with E! Entertainment Television, a cable channel. Other sites include search.com (a collection of search engines) and news.com (Internet and computer industry news).

C|NET went public in mid-1996 with an IPO that valued the company at about $175 million. Founder and chairman Halsey Minor, COO and CFO Shelby Bonnie, and EVP Kevin Wendle own 21%, 24%, and 7%, respectively; Microsoft cofounder Paul Allen owns 22%; and semiconductor giant Intel owns 4.5%.

Minor, who had earlier produced multimedia business training products, founded the company in 1992 to create cable programming on computers and technology. The name C|NET derives from "computer network"; Minor plans for C|NET to become an entire cable network of computer and technology programming. Bonnie and Wendle joined the firm in 1993 (Bonnie had been managing director of an investment firm; Wendle was a founder of Fox Broadcasting). An early deal gave the USA Network a 5% stake in C|NET in exchange for a half-hour time slot 6 times a week. The company's "c|net central" series hit the airwaves in the spring of 1995. Its first online site, cnet.com, was launched in mid-1995 and by the following March the

- Pioneer in use of television as a complementary medium to the Internet

- Generally focused on computer and Internet-related content and services

- Establishing a leading position in Internet-based software distribution

- Launching a new site with E!

- Internet advertising revenue eclipsed TV advertising revenue in 2nd quarter 1996

- 1st half, 1996 revenue up 400%

- Mounting losses
- Unproven business model
- Television deal with USA Networks calls for cost recovery only — no profits possible
- Market Cap of $140 million (8/96), 1st half 1996 sales of $4.3 million

C|NET, INC.
HQ: 150 Chestnut St.,
   San Francisco, CA 94111
Phone: 415-395-7800
Fax: 415-395-9205
Web site: www.cnet.com

OFFICERS

Chairman, President, and CEO:
   Halsey M. Minor, age 31, $175,000 pay

EVP; President, Television Division;
Executive Producer, Internet Division:
   Kevin Wendle, age 37, $212,500 pay

EVP Network Sales:
   Lon E. Otremba, age 39, $172,000 pay

EVP, COO, CFO, and Secretary:
   Shelby W. Bonnie, age 31, $160,000 pay

EVP Technology:
   Jonathan Rosenberg, age 44, $111,000 pay

Manager Human Resources: Nancy Guilbert
Auditors: KPMG Peat Marwick

SELECTED PRODUCTS AND SERVICES

Television Programming
   "c|net central" (magazine-format program about computers, digital technology, and the Internet)

Internet Content
   cnet.com (World Wide Web site providing feature stories, interviews, news, product information, and other information about computers, digital technology, and the Internet)

   E! Online (50%; joint venture with E! Entertainment Television, Inc.; in development)

   news.com (Internet and computer industry news)

   search.com (customizable collection of more than 250 search engines and directories)

   shareware.com (index and access to 185,000 freeware and shareware software titles)

KEY COMPETITORS

America Online	Netscape
CMP Publications	Pointcast
CompuServe	Prodigy
CyberSource	Sendai Media Group
Discovery Channel	Time Warner
IDT	Turner Broadcasting
International Data Group	Wired Ventures
Mecklermedia	
Microsoft	
NBC	

company had 3 sites in operation. That year it began c|net radio, an online audio news service based on Progressive Networks, Inc.'s RealAudio technology.

By mid-1996 more than 500,000 people had signed up for cnet.com's e-mail newsletter, Digital Dispatch. That year the company announced a host of new TV projects, including "The Web," covering the Internet and online topics; "The New Edge," exploring cyberspace and future technologies; and "TV.COM," a series on the Internet produced for television syndicator Golden Gate Productions (debuting in fall 1996). C|NET also developed Web sites covering software (download.com) and computer games (gamecenter.com).

C|NET: THE NUMBERS

Nasdaq symbol: CNWK FYE: December 31	Annual Growth	1990	1991	1992	1993	1994	1995
Sales ($ mil.)	—	—	—	—	0.0	0.0	3.5
Net income ($ mil.)	—	—	—	—	(0.9)	(2.8)	(8.6)
Income as % of sales	—	—	—	—	—	—	—
Employees	—	—	—	—	—	—	164

1995 YEAR-END

Debt ratio: 19.0%
Return on equity: —
Cash (mil.): $0.7
Current ratio: 1.52
Long-term debt (mil.): $0.5
No. of shares (mil.): —
Dividends
  Yield: —
  Payout: —
R&D as % of sales: 64.7%

QUARTER ENDED 6/30

	1996	1995
Sales ($ millions)	2.6	0.9
Net Income ($ millions)	(4.3)	(2.8)
Earnings Per Share ($)	(0.47)	(0.31)
No. of Shares (thou.)	9,216	9,216

6 MONTHS ENDED 6/30

	1996	1995
Sales ($ millions)	4.3	0.9
Net Income ($ millions)	(8.0)	(3.6)
Earnings Per Share ($)	(0.87)	(0.40)
No. of Shares (thou.)	9,216	9,216

STOCK PRICE HISTORY: High/Low/Close

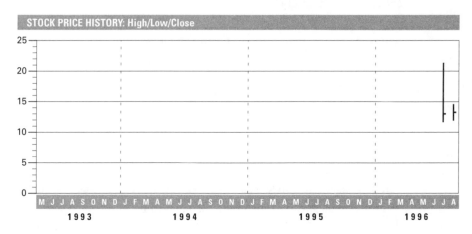

- #2 proprietary online service

- An estimated 1.5 million business subscribers

- Strong European presence

- New release of "CSI" (new name for CompuServe) software will link more closely to the Web

- Network Services business focuses on corporations and is growing at more than 30% annually

- Combination of corporate and consumer traffic smooths network usage around the clock

- Muddled strategy — continually creating and killing services

- Has suffered top management exodus in 1996

- Interface relatively difficult to use

- Web threatens to siphon off subscribers

- H&R Block wants to unload its 80% stake

- Monthly subscriber count declined for the first time in 1996

- Announced first quarter fiscal 1997 loss

 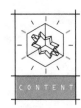 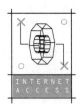 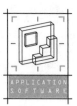

SPECIALIZED SERVICES   CONTENT   INTERNET ACCESS   APPLICATION SOFTWARE

CompuServe Corporation

The world's #2 consumer online service (after America Online) wants to know: how can we CompuServe you? The Columbus, Ohio-based company's flagship CompuServe Information Service (CSI) offers services such as airline reservations, e-mail, online shopping, and stock market information. In addition, the company is the leading online service provider in Europe, serves subscribers in Japan (through NiftyServe), and offers SPRYNET, an Internet-only service.

Jeffrey Wilkins started CompuServe in 1969 to computerize his father-in-law's insurance company. Eight years later he introduced MicroNet, a mainframe computer time-sharing network that eventually became one of the first true online services. H&R Block acquired CompuServe in 1980, providing the financing to aggressively develop online technology.

Through the 1980s the company initiated several now-standard services, including e-mail. Through a joint venture with Nissho Iwai and Fujitsu, the company debuted NiftyServe in 1987. During the late 1980s and early 1990s CompuServe expanded into Australia, Chile, Hungary, Israel, South Africa, South Korea, Taiwan, and the UK. In 1994 the firm acquired a stake in corporate Web site developer Network Publishing.

CompuServe purchased SPRY, developer of the popular Internet in a Box software, in 1995 and began offering World Wide Web access to CSI subscribers. Under shareholder pressure to maximize share value, H&R Block

CompuServe

COMPUSERVE CORPORATION
HQ: 5000 Arlington Centre Blvd.,
   Columbus, OH 43220
Phone: 614-457-8600
Fax: 614-457-0348
Web site: www.compuserve.com

OFFICERS

Chairman: Henry F. Frigon, age 61
President and CEO:
   Robert J. Massey, age 51, $470,358 pay
President, Online Services:
   Dennis D. Matteucci, age 57
President, CompuServe Europe:
   Steven P. Stanbrook, age 39
EVP Administration:
   Herbert J. Kahn, age 56, $285,673 pay
EVP Network Services Division:
   Peter F. Van Camp, age 40
EVP and CFO: Lawrence A. Gyenes, age 46
VP Human Resources: Judy Reinhard
Auditors: Deloitte & Touche LLP

SELECTED PRODUCTS AND SERVICES

Interactive Services
   CompuServe Information Service (CIS, online
      service targeted at experienced users)
   NiftyServe (Japanese counterpart to CIS)
   SPRYNET (Internet-access-only service)
   WOW! (online service targeted at home market)

Features and Information Providers
   Executive News Service (clips from AP, UPI, Dow
      Jones, Reuters, and others)
   Grolier's Academic American Encyclopedia
   Hoover's Company Database
   Knowledge Index (access to the text of more
      than 50,000 journals and 100 popular
      databases)
   Magazine Database Plus (articles from more
      than 100 popular magazines)
   TRAVELSHOPPER (airline schedules, fares, and
      booking; hotel and car rental information)

KEY COMPETITORS

America Online	EarthLink	MFS
AT&T	France Telecom	Communications
BBN	IBM	Microsoft
Bertelsmann	IDT	MindSpring
C|NET	International	NETCOM
Deutsche	Wireless	PSINet
Telekom	MCI	

partially spun off CompuServe in 1996. That year the online service firm announced a pact with Microsoft allowing CompuServe subscribers to use Microsoft's Internet Explorer to browse the Web, then said it would abandon its proprietary CompuServe software altogether and restructure itself in the Web's open environment.

COMPUSERVE: THE NUMBERS

Nasdaq symbol: CSRV FYE: April 30	Annual Growth	1991	1992	1993	1994	1995	1996
Sales ($ mil.)	29.2%	220.1	266.5	315.4	429.9	582.8	793.2
Net income ($ mil.)	10.8%	29.4	33.0	45.6	62.1	8.8	49.1
Income as % of sales	—	13.4%	12.4%	14.5%	14.4%	1.5%	6.2%
Employees	32.1%	—	1,200	1,500	2,200	2,500	3,650

1996 YEAR-END

Debt ratio: 0.0%
Return on equity: 7.2%
Cash (mil.): $310.0
Current ratio: 3.51
Long-term debt (mil.): $0.0
No. of shares (mil.): —
Dividends
  Yield: —
  Payout: —
Market value (mil.): —

QUARTER ENDED 7/31

	1996	1995
Sales ($ millions)	208.6	186.5
Net Income ($ millions)	(29.6)	26.8
Earnings Per Share ($)	(0.32)	0.36
No. of Shares (thou.)	92,600	74,200

3 MONTHS ENDED 7/31

	1996	1995
Sales ($ millions)	208.6	186.5
Net Income ($ millions)	(29.6)	26.8
Earnings Per Share ($)	(0.32)	0.36
No. of Shares (thou.)	92,600	74,200

STOCK PRICE HISTORY: High/Low/Close

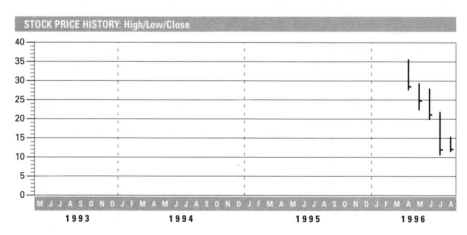

SPECIALIZED SERVICES

CyberCash, Inc.

CyberCash is committed to making Internet users' money not just virtually safe but actually secure. Conducting paper-free financial transactions through the Internet seems ideal, but the market demand has been slow to develop. Why? Individuals, merchants, and bankers fear losing the privacy of their financial information in such an unsecured, public environment or, worse, running the risk of theft. Reston, Virginia-based software developer CyberCash is working on providing a safe, convenient payment system on the Internet.

The company's Credit Card and its still-in-development Electronic Check and Electronic Coin services are Internet counterparts to traditional payment methods; it is integrating these with the existing transaction systems of financial institutions and businesses. CyberCash Wallet software allows consumers to buy an item on the Internet by sending encrypted credit card information to the merchant along with the order. The merchant processes the order and passes the still-coded payment information to CyberCash. Decoded, the information goes first to the merchant's bank and then to the credit card company. CyberCash, the merchant, and the consumer are then told that the purchase has been approved or denied. The whole process takes less than 20 seconds. CyberCash receives its revenues from transaction fees.

Led by Bill Melton, who previously set up financial software firms VeriFone and Transaction Network Systems, CyberCash was founded in 1994. Other

- Positioned in the middle of the potentially huge Web commerce industry
- Has relationships with most key credit card processing banks
- Has established a foothold in Europe
- CEO was the founder of VeriFone
- Marketing partners include CompuServe, GNN, and PSINet

- Immature market with no discernable leader, underdeveloped technical standards
- Current transaction solution is not elegant
- Susceptible to technology leapfrogging among market participants
- Competition from VeriFone looms
- Cofounder resigned 6 months after IPO
- Market cap of $310 million (8/96) vs. sales of $37,705 since inception

 **CyberCash**

CYBERCASH, INC.

HQ: 2100 Reston Pkwy., Ste. 430,
Reston, VA 22091
Phone: 703-620-4200
Fax: 703-620-4215
Web site: www.cybercash.com

OFFICERS

Chairman: Daniel C. Lynch, age 54
President and CEO:
William N. Melton, age 53, $100,000 pay
COO: Bruce G. Wilson, age 47, $170,000 pay
SVP: Stephen D, Crocker, age 51, $170,000 pay
General Counsel and Secretary:
Larry Gilbert, age 44, $138,545 pay
CFO: Gene Riechers, age 40
Auditors: Ernst & Young LLP

SELECTED PRODUCTS AND SERVICES

Electronic Payment
Credit Card
Electronic Check (under development)
Electronic Coin (under development)
Software
CyberCash Wallet

KEY COMPETITORS

CheckFree
DigiCash
First USA Paymentech
IBM
Intuit
Netbill
VeriFone
Virtual Open Network Environment

cofounders include Dan Lynch (founder of Interop, the top trade show for the networking industry), Steve Crocker, Magdalena Yesil, and Bruce Wilson.

The company hopes to grow along with use of the Internet. Its CyberCash Wallet software is distributed to individuals free of charge. CyberCash also provides merchants with free server software and works with financial institutions through its gateway server software. Its CyberCash wallet software is connected to 80% of the banks in the US. CyberCash began securing credit card transactions on the Internet in 1995, and it plans to put its electronic check and cash products on the market in 1997. CEO Melton holds 22% of the company, which went public in 1996. Software makers also have stakes: SOFTBANK owns 10%; VeriFone, 9%; and Cisco Systems, 6%. Also in 1996 CyberCash agreed for CyberCash Wallet to be integrated into America Online's service. With an eye toward geographical expansion, the company also conducted a series of cyberbanking seminars in Asia.

CYBERCASH: THE NUMBERS

Nasdaq symbol: CYCH FYE: December 31	Annual Growth	1990	1991	1992	1993	1994	1995
Sales ($ mil.)	—	—	—	—	—	0.0	0.0
Net income ($ mil.)	—	—	—	—	—	(1.2)	(10.0)
Income as % of sales	—	—	—	—	—	—	—
Employees	—	—	—	—	—	—	65

1995 YEAR-END

Debt ratio: 0.0%
Return on equity: —
Cash (mil.): $5.3
Current ratio: 2.51
Long-term debt (mil.): $0.0
No. of shares (mil.): —
Dividends
  Yield: —
  Payout: —

QUARTER ENDED 6/30

	1996	1995
Sales ($ millions)	0.0	0.0
Net Income ($ millions)	(6.2)	(2.0)
Earnings Per Share ($)	(0.59)	(0.50)
No. of Shares (thou.)	7,151	4,002

6 MONTHS ENDED 6/30

	1996	1995
Sales ($ millions)	0.0	0.0
Net Income ($ millions)	(10.8)	(3.8)
Earnings Per Share ($)	(1.28)	(0.95)
No. of Shares (thou.)	7,151	4,002

STOCK PRICE HISTORY: High/Low/Close

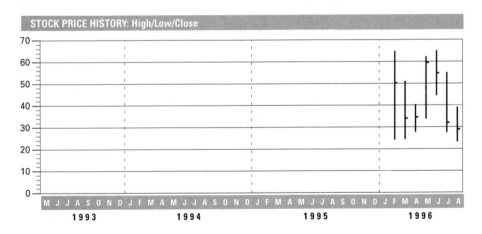

- Well-established leader in private-network security products

- Cisco, GTE, others, are integrating Cylink security technology into their hardware

- Will provide security for USPS's new postmarked e-mail service

- Security customers include US Federal Reserve, Bank of America, Credit Suisse

- Developing nations like Cylink's inexpensive wireless communications technology

- Would have lost money in the 2nd quarter of 1996 if not for interest on IPO cash

- RSA (Security Dynamics) public-key encryption technology is the industry standard

- Bitter legal battle with RSA shows no sign of ending

- Exclusive rights to Diffie-Hellman public-key encryption patents expire in 1997

- Hardware and software companies are embedding competing security in their products

- Company CEO Lewis Morris suffered a stroke in May, 1996

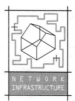

NETWORK
INFRASTRUCTURE

Cylink Corporation

Cyclops-like, Cylink has its eye on security. A leading provider of computer network security, Cylink offers products that allow for safe transmission of information across wireless remote access, the Internet, LANs, and WANs. The Sunnyvale, California-based company's core software is the Secure Enterprise Architecture Stack, which provides privacy, data integrity, authentication, and access control throughout a network. Cylink also makes the Airlink line of wireless products, such as modems and radio transmitters and receivers, which are used in activities such as voice and data connections to offshore oil rigs.

Cylink was founded in 1984 by former Xerox executive Lewis Morris and electrical engineering expert Jimmy Omura to provide data security products. That year Cylink pioneered the integration of public key technology (cryptography techniques first developed at Stanford in 1976) and centralized network management into enterprisewide information security products. The system soon became the network data encryption standard for high-speed WANs. The company launched the first public key management coprocessor in 1987.

Expanding into the wireless market, Cylink launched the AirLink family of wireless, long-range, digital microwave radio products in 1990.
The company is taking advantage of the shift from mainframe to client/server systems and the increasing use of shared public networks (such as the Internet). It expanded its product line in 1995, introducing a security

CYLINK CORPORATION
HQ: 910 Hermosa Ct.,
Sunnyvale, CA 94086
Phone: 408-735-5800
Fax: 408-735-6643
Web site: www.cylink.com

OFFICERS

President:
Lewis C. Morris, age 63, $157,790 pay

Chief Technical Officer and Acting CEO:
Jimmy K. Omura, age 55, $157,790 pay

VP Sales and Marketing:
David M. Morris, age 35, $183,165 pay

VP Engineering:
Harold S. Yang, age 54, $150,000 pay

**VP and General Manager, Wireless
Communications:** Steven H. Goldberg, age 42

General Counsel and Secretary:
Robert B. Fougner, age 43, $127,529 pay

CFO: John Daws
Manager Human Resources: Peggy Eger
Auditors: Price Waterhouse LLP

SELECTED PRODUCTS AND SERVICES

Security
SecureAccess (remote access management system)

SecureLAN (provides security from the desktop and throughout all points on the enterprise network: application layer, nodes, subnetworks, and internetworks)

SecureManager (easy-to-use enterprise management tools)

SecureWAN (wide-area internetworking products)

Wireless
AirLink Accessories
AirLink Modems
AirLink T1/E1 radio systems

KEY COMPETITORS

Cheyenne Software
Information Resource Engineering
Racal
Secure
Security Dynamics
Verisign
Virtual Open Network Environment

library for software developers, an access control system, a LAN security system, and the world's first asynchronous transfer mode (ATM) cell encryptor. However, costs related to increased R&D and legal bills for the protection of its patents pushed Cylink into the loss column in 1994 and 1995. Morris and Omura took the company public in 1996. Pittway Corp., a maker of alarm systems, owns 36% of the company, and director James Simons 19%. Omura and Morris own 6% and 4%, respectively. Omura took over as acting CEO in 1996, after Morris suffered a mild stroke.

CYLINK: THE NUMBERS

Nasdaq symbol: CYLK FYE: December 31	Annual Growth	1990	1991	1992	1993	1994	1995
Sales ($ mil.)	17.2%	—	18.5	17.2	26.3	26.6	34.9
Net income ($ mil.)	—	—	1.4	0.9	1.9	(0.7)	(1.1)
Income as % of sales	—	—	7.4%	5.4%	7.2%	—	—
Employees	—	—	—	—	—	—	265

1995 YEAR-END

Debt ratio: 8.9%
Return on equity: —
Cash (mil.): $6.1
Current ratio: 2.65
Long-term debt (mil.): $0.3
No. of shares (mil.): —
Dividends
 Yield: —
 Payout: —
R&D as % of sales: 29.2%

QUARTER ENDED 6/30

	1996	1995
Sales ($ millions)	12.3	8.5
Net Income ($ millions)	0.3	(0.1)
Earnings Per Share ($)	0.01	(0.00)
No. of Shares (thou.)	26,605	17,624

6 MONTHS ENDED 6/30

	1996	1995
Sales ($ millions)	20.8	16.2
Net Income ($ millions)	(1.0)	(0.7)
Earnings Per Share ($)	(0.04)	(0.03)
No. of Shares (thou.)	26,605	17,624

STOCK PRICE HISTORY: High/Low/Close

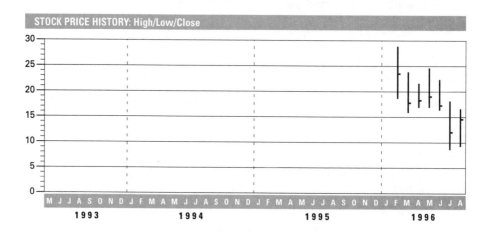

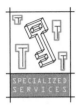
SPECIALIZED SERVICES

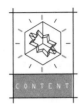
CONTENT

Data Broadcasting

Data Broadcasting Corporation (DBC) is an international provider of financial, sports, and gaming information to individual and professional investors and handicappers. The Jackson, Wyoming-based company, which has major operations in San Mateo, California, delivers instant stock and bond quotes, financial and sports news, currency and mutual fund data, betting odds, analyses, and commentaries to more than 30,000 subscribers via such low-cost distribution channels as satellite, cable TV, wireless FM, and the Internet. DBC also reaches a wider audience through the Internet via the Microsoft Network and World Wide Web pages for *USA Today* and Deloitte & Touche, among others. The company has the exclusive rights to Chinese financial data via wireless FM, which it intends to transmit throughout China and the company's North American network. DBC is looking at other overseas markets, such as Australia, Japan, and Singapore. Co-CEOs Alan Hirschfield and Allan Tessler control 7.7% and 8%, respectively, of the company's stock.

DBC was formed in 1992 as the successor to the Financial News Network (FNN), a bankrupt financial cable TV network. Hirschfield, former CEO of 20th Century Fox and Columbia Pictures, and Tessler, experienced in restructuring businesses, were brought in; they sold many of FNN's assets but held onto 2 financial information services, DBC West (stock data for private investors) and Shark Information Services (serving professional traders). The company has expanded its services and markets through key acquisitions. In 1994 it bought an online sports database firm, Computer Sports

- Claims that its Web site is the most visited quote site
- Private-label Web site deals have attracted partners including *USA Today*, *Washington Post*, Hoover's
- Has just begun selling advertising on its Web site
- New low-cost service could expand market for real-time quotes
- Has wireless, broadcast expertise from wireless quote services

- Faces serious, well-heeled competitors including Reuters and Bloomberg
- Low-cost, wireless Internet access could hurt DBC's lucrative wireless quote business
- Business Services Division revenues have been erratic

DATA BROADCASTING CORPORATION

HQ: 3490 Clubhouse Dr., PO Box 7443,
Jackson, WY 83001
Phone: 307-733-9742
Fax: 307-733-4935
Web site: www.dbc.com

OFFICERS

Co-chairman and co-CEO:
Alan J. Hirschfield, age 60, $711,341 pay
Co-chairman and co-CEO:
Allan R. Tessler, age 59, $711,341 pay
President, Information Services Division:
Edward M. Anderson
EVP Strategic Planning:
B. Douglas Smith, age 50, $365,000 pay
EVP and CFO:
Mark F. Imperiale, age 44, $335,000 pay
General Counsel and Corporate Secretary:
Reed L. Benson
Director Human Resources:
Michelle Grossman
Auditors: Price Waterhouse LLP

SELECTED PRODUCTS AND SERVICES

BMI (quotation and news service)
BondEdge (securities data and portfolio analysis)
BondWire (bond prices and commentaries)
CheckRite (automatic check and credit verification services)
Computer Sports World (DBC sports information database)
DBC Online (financial data, betting odds, and sports information on the Microsoft Network and World Wide Web)
ISN/Business TV (satellite delivery of communications services)
QuoTrek (portable wirelines quotation monitor)
Scorecast (sports database)
Signal (securities prices and news)
SignalCard (wireless delivery of quotes, headlines, and market commentary)
SporTrax (instant sports and horse racing updates; pregame odds)
SportSignal (instant sports updates)

KEY COMPETITORS

ADP	PC Quote
Bloomberg	Quote.com
Checkfree	Reuters
Dow Jones	Starwave
Individual Investor Group	Telescan
K-III	UPI
Knight-Ridder	

World, and a fixed income data and analysis company, Capital Management Sciences. DBC bought and merged with its chief rival, Broadcast International, in 1995. Later that year DBC bought a stake in Internet Financial Network, an online distributor of SEC filings from EDGAR, the commission's computer. The company sold Shark in 1995.

DATA BROADCASTING: THE NUMBERS

Nasdaq symbol: DBCC FYE: June 30	Annual Growth	1990[2]	1991[2]	1992[2]	1993	1994	1995
Sales ($ mil.)	7.1%	52.6	22.5	24.9	55.9	66.4	74.2
Net income ($ mil.)	154.1%	—	—	1.0	3.2	4.4	16.4
Income as % of sales	—	—	—	4.2%	5.8%	6.6%	22.0%
Earnings per share ($)	123.5%	—	—	0.06	0.15	0.19	0.67
Stock price – high ($)[1]	—	—	—	3.13	4.88	8.25	15.00
Stock price – low ($)[1]	—	—	—	1.00	2.25	3.50	3.50
Stock price – close ($)[1]	75.0%	—	—	2.31	4.13	4.13	12.38
P/E – high	—	—	—	52	33	43	22
P/E – low	—	—	—	17	15	18	5
Dividends per share ($)	—	—	—	0.00	0.00	0.00	0.00
Book value per share ($)	52.0%	—	—	0.94	1.13	1.79	3.30
Employees	39.4%	—	—	243	264	376	658

[1] Stock prices are for the prior calendar year. [2] Sales and earnings not comparable to later years (results of predecessor).

1995 YEAR-END

Debt ratio: 14.3%
Return on equity: 23.9%
Cash (mil.): $34.4
Current ratio: 0.96
Long-term debt (mil.): $8.9
No. of shares (mil.): 29.3
Dividends
  Yield: —
  Payout: —
Market value (mil.): $362.2
R&D as % of sales: 6.1%

QUARTER ENDED 6/30

	1996	1995
Sales ($ millions)	30.4	16.4
Net Income ($ millions)	2.0	3.5
Earnings Per Share ($)	0.06	0.15
Avg. Shares (thousands)	31,834	29,273

12 MONTHS ENDED 6/30

	1996	1995
Sales ($ millions)	114.6	74.2
Net Income ($ millions)	9.1	16.4
Earnings Per Share ($)	0.28	0.68
Avg. Shares (thousands)	31,834	29,273

STOCK PRICE HISTORY: High/Low/Close

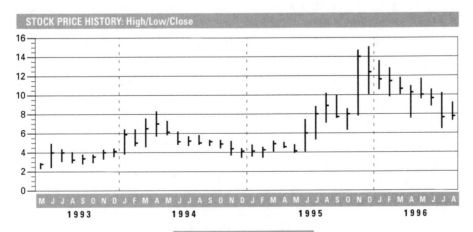

www·cyberstocks·com

- Relatively mature, proven business model

- 2nd quarter 1996 revenues up 48%, operating income up 181%, indicating strong operating leverage

- Focused on the high-margin corporate market

- Enjoys very low subscriber "churn"

- NewsEDGE/WEB intranet product has been well-received in tests

- Faces increasing competition, including low-end, free, Internet-based services

- P/E over 60 (8/96)

SPECIALIZED SERVICES

Desktop Data

If you are a news junkie, Desktop Data could be the ultimate pusher, delivering the goods right to you at work. Headquartered in Burlington, Massachusetts, the company provides a service called NewsEDGE, which delivers news from more than 500 different sources in real time directly to users' PCs via their companies' local area networks (LANs). Different from an online service, which requires users to dial out and retrieve news, NewsEDGE sends news directly to users, automatically monitoring and filtering the information according to preset preferences. When a story breaks that fits the user's criteria, a message is sent to that customer's PC. Desktop Data sells its service to financial institutions, including Merrill Lynch, Moody's Investment Services, and NationsBank; other corporate customers, such as AT&T and NYNEX; and government organizations, including the Department of Defense and the Department of the Treasury. Founder Donald McLagan owns 26.7% of the company.

A former executive with software maker Lotus and economic information provider Data Resources, McLagan combined his experience with computers and information to form Desktop Data in 1988. The following year the company introduced NewsEDGE. It entered a marketing agreement with IBM in 1990, with Big Blue selling NewsEDGE to its customers. The company continued to grow, adding more news services to its roster, and went public in 1995.

Keys to Desktop Data rapid growth are its relatively low-cost installation and its independence. While other services provide real-time news, many require special (and expensive) terminals. By using a company's existing

Desktop Data, Inc.

DESKTOP DATA, INC.
HQ: 80 Blanchard Rd.,
Burlington, MA 01803
Phone: 617-229-3000
Fax: 617-229-3030
Web site: www.desktopdata.com

OFFICERS

Chairman, President, and CEO:
Donald L. McLagan, age 53, $115,500 pay
VP Finance and Operations and Treasurer:
Edward R. Siegfried, age 50, $115,500 pay
VP Sales and Marketing:
Clifford M. Pollan, age 38, $115,500 pay
VP and Chief Technology Officer:
Daniel F. X. O'Reilly, age 48, $115,500 pay (prior
to promotion)
VP Development: Michael F. Kilgore
Director Human Resources: Jessica Wasner
Auditors: Andersen Worldwide

SELECTED PRODUCTS AND SERVICES

Selected News Sources
The Associated Press
Financial Times (UK)
Forbes
FORTUNE
Knight Ridder
The New York Times
Nihon Keizai Shimbun ("Nikkei English News")
Reuters
USA Today
The Wall Street Journal

Selected Customers
Andersen Worldwide
AT&T
Citibank
The Executive Office of the President of the U.S.
Merrill Lynch
Microsoft
NYNEX
Royal Dutch/Shell

KEY COMPETITORS

America Online	M.A.I.D.
Applix	Mainstream Data
Bloomberg	Microsoft
CompuServe	New York Times
Comtex	OneSource
Dow Jones	Pearson
Gannett	Prodigy
IBM	Reed Elsevier
Individual	Reuters
Knight-Ridder	Thomson Corp.

LAN, Desktop Data keeps installation costs low. And since it is independent, it can gather news from an array of sources, rather than pushing one particular source. In late 1995 the company introduced LinkEdge, which includes live video broadcasts and real-time SEC filings. In 1996 it launched an Intranet-based service called NewsEDGE/WEB.

DESKTOP DATA: THE NUMBERS

Nasdaq symbol: DTOP FYE: December 31	Annual Growth	1990	1991	1992	1993	1994	1995
Sales ($ mil.)	115.4%	0.5	2.0	4.2	7.7	14.4	23.2
Net income ($ mil.)	—	(2.5)	(1.8)	(1.4)	(1.3)	(0.3)	2.1
Income as % of sales	—	—	—	—	—	—	9.1%
Earnings per share ($)	—	—	—	—	—	(0.06)	0.43
Stock price – high ($)	—	—	—	—	—	—	38.00
Stock price – low ($)	—	—	—	—	—	—	21.00
Stock price – close ($)	—	—	—	—	—	—	24.50
P/E – high	—	—	—	—	—	—	88
P/E – low	—	—	—	—	—	—	49
Dividends per share ($)	—	—	—	—	—	—	0.00
Book value per share ($)	—	—	—	—	—	—	2.89
Employees	—	—	—	—	—	—	130

1995 YEAR-END

Debt ratio: 3.0%
Return on equity: 14.5%
Cash (mil.): $32.5
Current ratio: 2.59
Long-term debt (mil.): $0.5
No. of shares (mil.): 8.5
Dividends
  Yield: —
  Payout: —
Market value (mil.): $207.8
R&D as % of sales: 12.5%

QUARTER ENDED 6/30

	1996	1995
Sales ($ millions)	8.1	5.5
Net Income ($ millions)	1.0	0.3
Earnings Per Share ($)	0.12	0.04
Avg. Shares (thousands)	8,839	2,639

6 MONTHS ENDED 6/30

	1996	1995
Sales ($ millions)	15.4	10.5
Net Income ($ millions)	1.9	0.6
Earnings Per Share ($)	0.21	0.08
Avg. Shares (thousands)	8,839	2,639

STOCK PRICE HISTORY: High/Low/Close

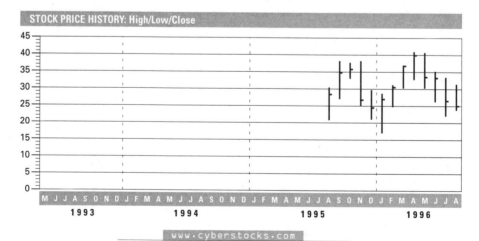

www·cyberstocks·com

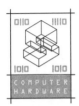

Diamond Multimedia

- A leading graphics card manufacturer
- Outlook for modem demand remains good
- Graphics cards consistently receive "best buy" ratings from PC magazines
- Has added videophone functions to Supra modem line

Diamond is finding the competition in the computer peripherals market a little rough. The San Jose-based company makes graphics accelerators, hardware that helps computers process power-sapping sound and graphics. Diamond also makes fax/modems and ISDN digital telephone adapters (for network access). Though sales have been rising, increased competition in the peripherals industry and costs related to acquisitions have left Diamond with a ruby-red bottom line. Investor groups Summit Partners and TA Associates own 15% and 9% of the company, respectively, while founder Chong-Moon Lee owns about 8%.

A descendant of King Sei-Jung (who Lee says created the Korean language in the 14th century), Lee started Diamond Computer Systems in 1982 to explore the possibility of running Apple software on IBM computers. The attempt failed, costing Lee his house, his marriage, and $2.7 million. In 1987 a member of IBM's board suggested to Lee that he find a niche for himself in multimedia. Renamed Diamond Multimedia Systems, the company's first product in the relatively new industry was a software driver, which Lee sold to computer maker Gateway 2000. Diamond made its hardware products domestically, so it beat its Asian competitors to the marketplace. Through the early 1990s the company focused on high-performance graphic accelerators.

Things happened quickly in the mid-1990s. In 1994 Lee sold stakes in Diamond to Summit Partners and TA Associates. The next year he took the

- Slowdown in US PC sales growth, weak European sales have hurt Diamond's sales growth
- Gross margins are under pressure from intense price competition in graphics card and modem markets
- Spea, acquired in late 1995, remains unprofitable
- Intel's incorporation of MMX multimedia features into Pentium chips could hurt graphics cards sales
- CFO announced resignation as of 10/96

DIAMOND MULTIMEDIA SYSTEMS, INC.
HQ: 2880 Junction Ave.,
San Jose, CA 95134-1922
Phone: 408-325-7000
Fax: 408-325-7070
Web site: www.diamondmm.com

OFFICERS
Chairman: Chong-Moon Lee, age 68
President and CEO:
William J. Schroeder, age 51, $450,000 pay
SVP and CFO:
Gary B. Filler, age 55, $360,270 pay
SVP and Chief Technical Officer:
Hyung Hwe Huh, age 43, $339,308 pay
SVP Worldwide Sales:
C. Scott Holt, age 54, $325,890 pay
VP and General Counsel:
Frank G. Hausmann
Controller (HR): Song Kim
Auditors: Coopers & Lybrand L.L.P.

SELECTED PRODUCTS AND SERVICES
3D accelerators
Diamond EDGE 3D
Fire GL
Fax/modems
Supra
TeleCommander
Graphics accelerators
Stealth
Viper
Internet products
Supra NetCommander ISDN adapters
Supra Simple Internet Kit

KEY COMPETITORS
3Com	S3
ATI Technologies	STB Systems
Boca Research	Trident Microsystems
Cirrus Logic	Tseng Labs
Hayes Microcomputer	U.S. Robotics
IEC Electronics	VLSI Technology
Number Nine Visual	Weitek
Oki Electric	Western Digital
PairGain	

company public. Also in 1995 Diamond bought Supra Corporation (fax/modems) for $54 million and SPEA Software (accelerators) for $61.5 million and launched a 3D animation accelerator and a telecommunications system that offered fax, modem, telephone, voice mail, and other capabilities in a single unit. In 1996 the company introduced its first ISDN device for PCs.

DIAMOND: THE NUMBERS

Nasdaq symbol: DIMD FYE: December 31	Annual Growth	1990	1991	1992	1993	1994	1995
Sales ($ mil.)	84.7%	—	40.2	74.5	130.3	203.3	467.6
Net income ($ mil.)	—	—	4.1	7.1	12.4	20.1	(41.3)
Income as % of sales	—	—	10.1%	9.5%	9.5%	9.9%	—
Earnings per share ($)	—	—	0.19	0.34	0.59	0.96	(1.55)
Stock price – high ($)	—	—	—	—	—	—	43.00
Stock price – low ($)	—	—	—	—	—	—	16.50
Stock price – close ($)	—	—	—	—	—	—	35.88
P/E – high	—	—	—	—	—	—	—
P/E – low	—	—	—	—	—	—	—
Dividends per share ($)	—	—	—	—	—	—	0.00
Book value per share ($)	—	—	—	—	—	—	6.02
Employees	110.6%	—	—	80	125	271	747

1995 YEAR-END

Debt ratio: 12.5%
Return on equity: —
Cash (mil.): $106.2
Current ratio: 2.49
Long-term debt (mil.): $11.7
No. of shares (mil.): 34.7
Dividends
  Yield: —
  Payout: —
Market value (mil.): $1,243.9
R&D as % of sales: 2.3%

QUARTER ENDED 6/30

	1996	1995
Sales ($ millions)	120.2	95.1
Net Income ($ millions)	(4.8)	7.8
Earnings Per Share ($)	(0.14)	0.30
Avg. Shares (thousands)	34,391	27,725

6 MONTHS ENDED 6/30

	1996	1995
Sales ($ millions)	307.8	175.4
Net Income ($ millions)	6.4	13.9
Earnings Per Share ($)	0.18	0.58
Avg. Shares (thousands)	34,391	27,725

STOCK PRICE HISTORY: High/Low/Close

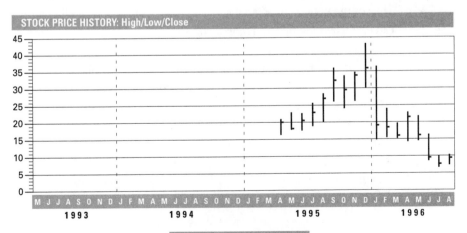

M J J A S O N D J F M A M J J A S O N D J F M A M J J A S O N D J F M A M J J A
1993   1994   1995   1996

- Broad WAN-access product line covers both public and private networks

- Significant inroads into the ISP WAN-access market

- Profitable since 1986

- Always invested heavily in R&D

- Early to market with Frame Relay, SMDS, ATM products

- Slow to release its W/ATM GateWay product for telcos

- MCI and BBN accounted for 37% of 1st half 1996 sales

- Gross margins are expected to continue to erode

- Company president resigned (10/95) and has not yet been replaced (8/96)

- Lawsuits add risk to the stock

- 1st half of 1996 sales up 2%, earnings down 46%

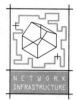

NETWORK
INFRASTRUCTURE

Digital Link Corporation

Digital Link is widely known in the wide-area networking (WAN) market. The Sunnyvale, California-based company makes digital access products that provide access to private WANs based on dedicated leased lines and to public WANs that use advanced technologies such as asynchronous transfer mode (ATM), frame relay, and switched multimegabit data service (SMDS). The company sells to end users, VARs, and OEMs. MCI and Siemens each account for more than 10% of Digital Link's sales; other customers include corporations such as Shell Oil and institutions such as Rice University and the US Army. Founder and chairwoman Vinita Gupta owns about 45% of Digital Link.

Digital Link depends on innovations — it spends 20% of revenues on R&D — to stay at the forefront of the rapidly changing WAN access marketplace. The company has gained an edge by making its products modular; units can easily be modified and upgraded.

Gupta, an electrical engineer and veteran of Northern Telecom's R&D operations, founded Digital Link in 1985. The company shipped its first products in 1985 and 2 years later introduced its data service units/channel service units (DSU/CSU) products, which control access to a WAN and translate data from one network standard to another. Digital Link began shipping SMDS access products in 1991 and ATM products the next year. Also in 1992 it won a subcontract to work with Sprint to supply ATM

DIGITAL LINK CORPORATION
HQ: 217 Humboldt Ct.,
     Sunnyvale, CA 94089
Phone: 408-745-6200
Fax: 408-745-6250
Web site: www.dl.com

OFFICERS

Chairman and CEO:
Vinita Gupta, age 45, $209,727 pay

VP Sales:
Timothy K. Montgomery, age 43, $200,957 pay

VP Operations:
Toni M. Bellin, age 50, $162,902 pay

VP Finance and Administration, CFO, and Secretary:
Stanley E. Kazmierczak, age 35, $127,491 pay

VP Engineering:
James W. Checco, age 61, $106,686 pay

VP Marketing: Jack A. Musgrove, age 46

Director Human Resources:
Diane Mastilock

Auditors: Coopers & Lybrand L.L.P.

SELECTED PRODUCTS AND SERVICES

Access multiplexers (devices that can transmit multiple signals over one or more WAN lines)

Data Service Units/Channel Services Units (DSUs/CSUs control WAN access and translate between networking standards)

Inverse multiplexers (devices that take a high-bit data stream, divide it, and retransmit it over multiple lower-speed transmission lines)

	1995 Sales % of total
End users	45
VARs	37
OEMs	18
Total	**100**

KEY COMPETITORS

ADC Telecommunications
ADTRAN
Fore
General DataComm
Lucent Technologies
Micom
Motorola
Newbridge Networks
Premisys
Tellabs

networks for NASA and the US Department of Energy. The company went public in 1994.

The following year Daniel Palmer stepped down as president and COO. Also in 1995 Digital Link formed an alliance with Cisco Systems to provide DSU cards for Cisco products. The 2 companies expanded their development and marketing agreement in 1996. Digital Link will provide DSU/CSU units for Cisco's new line of routers.

DIGITAL LINK: THE NUMBERS

Nasdaq symbol: DLNK FYE: December 31	Annual Growth	1990	1991	1992	1993	1994	1995
Sales ($ mil.)	39.5%	8.4	13.3	17.1	22.5	35.2	44.3
Net income ($ mil.)	36.9%	1.0	1.6	1.9	2.2	4.4	4.8
Income as % of sales	—	12.5%	11.8%	11.4%	9.8%	12.5%	10.9%
Earnings per share ($)	27.7%	0.15	0.23	0.28	0.31	0.48	0.51
Stock price – high ($)	—	—	—	—	—	29.50	34.00
Stock price – low ($)	—	—	—	—	—	7.75	13.75
Stock price – close ($)	—	—	—	—	—	26.88	14.13
P/E – high	—	—	—	—	—	61	67
P/E – low	—	—	—	—	—	16	27
Dividends per share ($)	—	—	—	—	—	0.00	0.00
Book value per share ($)	—	—	—	—	—	4.66	5.31
Employees	28.9%	—	—	—	127	187	211

1995 YEAR-END

Debt ratio: 0.0%
Return on equity: 10.9%
Cash (mil.): $19.4
Current ratio: 4.94
Long-term debt (mil.): $0.0
No. of shares (mil.): 9.0
Dividends
  Yield: —
  Payout: —
Market value (mil): $127.1
R&D as % of sales: 20.1%

QUARTER ENDED 6/30

	1996	1995
Sales ($ millions)	12.0	11.4
Net Income ($ millions)	0.9	1.4
Earnings Per Share ($)	0.09	0.15
Avg. Shares (thousands)	9,449	8,777

6 MONTHS ENDED 6/30

	1996	1995
Sales ($ millions)	22.2	21.8
Net Income ($ millions)	1.4	2.6
Earnings Per Share ($)	0.15	0.28
Avg. Shares (thousands)	9,449	8,777

STOCK PRICE HISTORY: High/Low/Close

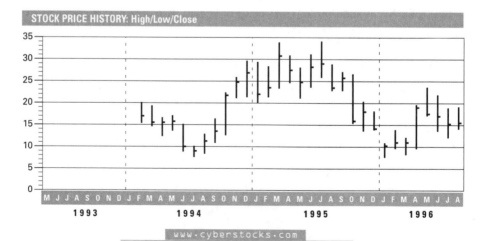

www.cyberstocks.com

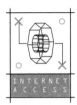

EarthLink
Network, Inc.

The sky's the limit for Sky Dayton, EarthLink's founder and chairman, who is steering the fast-growing Internet service provider on a rocket-like trajectory. Pasadena, California-based EarthLink specializes in fast and easy Internet access for individuals and businesses. The upstart company has grown from about 30,000 customers at the end of 1995 to more than 140,000 and has become a major player among the service providers market. Its strategy includes establishing relations with leading media and consumer products companies to promote EarthLink products to their customers. Through agreements with Netscape, Macmillan Publishing, and UUNET Technologies (which was bought by MFS Communications in August 1996), EarthLink provides Internet access in more than 270 cities across the country through its TotalAccess Internet software. EarthLink also offers an 800-number service for customers who do not have local access to the Internet.

Frustrated by the difficulty of getting onto the Internet, Dayton decided in 1994 (at age 23) to set up his own Internet access company. Earthlink Network was the 3rd business for the entrepreneur/wunderkind, who had already co-founded Cafe Mocha, a popular Los Angeles coffeehouse, and Dayton Walker Design, a high-tech computer-based advertising design firm. Founded on the idea that Internet access could be made easy for anyone, EarthLink sold its first Internet access account by the end of 1994. The next year EarthLink released TotalAccess, a package of leading Internet

- #3 independent Internet access provider
- Focused on building brand and consumer subscriber base, not networks
- As a pure reseller, has low capital requirements
- CEO is 24 years old
- First quarter 1996 sales up 1,768%

- Totally dependent on wholesalers for Internet access
- Balance sheet is low on assets
- Has never been profitable
- CEO
  * is 24 years old
  * never attended college
  * lists cafe management and advertising as previous business experience

EARTHLINK NETWORK, INC.
HQ: 3100 New York Dr., Ste. 201,
Pasadena, CA 91107
Phone: 818-296-2400
Fax: 818-296-2470
Web site: www.earthlink.com

OFFICERS

Chairman:
Sky D. Dayton, age 24, $114,299 pay

President and CEO:
Charles G. Betty, age 39

VP and CFO: Barry W. Hall, age 48

VP Sales and Marketing:
Robert E. Johnson, Jr., age 44, $109,224 pay

VP Operations:
David R. Tommela, age 57

VP Strategic Planning:
Brinton O.C. Young, age 44

Director Human Resources: Carol Cross
Auditors: Price Waterhouse LLP

SELECTED PRODUCTS AND SERVICES

TotalAccess Internet software (a package of leading Internet software applications including Netscape World Wide Web browser and Eudora Email)

TotalAccess 800 (Internet service from anywhere in the continental United States)

TotalAccess Canada (dial-up Internet service in most major Canadian cities)

TotalAccess USA (dial-up Internet Service available in over 260 US cities)

KEY COMPETITORS

America Online
AT&T
CompuServe
IBM
IDT
International Wireless
MCI
Mindspring
NETCOM

software including the popular Netscape World Wide Web browser and QUALCOMM's Eudora, the Internet's most widely-used e-mail program.

The company leases points of presence (locations which can access the Internet) from telecom partner UUNET. Macmillan Publishing and its parent, Viacom (the largest publishing conglomerate in the world), have agreed to sell TotalAccess disks in their Internet books. EarthLink has made similar deals to distribute its TotalAccess software with about 90 other partners. The company filed to go public in 1996. Dayton owns approximately 26% of the company, and other board members Kevin O'Donnell, Reed Slatkin, and Sidney Azeez own 19%, 19%, and 9%, respectively. The company signed a deal with struggling rival PSINet in 1996 giving EarthLink customers access to the Internet through PSINet's 237 locations in the US and Canada.

EARTHLINK: THE NUMBERS

FYE: December 31	Annual Growth	1990	1991	1992	1993	1994	1995
Sales ($ mil.)	—	—	—	—	—	0.1	3.0
Net income ($ mil.)	—	—	—	—	—	(0.1)	(6.1)
Income as % of sales	—	—	—	—	—	—	—
Employees	—	—	—	—	—	—	196

1995 YEAR-END

Debt ratio: 100.0%
Return on equity: —
Cash (mil.): $1.8
Current ratio: 0.53
Long-term debt (mil.): $1.5
No. of shares (mil.): —
Dividends
  Yield: —
  Payout: —
Market value (mil.): —

QUARTER ENDED 3/31

	1996	1995
Sales ($ millions)	3.4	0.2
Net Income ($ millions)	(4.9)	(0.3)
Earnings Per Share ($)	(0.35)	(0.02)
Avg. Shares (thousands)	13,717	12,594

3 MONTHS ENDED 3/31

	1996	1995
Sales ($ millions)	3.4	0.2
Net Income ($ millions)	(4.9)	(0.3)
Earnings Per Share ($)	(0.35)	(0.02)
Avg. Shares (thousands)	13,717	12,594

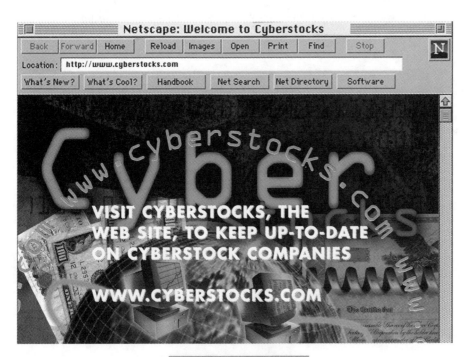

- Product combines live telephone sales or service with self-service Web experience

- Has been particularly successful in corporate human resources department applications

- Corporations are eager to use Web to lower customer service and support costs

- Has partnered with Visa to promote its Web banking product

- First half 1996 revenues up 109%

- Still unprofitable

- Market Cap $380 million vs. first half 1996 sales of $8.2 million

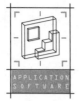

APPLICATION
SOFTWARE

Edify
Corporation

Edify Corporation is enlightening businesses on how to dovetail 2 major trends in the modern workplace — cutting costs and going online. The Santa Clara, California-based company is a major supplier of software that lets organizations provide automated services to customers, employees, and partners via the Internet. Edify's primary software, Electronic Workforce, enables users to give their affiliates access to information and services via phone, fax, PC, pager, and kiosk. In addition, Edify Electronic Banking System software allows banks and other financial institutions to offer banking services via the World Wide Web.

Electronic Workforce is used at more than 500 sites in customer service, human resources and other departments at a broad range of companies. Clients include AT&T, Bristol-Myers Squibb, DHL, IBM, Kodak, MCI, Office Depot, Nike, and the University of California. The company markets its products through a direct sales force and through value-added resellers, distributors, and system integrators.

Edify was cofounded in 1990 by Jeffrey Crowe, Robert Holmes, and Charles Jolissaint. Both Crowe and Jolissaint had been executives with telecommunications equipment maker Rolm Corp., and Holmes was formerly an engineer with IBM. The trio formed the company with the aim of developing software that allows computers to receive phone calls, process information, and respond to customer requests. It began shipping Edify Information Agent (later renamed Electronic Workforce) in 1992. This system was part

EDIFY CORPORATION
HQ: 2840 San Tomas Expwy.,
Santa Clara, CA 95051
Phone: 408-982-2000
Fax: 408-982-0777
Web site: www.edify.com

OFFICERS

President and CEO:
Jeffrey M. Crowe, age 39, $140,940 pay
VP Sales:
Terrance A. Shough, age 47, $290,333 pay
VP Engineering:
Martin G. Lane-Smith, age 48, $151,200 pay
VP Professional Services:
Alvin S. Begun, age 51, $147,152 pay
VP Finance and Administration, CFO:
Stephanie A. Vinella, age 41
VP Human Resources:
Patricia A. Tomlinson, age 38
Auditors: KPMG Peat Marwick LLP

SELECTED PRODUCTS AND SERVICES

Edify Electronic Banking System (software that offers financial institutions the means to deploy a suite of automated banking services via the World Wide Web)

Electronic Workforce (software that enables users to give their affiliates access to information and services via phone, fax, PC, pager, and kiosk)

KEY COMPETITORS

AT&T Corp.
Checkfree
Dun & Bradstreet
General Magic
Informix
InterVoice
Intuit
Microsoft
Netscape
Oracle
Periphonics
SAP
Sterling Commerce

voice mail, part database-querying system, and part information agent, allowing a company to create programs to respond to faxes, incoming phone calls, and e-mail requests for information. Edify added remote access to Lotus Notes in its 1993 upgrade and the next year teamed up with Big Six auditor KPMG Peat Marwick to jointly market the Electronic Workforce software.

Edify introduced Web-enabled software in 1995, and Unisys selected to provide Web-based human resource services to its worldwide workforce of 36,000. Edify went public in 1996. That year the company also teamed up with credit card king Visa to market its electronic banking system to Visa member banks around the world.

EDIFY: THE NUMBERS

Nasdaq symbol: EDFY FYE: December 31	Annual Growth	1990	1991	1992	1993	1994	1995
Sales ($ mil.)	—	—	0.0	1.6	4.0	8.4	16.0
Net income ($ mil.)	—	—	(2.5)	(4.2)	(4.5)	(1.7)	(0.1)
Income as % of sales	—	—	—	—	—	—	—
Employees	45.2%	—	—	—	65	77	137

1995 YEAR-END

Debt ratio: 7.4%
Return on equity: —
Cash (mil.): $6.2
Current ratio: 3.02
Long-term debt (mil.): $0.5
No. of shares (mil.): —
Dividends
  Yield: —
  Payout: —

QUARTER ENDED 6/30

	1996	1995
Sales ($ millions)	6.9	3.4
Net Income ($ millions)	(0.5)	(0.2)
Earnings Per Share ($)	(0.03)	(0.02)
Avg. Shares (thousands)	15,077	13,054

6 MONTHS ENDED 6/30

	1996	1995
Sales ($ millions)	12.7	6.1
Net Income ($ millions)	(1.1)	(0.7)
Earnings Per Share ($)	(0.07)	(0.05)
Avg. Shares (thousands)	15,077	13,054

STOCK PRICE HISTORY: High/Low/Close

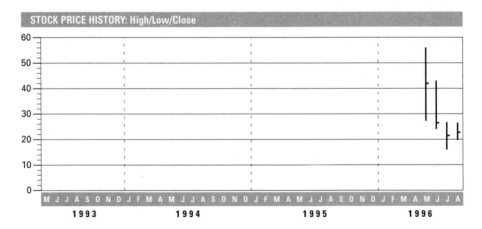

SPECIALIZED
SERVICES

E*TRADE Group

E*TRADE wants to make you rich, whether you trade stock through it or own stock in it. The Palo Alto, California-based Internet brokerage firm lets customers trade stock via America Online, CompuServe, the Internet, and even touch-tone telephones, with transactions posted directly to various stock markets. The company has more than 73,000 customers and is growing by more than 10% each month. In addition to trading, E*TRADE offers a growing list of cash and portfolio management services. Automation allows the company to offer deeply discounted services.

E*TRADE — whose revenues have grown an average of 125% annually since it was founded — went public in 1996 with an IPO filing that valued the company at more than $310 million. Following the IPO, chairman and founder William Porter will own 11% of the company, director emeritus Bernard Newcomb will own 8%, and president and CEO Christos Cotsakos, 5%. In addition, General Atlantic Partners will own 24%.

Porter (a physicist who holds 14 patents in communications and electronics) created Trade Plus, an electronic brokerage service bureau for stockbrokers, in 1982. He founded E*TRADE Securities as a Trade Plus subsidiary in 1991. The following year E*TRADE became CompuServe's first online securities trading service. Revenue took off immediately.

In 1996 Porter stepped down as CEO of E*TRADE but remained the com-

- Among the leaders in new online brokerage industry
- Automated brokerage service allows low commissions
- Claims brokerage technology may be used for insurance processing, cash transfers over the Internet
- Plans to take small companies public over the Internet
- 9-month revenues up 128%1996 FY end is September 30.

- Breakneck growth could lead to operational problems
- Has experienced systems problems, customer ire, legal threats
- Service is susceptible to Internet overload and reliability problems
- Faces competition from more established firms including Schwab, Lombard
- New management team just installed
- Has become unprofitable in 1996

E*TRADE GROUP, INC.

HQ: 4 Embarcadero Place, 2400 Geng Rd.,
Palo Alto, CA 94303
Phone: 415-842-2500
Fax: 415-842-2575
Web site: www.etrade.com

OFFICERS

Chairman:
William A. Porter, age 67, $163,108 pay

President and CEO:
Christos M. Cotsakos, age 47

SVP Finance and Administration and CFO:
Stephen C. Richards, age 42

SVP; President and COO, E*TRADE Securities, Inc.: Kathy Levinson, age 41

SVP; President and COO, E*TRADE Online Ventures: David M. Traversi, age 37

SVP Systems and Chief Information Officer:
David R. Ewing, age 40

VP Corporate Investor Relations:
Wayne H. Heldt, age 56, $149,164 pay

VP Human Resources: Robin N. Rosenberg
Auditors: Deloitte & Touche LLP

SELECTED PRODUCTS AND SERVICES

Cash management
Automatic deposits (proposed)
Checking services
Credit interest programs and money market funds
Electronic funds transfer (proposed)

Market data
Portfolio tracking and records management
Stock and option trading

	1995 Sales	
	$ mil.	% of total
Transactions	20.8	89
Computer services	1.4	6
Interest & other	1.1	5
Total	**23.3**	**100**

KEY COMPETITORS

Charles Schwab
Donaldson, Lufkin & Jenrette
eBroker
Fidelity Brokerage Services
Institutional Brokerage
Pacific Brokerage Services
Quick & Reilly
Sherwood Securities
TransTerra Waterhouse

pany's chairman. Former A.C. Nielsen co-CEO Christos Cotsakos was named E*TRADE president and CEO.

Rapid growth (monthly trading volume tripled from 50 million to 170 million shares in the first half of 1996) has E*TRADE scrambling to keep services timely. In mid-1996 a computer hardware failure left some users without trading access for more than 2 hours; the company covered $1.7 million in customer market losses. Soon after, E*TRADE added a backup computer facility near Sacramento. As competition among online services heated up, the firm cut its comission by 25%, making transaction fees about $15 for AMEX and NYSE trading and about $20 for Nasdaq orders.

E*TRADE: THE NUMBERS

Nasdaq symbol: EGRP FYE: September 30	Annual Growth	1990	1991	1992	1993	1994	1995
Sales ($ mil.)	132.3%	—	0.8	0.8	3.0	10.9	23.3
Net income ($ mil.)	—	—	(0.1)	(0.3)	0.1	0.8	2.6
Income as % of sales	—	—	—	—	3.3%	7.2%	11.1%
Employees	250.0%	—	—	—	20	44	245

1995 YEAR-END

Debt ratio: 0.6%
Return on equity: 46.7%
Cash (mil.): $9.6
Current ratio: 4.05
Long-term debt (mil.): $0.0
No. of shares (mil.): —
Dividends
  Yield: —
  Payout: —
Market value (mil.): —

QUARTER ENDED 6/30

	1996	1995
Sales ($ millions)	15.6	6.8
Net Income ($ millions)	(2.4)	1.1
Earnings Per Share ($)	(0.09)	0.04
Avg. Shares (thousands)	28,550	25,577

9 MONTHS ENDED 6/30

	1996	1995
Sales ($ millions)	34.5	15.1
Net Income ($ millions)	(1.3)	2.2
Earnings Per Share ($)	(0.05)	0.08
Avg. Shares (thousands)	28,550	25,577

STOCK PRICE HISTORY: High/Low/Close

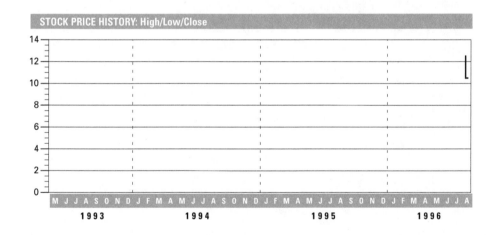

- Leading-edge products have extensive intranet and Internet applications

- ConQuest acquisition netted plain-English query technology

- Expanding rapidly in Europe

- Trying to make a transition from direct sales to strategic partnering

- Dramatic slowdown in sales growth so far in fiscal 1997

- Revenue from IBM partnership appears to be winding down

- Heavy R&D, marketing spending has yet to pay off in fiscal 1997

- Cash burn is troublesome

APPLICATION
SOFTWARE

Excalibur Technologies

Excalibur is making cybersurfing more intuitive. Based in Vienna, Virginia, the company offers "fuzzy searching" — information search technology that approximates that of biological organisms. Its Adaptive Pattern Recognition Processing (APRP) technology identifies and indexes underlying patterns in digital data, allowing a variety of text, image, video, and sound searches, including misspelled words. In addition, Excalibur's recently acquired subsidiary, ConQuest, pioneered semantic networks — a search tool that not only identifies specific words but concepts related to those words as well. Excalibur's customers include *Fortune* 500 companies, federal government organizations, and electronic publishers and information vendors.

Excalibur was founded in 1980 by James Dowe III, a dyslexic computer programmer who needed a device that could handle spelling problems. During the early 1980s Excalibur developed technology to locate information despite misspellings, bad handwriting, and even messy graphic images. By 1984 the company had reached $10 million in sales.

The next year Excalibur signed its first distribution agreement with Nikkei Information System Co. Nikkei provided research and development funds in exchange for exclusive distribution rights in Japan. The company released 3 software libraries based on its technology in the US and Japan in 1988, and the next year it signed a distribution agreement with Digital

EXCALIBUR
TECHNOLOGIES

EXCALIBUR TECHNOLOGIES CORPORATION

HQ: 1921 Gallows Rd., Ste. 200,
Vienna, VA 22182
Phone: 619-438-7900
Fax: 619-438-7901
Web site: www.excalib.com

OFFICERS

Chairman: Richard M. Crooks Jr., age 56
President and CEO:
Patrick C. Condo, age 39, $192,961 pay
EVP: Edwin R. Addison, age 39, $165,750 pay
Chief Scientist:
James W. Dowe III, age 54, $125,000 pay
VP, CFO, Secretary, and Treasurer:
James H. Buchanan, age 40, $51,705 pay
VP Worldwide Sales and Service:
John T. Cannington Jr.
VP Online Sales: Shelly Talbott
Auditors: Andersen Worldwide

SELECTED PRODUCTS AND SERVICES

Electronic Filing Software (EFS software applications for document imaging and information retrieval)
EFS Webfile (information search and retrieval on the World Wide Web)
RetrievalWare (information retrieval software suite)
RetrievalWare Image Servers
RetrievalWare Profiling Server
RetrievalWare Software Developer's Kit (SDK)
RetrievalWare TextServers
RetrievalWare Web Server
RetrievalWare

KEY COMPETITORS

America Online	General Magic
DataWare	Information Dimension
DEC	Open Text
Folio	Oracle
Fulcrum Technologies	Verity

Equipment Corporation. Excalibur went overseas in 1992, establishing a wholly owned subsidiary Excalibur Technologies International, Ltd , in the UK.

The company acquired ConQuest Software (natural language text management software) in 1995 and moved its headquarters to Virginia. It also expanded its distribution, shipping products that support non-English languages to Europe, the Pacific Rim, Australia, and Central and South America. In 1996 Excalibur continued to expand its market, signing joint development and marketing agreements with IBM and providing its software to major online technology companies such as EarthWeb and Bell & Howell.

EXCALIBUR: THE NUMBERS

Nasdaq symbol: EXCA FYE: January 31	Annual Growth	1991	1992	1993	1994	1995	1996
Sales ($ mil.)	59.7%	1.8	4.9	7.9	10.7	10.8	18.7
Net income ($ mil.)	—	(3.4)	(3.9)	(7.6)	(6.7)	(6.9)	(0.9)
Income as % of sales	—	—	—	—	—	—	—
Earnings per share ($)	—	(0.51)	(0.53)	(0.91)	(0.73)	(0.72)	(0.08)
Stock price – high ($)[1]	—	16.63	21.75	19.25	17.25	12.25	39.75
Stock price – low ($)[1]	—	7.25	8.75	9.00	11.00	4.75	6.00
Stock price – close ($)[1]	32.3%	9.00	16.75	12.75	11.75	5.75	36.50
P/E – high	—	—	—	—	—	—	—
P/E – low	—	—	—	—	—	—	—
Dividends per share ($)	—	0.00	0.00	0.00	0.00	0.00	0.00
Book value per share ($)	(9.3%)	2.09	1.58	2.00	1.50	1.23	1.28
Employees	12.5%	—	78	102	121	92	125

[1] Stock prices are for the prior calendar year.

1995 YEAR-END

Debt ratio: 0.0%
Return on equity: —
Cash (mil.): $13.2
Current ratio: 2.66
Long-term debt (mil.): $0.0
No. of shares (mil.): 12.0
Dividends
  Yield: —
  Payout: —
Market value (mil.): $436.3
R&D as % of sales: 26.6%

QUARTER ENDED 4/30

	1996	1995
Sales ($ millions)	4.0	2.8
Net Income ($ millions)	(1.7)	(0.5)
Earnings Per Share ($)	(0.14)	(0.05)
Avg. Shares (thousands)	12,340	9,898

3 MONTHS ENDED 4/30

	1996	1995
Sales ($ millions)	4.0	2.8
Net Income ($ millions)	(1.7)	(0.5)
Earnings Per Share ($)	(0.14)	(0.05)
Avg. Shares (thousands)	12,340	9,898

STOCK PRICE HISTORY: High/Low/Close

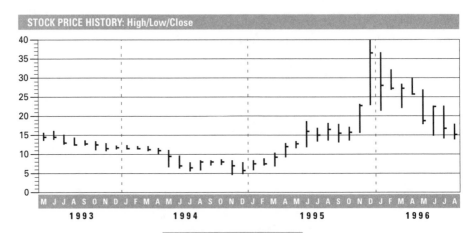

SPECIALIZED SERVICES

CONTENT

Excite Inc.

What's so exciting? A World Wide Web with hundreds of thousands of sites representing a truly global community — and services such as Excite that make online globe-trotting easy. Mountain View, California-based Excite (formerly Architext Software) provides a variety of navigational tools for the Web, including customizable and regional search aids. The company's proprietary Excite search engine scouts for subjects by concept, providing a broader search capability than the keyword-based engines of its rivals. Excite has entry points on such leading services as America Online and the Microsoft Network and on Netscape's NetDirectory. Among its content providers are Times Mirror's *Los Angeles Times* and Reuters. The company has signed up more than 50 advertisers, including AT&T, Honda, L.L. Bean, and Microsoft. Prior to its April 1996 initial public offering, the company was valued at a healthy $130 million by Wall Street analysts. After the offering, venture capital firms Kleiner Perkins Caufield and Byers and Institutional Venture Partners each own 23% of the company, America Online owns 13%, the Tribune Company has 8%, and cofounder and chief technical officer Graham Spencer owns 6%.

Six Stanford dorm mates (Joe Kraus, Ben Lutch, Ryan McIntyre, Martin Reinfried, Mark Van Haren, and Spencer) came up with the idea for Architext Software in 1993. They formed the company in mid-1994 to fulfill a $100,000 contract for an online project from computer magazine publisher International Data Group. Architext spent the next year fulfilling its contract, developing its search engine, and recruiting key staff members, including Jeffrey McFadden, a former Sun Microsystems executive, as VP of business development. In October 1995 the company launched its

- 2nd quarter revenues up 85% over first quarter in 1996
- Claims that Magellan acquisition makes Excite #2 in search traffic
- Magellan acquisition provides
  * 2 of 5 search site choices linked to Netscape browser
  * 2 of 4 search site choices offered by America Online
- Balance sheet shows $4 per share in cash (before Magellan acquisition)

- Losses are accelerating
- Magellan was doing poorly before the acquisition
- Relatively low technical barriers to entry into market
- Unproven advertising-based business model
- Both search sites are heavily dependent on traffic generated by Netscape
- Browser companies can influence traffic flow or compete
- Market cap of $64 million (8/96) vs. trailing 12-month sales of $2.7 million

EXCITE INC.
HQ: 1091 N. Shoreline Blvd.,
 Mountain View, CA 94043
Phone: 415-934-3611
Fax: 415-934-3610
Web site: www.excite.com

OFFICERS

President and CEO: George Bell, age 39
SVP Business Development:
 Joseph R. Kraus IV, age 24, $62,156 pay
SVP Marketing and Sales:
 Brett T. Bullington, age 42
VP Business Development:
 Jeffrey A. McFadden, $137,236 pay
VP Technology and Chief Technical Officer:
 Graham F. Spencer, age 24
VP Engineering: Cary H. Masatsugu, age 39
Director Finance, Acting CFO, and Secretary
(HR): Richard B. Redding, age 40
Human Resources Manager:
 Nancy Shearer-Schroeder
Auditors: Ernst & Young LLP

SELECTED PRODUCTS AND SERVICES

City.Net (geographically organized database for locating local and regional content)

Excite Bulletin (online newspaper)

NetDirectory (reviews of more than 50,000 Web sites)

NetSearch (document search and Web browsing service)

Personal Excite (personal interface for monitoring selected information, including NetDirectory categories, news topics, and stock quotes)

	1995 Sales	
	$ thou.	% of total
Contracts	291.0	67
Advertising	143.5	33
Total	**434.5**	**100**

KEY COMPETITORS

America Online
CompuServe
DEC
Individual
Infonautics
Infoseek

Lycos
Wired Ventures
Wolff New Media
Yahoo!

NetDirectory site reviews and NetSearch indexing service and released EWS, companion software to its search service. At that time it also started selling advertising. The following month Architext purchased the City.Net (an online resource for local and regional information such as entertainment, dining, and cultural events) and added it to its services.

In early 1996 Personal Excite, a customizable search tool, went online, and George Bell, a former SVP at the Times Mirror Co., was named president and CEO. The company changed its name to Excite in 1996 and began trading in April of that year, raising $34 million. Later in 1996 Excite announced plans to purchase McKinley Group, operator of the Magellan search site, for $10 million in stock.

EXCITE: THE NUMBERS

Nasdaq symbol: XCIT FYE: December 31	Annual Growth	1990	1991	1992	1993	1994	1995
Sales ($ mil.)	—	—	—	—	—	0.1	0.4
Net income ($ mil.)	—	—	—	—	—	(0.1)	(3.3)
Income as % of sales	—	—	—	—	—	—	—
Employees	—	—	—	—	—	—	38

1995 YEAR-END

Debt ratio: —
Return on equity: —
Cash (mil.): $0.6
Current ratio: 1.28
Long-term debt (mil.): $0.4
No. of shares (mil.): —
Dividends:
  Yield: —
  Payout: —
R&D as % of sales: 17.6%
Advertising as % of sales: 33.1%

QUARTER ENDED 6/30

	1996	1995
Sales ($ millions)	2.1	0.0
Net Income ($ millions)	(7.0)	(0.2)
Earnings Per Share ($)	(0.63)	(0.02)
No. of Shares (thou.)	11,068	10,652

6 MONTHS ENDED 6/30

	1996	1995
Sales ($ millions)	3.3	0.3
Net Income ($ millions)	(10.6)	(0.3)
Earnings Per Share ($)	(0.98)	(0.03)
No. of Shares (thou.)	11,068	10,652

STOCK PRICE HISTORY: High/Low/Close

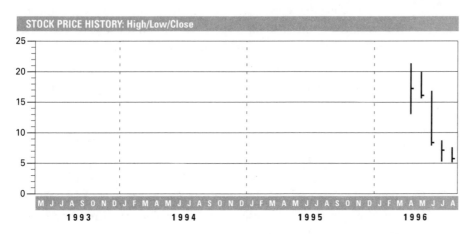

- #3 credit card processor for merchant accounts

- Owns 50% stake in Internet payment processor First Virtual

- Positioned to use existing credit card processing infrastructure for payments over the Internet

- Promoting business-to-business credit card concept

- Acquiring businesses and technology with electronic commerce applications

- Excellent track record, fiscal 1996 earnings per share rose 69%

- P/E over 60 (8/96)

First USA Paymentech

What happens when the sales clerk runs your credit card through the card reader? A network of computer connections contacts your issuer, confirms your creditworthiness, and authorizes payment; then it posts the sales amount with Visa or MasterCard as a credit for the merchant. The charge is then posted as a debit with your bank through the card issuer.

However, the company that processes the transaction for the merchant may not be the one that bills you. First USA Paymentech processes transactions for the merchant; its parent, First USA (which owns about 78% of the company), issues cards and processes transactions on the consumer side. The merchant processor also assembles the authorization network and recruits merchants. It owns 50% of First Virtual Holdings, an Internet secured payment company.

First USA Paymentech was created in 1996 as a holding company for First USA's Merchant Processing Services (the 3rd largest, after First Data and National City Corp.) and newly created First USA Financial, Inc. (which was founded to enter the growing corporate card business). Transaction processing is technologically intensive. First USA's technical operations were developed by Pamela Patsley (who became Paymentech's president).

In 1995, as consolidation in the industry increased, First USA made several acquisitions, including Litle & Co. and DGMT, both based in New Hampshire and specializing in direct marketing sales processing. The fol-

FIRST USA PAYMENTECH, INC.
HQ: 1601 Elm St., Dallas, TX 75201
Phone: 214-849-2000
Fax: 214-849-3748
Web site: www.fusa.com/

OFFICERS

Chairman: John C. Tolleson, age 47
President and CEO:
Pamela H. Patsley, age 39, $393,750 pay
Group Executive, Marketing:
Susan H. Cerpanya, age 45, $187,500 pay
Group Executive, Technology:
Raymond J. McArdle, age 57, $173,250 pay
Group Executive, Portfolio Management:
Elena R. Anderson, age 36, $145,500 pay
Group Executive, Direct Marketing:
Michael P. Duffy, age 37
National Sales Manager:
Thomas J. Lupinacci, age 48, $202,500 pay
CFO and Secretary: David W. Truetzel, age 39
Director Human Resources:
Bonnie Johnston
Auditors: Ernst & Young LLP

SELECTED SUBSIDIARIES AND AFFILIATES

First USA Financial Services, Inc. (commercial credit cards and corporate purchasing cards)

First USA Merchant Services, Inc. (merchant credit card transaction processing)

First Virtual Holdings, Inc. (50%; Internet secured payment systems)

KEY COMPETITORS

American Express
AT&T Corp.
BSI Business Services
Checkfree
Citicorp
Concord EFS
CyberCash
DigiCash
First Bank System
Moneygram Payment Services
National City Corp.
National Processing
Nova Corp.
PMT Services
SPS Transaction Services
Total System Services
Verifone

lowing year First USA decided to separate the 2 sides of its business and take Paymentech public. This allowed the company to raise money for acquisitions as well as providing a way to recoup previous acquisition costs. First USA Paymentech began moving immediately after going public. It made several portfolio purchases, including one worth $700 million per year from Mercantile Bancorp of St. Louis, and bought Gensar, a transaction processing company based in Philadelphia.

FIRST USA: THE NUMBERS

NYSE symbol: PTI FYE: June 30	Annual Growth	1990	1991	1992	1993	1994	1995
Sales ($ mil.)	24.0%	—	36.6	44.6	51.3	63.7	86.6
Net income ($ mil.)	26.3%	—	3.1	4.3	4.1	6.4	7.9
Income as % of sales	—	—	8.4%	9.5%	8.0%	10.0%	9.1%
Employees	—	—	—	—	—	—	800

1995 YEAR-END

Debt ratio: 7.8%
Return on equity: 17.7%
Cash (mil.): $4.6
Current ratio: 0.94
Long-term debt (mil.): $4.0
No. of shares (mil.): —
Dividends:
  Yield: —
  Payout: —
Market value ($ mil.): —

QUARTER ENDED 6/30

	1996	1995
Sales ($ millions)	33.9	21.7
Net Income ($ millions)	5.4	2.0
Earnings Per Share ($)	0.17	0.08
No. of Shares (thou.)	32,080	24,411

12 MONTHS ENDED 6/30

	1996	1995
Sales ($ millions)	121.2	86.6
Net Income ($ millions)	14.3	7.9
Earnings Per Share ($)	0.54	0.32
No. of Shares (thou.)	32,080	24,411

STOCK PRICE HISTORY: High/Low/Close

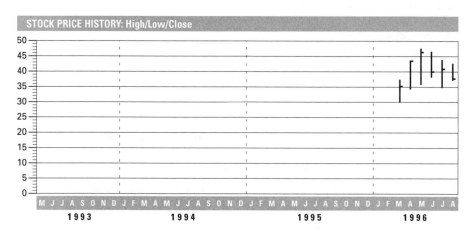

M J J A S O N D J F M A M J J A S O N D J F M A M J J A S O N D J F M A M J J A
1993   1994   1995   1996

NETWORK
INFRASTRUCTURE

FORE Systems

FORE Systems is foremost among makers of networking products based on ATM (asynchronous transfer mode, a high-speed, high-volume networking protocol). Warrendale, Pennsylvania-based FORE makes both hardware and software to help companies create LANs and WANs. It sells primarily to corporate end users; customers include AT&T, Ford Motor Co., General Electric, Motorola, Northern Telecom, and Sprint.

The company was founded in 1990 by 4 Carnegie Mellon researchers studying computer technologies: Francois Bitz, Onat Menzilcioglu, Robert Sansom, and Eric Cooper (their first initials gave FORE its name). It shipped its initial products, a line of ATM adapter cards, in 1991 and unveiled its ATM switching products the following year. FORE went public in 1994. The founders together own about 16% of the company's stock. FORE secured its leading-edge position by developing alliances with other developers of high-tech applications, including Cabletron and Northern Telecom. In 1994 the company joined with Microsoft and Tele-Communications, Inc. (the US's largest cable operator), to test an interactive television system, including home shopping and movies on demand.

In 1995 FORE moved to counter the threat of Ethernet, a rival technology, by acquiring Applied Network Technology, a developer of Ethernet switching products. That year it also bought RainbowBridge Communications, a

- Leader in nascent LAN ATM switching market
- Alantec gives FORE better access to prospects with Ethernet LANs
- Nortel resells FORE switches to RBOCs, other telecomms
- Company is focused on ATM technology

- Lack of standards, high cost, and difficult setup slow ATM deployment
- Most customers buy LAN ATM switches for backbone applications only
- Competitors are much larger, more established, well-financed
- P/E over 50 (8/96)

FORE SYSTEMS, INC.

HQ: 174 Thorn Hill Rd.,
Warrendale, PA 15086-7535
Phone: 412-772-6600
Fax: 412-772-6500
Web site: www.fore.com

OFFICERS

Chairman and CEO:
Eric C. Cooper, age 37, $256,157 pay

President:
Onat Menzilcioglu, age 37, $224,750 pay

VP Engineering:
Francois J. Bitz, age 36, $182,313 pay

VP Engineering and Secretary:
Robert D. Sansom, age 36, $182,313 pay

VP Sales and Marketing:
Michael I. Green, age 48, $210,709 pay

VP Finance, CFO, and Treasurer:
Thomas J. Gill, age 38

VP Human Resources: Thomas Armour
Auditors: Price Waterhouse LLP

SELECTED PRODUCTS AND SERVICES

Selected ATM Products

CellPath WAN multiplexers (aggregate network traffic onto wide area transmission lines)

ForeRunner ATM adapter cards (allow computers to communicate over ATM networks)

ForeRunner ATM switches (workgroup, LAN backbone, and WAN-access switches for up to 96 computers or other networking devices)

ForeThought software (includes control software for FORE's ATM switches and the device driver for its ATM adapter cards)

ForeView software (network management)

PowerHub LAN switches (intelligent switches for Ethernet, Fast Ethernet, FDDI, and ATM networks)

KEY COMPETITORS

3Com	DSC Communications
Bay Networks	General Datacomm
Cabletron	IBM
Cascade Communications	Interphase
Cisco Systems	Newbridge Networks
DEC	Sun Microsystems
Digital Link	Xylan

developer of network routing software, and Cell-Access Technology, a supplier of digital-access products.

The company acquired Alantec, a leading vendor of Ethernet products, in 1996. That year it formed an alliance with telecommunications equipment maker General Instrument to develop a system for home use that delivers computer images without a time delay. Also in 1996 communications giant MCI chose FORE's ForeRunner ASX-1000 ATM switch for MCI's Internet network.

FORE SYSTEMS: THE NUMBERS

Nasdaq symbol: FORE FYE: March 31	Annual Growth	1991	1992	1993	1994	1995	1996
Sales ($ mil.)	372.4%	0.1	1.0	5.5	23.5	75.6	235.2
Net income ($ mil.)	—	0.0	0.1	0.3	2.1	7.4	9.7
Income as % of sales	—	—	8.9%	5.4%	8.8%	9.7%	4.1%
Earnings per share ($)	48.3%	—	—	—	0.05	0.14	0.11
Stock price – high ($)[1]	—	—	—	—	—	17.88	33.88
Stock price – low ($)[1]	—	—	—	—	—	5.00	12.75
Stock price – close ($)[1]	—	—	—	—	—	16.88	29.75
P/E – high	—	—	—	—	—	132	308
P/E – low	—	—	—	—	—	37	116
Dividends per share ($)	—	—	—	—	—	0.00	0.00
Book value per share ($)	—	—	—	—	—	1.05	3.82
Employees	88.4%	—	—	146	165	357	977

[1] Stock prices are for the prior calendar year.

1996 YEAR-END

Debt ratio: 0.0%
Return on equity: 4.5%
Cash (mil.): $296.2
Current ratio: 4.52
Long-term debt (mil.): $0.0
No. of shares (mil.): 88.0
Dividends
 Yield: —
 Payout: —
Market value (mil.): $2,617.5
R&D as % of sales: 13.3%

QUARTER ENDED 6/30

	1996	1995
Sales ($ millions)	83.4	31.7
Net Income ($ millions)	11.4	1.5
Earnings Per Share ($)	0.12	0.03
No. of Shares (thou.)	89,370	54,360

3 MONTHS ENDED 6/30

	1996	1995
Sales ($ millions)	83.4	31.7
Net Income ($ millions)	11.4	1.5
Earnings Per Share ($)	0.12	0.03
No. of Shares (thou.)	89,370	54,360

STOCK PRICE HISTORY: High/Low/Close

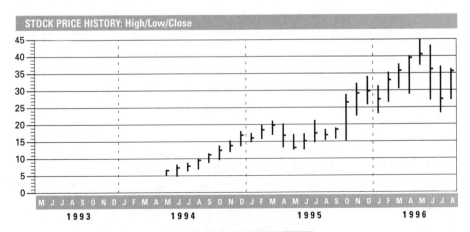

1993   1994   1995   1996

- Quickly becoming a pure play in Web productivity software

- Popular WebWhacker off-line browser is being retooled for intranet use

- Integration of WebSeeker "meta search" capabilities with WebWhacker is possible

- Recent acquisitions add retail and direct distribution channels

- Demand for collaboration software, such as RoundTable, is expected to grow rapidly

- Microsoft has licensed some of ForeFront's software

- WebWhacker's main features are not unique and the product may not be long-lived

- Web utility functionality is often easily incorporated into browsers

- Many big guns are competing in collaboration software

- Still unprofitable

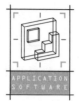

APPLICATION
SOFTWARE

The ForeFront Group, Inc.

A headstart on its competitors has put the ForeFront Group at the forefront of Internet software development. The Houston-based company makes software to help users find, capture, organize, and view information on the World Wide Web and then collaborate with others in real time in using the information. Computer users can "try before they buy" most of the software, downloading demos of the product off the Web. Major products include GrabNet (graphical bookmarker), WebWhacker (offline Web browser), WebSeeker (Web search unifier), and RoundTable (online conferencing).

ForeFront's first product, the Virtual Notebook System (VNS), began life in 1986 at Houston's Baylor College of Medicine as an electronic version of a research scientist's paper notebook that would allow geographically dispersed medical researchers to access and share their data. Anthony Gorry, a Rice professor who was primarily responsible for the VNS architecture (now chairman), and VP Andrew Burger founded ForeFront in 1990 to commercialize the VNS, introducing it in 1992 as a general-purpose workgroup productivity tool that could be shared over private networks. However, the company's progress stalled in the face of hurdles such as widespread reluctance to accept electronic recordkeeping.

In 1995 ForeFront rethought its position. Recognizing that the underlying structure of VNS resembled that of the Internet, the company decided to become an Internet software developer. (It still sells the VNS but no longer

ForeFront

THE FOREFRONT GROUP, INC.

HQ: 1360 Post Oak Blvd., Ste. 1660,
Houston, TX 77056
Phone: 713-961-1101
Fax: 713-961-1149
Web site: www.ffg.com

OFFICERS

Chairman and Chief Technical Advisor:
G. Anthony Gorry, age 54

President and CEO: David Sikora, age 34
EVP and CTO: Andrew M. Burger, age 39
VP Engineering: Julie Garrison, age 39
VP Sales and Marketing: John Bertero, age 36
CFO: Ernest D. Rapp, age 34
Auditors: Andersen Worldwide

SELECTED PRODUCTS AND SERVICES

FreeForm Canvas (computer palette for displaying graphics and text)

GrabNet (graphical bookmarker that organizes Web sites)

RoundTable (online text and graphics real-time conferencing/collaboration package)

Virtual Notebook System (integrated software for collecting and sharing information)

WebSeeker (automatic Web searcher that combines results from more than 20 search engines)

WebWhacker (offline Web browser that saves pages, text, or graphics to a PC)

KEY COMPETITORS

DEC	Netscape
Excite	Novell
First Floor Software	Pointcast
FTP Software	Quarterdeck
ichat	Reach Networks
Individual	SoftQuad
Infoseek	Spyglass
Internet Solutions	Traveling Software
Lycos	Yahoo!
Microsoft	
NetManage	

actively markets it.) ForeFront applied its Internet knowledge and within a few months had introduced two products.

Distribution has been a problem for ForeFront. The company's solution has been to license its technology (DEC, 1993; Microsoft, 1996), bundle its products (Brother, 1996), enter into alliances (Tripos, 1995; Seiko Epson and CE Software, 1996), and acquire competitors or companies with complementary products. ForeFront, which has yet to make a profit, went public in 1995 and, in a 3-month period in 1996, acquired Internet search engine maker Blue Squirrel, booklet software maker Bookmaker, and PC troubleshooting software maker AllMicro.

FOREFRONT GROUP: THE NUMBERS

Nasdaq symbol: FFGI FYE: December 31	Annual Growth	1990	1991	1992	1993	1994	1995
Sales ($ mil.)	44.2%	—	—	0.1	0.6	0.5	0.3
Net income ($ mil.)	—	—	—	(0.3)	(0.4)	(1.5)	(1.5)
Income as % of sales	—	—	—	—	—	—	—
Earnings per share ($)	—	—	—	(0.17)	(0.12)	(0.46)	(0.46)
Stock price – high ($)	—	—	—	—	—	—	9.25
Stock price – low ($)	—	—	—	—	—	—	8.22
Stock price – close ($)	—	—	—	—	—	—	8.38
P/E – high	—	—	—	—	—	—	—
P/E – low	—	—	—	—	—	—	—
Dividends per share ($)	—	—	—	—	—	—	0.00
Book value per share ($)	—	—	—	—	—	—	2.65
Employees	—	—	—	—	—	14	31

1995 YEAR-END

Debt ratio: 0.0%
Return on equity: —
Cash (mil.): $12.9
Current ratio: 19.13
Long-term debt (mil.): $0.0
No. of shares (mil.): 4.7
Dividends
  Yield: —
  Payout: —
Market value (mil.): $39.4
R&D as % of sales: 301.9%

QUARTER ENDED 6/30

	1996	1995
Sales ($ millions)	0.8	0.0
Net Income ($ millions)	(3.2)	(0.3)
Earnings Per Share ($)	(0.65)	(0.10)
No. of Shares (thou.)	5,059	3,260

6 MONTHS ENDED 6/30

	1996	1995
Sales ($ millions)	1.2	0.2
Net Income ($ millions)	(4.0)	(0.6)
Earnings Per Share ($)	(0.83)	(0.22)
No. of Shares (thou.)	5,059	3,260

STOCK PRICE HISTORY: High/Low/Close

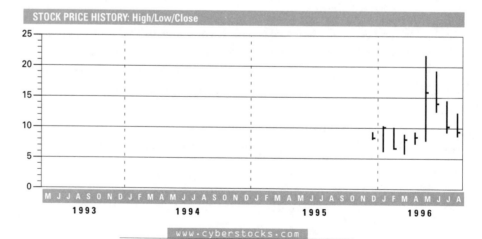

M J J A S O N D J F M A M J J A S O N D J F M A M J J A S O N D J F M A M J J A
1993   1994   1995   1996

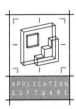

APPLICATION
SOFTWARE

FTP Software

Collaboration used to mean putting people in the same place so they could work together on a project. These days, collaborators can be in different buildings or even on different continents if their computers are linked and they've got the right software. That's where FTP Software comes in. The market leader in desktop open networking, FTP makes connectivity products that help computers talk to each other and is expanding into collaboration products that help users share resources. Its main products are the PC/TCP and OnNet information sharing software families.

FTP, which takes its name from the Internet term "file transfer protocol," has its roots in the mid-1980s at MIT. Several students wrote a version of networking language TCP/IP that allowed DOS-based IBM PCs to communicate with mainframes. Seeing profit potential in adapting it to other systems, 5 graduates founded FTP (all have since left the company). When firms began replacing mainframes with PCs, FTP was ready to link them into networks. The company went public in 1993.

FTP has tried to keep ahead of competitors by developing new products, upgrading old ones, and licensing or acquiring others. It licensed a version of Spyglass's Mosaic Internet browser in 1994. The next year FTP divided its business into 2 units: Networking Products, which is extending PC/TCP and OnNet product lines to new platforms and arenas, and New Ventures, which will develop or acquire new technologies.

The early-1996 acquisitions of the Mariner product line (Internet search capabilities) from Network Computing Devices and HyperDesk's GroupWorks

- Both an intranet and Internet play
- Firefox adds a complementary product line, sales channel, and customer base
- Acquiring technology to create a complete client/server TCP/IP software suite
- Marketing partners include Hewlett-Packard, Spyglass, and Siemens
- Projects a return to profitability in 2nd half of 1996, EPS of $.57 in 1997

- Many of its products compete with "freeware," "shareware," and bundled software
- Could get caught in the crossfire between Microsoft and Netscape
- Sales are down, gross margins are declining
- Firefox products currently do not work with Windows NT
- Government sales are faltering

FTP SOFTWARE, INC.
HQ: 2 High St., North Andover, MA 01845
Phone: 508-685-4000
Fax: 508-794-4488
Web site: www.ftp.com

OFFICERS

Chairman and CEO:
David H. Zirkle, age 59, $300,000 pay

President and COO:
Glenn C. Hazard, age 45

SVP Global Engineering and Development:
John H. Keller, age 44, $201,776 pay

SVP Business Development and Planning, General Counsel, and Clerk:
Douglas F. Flood, age 38, $179,673 pay

SVP, CFO, and Treasurer:
John J. Warnock Jr., age 40

VP Customer Services:
Dean L. Carmeris, age 53, $167,500 pay

VP Business Development/Alliances:
Penelope C. Leavy, age 32, $140,000 pay

VP Human Resources and Investor Relations: Karen A. Wharton, age 41

Chief Technical Officer:
Peter R. Simkin, age 43

Auditors: Coopers & Lybrand L.L.P.

SELECTED PRODUCTS AND SERVICES

Networking Products
InterDrive (networking applications)
LANCatch (network utility)
LANWatch (network analyzer)
OnNet (internetworking)
PC/Bind (DOS-based domain name server)
PC/SNMP Tools (network management)
PC/TCP (internetworking)
Services OnNet (configuration management)
X OnNet (applications access)

New Ventures
Esplanade (Web server)
Explore (Internet access)
FrontPage (Web page development)
GroupWorks (project team management utility)
KEYpak (document interchange and conversion)
KEYview (e-mail utility)
Mariner (Internet search)

KEY COMPETITORS

Adobe	NetManage
Attachmate	Netscape
CompuServe	Novell
DEC	ON Technology
ForeFront	QUALCOMM
Frontier Technologies	Quarterdeck
General Magic	SoftQuad
IBM	Spyglass
ichat	Sun Microsystems
Ipswitch	Wall Data
Microsoft	

(project team management utility) helped the company move toward products to help users work together on projects. FTP acquired Firefox Communications in mid-1996, complementing its TCP/IP client-based products with Firefox's TCP/IP server-based software.

FTP SOFTWARE: THE NUMBERS

Nasdaq symbol: FTPS FYE: December 31	Annual Growth	1990	1991	1992	1993	1994	1995
Sales ($ mil.)	65.2%	11.1	21.4	33.1	58.7	93.2	136.4
Net income ($ mil.)	49.4%	3.3	5.4	10.6	16.3	23.0	24.6
Income as % of sales	—	29.4%	25.2%	24.3%	27.8%	24.6%	18.1%
Earnings per share ($)	40.3%	0.16	0.24	0.34	0.60	0.79	0.87
Stock price – high ($)	—	—	—	—	27.75	33.50	40.63
Stock price – low ($)	—	—	—	—	22.50	11.50	20.25
Stock price – close ($)	4.6%	—	—	—	26.50	31.63	29.00
P/E – high	—	—	—	—	46	42	47
P/E – low	—	—	—	—	38	15	23
Dividends per share ($)	—	—	—	—	0.00	0.00	0.00
Book value per share ($)	33.1%	—	—	—	3.51	4.83	6.22
Employees	34.7%	—	—	—	408	474	740

1995 YEAR-END

Debt ratio: 1.0%
Return on equity: 17.8%
Cash (mil.): $66.6
Current ratio: 4.60
Long-term debt (mil.): $0.8
No. of shares (mil.): 26.5
Dividends
 Yield: —
 Payout: —
Market value (mil.): $768.7
R&D as % of sales: 22.6%

QUARTER ENDED 6/30

	1996	1995
Sales ($ millions)	28.1	34.1
Net Income ($ millions)	(13.1)	9.3
Earnings Per Share ($)	(0.49)	0.33
No. of Shares (thou.)	26,967	24,952

6 MONTHS ENDED 6/30

	1996	1995
Sales ($ millions)	57.1	65.4
Net Income ($ millions)	(21.6)	17.2
Earnings Per Share ($)	(0.80)	0.61
No. of Shares (thou.)	26,967	24,952

STOCK PRICE HISTORY: High/Low/Close

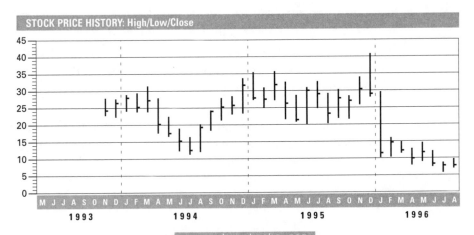

www·cyberstocks·com

Cyberstocks: An Investor's Guide to Internet Companies • 195

- Has established a foothold in the rapidly growing ATM WAN switching market
- ATM product sales grew by 80% in the first 9 months of fiscal 1996
- Lucent, DSC Communications, Ericsson resell GDC's products
- Has forecast a rebound in gross margins

- Has been unprofitable since 1993
- Growth in sales of older, analog products is slowing
- Domestic sales are declining

NETWORK
INFRASTRUCTURE

General DataComm

General DataComm (GDC) is spreading out hot asphalt for the information superhighway. The Middlebury, Connecticut-based company designs, assembles, markets, and services WAN (wide area network) and telecommunications products, which enable telecommunications systems operators, commercial institutions, and governments to build, upgrade, and manage their global telecommunications networks. Its line of ATM (asynchronous transfer mode) switches, modems, multiplexers, and other internetworking devices integrate voice, video, and data information on the same network to facilitate multimedia applications. GDC suffered a loss in 1995 as a result of the high cost of developing ATM technology, slower-than-expected sales of ATM switches, and a devaluation of first-generation switches still in inventory. Chairman Charles Johnson owns 8% of the company.

Johnson, an electrical engineer who was introduced to communications and electronics while serving in the US Navy, started the operation in 1969. Its first products were modems and other data communications devices. The company went public in 1971. Through the 1970s and 1980s GDC increased international sales of its products.

In 1991 it acquired 2 of its foreign distributors: Eurotech France (a unit of Bell Atlantic) and Mexico-based General Telecomm (a majority stake). To

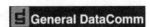

**GENERAL DATACOMM
INDUSTRIES, INC.**
HQ: 1579 Straits Tpke.,
     Middlebury, CT 06762-1299
Phone: 203-574-1118
Fax: 203-758-8507
Web site: www.gdc.com

OFFICERS

Chairman and CEO:
  Charles P. Johnson, age 68, $587,918 pay

President and COO:
  Ross A. Belson, age 59, $312,575 pay

SVP Marketing:
  Michael C. Thurk, age 43, $239,940 pay

SVP US Sales:
  V. Jay Damiano, age 50, $179,900 pay

VP Finance and CFO:
  William S. Lawrence, age 52, $201,471 pay

VP Technology: Frederick R. Cronin, age 64

VP and Treasurer: Dennis J. Nesler, age 52

VP Human Resources:
  Robert H. Dorion Jr., age 41

Auditors: Coopers & Lybrand L.L.P.

SELECTED PRODUCTS AND SERVICES

Analog modems (digital computer signal conversion for telephone line transmission)

ATM switches (signal processing and direction)

Digital data sets (signal conversion from computers and communications equipment for telecommunications transmission)

Multiplexers (signal consolidation on a single transmission line)

	1995 Sales % of total
Product sales	80
Service revenues	17
Product leasing	3
Total	**100**

KEY COMPETITORS

ADC Telecommunications	FORE Systems
Alcatel Alsthom	Fujitsu
Ascend	Hitachi
Ascom Group	IBM
Bay Networks	Lucent
Cascade Communications	Newbridge
Cisco Systems	Northern Telecom
Digital Equipment	Premisys
DSC Communications	Siemens
ECI Telecom	Tellabs
Ericsson	

expedite the development of ATM switches in 1993, the company acquired its ATM distribution and technology partner, Netcomm Ltd.

In 1995, a year in which sales outside the US and Canada accounted for 40% of the total, GDC introduced an enhanced operating system for its line of ATM switches. The new system enables video communications transmissions over telecommunications networks and facilitates the connection of LANs (local area networks) to established WAN systems.

GENERAL DATACOMM: THE NUMBERS

NYSE symbol: GDC FYE: September 30	Annual Growth	1990	1991	1992	1993	1994	1995
Sales ($ mil.)	1.9%	201.5	191.7	197.9	211.8	211.0	221.2
Net income ($ mil.)	—	0.4	0.6	2.6	6.1	(1.9)	(27.6)
Income as % of sales	—	0.2%	0.3%	1.3%	2.9%	—	—
Earnings per share ($)	—	0.03	0.04	0.17	0.36	(0.11)	(1.40)
Stock price – high ($)	—	5.00	3.88	6.38	15.75	34.88	35.88
Stock price – low ($)	—	1.63	2.00	2.88	6.25	8.25	9.25
Stock price – close ($)	51.7%	2.13	3.25	6.38	10.38	32.38	17.13
P/E – high	—	167	97	38	44	—	—
P/E – low	—	54	50	17	17	—	—
Dividends per share ($)	—	0.00	0.00	0.00	0.00	0.00	0.00
Book value per share ($)	8.5%	3.81	3.76	3.91	4.22	4.72	5.73
Employees	(2.0%)	1,975	1,737	1,788	1,820	1,824	1,781

1995 YEAR-END

Debt ratio: 23.5%
Return on equity: —
Cash (mil.): $18.4
Current ratio: 2.20
Long-term debt (mil.): $23.4
No. of shares (mil.): 20.4
Dividends
 Yield: —
 Payout: —
Market value (mil.): $350.2
R&D as % of sales: 12.8%

QUARTER ENDED 6/30

	1996	1995
Sales ($ millions)	56.6	48.1
Net Income ($ millions)	(7.8)	(16.6)
Earnings Per Share ($)	(0.37)	(0.82)
No. of Shares (thou.)	20,853	20,332

9 MONTHS ENDED 6/30

	1996	1995
Sales ($ millions)	175.5	162.8
Net Income ($ millions)	(12.3)	(22.4)
Earnings Per Share ($)	(0.60)	(1.15)
No. of Shares (thou.)	20,853	20,332

STOCK PRICE HISTORY: High/Low/Close

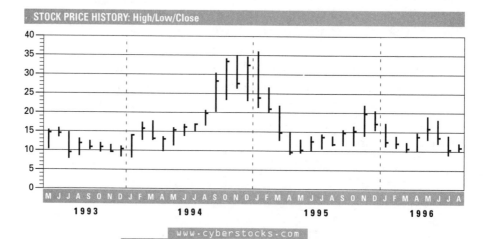

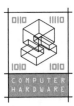

COMPUTER
HARDWARE

General Instrument

General Instrument (GI) wants your PC to act like a TV. The Chicago-based company — a leading developer of interactive data, video, and voice transmission products — pioneered video digital compression. Now GI is working with networking maven FORE Systems to improve image transmissions to home computers. GI is covering its bases by marketing to all segments of the converging communications industry: it supplies equipment for GTE's video network as well as equipment that allows cable TV companies to transmit telephone signals. GI's divisions include GI Communications, the world's top provider of cable TV systems and subscriber terminals; CommScope, a leading supplier of coaxial and fiber-optic cable for TV; and Power Semiconductor, a maker of electrical power-handling equipment.

GI was founded in New York in 1923 by Austrian immigrant Abraham Blumenkrantz to make variable condensers for tuning radios. Soon the company was also making earphone jacks and tube sockets. It went public in 1939. During WWII GI (called "Genius Incorporated" for its amazing innovations) supplied parts for bombs. It added phonograph record changers and television components to its line in the 1940s. By the 1950s GI made more than a thousand items, including a converter box for the new UHF TV channels.

GI acquired Jerrold Communications (CATV equipment) and American Totalisator, (pari-mutuel betting machines) in 1967. The company soon

- Dominant supplier of set-top converters
- Major producer of cable- and satellite-TV infrastructure equipment
- A technology leader in video compression, satellite-TV encryption
- Telecommunications deregulation could speed deployment of interactive TV systems
- Big international opportunity in cable-TV
- Makes equipment for high-speed cable Internet access

- Deployment of interactive cable TV has been very slow
- Digital TV communications standards could commoditize some market segments
- Remember HDTV?

GI General Instrument

GENERAL INSTRUMENT CORPORATION
HQ: 8770 W. Bryn Mawr Ave., Ste. 1300,
Chicago, IL 60631
Phone: 312-695-1000
Fax: 312-695-1001
Web site: www.gi.com

OFFICERS

Chairman and CEO:
Richard S. Friedland, age 45, $804,028 pay

Chairman, President, and CEO, CommScope:
Frank M. Drendel, age 51, $524,201 pay

VP; President, Power Semiconductor:
Ronald A. Ostertag, age 55, $500,810 pay

VP, General Counsel, and Chief Administrative Officer:
Thomas A. Dumit, age 53, $409,120 pay

VP and CFO: Charles T. Dickson, age 41
VP and Controller: Paul J. Berzenski, age 43
VP Taxes and Treasurer:
Richard C. Smith, age 51

VP Human Resources: Clark E. Tucker, age 46
Auditors: Deloitte & Touche LLP

SELECTED PRODUCTS AND SERVICES

Broadband Communications
CommScope (coaxial cable for cable TV applications)
GI Communications
Analog and digital satellite products (scrambling and descrambling products for satellite-based distribution of television programming)
Analog and digital terrestrial products (allow cable TV operators to control subscribers' cable service from a central computer and to increase channel capacity, upgrade signal quality, and improve security)
Next Level Communications (broadband access system for telephony, video, and data)

Power Semiconductors
Power Semiconductor Division (power rectifying and transient voltage suppressing components)

KEY COMPETITORS

ADC Telecommunications	Motorola
American Power Conversion	Scientific-Atlanta
	SGS-Thomson
Antec	Siemens
Belden	Stanford
Cable Design Technologies	Telecommunications
Essex Group	

began to focus on cable TV and gaming, and during the 1980s the firm added major cable TV equipment operations.

The company was acquired in a leveraged buyout in 1990 by Forstmann Little & Co., which took it public again in 1992. In 1995 it acquired Next Level Communications, a maker of digital telephone equipment designed to carry voice, video, and data. In 1996, GI bought the the Magnitude MPEG product line from Compression Labs. MPEG is a compression standard for transmitting entertainment and information services over cable, satellite, and telephone networks.

GENERAL INSTRUMENT: THE NUMBERS

NYSE symbol: GIC FYE: December 31	Annual Growth	1990[1]	1991	1992	1993	1994	1995
Sales ($ mil.)	21.6%	916.1	928.8	1,074.7	1,392.5	2,036.3	2,432.0
Net income ($ mil.)	—	(236.6)	(110.7)	(53.0)	90.4	248.5	123.8
Income as % of sales	—	—	—	—	6.5%	12.2%	5.1%
Earnings per share ($)	—	(3.43)	(1.52)	(0.54)	0.74	1.89	0.96
Stock price – high ($)	—	—	—	12.94	30.13	34.63	41.63
Stock price – low ($)	—	—	—	5.75	11.63	21.25	18.25
Stock price – close ($)	22.4%	—	—	12.75	28.25	30.00	23.38
P/E – high	—	—	—	—	41	18	43
P/E – low	—	—	—	—	16	11	19
Dividends per share ($)	—	—	—	0.00	0.00	0.00	0.00
Book value per share ($)	43.2%	—	—	2.48	3.24	5.54	7.28
Employees	10.2%	—	—	9,200	10,100	12,300	12,300

[1] 10-month fiscal year

1995 YEAR-END

Debt ratio: 44.8%
Return on equity: 15.5%
Cash (mil.): $36.4
Current ratio: 1.78
Long-term debt (mil.): $738.6
No. of shares (mil.): 125.8
Dividends
 Yield: —
 Payout: —
Market value (mil.): $2,941.2
R&D as % of sales: 6.1%

QUARTER ENDED 6/30

	1996	1995
Sales ($ millions)	675.2	611.6
Net Income ($ millions)	(58.1)	54.1
Earnings Per Share ($)	(0.45)	0.44
No. of Shares (thou.)	136,730	122,824

6 MONTHS ENDED 6/30

	1996	1995
Sales ($ millions)	1,291	1,220.4
Net Income ($ millions)	(26.9)	111.1
Earnings Per Share ($)	(0.21)	0.90
No. of Shares (thou.)	136,730	122,824

STOCK PRICE HISTORY: High/Low/Close

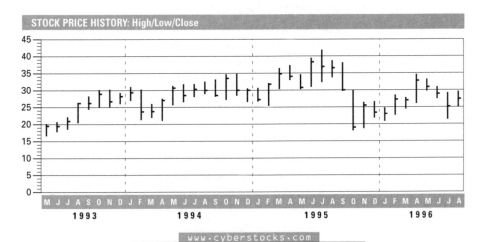

www.cyberstocks.com

- Shifted strategic focus to Internet and intranet markets

- Agent products appear to be best suited for wireless, mobile access applications

- Strong brand recognition

- Equity interests held by major tech companies including Fujitsu, Mitsubishi, Motorola, Apple, AT&T, Sony

- Balance sheet shows $90 million (approximately $3.50 per share) in cash

- Recent strategy switch was caused by failure of heavily hyped, PDA-based strategy

- Faces more competition in Internet agent market than in PDA agent market

- Until PCS systems are deployed, wireless Internet access may remain expensive and slow

- Poor market acceptance of Tabriz product would leave the company with little but cash

- Has sustained heavy losses since inception, predicts losses at least through 1997

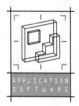

APPLICATION SOFTWARE

General Magic

If General Magic doesn't pull off its next trick, it may find itself doing a disappearing act. The Sunnyvale, California-based company has developed 2 object-oriented software programs, Magic Cap (which combines e-mail, fax, paging, and telephone capabilities) and Telescript (which creates intelligent software "agents" to perform various tasks for computer network users, such as data searching). When major customers Sony (which owns 7% of the firm) and AT&T (6%) abandoned products that use the company's programs, General Magic waved its wand and turned itself into an Internet company (intending to leverage the power of its software online).

Marc Porat (who owns 8% of the company), Andrew Hertzfeld (7%), and William Atkinson worked at Apple (which owns 10%), where Hertzfeld and Atkinson helped develop the Macintosh operating system. They wanted to invent an electronic communication system contained in an instrument the user could take anywhere. In 1990 Apple was intrigued, so it set them up in their own company, General Magic. With backing from several interested giants, including AT&T, Sony, and Motorola (6%) they set to work. Three years and $53 million later they unveiled a prototype, which was skeptically received, and in 1994 there was finally a product. By then, however, Apple had come out with the Newton. Worse, the point-and-click office interface that General Magic envisioned had already appeared in Microsoft's Bob.

In 1994 Sony introduced the Magic Link, and Motorola launched the Envoy (hand-held communicators that used the firm's software). AT&T also

General Magic

GENERAL MAGIC, INC.

HQ: 420 N. Mary Ave.,
Sunnyvale, CA 94086
Phone: 408-774-4000
Fax: 408-774-4010
Web site: www.genmagic.com

OFFICERS

Chairman and CEO:
Marc Porat, age 48, $175,481 pay

President and COO: Robert Kelsch, age 50

VP and General Manager, Worldwide Field Operations Division:
William Keating, age 39, $150,000 pay

VP and General Manager, Magic Cap Division: Steven Schramm, age 36

VP Magic Cap Technologies and Software Wizard: Andrew Hertzfeld, age 42, $135,096

VP Business Affairs and General Counsel:
Michael Stern, $133,019 pay

VP Internet Business Development:
Tony Rutkowski, age 52

VP Human Resources: Stephen Hams

Controller and Acting CFO:
Wendy Olszewski

Auditors: KPMG Peat Marwick LLP

SELECTED PRODUCTS AND SERVICES

Magic Cap (application platform that integrates e-mail, fax, paging, telephone, and other communication methods with a simple user interface)

Presto!Links and Presto!Mail (a mobile Internet platform that integrates calendars, contacts, e-mail, and Web browser on Magic Cap communicators)

SoftModem (software that can perform data and fax modem functions on general-purpose microprocessors independent of an operating system)

Tabriz Agent Tools (software developer tools for creating agent-based applications at Tabriz Web sites)

Telescript (object-oriented software that enables intelligent "agents" to perform various tasks for computer network users, such as carrying messages, seeking information, and executing transactions)

KEY COMPETITORS

Edify
Forte Software
FTP Software
Geoworks
Microsoft
Oracle
Parc Place
Verity

introduced Telescript-based PersonaLink Services. The following year General Magic went public. But customers' product sales languished.

In 1996 Sony and AT&T terminated products that used General Magic software. Later that year General Magic decided to put its remaining $100 million in cash to work transferring its know-how to the Internet. As part of that strategy, the company modified Telescript to allow its agents to automatically search the Internet for goods, services, and other specific information.

GENERAL MAGIC: THE NUMBERS

Nasdaq symbol: GMGC FYE: December 31	Annual Growth	1990	1991	1992	1993	1994	1995
Sales ($ mil.)	—	—	0.0	0.0	0.0	2.5	14.2
Net income ($ mil.)	—	—	(3.6)	(10.1)	(17.4)	(21.5)	(20.6)
Income as % of sales	—	—	—	—	—	—	—
Earnings per share ($)	—	—	—	—	—	—	(0.84)
Stock price – high ($)	—	—	—	—	—	—	32.00
Stock price – low ($)	—	—	—	—	—	—	9.88
Stock price – close ($)	—	—	—	—	—	—	10.63
P/E – high	—	—	—	—	—	—	—
P/E – low	—	—	—	—	—	—	—
Dividends per share ($)	—	—	—	—	—	—	0.00
Book value per share ($)	—	—	—	—	—	—	3.45
Employees	—	—	—	—	—	—	208

1995 YEAR-END

Debt ratio: 2.2%
Return on equity: —
Cash (mil.): $104.7
Current ratio: 13.08
Long-term debt (mil.): $1.2
No. of shares (mil.): 25.8
Dividends
 Yield: —
 Payout: —
Market value (mil.): $274.1
R&D as % of sales: 136.2%

QUARTER ENDED 6/30

	1996	1995
Sales ($ millions)	1.1	1.9
Net Income ($ millions)	(11.6)	(6.5)
Earnings Per Share ($)	(0.45)	(0.26)
No. of Shares (thou.)	26,039	25,043

6 MONTHS ENDED 6/30

	1996	1995
Sales ($ millions)	3.9	6.1
Net Income ($ millions)	(18.7)	(10.1)
Earnings Per Share ($)	(0.72)	(0.43)
No. of Shares (thou.)	26,039	25,043

STOCK PRICE HISTORY: High/Low/Close

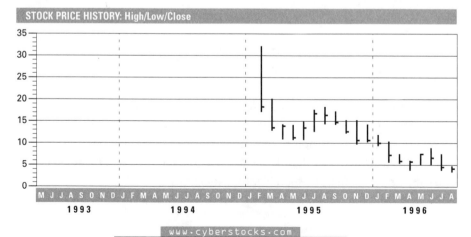

www.cyberstocks.com

NETWORK INFRASTRUCTURE

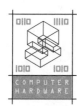

COMPUTER HARDWARE

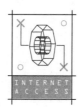

INTERNET ACCESS

Global Village Communication

Global Village has a new Window on the world. The Sunnyvale, California-based company has made its name and fortune supplying fax modems for Macintoshes, produced by now troubled Apple Computer. While the majority of Global Village's sales are still derived from its OneWorld, PowerPoint, and TelePort products (all designed for Apples), CEO Neil Selvin has planted the seeds for an even larger customer base of PC users. Global Village is also expanding its international presence and its stable of technologies through acquisitions and partnerships. Investor Michael O'Neill owns 5% of the company.

Founded in 1989 by chairman Len Lehmann and 2 others, the company took its name from Marshall McLuhan's metaphor of a world made small and interconnected by a vast electronic communications network. In 1992 Global signed a deal with Apple allowing the company to develop software for Apple products. Global brought in Neil Selvin (formerly director of marketing at Apple for PowerBook products) as president and CEO in 1993. Global's strongest market edge is that it is the only maker of integrated fax servers for Macintoshes. Global went public in 1994.

That year Global broke out of its Mac-only mold with the $13.5 million acquisition of SoftNet, a developer of communications software for DOS, Windows, and OS/2 PCs (networked or stand-alone). In 1995 Global released GlobalFax 2.5, with 40 new features. The company also agreed to

- A leading maker of modems for Apple computers

- Efforts to diversify beyond Apple products include:

  * Creation of communications software package for Windows/Windows 95

  * Launch of Global Center plug-and-play Internet connectivity for small businesses

  * Entry into remote access market

  * Licensing of technology for wireless communications services and products

- Heavily dependent on shrinking ranks of Apple computer buyers

- Growth has slowed significantly

- Faces increased price competition in Apple modem market

- Gross margins are declining

- Has become unprofitable

GLOBAL VILLAGE COMMUNICATION, INC.

HQ: 1144 E. Arques Ave.,
Sunnyvale, CA 94086-4602
Phone: 408-523-1000
Fax: 408-523-2407
Web site: www.globalvillag.com

OFFICERS

Chairman: Leonard A. Lehmann, age 41
President and CEO:
Neil Selvin, age 42, $423,629 pay
VP Finance, CFO, and Secretary:
James M. Walker, age 47, $247,337 pay
VP and General Manager, Communications Systems Division:
Charles R. Oppenheimer, age 37, $254,171 pay
VP Operations:
James Brown, age 41, $217,795 pay
VP Sales:
Douglas Dennerline, age 37, $197,083 pay
VP Customer Satisfaction:
Marsha Raulston, age 47
Manager Human Resources: Mary Cravalho
Auditors: KPMG Peat Marwick LLP

SELECTED PRODUCTS AND SERVICES

TelePort Gold II (14,400-bps)
TelePort Platinum (28,800-bps)
PowerPort Mercury (19,200-bps)
Integrated communications software
FaxWorks for Windows
FocalPoint for Windows 3.1 and Windows 95
(data, e-mail, fax, paging, speakerphone, and
voice mail capabilities in one interface)
FaxWorks Pro LAN for OS/2
FaxWorks Pro LAN for Windows NT
OneWorld Combo (network modem, fax, and
ARA 1.0/2.0 for
Ethernet and LocalTalk networks)
ISDN products
GlobalCenter Internet access service
GlobalFax 2.5 software

KEY COMPETITORS

3Com	Cypress	Netscape
America Online	Semiconductor	Prodigy
Apex Data	DATA RACE	PSINet
Apple	Diamond	Shiva
Ascend	Multimedia	Smith Micro
Communications	Matsushita	Symantec
AT&T Corp.	MFS	System
Bay Networks	Communications	Connection
Boca Research	Motorola	U.S. Robotics
Brooktrout	Multi-Tech	Xerox
Technology	Systems	Zoom Telephonics
Cisco Systems	NEC	
CompuServe	NETCOM	

bundle its TelePort Gold internal telecommunications card with Apple's latest Performa PC products.

In 1996 Global Village introduced FocalPoint; hailed by some analysts as the first truly integrated communication software, it includes fax, e-mail, Internet, voice-mail, and paging capabilities. Also that year the company formed a new subsidiary (GlobalCenter) from its Internet services division, and Internet service provider UUNET bought a 20% interest in the the unit.

GLOBAL VILLAGE: THE NUMBERS

Nasdaq symbol: GVIL FYE: March 31	Annual Growth	1991[2]	1992	1993	1994	1995	1996
Sales ($ mil.)	210.6%	0.5	4.2	22.9	46.6	80.0	144.5
Net income ($ mil.)	—	(0.5)	(0.7)	1.5	4.3	(6.2)	8.8
Income as % of sales	—	—	—	6.5%	9.2%	—	6.1%
Earnings per share ($)	—	(0.13)	(0.19)	0.12	0.37	(0.45)	0.49
Stock price – high ($)[1]	—	—	—	—	—	12.50	25.75
Stock price – low ($)[1]	—	—	—	—	—	5.75	8.88
Stock price – close ($)[1]	—	—	—	—	—	9.13	19.38
P/E – high	—	—	—	—	—	—	53
P/E – low	—	—	—	—	—	—	18
Dividends per share ($)	—	—	—	—	—	0.00	0.00
Book value per share ($)	—	—	—	—	—	2.53	2.86
Employees	33.4%	—	—	125	122	225	297

[1] Stock prices are for the prior calendar year. [2] 15-month period ended March 31, 1991.

1996 YEAR-END

Debt ratio: 0.2%
Return on equity: 20.7%
Cash (mil.): $37.7
Current ratio: 2.29
Long-term debt (mil.): $0.0
No. of shares (mil.): 16.7
Dividends
  Yield: —
  Payout: —
Market value (mil.): $324.4
R&D as % of sales: 11.3%

QUARTER ENDED 6/30

	1996	1995
Sales ($ millions)	30.4	27.6
Net Income ($ millions)	(5.1)	2.3
Earnings Per Share ($)	(0.30)	0.14
No. of Shares (thou.)	16,814	15,010

3 MONTHS ENDED 6/30

	1996	1995
Sales ($ millions)	30.4	27.6
Net Income ($ millions)	(5.1)	2.3
Earnings Per Share ($)	(0.30)	0.14
No. of Shares (thou.)	16,814	15,010

STOCK PRICE HISTORY: High/Low/Close

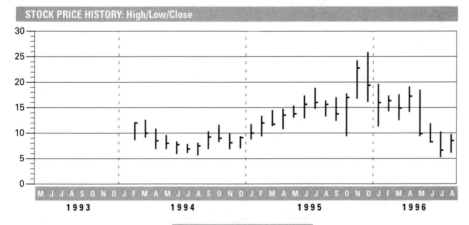

- A leader in neural network application software for client/server environments

- Transaction-based decision products appear well-suited to Internet commerce

- Long-term support contracts represent a substantial proportion of sales

- Rapidly applying its technology to new areas of commerce

- Has formed marketing partnership with Infoseek

- First Data Resources accounted for 15% of 1995 sales

- Flagship product faces new, direct competition from Mastercard in credit card fraud detection software

- P/E over 90 (8/96)

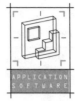

APPLICATION
SOFTWARE

HNC Software

Lost your credit card? Don't worry. HNC Software's products detect debit and credit card fraud. They also manage merchant risk and retail inventories, automate lending decisions and home valuations, and extract information from customer databases. The San Diego-based company develops client/server software that uses neural network technology, a statistical technique that emulates the human brain to recognize patterns in streams of electronic data. By using predictive models based on neural network technology, HNC's software goes beyond gathering information; it comes up with recommendations and actions. The company has focused primarily on financial services organizations, but it is broadening its product lines. It has applied its technology to Internet and intranet applications by creating a search engine that can do sophisticated searches for text and images.

Robert Hecht-Nielsen and Todd Gutschow, both veterans of high-tech company TRW's neurocomputing research and development program, founded Hecht-Nielsen Neurocomputer Corporation in 1986. The company, which changed its name to HNC, Inc., in 1987, offered training in neural network technology, software, and hardware to help developers design and build their own software. HNC then changed its business strategy from the delivery of tools to the development and marketing of intelligent decision-support application software. In 1992 the company formed a unit to develop inventory control products for the retail market. It became HNC Software

HNC SOFTWARE INC.

HQ: 5930 Cornerstone Ct. West,
  San Diego, CA 92121-3728
Phone: 619-546-8877
Fax: 619-452-6524
Web site: www.hncs.com

OFFICERS

President and CEO:
  Robert L. North, age 60, $238,528 pay

President, Text Analysis System:
  Michael A. Thiemann, age 39, $151,139 pay

VP Sales: Lee E. Martin, age 34, $310,745 pay

VP Payment Systems:
  Krishna Gopinathan, age 30, $143,765 pay

VP Finance and Administration, CFO, and Secretary:
  Raymond V. Thomas, age 53

VP Technology Development:
  Todd W. Gutschow, age 35

VP Strategic Business Development:
  Larry A. Spelhaug, age 56

Auditors: Price Waterhouse LLP

SELECTED PRODUCTS AND SERVICES

Selected Software

  Colleague, AREAS (for automating lending decisions)

  DataBase Mining Workstation and Marksman (for enabling neural-network model development)

  Eagle (for managing merchant risk)

  Falcon (for detecting credit/debit card fraud)

  Falcon Sentry (for detecting credit card application fraud)

  ProfitMax (for determining card transaction profitability)

  SkuPLAN (for retail inventory)

	1995 Sales	
	$ mil.	% of total
Software licenses & installation	16.0	63
Contracts & other	9.2	37
Total	**25.2**	**100**

KEY COMPETITORS

BehavHeuristics	MasterCard
Eastman Kodak	Nestor
Fair, Isaac	NeuralTech
Fannie Mae	Neuralware
Freddie Mac	Norwest
HyperLogic	PMI Group
IBM	Policy Management
Manugistics	Visa

in 1994. That year another TRW veteran, Robert North, took over as CEO. The company went public in 1995.

HNC is hoping to triple its market size with new product offerings such as its Eagle merchant profitability system and its Colleague mortgage underwriting decision application. It also is aiming to boost its overseas sales (about 15% of total revenues). In 1996 HNC teamed up with Infoseek, a popular Web research service, to jointly design and market an intelligent advertising and audience management server for the World Wide Web.

HNC SOFTWARE: THE NUMBERS

Nasdaq symbol: HNCS FYE: December 31	Annual Growth	1990	1991	1992	1993	1994	1995
Sales ($ mil.)	43.2%	—	6.0	8.5	10.3	16.5	25.2
Net income ($ mil.)	—	—	(2.6)	0.4	0.9	1.9	4.5
Income as % of sales	—	—	—	4.5%	8.8%	11.7%	17.7%
Earnings per share ($)	—	—	—	—	—	0.16	0.31
Stock price – high ($)	—	—	—	—	—	—	24.50
Stock price – low ($)	—	—	—	—	—	—	9.88
Stock price – close ($)	—	—	—	—	—	—	23.88
P/E – high	—	—	—	—	—	—	79
P/E – low	—	—	—	—	—	—	32
Dividends per share ($)	—	—	—	—	—	—	0.00
Book value per share ($)	—	—	—	—	—	—	3.28
Employees	—	—	—	—	—	152	195

1995 YEAR-END

Debt ratio: 0.0%
Return on equity: 15.2%
Cash (mil.): $34.5
Current ratio: 8.13
Long-term debt (mil.): $0.0
No. of shares (mil.): 14.7
Dividends
  Yield: —
  Payout: —
Market value (mil.): $351.4
R&D as % of sales: 18.3%

QUARTER ENDED 6/30

	1996	1995
Sales ($ millions)	8.7	5.9
Net Income ($ millions)	1.0	0.5
Earnings Per Share ($)	0.06	0.04
No. of Shares (thou.)	16,989	13,470

6 MONTHS ENDED 6/30

	1996	1995
Sales ($ millions)	16.5	11.0
Net Income ($ millions)	1.8	0.9
Earnings Per Share ($)	0.11	0.07
No. of Shares (thou.)	16,989	13,470

STOCK PRICE HISTORY: High/Low/Close

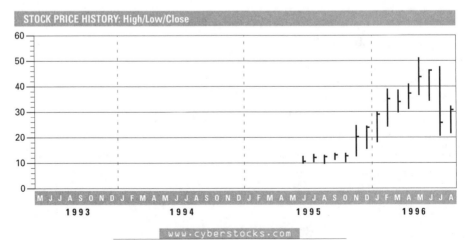

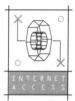 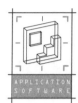 

INTERNET ACCESS   APPLICATION SOFTWARE   CONTENT

IDT Corporation

A godsend for lonely expatriates, IDT lets callers outside the US phone anywhere in the world more cheaply than the major phone companies. IDT's technology allows callers to bypass overseas phone carriers (and high rates) and make international calls routed through its Hackensack, New Jersey headquarters. It provides the service to more than 11,000 customers in 120 countries. Fast-growing IDT also provides Internet access to more than 70,000 subscribers in the US and to 103 business clients in the US, France, Italy, and South Korea.

As a high school student, company founder Howard Jonas sold hot dogs outside a Bronx methadone clinic. He began a publishing business in 1978, beginning with trade magazine *Auto and Flat Glass Journal*. Spurred by an $8,000 phone bill he had run up while trying to set up a sales office in Israel, Jonas bought $300 worth of components and rigged up an automatic dialing apparatus that slashed the cost of calls by 75%. Using this technology, in 1990 Jonas established International Discount Telecommunications Corp. and moved into the international call reorigination business to take advantage of the cheaper rates available in the US telephone markets. International Discount Telecommunications began selling the service in 1991 and quickly built up a European distributor network of about 150 corporations, such as National Semiconductor and PepsiCo. International aid agency The World Bank signed on in 1992, and by 1993 the company had more than 1,000 customers in some 60 countries.

The company began providing Internet access to businesses and individuals in 1994. The following year, Jonas launched a new telephone system that

- International call-back telephone service is growing rapidly
- Demand appears strong for new, Internet-based, PC-to-handset telephone service
- Genie acquisition adds content, services to IDT's Internet offerings
- Can bill customers for services through debit card system
- New access deal with PSINet could lower costs
- Revenues for the 9 months ended 4/30/96 were up 396%

- Still unprofitable
- Recently acquired Genie online service never took off
- New www.genie.com premium service seeks to compete with America Online, CompuServe
- Losses exceed revenues in Internet operations

IDT CORPORATION

HQ: 294 State St., Hackensack, NJ 07601
Phone: 201-928-1000
Fax: 201-928-1057
Web site: www.idt.net

OFFICERS

Chairman, President, and CEO:
Howard S. Jonas, age 39

COO: Howard S. Balter, age 34

CFO: Stephen R. Brown, age 39

Chief Information Officer:
Kenneth Scharf, age 45

Chief Technical Officer: Eric L. Raab, age 35

VP: Mark E. Knoller, age 35

Secretary: Joyce J. Mason, age 36

Human Resources Director:
Howard Millendorf

Auditors: Ernst & Young LLP

SELECTED PRODUCTS AND SERVICES

Internet
International dedicated Internet access
US dedicated Internet access
US dial-up Internet access
Value-added Internet services

Internet Telephony
Net2Phone (PC-to-telephone communications via the Internet)

Telecommunications
Domestic long-distance resale
Global carrier rate arbitrage
International long distance telephone service, via call-back

KEY COMPETITORS

America Online	MCI
AT&T	MFS Communications
BBN	Microsoft
BT	MindSpring
CompuServe	NETCOM
EarthLink	PSINet
IBM	VocalTec
International Wireless	

cuts the cost of international calls by using a PC to digitize speech and then transmit it to phone networks in the US via the Internet. Buoyed by the growing number of subscribers, Jonas took the company public in 1996 and renamed it IDT Corp. (He owns 53% of the company.) That year, in a move that will double the size of its business, IDT agreed to buy closely held Econophone, a provider of long-distance phone service in the UK with operations in the US. Later that year, IDT agreed to acquire the Genie online service.

IDT: THE NUMBERS

Nasdaq symbol: IDTC FYE: July 31	Annual Growth	1990	1991	1992	1993	1994	1995
Sales ($ mil.)	239.1%	—	—	0.3	1.7	3.2	11.7
Net income ($ mil.)	—	—	—	(0.3)	0.3	(0.3)	(2.1)
Income as % of sales	—	—	—	—	18.0%	—	—
Employees	—	—	—	—	—	—	337

1995 YEAR-END

Debt ratio: 0.5%
Return on equity: —
Cash (mil.): $0.2
Current ratio: 0.73
Long-term debt (mil.): $0.0
No. of shares (mil.): —
Dividends
  Yield: —
  Payout: —
Market value (mil.): —

QUARTER ENDED 4/30

	1996	1995
Sales ($ millions)	18.2	3.3
Net Income ($ millions)	(4.4)	(0.3)
Earnings Per Share ($)	(0.24)	(0.02)
No. of Shares (thou.)	20,841	15,666

9 MONTHS ENDED 4/30

	1996	1995
Sales ($ millions)	34.5	7.0
Net Income ($ millions)	(11.0)	(1.3)
Earnings Per Share ($)	(0.64)	(0.08)
No. of Shares (thou.)	20,841	15,666

STOCK PRICE HISTORY: High/Low/Close

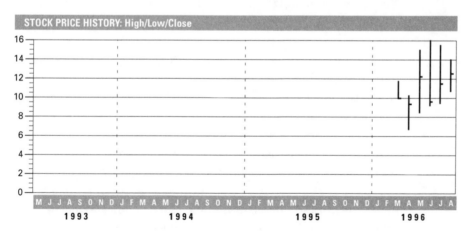

- A growing Internet keeps expanding the market for customized business news retrieval services

- Has added advertising to revenue stream

- Netscape has incorporated NewsPage Direct e-mail service into its Navigator Web browser

- Acquisition of FreeLoader adds off-line browsing service, agent technology

- Has strategic relationship with Microsoft

- Market for personalized information retrieval is becoming more competitive

- Still somewhat dependent on Lotus Notes as a distribution channel

- Advertising-based services may be cannibalizing lucrative subscription services

- Heavy turnover in corporate offices

- Remains unprofitable, FreeLoader acquisition will not help

SPECIALIZED SERVICES

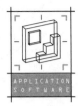

APPLICATION SOFTWARE

Individual, Inc.

The Internet: a land of measureless opportunity waiting to be tapped, or a land mine waiting to explode? Joseph (Yosi) Amram, founder of Individual, and company directors have found it to be a little of both. The Burlington, Massachusetts-based company is the leading provider of daily news personalized to the interests of its clients and delivered by fax, e-mail, or other electronic means. While Amram dreamed of unlocking the Internet's potential, particularly through acquisitions, directors wanted to start making money (the company has yet to make a profit, even though sales have lately grown around 100% per year). The dream went bust when the company ousted Amram and began seeking a new CEO.

Individual gathers some 20,000 business stories a day from more than 600 sources ranging from trade publications to newspapers. A computer filters articles according to the individual or corporate subscriber's preferences, and they arrive at the subscriber's computer or fax machine the next morning. Products include the company's flagship First! (for corporations), HeadsUp (for individuals), Physician's NewScan (about health care), and BookWire (about the book industry).

Amram owns 13% of the company; Microsoft and Knight-Ridder Information, which have partnership arrangements with Individual, own 9% and 8%, respectively; and several investment firms own another 41%. Founded in 1989, Individual had its first office in Amram's apartment; its 2nd was an examining room subleased from a doctor. Born and reared in Israel, Amram earned 2 degrees from MIT and an MBA from Harvard on coming to the US. The company got its name from the fact that individual

INDIVIDUAL, INC.
HQ: 8 New England Executive Park West,
Burlington, MA 01803
Phone: 617-273-6000
Fax: 617-273-6060
Web site: www.individual.com

OFFICERS

Chairman: Andy Devereaux
EVP, CFO, and Treasurer:
Bruce D. Glabe, age 47, $137,850 pay
SVP and General Manager Enterprise Services:
Annette E. Lissauer, age 50, $112,763 pay
SVP and General Manager Internet and Single-User Services:
Janesse T. Bruce, age 39
VP Marketing:
Richard C. Vancil, age 35, $111,398 pay
VP Business Development and Secretary:
John S. Zahner, age 44, $108,101 pay
VP Editorial and Operations:
Majed G. Tomeh, age 36
VP Engineering: Jacques Bouvard, age 60
VP Finance: Robert L. Lentz, age 45
Auditors: Coopers & Lybrand L.L.P.

SELECTED PRODUCTS AND SERVICES

Alert (news service on e-mail)
BookWire (Internet site on books and book industry for individual users)
First! (news service for corporations)
First! Intranet (enterprise-wide news service via intranet)
FreeLoader (off-line Internet delivery service)
HeadsUp (news service for individual users)
iNews (business-oriented news service for individual users)
NewsPage (news site on the Internet for individual users)
NewsPage Direct (news service to Microsoft Network [MSN] subscribers)
Personal NewsPage Direct (news service to NETCOM subscribers)
Physician's NewScan (health care industry news service for individual users)

KEY COMPETITORS

America Online	Excite	Open Text
ClariNet	ForeFront	Pearson
CompuServe	Gannett	Prodigy
Data Broadcasting	Infoseek	Reed Elsevier
	Knight-Ridder	Reuters
DEC	Lycos	Thomson
Desktop Data	M.A.I.D.	Yahoo!
Dow Jones	Mobile Media	

users, even in a corporate setting, select the kinds of stories they want to receive. Over the years Individual had developed partnerships with such companies as Apple, Lotus, Motorola, and Prodigy, but its biggest coup was the 1996 deal to make its e-mail news available on the one-million-plus-subscriber Microsoft Network (MSN). In mid-1996 Amram was pushed out of the firm in a disagreement over the company's expansion strategy.

INDIVIDUAL: THE NUMBERS

Nasdaq symbol: INDV FYE: December 31	Annual Growth	1990	1991	1992	1993	1994	1995
Sales ($ mil.)	113.8%	—	0.8	1.9	4.1	9.1	16.7
Net income ($ mil.)	—	—	(1.6)	(1.7)	(3.0)	(4.3)	(6.4)
Income as % of sales	—	—	—	—	—	—	—
Employees	—	—	—	—	—	—	157

1995 YEAR-END

Debt ratio: 100.0%
Return on equity: —
Cash (mil.): $17.5
Current ratio: 1.73
Long-term debt (mil.): $11.0
No. of shares (mil.): —
Dividends
  Yield: —
  Payout: —
Market value (mil.): —
R&D as % of sales: 15.5%

QUARTER ENDED 6/30

	1996	1995
Sales ($ millions)	5.6	4.1
Net Income ($ millions)	(38.3)	(1.4)
Earnings Per Share ($)	(3.09)	(0.15)
No. of Shares (thou.)	12,424	9,495

6 MONTHS ENDED 6/30

	1996	1995
Sales ($ millions)	10.7	7.6
Net Income ($ millions)	(40.8)	(3.0)
Earnings Per Share ($)	(3.67)	(0.32)
No. of Shares (thou.)	12,424	9,495

STOCK PRICE HISTORY: High/Low/Close

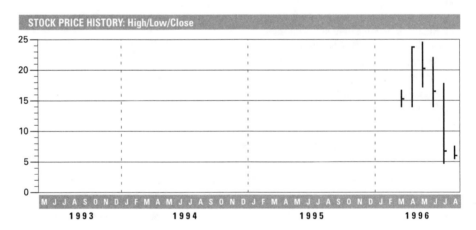

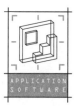
APPLICATION
SOFTWARE

SPECIALIZED
SERVICES

Infonautics

Infonautics helps information seekers (infonauts) explore easy-to-use and affordable reference services on the Internet and online services. Wayne, Pennsylvania-based Infonautics operates Homework Helper (the world's most extensive online library for kids), which accesses newspapers, nearly 800 magazines, 10 news wires, reference books, maps, photographs, major works of literature and art, and the Electric Library, an online reference library for students of all ages.

The company was spun off in 1992 from Telebase Systems, an online database search company set up in 1984, to develop Homework Helper, a subscription-based educational online service. The founders of Infonautics were Marvin Weinberger, a cofounder of Telebase and the project leader of Homework Helper, former Telebase chairman Israel Melman, and Joshua Kopelman, who worked with Weinberger in developing Homework Helper. Telebase retained financial interests in and cross-licensing agreements with Infonautics following the spinoff.

In 1994 Infonautics introduced the Electronic Printing Press, a proprietary system for data creation, archiving, customer access, billing, and other operations leased to publishers to allow them to create, operate, and market their online information services. The next year Homework Helper was launched exclusively on Prodigy, accessible to consumers for a fee.

The company signed up software developer Quarterdeck Corp. in 1995 to sell Homework Helper both in the US and internationally. The

- Focused on home and institutional education markets
- Forming direct sales organization to sell to schools and libraries
- Charges relatively low prices for search and retrieval
- Pledged to give 5% of gross Internet revenue to needy schools
- Balance sheet shows $4 per share in cash

- Extremely competitive market
- Prodigy is rapidly fading, hurting prospects for Homework Helper
- Pledged to give 5% of gross Internet revenue to needy schools
- Losses continue to mount

INFONAUTICS, INC.
HQ: 900 W. Valley Rd., Ste. 1000,
Wayne, PA 19087-1830
Phone: 610-971-8840
Fax: 610-971-8859
Web site: www.infonautics.com

OFFICERS
Chairman and CEO:
Marvin I. Weinberger, age 41, $133,750 pay
President and COO:
David Van Riper "Van" Morris, age 41
EVP and Secretary:
Joshua M. Kopelman, age 25
VP Engineering:
James T. Beattie, age 47, $126,667 pay
VP Finance, Administration, and CFO:
Ronald A. Berg, age 39
Corporate Communications Manager (HR):
Robert Palmer
Auditors: Coopers & Lybrand L.L.P.

SELECTED PRODUCTS AND SERVICES
Electric Library (research vehicle with access to 150 full-text newspapers, nearly 800 full-text magazines, 10 news wires, reference books, maps, photographs, and major works of literature and art)

Electronic Printing Press (proprietary system for data creation, archiving, customer access, billing, and other operations leased to publishers to allow them to create, operate, and market their online information services)

E.P.I.C. The Infonautics Electric Publishing Innovation Campaign (grant program to recognize and promote excellence in electronic publishing)

Homework Helper (online library for kids)

KEY COMPETITORS

America Online	Infoseek	Schuster
CompuServe	Lycos	Thomson Corp.
DEC	Open Text	Verity
Encyclopaedia	Primark	Wired Ventures
Britannica	Reed Elsevier	Wolff New
Grolier	Scholastic	Media
Individual	Simon &	Yahoo!

Electric Library was placed on the World Wide Web and the Microsoft Network in 1996. Although most of the company's revenues have been generated by its consumer products, Infonautics's long-term strategy is to capture a leading market share in the school, library, and academic institution online markets as well. The company boosted its Electric Library resources in 1996 when it signed agreements with several top publishers, including *U.S. News & World Report* and *the Washington Times National Weekly Edition*. That year the company launched E.P.I.C., a $1 million program that will provide publishers, individual authors, and photographers the means to digitize and prepare their works for the Internet. Infonautics went public in 1996. Weinberger owns almost 19% of the company.

INFONAUTICS: THE NUMBERS

Nasdaq symbol: INFO FYE: December 31	Annual Growth	1990	1991	1992	1993	1994	1995
Sales ($ mil.)	—	—	—	—	0.0	0.0	0.4
Net income ($ mil.)	—	—	—	—	(0.6)	(3.7)	(7.5)
Income as % of sales	—	—	—	—	—	—	—
Employees	—	—	—	—	—	—	67

1995 YEAR-END

Debt ratio: 100.0%
Return on equity: —
Cash (mil.): $1.0
Current ratio: 0.49
Long-term debt (mil.): $0.1
No. of shares (mil.): —
Dividends
  Yield: —
  Payout: —
Market value (mil.): —

QUARTER ENDED 6/30

	1996	1995
Sales ($ millions)	0.4	0.1
Net Income ($ millions)	(2.6)	(1.8)
Earnings Per Share ($)	(0.31)	(0.31)
No. of Shares (thou.)	6,036	6,036

6 MONTHS ENDED 6/30

	1996	1995
Sales ($ millions)	0.6	0.2
Net Income ($ millions)	(5.6)	(3.6)
Earnings Per Share ($)	(0.78)	(0.62)
No. of Shares (thou.)	6,036	6,036

STOCK PRICE HISTORY: High/Low/Close

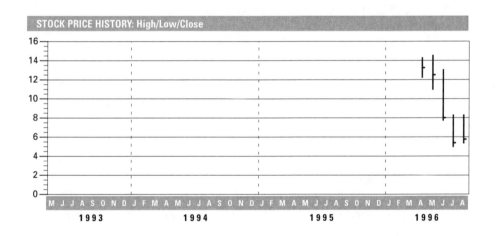

- Pure play in the rapidly growing Internet security market

- Strong in remote-access (dial-in) security

- New alliance pairs CyberGuard's firewall with IRE's Internet security product

- Impressive client list includes 7 of 10 largest US banks, US Treasury, FBI

- Called with MCI to market security solutions to banks and governments

- Engaged in rapid international expansion

- R&D and production start-up expenses led to a 1st quarter 1996 loss

- The US severely restricts exports of encryption products

- MCI accounted for 88% of IRE backlog at the end of the 1st quarter

- Sells for 4-to-5 times estimated 1996 revenue (as of 8/96)

NETWORK
INFRASTRUCTURE

Information Resource

Playing with secret codes straight out of a James Bond movie is big business for Baltimore, Maryland-based Information Resource Engineering (IRE). The company manufactures computer security systems that protect network data by using encryption technology (scrambling or coding systems that use mathematical algorithms). Its products are used by the US Department of the Treasury, the Secret Service, and the FBI. The company also sells products to 7 of the 10 largest US banks, including J.P. Morgan and Citibank, and to telecommunications giants MCI and AT&T. President and CEO Anthony Caputo owns about 11% of the company.

IRE, originally named Industrial Resource Engineering, was founded in 1983 by former National Security Agency engineers Douglas Kozlay and Alan Hastings. Interested in their idea to take the spy game mainstream, Caputo invested in the company in 1986 and became CEO in 1987. Caputo took the company out of the shadows and masterminded its initial public offering in 1989.

The company was one of the first to offer products for securing dial-up and packet-switched networks and in 1994 introduced the first portable secure modem for users on the go. In 1995 the company made a deal (worth more than $10 million) with MCI to provide SafeNet, IRE's Internet security

**INFORMATION RESOURCE
ENGINEERING INC.**
HQ: 8029 Corporate Dr.,
　　Baltimore, MD 21236
Phone: 410-931-7500
Fax: 410-931-7524
Web site: www.ire.com

OFFICERS

Chairman, President, and CEO:
　Anthony A. Caputo, age 54, $285,486 pay
SVP: Jill Leukhardt, age 39, $170,026 pay
SVP: Charles D. Brown, age 37, $129,355 pay
**VP Finance and Administration, Secretary,
and Treasurer (HR):**
　David A. Skalitzky, age 60
Principal Engineer: Douglas E. Kozlay, age 56
Auditors: KPMG Peat Marwick LLP

SELECTED PRODUCTS AND SERVICES

enterprISDN (hardware and software to provide
　communications over ISDN networks)
GRETACODER Link Encryptors (protection
　systems for synchronous or asynchronous
　communications)
Link Security Systems (protection systems for
　synchronous or asynchronous communications)
SafeNet (Internet information protection)
Secure Dial Access Systems (security systems
　for remote users accessing host computers)
Secure Modems (portable modem with internal
　security features)
X.25 Security Systems (networks that use
　encryption technology)

KEY COMPETITORS

America Online	Netscape	Secure
Ascend	Network	Security
AXENT	Systems	Dynamics
Check Point	Open Market	Trusted
Software	Rainbow	Information
Cylink	Technology	Virtual Open

system, which includes a firewall (for screening data at access points), a portable security modem, and a central security management system. In 1996 the company teamed up with Sun Microsystems to equip IRE's pocket modems with Sun's Internet security firewall to protect communications between remote users and host computers.

IRE would like to expand into a broader market as companies increase their use of electronic commerce (such as purchasing goods over the Internet). The company signed an agreement in 1996 with firewall company CyberGuard to develop security products for Internet business communications.

IRE: THE NUMBERS

Nasdaq symbol: IREG FYE: December 31	Annual Growth	1990	1991	1992	1993	1994	1995
Sales ($ mil.)	44.2%	1.3	2.1	3.1	2.6	3.4	8.1
Net income ($ mil.)	—	(0.3)	0.4	0.7	(0.1)	(0.8)	(0.8)
Income as % of sales	—	—	19.6%	21.9%	—	—	—
Earnings per share ($)	—	(0.13)	0.17	0.27	(0.02)	(0.25)	(0.20)
Stock price – high ($)	—	—	—	4.75	6.63	6.63	29.00
Stock price – low ($)	—	—	—	4.19	3.25	3.63	5.88
Stock price – close ($)	74.1%	—	—	4.69	5.50	6.06	24.75
P/E – high	—	—	—	18	—	—	—
P/E – low	—	—	—	16	—	—	—
Dividends per share ($)	—	—	—	0.00	0.00	0.00	0.00
Book value per share ($)	3.3%	—	—	1.76	1.35	1.49	1.94
Employees	38.0%	18	22	29	33	47	90

1995 YEAR-END

Debt ratio: 33.7%
Return on equity: —
Cash (mil.): $2.7
Current ratio: 1.30
Long-term debt (mil.): $0.0
No. of shares (mil.): 4.2
Dividends
  Yield: —
  Payout: —
Market value (mil.): $105.1

QUARTER ENDED 6/30

	1996	1995
Sales ($ millions)	5.1	1.1
Net Income ($ millions)	(0.2)	(0.4)
Earnings Per Share ($)	(0.04)	(0.11)
No. of Shares (thou.)	5,417	3,701

6 MONTHS ENDED 6/30

	1996	1995
Sales ($ millions)	8.4	2.7
Net Income ($ millions)	(1.1)	(0.3)
Earnings Per Share ($)	(0.22)	(0.11)
No. of Shares (thou.)	5,417	3,701

STOCK PRICE HISTORY: High/Low/Close

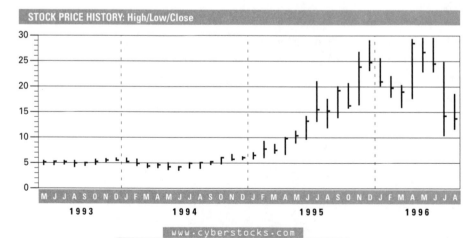

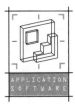

Informix
Corporation

- Positioned as technological leader, moving up-market

- Universal server is extremely well-suited to Internet/intranet application development

- Key partnerships with Netscape, Hewlett-Packard

- SAP alliance extends business into packaged applications

- Rival Sybase is in trouble

Informix puts information at your fingertips. The Menlo Park, California-based company is one of the largest database management software companies in the US. It develops open systems software that can handle vast amounts of information and can be accessed from a variety of computer systems. It also produces software that allows for easy data transfer from personal computers to mainframes and makes development tools for client/server production applications.

Informix was founded in 1980 by Roger Sippl, who had been diverted from the study of medicine by a bout with Hodgkin's disease. After a stint with Cromenco, a microcomputer maker, Sippl scraped up enough capital to start his own company. It grew quickly and went public in 1986. In 1988 Informix introduced OnLine Dynamic Server, the parallel database server that is its core product. That year it merged with Innovative Software, of Kansas City, but instead of lower costs and more business, Informix wound up with duplicated operations and an inflated organization. Realizing that Informix had outgrown his ability to run it, Sippl brought in Phillip White as CEO in 1989. White turned the organization around. In 1992 Sippl, an entrepreneur at heart, stepped down as chairman and went on to found Visigenic Software.

Informix expanded its global presence in 1994 when it acquired distributors NextWare (Malaysia) and Garmhausen and Partners (Germany). The company formed alliances with MicroStrategy, Spider Technologies, and Sun

- Must contend with Microsoft at low end Oracle, IBM, others at high end of market

- Market is becoming increasingly price competitive

- Turnover in executive offices

- Flat earnings in 1st half of 1996

Informix

INFORMIX CORPORATION
HQ: 4100 Bohannon Dr.,
 Menlo Park, CA 94025
Phone: 415-926-6300
Fax: 415-926-6564
Web site: www.informix.com

OFFICERS

Chairman, President, and CEO:
 Phillip E. White, age 53, $821,667 pay

**SVP Product Management and
Development:**
 Mike Saranga, age 58, $397,333 pay

SVP Finance and CFO:
 Howard H. Graham, age 48, $444,333 pay

SVP International:
 D. Kenneth Coulter, age 51, $421,202 pay

SVP Japan Operations:
 Edwin C. Winder, age 46, $352,392 pay

**VP Legal and Corporate Services, General
Counsel, and Secretary:**
 David H. Stanley, age 49

VP Human Resources: Ira H. Dorf, age 55
Auditors: Ernst & Young LLP

SELECTED PRODUCTS AND SERVICES

Connectivity products (INFORMIX-Gateway,
 INFORMIX-STAR)

Database application development products
 (INFORMIX-NewEra, INFORMIX-4GL)

Object-relational products (Universal Server,
 DataBlade)

	1995 Sales	
	$ mil.	% of total
License fees	536.9	76
Services	173.1	24
Total	**709.0**	**100**

KEY COMPETITORS

Computer Associates
Dynasty Technology
Forte Software
Gupta
IBM
Microsoft
Object Design
Oracle
PLATINUM technology
Progress Software
Red Brick
Software AG
Spyglass
Sybase

Microsystems in 1995. Also that year Informix purchased Stanford Technology Group to take advantage of the burgeoning market for data warehouse products, which organize and save data from multiple sources. The company acquired Illustra Information Technologies for about $350 million in 1996 in its bid to take the lead in the fast growing market for multimedia database products for use on the Internet.

INFORMIX: THE NUMBERS

Nasdaq symbol: IFMX FYE: December 31	Annual Growth	1990	1991	1992	1993	1994	1995
Sales ($ mil.)	37.2%	146.1	179.8	283.6	352.9	468.7	709.0
Net income ($ mil.)	—	(23.1)	12.2	47.8	56.1	66.2	105.3
Income as % of sales	—	—	6.8%	16.9%	15.9%	14.1%	14.9%
Earnings per share ($)	—	(0.23)	0.11	0.38	0.42	0.49	0.76
Stock prices – high ($)	—	2.19	1.98	9.44	13.63	16.06	34.38
Stock prices – low ($)	—	0.44	0.33	1.66	6.69	7.13	14.56
Stock prices – close ($)	121.7%	0.56	1.72	9.06	10.63	16.06	30.00
P/E – high	—	—	19	25	33	33	45
P/E – low	—	—	3	4	16	15	19
Dividends per share ($)	—	0.00	0.00	0.00	0.00	0.00	0.00
Book value per share ($)	54.1%	0.36	0.48	1.06	1.60	2.10	3.13
Employees	21.0%	1,242	1,121	1,445	1,718	2,212	3,219

1995 YEAR-END

Debt ratio: 0.3%
Return on equity: 30.2%
Cash (mil.): $252.2
Current ratio: 2.09
Long-term debt (mil.): $0.8
No. of shares (mil.): 135.3
Dividends
    Yield: —
    Payout: —
Market value (mil.): $4,059.9
R&D as % of sales: 11.2%

QUARTER ENDED 6/30

	1996	1995
Sales ($ millions)	226.3	163.6
Net Income ($ millions)	21.6	22.1
Earnings Per Share ($)	0.14	0.16
No. of Shares (thou.)	155,046	133,640

6 MONTHS ENDED 6/30

	1996	1995
Sales ($ millions)	430.3	311.4
Net Income ($ millions)	37.5	41.2
Earnings Per Share ($)	0.24	0.30
No. of Shares (thou.)	155,046	133,640

STOCK PRICE HISTORY: High/Low/Close

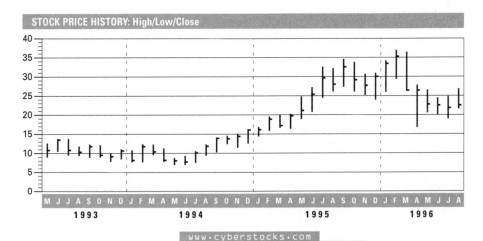

- Pay-by-the-piece business model is appealing to content providers

- New strategy embaces the Internet and intranets

- Formed marketing partnerships with Reed Elsevier, 3M

- Has very few customers

- Has never been profitable

- Faces stiff competition from many other online security and transaction techniques

- Sales plunged by more than 50% in the first 9 months of fiscal 1996

- Accountants issued "going concern" warning in fiscal 1995 audit report

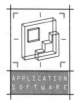

APPLICATION SOFTWARE

Infosafe Systems, Inc.

Infosafe's vending machines are full of information, not candy bars. Headquartered in New York City, the company makes the Design Palette pay-per-use CD-ROM library system, which contains $1.2 million worth of graphic design content, including artwork, photographs, and typefaces. The company provides the systems (which have 40 or more CD-ROMs and which are connected to users' PCs) free of charge and bills only for the content that the customer decides to use. Advertising agencies, corporate communications departments, graphic designers, and publishers make up the company's primary market. Infosafe also provides the systems to companies that want to provide pay-per-use access to their own databases. So far, R&D and marketing spending has outpaced sales by more than 300%. CEO Thomas Lipscomb owns about 41% of the company, and CFO Alan Alpern owns about 10%.

A veteran of the publishing industry and cofounder of data security innovator Wave Systems, Lipscomb teamed with computer scientist and brain researcher Robert Nagel to start Infosafe in 1991. The company began developing a system to provide digital information, while keeping track of the content used, without going through a commercial online service. Initial customers included the American Trucking Association, which

INFOSAFE SYSTEMS, INC.

HQ: 342 Madison Ave., Ste. 622,
New York, NY 10173
Phone: 212-867-7200
Fax: 212-867-7227
Web site: www.infosafe.com

OFFICERS

President and CEO:
Thomas H. Lipscomb, age 57, $151,749 pay

CFO: Alan Alpern, age 68, $101,747 pay
EVP Technology: Robert H. Nagel
EVP Marketing: Charlton H. Calhoun III
Controller and Secretary: Patrick Brosnan
Manager Human Resources: Alistair Wier
Auditors: Richard A. Eisner & Company, LLP

SELECTED PRODUCTS AND SERVICES

Clearinghouse systems (processes electronic transactions)

Design Palette (graphic arts metering system)

Electronic tracking systems (processes data interchange and document management)

Electronic vending machines (digital content system)

Internal security and information management systems

KEY COMPETITORS

IBM
Microsoft
Netscape
Reed Elsevier
Thomson Corp.
Wave Systems

wanted one of the company's systems to sell training and regulatory information to its members, and International Typeface Corporation, which used the system to license its fonts.

In 1995 the company went public. That year Infosafe received a patent for its digital information monitoring and retrieval system. Also in 1995 the firm introduced the Design Palette desktop system, which contained more than 30,000 separately priced graphic arts products. In 1996 the company expanded the offerings included in the Design Palette and announced plans to sell its products over the Internet. Infosafe has also announced plans to use its technology to move into Internet transaction security.

INFOSAFE: THE NUMBERS

Nasdaq symbol (SC): ISFEA FYE: July 31	Annual Growth	1990	1991	1992	1993	1994	1995
Sales ($ mil.)	—	—	—	—	0.0	0.4	0.1
Net income ($ mil.)	—	—	—	—	(1.1)	(0.8)	(2.6)
Income as % of sales	—	—	—	—	—	—	—
Earnings per share ($)	—	—	—	—	(0.93)	(0.54)	(1.15)
Stock price – high ($)	—	—	—	—	—	—	8.50
Stock price – low ($)	—	—	—	—	—	—	5.00
Stock price – close ($)	—	—	—	—	—	—	6.75
P/E – high	—	—	—	—	—	—	—
P/E – low	—	—	—	—	—	—	—
Dividends per share ($)	—	—	—	—	—	—	0.00
Book value per share ($)	—	—	—	—	—	—	1.48
Employees	—	—	—	—	—	—	17

1995 YEAR-END

Debt ratio: 5.2%
Return on equity: —
Cash (mil.): $3.9
Current ratio: 5.21
Long-term debt (mil.): $0.1
No. of shares (mil.): 3.1
Dividends
  Yield: —
  Payout: —
Market value: $21.2
R&D as % of sales: 382.2%

QUARTER ENDED 4/30

	1996	1995
Sales ($ millions)	0.0	0.1
Net Income ($ millions)	(1.3)	(0.7)
Earnings Per Share ($)	(0.38)	(0.25)
No. of Shares (thou.)	6,899	5,116

9 MONTHS ENDED 4/30

	1996	1995
Sales ($ millions)	0.1	0.1
Net Income ($ millions)	(2.7)	(1.9)
Earnings Per Share ($)	(0.80)	(0.94)
No. of Shares (thou.)	6,899	5,116

STOCK PRICE HISTORY: High/Low/Close

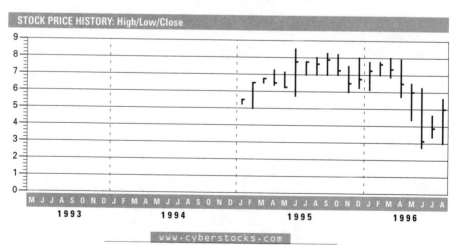

www·cyberstocks·com

228 • Cyberstocks: An Investor's Guide to Internet Companies

Infoseek Corporation

Want to ride the infowave? Try power-surfing with Infoseek's Internet search service. The Santa Clara, California-based company's Infoseek Guide is a powerful indexing and text-retrieval service linked to more than one million Web pages as well as commercial databases, business news services, computer publications, newspapers, and Usenet groups. Its prominent position as part of Netscape's Web browser site made Infoseek's search engine one of the most frequently used on the Web. It has also been rated one of the most effective. Infoseek went public in June 1996; its IPO valued the company at over $270 million. After the offering, chairman Steve Kirsch owned 24% of the company and venture capital firms Menlo Ventures and Battery Ventures owned 19% and 10%, respectively.

The Infoseek Search proprietary search engine is based on natural language, which allows users to make queries in plain English using key words and phrases. Some Infoseek services are subscription based, but the company is working to expand its free (advertiser-sponsored) services. It has signed up more than 100 advertisers, including Microsoft, IBM, Nissan, and Saturn. Among Infoseek's content providers are Business Wire, Information Access, InfoWorld Publishing, and Hoover's, Inc. (publisher of this book).

The company was founded in 1993 by Steven Kirsch, a high-tech entrepreneur who had started Mouse Systems (1982), developer of an optical mouse (which uses a laser instead of the traditional trackball), and Frame Technology (1986), a publishing software company acquired in 1995 by

- Vying with Yahoo! for most advertising revenue from a search site

- Has a large and effective advertising sales force

- Exclusive HNC neural network software deal will enable

  * automated directory maintenance (lower costs)

  * targeting of advertising at individual users (higher ad rates)

- After loss of preferred position on Netscape browser, traffic has declined by 50%

- Relatively low technical barriers to entry into market

- Unproven advertising-based business model

- Browser companies can influence traffic flow or compete

- 10% of 2nd quarter 1996 sales were from barter deals

- Market cap of $160 million (8/96) vs. trailing 12 months sales of $6 million

INFOSEEK CORPORATION

HQ: 2620 Augustine Dr., Ste. 250,
Santa Clara, CA 95054
Phone: 408-567-2700
Fax: 408-986-1889
Web site: www.infoseek.com

OFFICERS

Chairman:
Steven T. Kirsch, age 39, $82,500 pay
President and CEO:
Robert E. L. "Robin" Johnson III, age 38
EVP Finance and CFO:
Leonard J. LeBlanc, age 55
VP Administration and Finance (HR):
Victoria Blakeslee
Auditors: Ernst & Young LLP

SELECTED PRODUCTS AND SERVICES

Infoseek Guide (free Internet search service)

Infoseek Net Search (free search service with access to 30 commercial information databases, 13,000 Usenet newsgroups, and more than 100 computer publications)

Infoseek Professional (subscription-based access to business, computer, and medical information)

Personal Newswire (news service that lets subscribers track specific topics)

KEY COMPETITORS

America Online	Individual
CompuServe	Infonautics
DataWare	Lycos
DEC	Open Text
Excalibur	Wired Ventures
Excite	Wolff New Media
Fulcrum Technologies	Yahoo!

Adobe Systems. The service went online in February 1995 and debuted its Personal Newswire service that summer. In mid-1995 Infoseek raised $6 million in venture financing from Menlo Park, California-based Menlo Ventures and Boston-based Battery Ventures. That August Microsoft licensed the company's Net Search service for the Microsoft Network. Robin Johnson, former SVP of corporate development at Time, Inc., was hired as CEO in late 1995 to head a team of communications and high-tech industry veterans.

In April 1996 Infoseek sold a 5% stake to NYNEX, which plans to incorporate Infoseek Guide into its new online shopping directory, BigYellow. Until it began sharing its preferred position with 4 other search services, the company had been receiving more than 7 million requests for information a day. After the change, information request volume dropped to approximately 3.5 million per day. Johnson has projected 1996 revenues at over $20 million, 95% of it from advertising.

INFOSEEK: THE NUMBERS

Nasdaq symbol: SEEK FYE: December 31	Annual Growth	1990	1991	1992	1993	1994	1995
Sales ($ mil.)	—	—	—	—	—	0.0	1.0
Net income ($ mil.)	—	—	—	—	—	(1.5)	(3.1)
Income as % of sales	—	—	—	—	—	—	—
Employees	—	—	—	—	—	11	54

1995 YEAR-END

Debt ratio: 33.4%
Return on equity: —
Cash (mil.): $1.6
Current ratio: 1.04
Long-term debt (mil.): $0.7
No. of shares (mil.): —
Dividends
  Yield: —
  Payout: —
Market value (mil.): —
R&D as % of sales: 113.8%

QUARTER ENDED 6/30

	1996	1995
Sales ($ millions)	3.3	0.1
Net Income ($ millions)	(4.7)	(0.6)
Earnings Per Share ($)	(0.52)	(0.02)
No. of Shares (thou.)	25,863	25,862

6 MONTHS ENDED 6/30

	1996	1995
Sales ($ millions)	5.0	0.1
Net Income ($ millions)	(8.3)	(1.0)
Earnings Per Share ($)	(0.47)	(0.04)
No. of Shares (thou.)	25,863	25,862

STOCK PRICE HISTORY: High/Low/Close

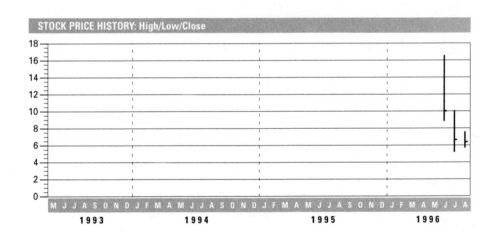

- Addresses desperate need of high-tech Web marketers for information

- Internet studies have raised the company's profile

- Subscription revenues are running at about 1/3 of total revenue

- Pipeline acquisition bolsters registration services, international presence

- Faces competition from industry giants including Nielsen

- Recently-acquired Pipeline is losing money

- Dependent on a relatively low number of customers

- Market Cap of $180 million (8/96) vs 1st half, 1996 sales of $8.8 million

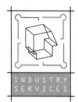

INDUSTRY
SERVICES

IntelliQuest Information

Who uses computers and other high-tech products? Why do people buy one brand and not another? What information do they use to make a decision? Austin, Texas-based IntelliQuest has the answers, gleaned from surveys of industry professionals.

Its offerings fall into 3 main categories: subscription-based products (which give clients the results of industry surveys), customized subscription software (providing product statistics and registration data), and commissioned research for individual customers. Microsoft and IBM are its 2 largest customers, accounting for 17% and 11%, respectively, of its business. Founder Peter Zandan owns about 15% of the company's stock.

Zandan was a University of Texas instructor in the mid-1980s when he accepted a consulting job to study customers for software developer Ashton-Tate. He discovered there were no marketing companies specializing in high tech, so in 1985 he started one, HiMark (renamed IntelliQuest in 1988). The company provided custom surveys for individual clients until 1991, when it began offering generalized studies to a wider audience. Two years later Microsoft and Intel commissioned IntelliQuest to conduct a survey of the computer industry — the Computer Industry Media Study (CIMS). CIMS

@INTELLIQUEST

INTELLIQUEST INFORMATION GROUP, INC.

HQ: 1250 Capital of Texas Hwy. South,
Bldg. 2, Plaza One, Austin, TX 78746
Phone: 512-329-0808
Fax: 512-329-0888
Web site: www.intelliquest.com

OFFICERS

Chairman and CEO:
Peter Zandan, age 43, $305,900 pay

President:
Brian Sharples, age 35, $312,400 pay

COO and CFO:
James Schellhase, age 37, $199,850 pay

Director Human Resources:
Bobbi Garrison

Auditors: Price Waterhouse LLP

SELECTED PRODUCTS AND SERVICES

CIMS (media readership database)

Customer Registration Programs (purchase registration information database)

IntelliTrack IQ (marketing statistics software)

Longitudinal Tracking Studies (brand, advertising, customer, and product tracking systems designed for specific clients)

Proprietary research projects (custom market surveys to analyze market opportunities, market segments, pricing and profitability, and advertising effectiveness)

ReplySat (customer satisfaction survey software)

Technology Panel (10,000-person industry survey group)

KEY COMPETITORS

A.C. Nielsen	International Data Group
FIND/SVP	META Group
Forrester Research	MRB Group
Gartner Group	NFO Research
Information Resources	Virtual Media Resources

raised IntelliQuest's profile and became the basis of an annual subscription product.

The company took advantage of a mania for public offerings in 1996 and sold about 60% of itself to the public. It planned to use the proceeds to buy other companies and expand overseas. Almost immediately it bought an electronic customer registration company, Pipeline Communications, Inc., for about $18 million in stock. This purchase not only increased IntelliQuest's penetration of the customer registration market, it also fulfills the goal of foreign expansion, since Pipeline operates in 90 countries.

Recognizing the lack of hard information about what's hot and what's not in cyberspace, IntelliQuest that year announced a new product, Web Score, to help customers figure out what makes a successful Web site.

INTELLIQUEST: THE NUMBERS

Nasdaq symbol: IQST FYE: December 31	Annual Growth	1990	1991	1992	1993	1994	1995
Sales ($ mil.)	66.7%	—	2.2	3.9	6.1	13.0	17.0
Net income ($ mil.)	—	—	(0.1)	(0.2)	(0.5)	0.0	0.9
Income as % of sales	—	—	—	—	—	—	5.4%
Employees	—	—	—	—	—	—	113

1995 YEAR-END

Debt ratio: —
Return on equity: —
Cash (mil.): $0.6
Current ratio: 1.30
Long-term debt (mil.): $0.1
No. of shares (mil.): —
Dividends
  Yield: —
  Payout: —
Market value (mil.): —

QUARTER ENDED 6/30

	1996	1995
Sales ($ millions)	4.7	3.6
Net Income ($ millions)	0.3	0.0
Earnings Per Share ($)	0.04	0.00
No. of Shares (thou.)	6,997	3,245

6 MONTHS ENDED 6/30

	1996	1995
Sales ($ millions)	8.8	7.0
Net Income ($ millions)	0.4	0.0
Earnings Per Share ($)	0.06	0.01
No. of Shares (thou.)	6,997	3,245

STOCK PRICE HISTORY: High/Low/Close

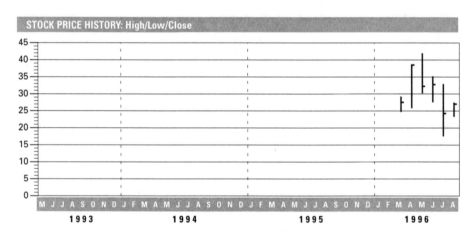

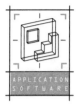

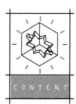

APPLICATION SOFTWARE | SPECIALIZED SERVICES | CONTENT

Intuit Inc.

Following a failed merger attempt with Microsoft, Menlo Park, California-based Intuit is playing hardball. The company, which is the #1 maker of accounting (QuickBooks), personal finance (Quicken), and tax (MacInTax and TurboTax) software, has stepped up to the plate with a major new service — online banking. The firm also offers automated financial services such as the Quicken Visa Card with IntelliCharge. (IntelliCharge is software that transmits expenditure data to the cardholder via modem.) Expenses related to the never-completed merger and subsequent acquisitions led Intuit to a net loss in 1995. Chairman Scott Cook owns 19% of the company.

After Cook got his MBA, he spent 3 years at Procter & Gamble and 4 years at Bain & Co. consulting. In 1983 he decided to apply to the software business the sort of brand management he had learned at P&G. Market research taught Cook that people wanted a very easy-to-use personal finance software package. The result was Quicken, introduced in 1984. Intuit was near collapse in 1986 when it received its first big order (from software retailer Egghead, Inc.), but by 1990 Quicken was the market leader. The company released its QuickBooks software in 1992. It went public in 1993 and later that year acquired ChipSoft, a tax preparation software developer. In 1994 Intuit bought Best Programs (professional tax preparation software) and National Payment Clearinghouse (automated bill payment services).

After the busted Microsoft merger, which was halted by a Justice Department antitrust lawsuit in 1995, Intuit sold over one million shares of stock to raise capital. Also that year the firm launched its online banking service through 21 of the largest national financial institutions, whose cus-

- #1 in personal finance, tax software for PCs
- Emphasizing OEM deals with Quicken product to expand user base
- Long-term strategy calls for selling Quicken users upgrades, online home banking services
- Has home-banking alliance with America Online
- Agreed to buy Galt Technologies, operator of popular NETworth financial information Web site

- Increased OEM distribution is hurting retail sales, gross margins
- Microsoft has stepped up competitive effort in home banking
- Having trouble with German operations
- Spending heavily to build home banking service
- Operating around breakeven

INTUIT INC.

HQ: 155 Linfield Ave.,
 Menlo Park, CA 94025
Phone: 415-322-0573
Fax: 415-329-2788
Web site: www.intuit.com

OFFICERS

Chairman: Scott D. Cook, age 43, $590,385 pay
President and CEO:
 William V. Campbell, age 55, $744,769 pay
EVP: William H. Harris Jr., age 39, $342,401 pay
CFO: James J. Heeger, age 39
General Counsel:
 Catherine L. Valentine, age 43
VP Sales: Alan A. Gleicher, age 43
VP; General Manager, Automated Financial Services:
 Stephen D. Pelletier, age 42, $278,577 pay
VP; General Manager, Business Products Group: John Monson, age 40
VP Human Resources:
 Michael A. Ahearn, age 48
Auditors: Ernst & Young LLP

SELECTED PRODUCTS AND SERVICES

Personal Fianance Software
 Quicken (DOS, Windows, and Macintosh)
 Quicken Financial Planner (retirement planning)
 Quicken Parents' Guide to Money
 Your Mutual Fund Selector

Small Business Accounting Software
 QuickBooks
 QuickBooks Pro
 QuickPay (payroll add-on)

Tax Preparation Software
 MacInTax
 TurboTax
 TurboTax ProSeries

Services
 Electronic Bill Payment
 Online banking & bill payment
 Payroll Tax Table Update Service
 Quicken Visa Card with IntelliCharge (credit management)

KEY COMPETITORS

Best Programs	Lacerte Software
Charles Schwab	Microsoft
Checkfree	Moore Business Forms
Citicorp	NEBS
Computer Associates	Sterling Commerce
Fidelity Investments	Taasc
H&R Block	ValueLine
IBM	Visa

tomers include about 90% of the US population. In addition, Intuit entered the world's 2nd largest personal computer market — Japan — with the purchase of Tokyo-based financial software firm Milky Way KK, for $50.4 million in stock. It also acquired PNI, a developer of online investment research technology.

INTUIT: THE NUMBERS

Nasdaq symbol: INTU FYE: July 31	Annual Growth	1990	1991	1992	1993	1994[1]	1995
Sales ($ mil.)	64.3%	33.1	44.5	83.8	121.4	194.1	395.7
Net income ($ mil.)	—	3.6	4.3	5.3	8.4	(176.6)	(45.4)
Income as % of sales	—	10.8%	9.6%	6.3%	6.9%	—	—
Earnings per share ($)	—	0.18	0.21	0.25	0.37	(5.22)	(1.11)
Stock price – high ($)	—	—	—	—	23.25	36.63	89.25
Stock price – low ($)	—	—	—	—	12.00	13.50	28.94
Stock price – close ($)	91.3%	—	—	—	21.31	33.38	78.00
P/E – high	—	—	—	—	63	—	—
P/E – low	—	—	—	—	32	—	—
Dividends per share ($)	—	—	—	—	0.00	0.00	0.00
Book value per share ($)	70.7%	—	—	—	2.20	4.83	6.41
Employees	90.1%	110	175	484	589	1,228	2,732

[1] 10-month fiscal year

1995 YEAR-END

Debt ratio: 1.5%
Return on equity: —
Cash (mil.): $191.4
Current ratio: 2.64
Long-term debt (mil.): $4.4
No. of shares (mil.): 43.9
Dividends
  Yield: —
  Payout: —
Market value (mil.): $3,421.6
R&D as % of sales: 13.5%

QUARTER ENDED 4/30

	1996	1995
Sales ($ millions)	136.5	98.9
Net Income ($ millions)	(0.3)	(3.8)
Earnings Per Share ($)	(0.01)	(0.09)
No. of Shares (thou.)	45,318	40,882

9 MONTHS ENDED 4/30

	1996	1995
Sales ($ millions)	461.8	329.9
Net Income ($ millions)	1.3	(43.0)
Earnings Per Share ($)	0.03	(1.07)
No. of Shares (thou.)	45,318	40,882

STOCK PRICE HISTORY: High/Low/Close

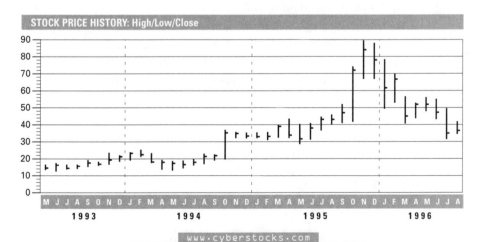

www.cyberstocks.com

- Has a head start over most competitors in interactive advertising

- Positioned to benefit from "narrowcasting" of advertising on the Internet

- Can sell traditional agency work to new media clients

- Believes its flat organizational structure results in better client service

- Small agency faces many competitors, large and small

- 4 clients accounted for more than 85% of 1st half, 1996 revenue

- Engaged in legal dispute with musical group the Spin Doctors

- 1st half earnings declined

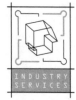

The Leap Group

Will a creative frog turn out to be a financial prince? Chicago-based Leap Group, an ad agency that uses a frog as its logo, hopes so. Leap styles itself as a specialty agency that concentrates on marrying brand strategy and creative ideas but leaves market research and media buying — as well as high overhead and layers of management — to others. It filed to go public in mid-1996 with an IPO that values the company at about $170 million. Founders George Gier, Joe Sciarrotta, Fred Smith, and Rick Lutterbach will each hold about 17% of the shares after the offering, and President Tom Sharbaugh will hold about 10%. Proceeds from the IPO will be used to pay debt and make acquisitions.

The company was started as Leap Partnership in 1993. Gier, Smith, and Sciarrotta (who claims that "Bewitched"'s Darrin Stephens character inspired him to become an ad man) had worked together at superagency DDB Needham Worldwide, where they had just created the Bud Light television ad character known for the line "Yes, I am." The new company's name came from the leap of faith it took to leave DDB Needham. Lutterbach, an old friend of Smith who had made millions in real estate, brought a businessman's perspective to the creative team. Anheuser-Busch helped kickstart the company by ordering television ads in late 1993.

In 1994 Miller Brewing, Papa John's Pizza, Boston Chicken, and the University of Notre Dame hired Leap. The company added Nike to its client roster in 1995. Late that year Leap resigned from the $30 million Miller

The Leap Partnership

THE LEAP GROUP, INC.
HQ: 22 W. Hubbard St., Chicago, IL 60610
Phone: 312-494-0300
Fax: 312-494-0120
Web site: www.leapnet.com

OFFICERS

Chairman and CEO:
R. Steven Lutterbach, age 46, $201,000 pay
VC and COO:
Frederick Smith, age 42, $201,000 pay
President: Thomas R. Sharbaugh, age 52
EVP and Chief Creative Officer:
Joseph Al Sciarrotta, age 34, $221,226 pay
EVP and Chief Marketing and Information Officer:
George Gier, age 35, $201,000 pay
CFO and Treasurer: Peter Vezmar, age 39
Chief Legal and Strategic Officer and Secretary:
Robert C. Bramlette, age 46
Creative Partner (HR): Nikki Fletcher
Auditors: Andersen Worldwide

SELECTED PRODUCTS AND SERVICES

Creative content development (advertising, entertainment programming, graphic design, marketing, and promotional programs for new and traditional media)

Strategic brand management (brand development and integrated marketing campaigns)

Selected Clients

Chicago Tribune Co.
Cincinnati Bell Telephone
Miller Brewing Co.
Nike
The One Show
Papa John's Pizza
Pizza Hut
R.J. Reynolds
Tommy Armour Golf Co.
University of Notre Dame
U.S. Robotics

KEY COMPETITORS

Bozell, Jacobs	Dentsu	Organic Online
BroadVision	Grey Advertising	Poppe Tyson
Bronner Slosberg	Interpublic Group	True North
CKS	Leo Burnett	WPP Group
Cordiant	Modem Media	Young &
Corinthian	Omnicom Group	Rubicam
D'Arcy Masius	On Ramp	Ziff-Davis

account (which had contributed 2/3 of that year's revenues), blaming a drop in Miller's ad dollars for Lite Ice.

In 1996 Sharbaugh, a former executive at Sears and Anheuser-Busch (where he had guided the "Spuds McKenzie" campaign), became Leap's president. That year the company widened its new media focus when it purchased Tanagram, a Chicago graphic design firm that specializes in interactive media.

LEAP GROUP: THE NUMBERS

FYE: January 31	Annual Growth	1991	1992	1993	1994	1995	1996
Sales ($ mil.)	352.8%	—	—	—	0.4	4.7	8.2
Net income ($ mil.)	—	—	—	—	(0.1)	(1.1)	0.7
Income as % of sales	—	—	—	—	—	—	8.5%
Employees	59.2%	—	—	—	15	27	38

1996 YEAR-END

Debt ratio: 100.0%
Return on equity: —
Cash (mil.): $0.0
Current ratio: 0.52
Long-term debt (mil.): $0.4
No. of shares (mil.): —
Dividends
  Yield: —
  Payout: —
Market value (mil.): —

QUARTER ENDED 7/31

	1996	1995
Sales ($ millions)	5.3	2.4
Net Income ($ millions)	0.4	0.4
Earnings Per Share ($)	—	—
No. of Shares (thou.)	—	—

6 MONTHS ENDED 7/31

	1996	1995
Sales ($ millions)	7.3	5.6
Net Income ($ millions)	0.3	0.7
Earnings Per Share ($)	—	—
No. of Shares (thou.)	—	—

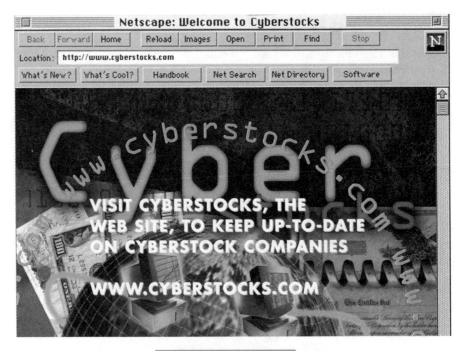

 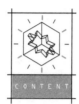

SPECIALIZED SERVICES

CONTENT

Lycos, Inc.

To use a library of information as vast as the World Wide Web, you need a good card catalog. Marlborough, Massachusetts-based Lycos's online search engine has cataloged 91% of the Web's contents (10.8 million addresses). The company also provides the a2z Directory, a cyberguide arranged by category, and Point Reviews, which offer critiques of the Web's most popular sites. Lycos's service is free; the company generates revenues by licensing its technology (10% of sales) and by selling advertising (90% of sales) at around $20,000 a month for a package that covers one million viewings of an ad (smaller packages are available). More than 50 companies — including IBM, MasterCard, and NYNEX — advertise on Lycos.

The company went public in April 1996 with a IPO that valued the company at an astonishing $177 million. CMG@Ventures, a Wilmington, Massachusetts-based venture firm, owns nearly 59% of the company; Carnegie Mellon University, which underwrote the original research for Lycos, and Michael Mauldin, the company's chief scientist who developed the technology, each own about 8%.

Mauldin, a researcher at Carnegie Mellon's Center for Machine Translation, formulated the Lycos search engine in 1994. The name comes from the wolf spider family (Lycosidae), which chases its prey (the company likens its indexing process to spiders crawling through the Web and retrieving information). The first commercialization of Lycos came in mid-1995, when both Microsoft and the Library Corp. licensed the technology. Lycos, Inc., was formed in June 1995 when CMG@Ventures purchased exclusive rights to the technology. At that time Robert Davis, a veteran of add-on-memory

- Appears to be the biggest beneficiary of the change in Netscape Premier Provider program
- Traffic has grown faster than most competitors in recent months
- Has established an international presence, including a deal with Bertelsmann
- CMG relationship could give lead to favorable alliances and deals in the future
- Balance sheet (4/96) showed about $3 per share

- Relatively low technical barriers to entry into market
- Unproven advertising-based business model
- Sales and marketing expense is running at more than 50% of revenue
- Browser companies can influence traffic flow or compete
- Market cap of $93 million (8/96) vs. 9 months sales of $2.6 million year

LYCOS, INC.
HQ: 293 Boston Post Rd. West,
Marlborough, MA 01752
Phone: 508-229-0717
Fax: 508-229-2866
Web site: www.lycos.com

SELECTED PRODUCTS AND SERVICES

a2z Directory (provides links to popular Web sites grouped into categories)

Lycos Catalog (Web index with hypertext links to more than 10.8 million Web pages)

Point Reviews (reviews of the Web's most popular sites)

KEY COMPETITORS

America Online
CompuServe
DEC
Excite
Individual
Infonautics
Infoseek
Open Text
Wired Ventures
Wolff New Media
Yahoo!

maker Cambex and computer maker Wang, was named president and CEO. In late 1995 Lycos acquired Point Communications Corp., which publishes online Web-site reviews called Point Reviews. The company, now a Lycos subsidiary, is known for its "Top 5% Web Site" icon found on many Web pages. in 1996 CompuServe licensed Lycos's search technology, the a2z Directory, and Point Reviews for integration into its WOW! online service. By early 1996 the Lycos Catalog was serving more than 47 million requests a month. In March of that year the company disclosed details of a deal with Netscape that guarantees it 700 million referrals from the Netscape web site per year in exchange for $5 million. The deal, which Netscape also struck with four other Web-Search companies, also guarantees Lycos prominent placement on the Netscape site.

Shortly following the public offering, Lycos announced that AT&T Corp. will license its Internet directories for its WorldNet Internet-access service.

LYCOS: THE NUMBERS

Nasdaq symbol: LCOS FYE: July 31	Annual Growth	1990	1991	1992	1993	1994	1995
Sales ($ mil.)	—	—	—	—	—	—	0.0
Net income ($ mil.)	—	—	—	—	—	—	(0.1)
Income as % of sales	—	—	—	—	—	—	—
Employees	—	—	—	—	—	—	28

1995 YEAR-END

Debt ratio: 0.0%
Return on equity: —
Cash (mil.): $0.4
Current ratio: 3.7
Long-term debt (mil.): $0.0
No. of shares (mil.): —
Dividends
  Yield: —
  Payout: —
Market value (mil.): —
R&D as % of sales: 319.0%

QUARTER ENDED 4/30

	1996	1995
Sales ($ millions)	1.6	—
Net Income ($ millions)	(1.6)	—
Earnings Per Share ($)	(0.13)	—
No. of Shares (thou.)	13,793	—

9 MONTHS ENDED 4/30

	1996	1995
Sales ($ millions)	2.6	—
Net Income ($ millions)	(2.9)	—
Earnings Per Share ($)	(0.25)	—
No. of Shares (thou.)	13,793	—

STOCK PRICE HISTORY: High/Low/Close

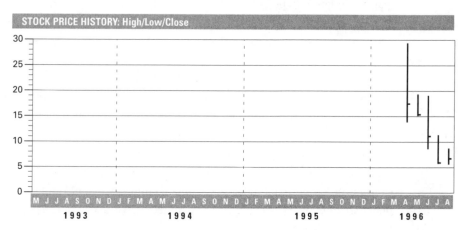

- A leader in multimedia development tools

- Shockwave to be integrated into Netscape browser and America Online, bundled with Microsoft Explorer

- Claims Shockwave has 9 million users, predicts 30 million by year-end

- Authors must use Macromedia software tools to create Shockwave applications

- Strong international presence

- Macintosh versions of Macromedia's products still dominate the sales mix

- Competition includes heavyweights Adobe, Corel, and Microsoft

- Recent price cuts could mark the beginning of a trend

APPLICATION
SOFTWARE

Macromedia

Macromedia has filled its studio with all the digital tools a cyberartist could want: pen, paintbrush, sound, and video. Now the San Francisco-based company is focused on making its software pervasive. Macromedia's software tools enable developers to create multimedia applications for CD-ROM, film, the Internet, print, and videotape. The company has focused on marketing over the Internet, direct mail advertising, and agreements with big kids like Microsoft to push sales skyward. However, Apple Computer's woes have slowed demand from Macromedia's biggest stable of customers: graphic designers (who favor the Apple Macintosh over IBM clones). Former Altsys executives James Von Ehr and Kevin Crowder own about 9% and 5% of the company, respectively.

The company was created in 1992 from the merger of Authorware and MacroMind/Paracomp. Michael Allen founded Authorware in 1985 to make multimedia authoring software. MacroMind, which developed multimedia software tools for PCs (set up by Marc Canter in 1984) and Paracomp, a creator of design and visualization software products (founded in 1986 by William Woodward), had merged in 1991. Macromedia purchased Farallon Computing's SoundEdit and MacRecorder technology in 1992 and went public in 1993. The following year it acquired Altsys, maker of the popular FreeHand illustration program.

In 1995 Macromedia bought Fauve Software (for its xRes image editing software and Matisse paint program) and joined Netscape to integrate the company's Director multimedia playback software into the Netscape Navigator

M̶ MACROMEDIA®

MACROMEDIA, INC.
HQ: 600 Townsend St.,
San Francisco, CA 94103-4945
Phone: 415-252-2000
Fax: 415-626-0554
Web site: www.macromedia.com

OFFICERS

Chairman, President, and CEO:
John C. Colligan, age 41, $354,789 pay
SVP Engineering: Norman Meyrowitz, age 36
VP Worldwide Sales:
Susan Gordon Bird, age 36, $314,439 pay
VP Operations, CFO, and Secretary:
Richard B. Wood, age 47, $244,833 pay
**VP Corporate Marketing and Customer
Support:**
Miles C. Walsh, age 44, $240,833 pay
VP Product Development/JAVA:
James R. Von Ehr II, age 45
VP Product Integration:
Kevin F. Crowder, age 41
VP Digital Arts Products:
Samantha Seals-Mason, age 28
VP Multimedia Products:
Steve Kusmer, age 39
VP Corporate Development: Jim Funk, age 38
Director Human Resources: Denise Minaberry
Auditors: KPMG Peat Marwick LLP

SELECTED PRODUCTS
AND SERVICES

Authorware Interactive Studio (suite of tools for
interactive applications)
Authorware 3.0 (software for writing interactive
applications)
Backstage Designer Plus (for Windows; software
for creating Web pages)
Backstage Internet Studio (suite of tools for
building Web tools)
Director Multimedia Studio (suite of tools for
multimedia and the Internet)
Fontographer (software for designing and
modifying fonts)
FreeHand (graphic design, illustration, and page
layout software)
Macromedia xRes 2.0 (software for designing
high-resolution images)
Shockwave (compression standard technology
for playing audio and graphics files created
with Macromedia tools over the World Wide
Web)

KEY COMPETITORS

Adobe	Innovex
Asymetrix	International Computers
Avid Technology	Metatec
Chyron	Micrografx
Corel	Microsoft
Dynatech	Netscape
Evans & Sutherland	Silicon Graphics
Horizons Technology	Sun Microsystems
IBM	

Web browser. Macromedia also bought OSC (digital audio production software) in 1995. The company debuted Shockwave, an application that enables Macromedia software-based productions to be used on the Web, in 1996. It also acquired iband (software for designing and linking Web pages).

MACROMEDIA: THE NUMBERS

Nasdaq symbol: MACR FYE: March 31	Annual Growth	1991	1992	1993	1994	1995	1996
Sales ($ mil.)	50.1%	15.3	24.7	25.3	30.1	53.7	116.7
Net income ($ mil.)	—	(7.6)	(12.0)	(0.2)	3.1	6.5	23.0
Income as % of sales	—	—	—	—	10.4%	12.2%	19.7%
Earnings per share ($)	—	—	—	(0.02)	0.15	0.19	0.59
Stock price – high ($)[1]	—	—	—	—	8.88	13.88	63.75
Stock price – low ($)[1]	—	—	—	—	6.38	3.75	10.56
Stock price – close ($)[1]	149.7%	—	—	—	8.38	12.75	52.25
P/E – high	—	—	—	—	61	73	108
P/E – low	—	—	—	—	44	20	18
Dividends per share ($)	—	—	—	—	0.00	0.00	0.00
Book value per share ($)	84.1%	—	—	—	1.08	1.28	3.66
Employees	37.7%	80	138	151	155	262	396

[1] Stock prices are for the prior calendar year.

1996 YEAR-END

Debt ratio: 0.0%
Return on equity: 26.6%
Cash (mil.): $116.7
Current ratio: 6.44
Long-term debt: $0.0
No. of shares (mil.): 36.4
Dividends
  Yield: —
  Payout: —
Market value (mil.): $1,902.6
R&D as % of sales: 17.2%

QUARTER ENDED 6/30

	1996	1995
Sales ($ millions)	35.0	22.3
Net Income ($ millions)	7.1	4.4
Earnings Per Share ($)	0.18	0.13
No. of Shares (thou.)	36,621	31,541

3 MONTHS ENDED 6/30

	1996	1995
Sales ($ millions)	35.0	22.3
Net Income ($ millions)	7.1	4.4
Earnings Per Share ($)	0.18	0.13
No. of Shares (thou.)	36,621	31,541

STOCK PRICE HISTORY: High/Low/Close

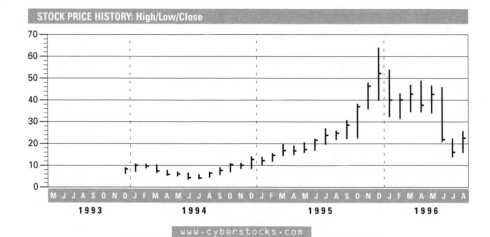

www.cyberstocks.com

SPECIALIZED
SERVICES

M·A·I·D plc

London-based M.A.I.D has made a name for itself as a worldwide provider of online market research reports, news, company statistics, and market and commodity prices. The company's major product is Profound, a Windows-based, easy-to-use business information online service. Profound offers economic data on more than 100 countries and approximately 20,000 companies. It also provides news articles from 4,000 magazines, newspapers, and journals and gives financial reports on 4 million companies. M.A.I.D's other products include M.A.I.D for Notes, a Lotus Notes add-on; NewsBase, a CD-ROM version of the M.A.I.D information service; and Brokerline, a database source for brokers.

Entrepreneur Daniel Wagner saw an opportunity in 1983 when, as a 19-year-old researcher, he experienced difficulty in getting market research reports to clients in an orderly and efficient manner. Keen to explore computer exchange of business information, he gathered about 300 reports from market research companies and launched M.A.I.D in 1985 to provide clients access to a database of market research reports for the advertising and marketing industries.

Slow to take off in the UK, M.A.I.D (an acronym for Market Analysis Information Database) had success in the more computer-literate US, where Wagner won contracts with Citibank and Colgate in 1986. M.A.I.D launched Infodynamics, an online business service in 1992. Wagner ap-

- All search and retrieval services focus on business content
- Subscriber base is growing fast; retention rate is high (85%)
- Enjoys a global customer base
- Recently launched an Internet-based search and retrieval service
- Internet service has potential as an intranet application
- Has inked deals to provide in-room Internet services to European hotel chains

- Faces competition on high end from large rivals such as Reuters, Dow Jones
- Faces competition on low end from free, advertising-based services
- Has become unprofitable
- Market cap of $440 million (8/96) vs. 1st half 1996 sales of $14 million

m·a·i·d

M.A.I.D. PLC

HQ: The Communications Bldg., 48
Leicester Sq., London, WC2H 7DB, UK

Phone: +44-171-930-6900

Fax: +44-171-930-6006

US HQ: 655 Madison Avenue
New York, NY 10021

US Phone: 212-750-6900

US Fax: 212-750-0660

Web site: www.maid-plc.com/

OFFICERS

Chairman:
Michael S. Mander, age 60, $57,333 pay

CEO: Daniel M. Wagner, age 32, $207,517 pay

Director Finance and Secretary:
David G. Mattey, age 33, $157,385 pay

Director Corporate Development:
Thomas A. Teichman, age 48, $155,677 pay

Director Product Development:
Bill A. Nash, age 32, $156,598 pay

President, US Operations:
John R. Wagner, age 61, $155,677 pay

Head of Information Technology:
Stephen Maller, age 37, $111,865 pay

Auditors: Price Waterhouse LLP

SELECTED PRODUCTS AND SERVICES

Brokerline (database source for brokers)

M.A.I.D for Notes (Lotus Notes)

NewsBase (CD-ROM version of the M.A.I.D information service)

Profound (Windows-based online information service)

	1995 Sales	
	$ mil.	% of total
Usage	10.5	50
Subscriptions	9.2	43
Other	1.4	7
Total	**21.1**	**100**

KEY COMPETITORS

America Online
Bloomberg
CompuServe
Data Times
Dow Jones
Dun & Bradstreet
Hoovers, Inc.
Knight-Ridder
Morningstar
Pearson
Primark
Reed Elsevier
Reuters
Thomson Corp.
Value Line

pointed his father John as president of his US business in 1993. The company has formed alliances with companies that complement its services, such as Adobe, Netscape, and Internet access provider Easynet.

In 1994 the company went public on the London Stock Exchange and started trading on the Nasdaq in 1995. Wagner owns about 19% of the company. M.A.I.D launched its Web-accessible Profound system in 1996. Expenses related to this launch resulted in a net loss in 1995.

M·A·I·D·: THE NUMBERS

Nasdaq symbol: MAIDY FYE: December 31	Annual Growth	1990	1991	1992	1993	1994	1995
Sales ($ mil.)	45.8%	3.2	4.5	5.3	8.5	13.9	21.1
Net income ($ mil.)	—	0.1	0.4	0.4	0.6	1.4	(5.6)
Income as % of sales	—	2.5%	9.0%	7.7%	7.1%	9.9%	—
Earnings per share ($)	—	0.01	0.03	0.03	0.04	0.07	(0.27)
Stock price – high ($)[1]	—	—	—	—	—	—	18.38
Stock price – low ($)[1]	—	—	—	—	—	—	12.75
Stock price – close ($)[1]	—	—	—	—	—	—	14.50
P/E – high	—	—	—	—	—	—	—
P/E – low	—	—	—	—	—	—	—
Dividends per share ($)	—	—	—	—	—	—	0.00
Book value per share ($)	—	—	—	—	—	—	2.14
Employees	98.8%	—	—	—	42	85	166

[1] Stock prices are for the prior calendar year.

1995 YEAR-END

Debt ratio: 7.9%
Return on equity: —
Cash (mil.): $34.1
Current ratio: 4.80
Long-term debt (mil.): $2.5
No. of shares (mil.): 22.9
Dividends
  Yield: —
  Payout: —
Market value (mil.): $332.5
R&D as % of sales: 19.4%

QUARTER ENDED 6/30

	1996	1995
Sales ($ millions)	7.6	4.3
Net Income ($ millions)	(3.9)	(4.5)
Earnings Per Share ($)	(0.17)	(0.22)
No. of Shares (thou.)	23,138	20,329

6 MONTHS ENDED 6/30

	1996	1995
Sales ($ millions)	14.0	8.4
Net Income ($ millions)	(7.7)	(7.6)
Earnings Per Share ($)	(0.34)	(0.37)
No. of Shares (thou.)	23,138	20,329

STOCK PRICE HISTORY: High/Low/Close

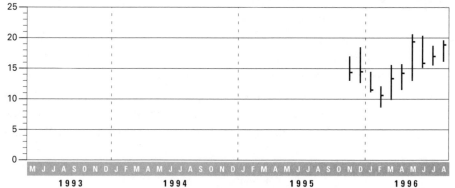

- #2 Long-distance provider

- Deregulation opens up local service markets

- Strong and rapidly growing international operations

- Stands to benefit from growth in outsourcing of networking services

- Has made large financial commitment to rapidly growing network services business

- Employs "father of the Internet" Vinton Cerf as Senior Vice President of Data Architecture

- Deregulation opens up long-distance market to more competitors

- Must spend billions of dollars to execute local service, wireless strategies

- Consumer-oriented Internet product offerings have been poorly received

- Internet telephony poses possible threat to long-distance business

- New ventures remain unprofitable

INTERNET ACCESS

MCI
Communications

MCI Communications and its partner phone giant British Telecommunications (BT) have gone fishing with the Internet. The 2 companies plan to catch many customers in their global net by jointly establishing 20 Internet hubs around the world, including locations in Australia, Germany, the UK, and the US. Through its Concert Communications joint venture with BT, it plans to use the improved network to offer high-speed service to corporations and to other Internet service providers.

The Washington, D.C.-based long-distance provider (#2 in the US, after nemesis AT&T) operates the nation's largest Internet backbone (high-speed lines that connect networks together). MCI's range of services includes Nationwide Cellular Service, the US's largest cellular reseller; local phone service through subsidiary MCImetro; and computer-network integration services through SHL Systemhouse. BT owns about 20% of MCI.

Consultant William McGowan founded MCI Communications in 1968; it began service in 1972 and went public in 1986. By the following year MCI's network reached more than 40 cities, but since it could not provide switched services, it had to be connected to the AT&T system. MCI won interconnection rights at its own facilities in 1976. MCI acquired businesses that competed directly with AT&T, including Western Union International (1982), a telex provider; Satellite Business Systems (1986), a satellite-based

**MCI COMMUNICATION
CORPORATION**

HQ: 1801 Pennsylvania Ave. NW,
Washington, DC 20006
Phone: 202-872-1600
Fax: 202-887-3140
Web site: www.mci.com

OFFICERS

Chairman and CEO:
Bert C. Roberts Jr., age 53, $2,190,000 pay

President and COO:
Gerald H. Taylor, age 54, $1,325,000 pay

**President and COO, MCI
Telecommunications Corporation:**
Timothy F. Price, age 42, $1,000,000 pay

President, MCI International, Inc.:
Seth D. Blumenfeld, age 55

President and COO, SHL Systemhouse Inc.:
Scott B. Ross

SVP and Chief Human Resources Officer:
William D. Wooten

Auditors: Price Waterhouse LLP

SELECTED PRODUCTS AND SERVICES

Concert Virtual Network Services (intranets for large international businesses)

Friends & Family (25% savings promotion on regular long-distance tolls)

internetMCI (Internet-access provider)

MCI One (linking of phone and computer services)

MCI Personal 500 (call forwarding to one's home, office, car, hotel, fax, or pager)

MCI PrePaid (prepaid calling card)

MCI Proof Positive (periodic account reviews and recommendations for savings)

KEY COMPETITORS

360 Degrees	Telephone	MindSpring
AirTouch	CompuServe	NETCOM
America Online	EarthLink	NYNEX
Ameritech	EDS	Pacific Telesis
Andersen	Frontier Corp.	PSINet
Consulting	GTE	SBC
AT&T Corp.	IBM	Communications
BBN	IDT	Sprint
Bell Atlantic	International	Telephone and
BellSouth	Wireless	Data Systems
Cable & Wireless	MFS	U.S. Long
Century	Communications	Distance

long-distance carrier; and RCA Global Communications (1988), a data communications service provider.

BT and MCI formed a joint venture (Concert) in 1993 to sell communications services globally. The next year MCI lost 1.1 million customers to AT&T — spurring its diversification strategy. The company unveiled internetMCI in 1995, a line of products and services including software and dial-up access. MCI also invested $1 billion in Rupert Murdoch's News Corp. to develop a $1.3 billion global direct-broadcast satellite television network. The Telecommunications Act of 1996 required the Baby Bells to open their local-access territories to competition. MCI became the first to offer a bundle of computer and telephone services under one brand name (MCI One).

MCI: THE NUMBERS

Nasdaq symbol: MCIC FYE: December 31	Annual Growth	1990	1991	1992	1993	1994	1995
Sales ($ mil.)	14.7%	7,680	8,433	10,562	11,921	13,338	15,265
Net income ($ mil.)	12.9%	299	551	609	627	795	548
Income as % of sales	—	3.9%	6.5%	5.8%	5.3%	6.0%	3.6%
Earnings per share ($)	8.6%	0.53	1.01	1.11	1.12	1.32	0.80
Stock price – high ($)	—	22.44	15.94	20.44	29.88	29.00	27.50
Stock price – low ($)	—	9.25	8.94	14.75	18.81	17.25	17.38
Stock price – close ($)	21.3%	9.94	15.13	19.81	28.25	18.38	26.13
P/E – high	—	42	16	18	27	22	34
P/E – low	—	18	9	13	17	13	22
Dividends per share ($)	—	0.05	0.05	0.05	0.05	0.05	0.05
Book value per share ($)	24.9%	4.60	5.71	5.99	8.71	13.24	14.00
Employees	15.5%	24,509	27,857	30,964	36,235	41,000	50,367

1995 YEAR-END

Debt ratio: 29.1%
Return on equity: 5.9%
Cash (mil.): $844
Current ratio: 0.93
Long-term debt (mil.): $3,444
No. of shares (mil.): 686
Dividends
  Yield: 0.2%
  Payout: 6.3%
Market value (mil.): $17,922

QUARTER ENDED 6/30

	1996	1995
Sales ($ millions)	4,565	3,706
Net Income ($ millions)	300	260
Earnings Per Share ($)	0.43	0.38
No. of Shares (thou.)	688,000	729,000

6 MONTHS ENDED 6/30

	1996	1995
Sales ($ millions)	9,056	7,267
Net Income ($ millions)	595	504
Earnings Per Share ($)	0.85	0.74
No. of Shares (thou.)	688,000	729,000

STOCK PRICE HISTORY: High/Low/Close

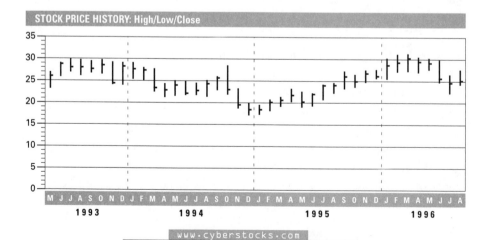

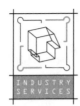

CONTENT

INDUSTRY SERVICES

Mecklermedia Corporation

Mecklermedia has given itself a subtitle: The Internet Media Company. Circulation for the Westport, Connecticut-based publisher's flagship magazine, *Internet World*, hit 250,000 in late 1995, and the company has added 2 new publications, *Web Developer* and *Web Week*. Mecklermedia's site on the World Wide Web, iWorld, is a top source of online Internet information, receiving more than a million hits a week. The firm also conducts trade shows in nearly a dozen countries for Internet and World Wide Web users and developers. Founder and CEO Alan Meckler owns about 31% of the company; VP James Mulholland III and his family own about 15%.

Meckler started the Meckler Corporation in 1971 to publish library science journals and reference books. As information technology evolved in the 1980s, the company moved into new areas, such as CD-ROMs. In the early 1990s the firm sold many of its scholarly library titles and began focusing on the Internet, CD-ROM technology, and virtual reality. It launched *Internet World* and *VR World* in 1993. That year the Mulhollands purchased about 1/3 of Meckler Corporation. The company became Mecklermedia in December 1993 and went public in 1994. It launched MecklerWeb (now iWorld) in 1994 with plans to charge as much as $50,000 to help companies develop online advertising. When advertisers failed to materialize, Alan

- Making progress toward becoming the Ziff-Davis of the Internet industry

- Magazines, especially *Internet World*, and trade shows are successful and growing rapidly

- Does not depend directly on the Internet for most revenues

- Deal with VNU should enable rapid European expansion

- Revenue for first 9 months of 1996 increased by 111%

- Faces intense competition in Internet-oriented print and online magazines

- Ballooning expenses and new trade show launches have resulted in losses so far in 1996

- Market cap of $155 million (8/96) vs. 9-month sales of $11.6 million

MECKLERMEDIA CORPORATION
HQ: 20 Ketchum St., Westport, CT 06880
Phone: 203-226-6967
Fax: 203-454-5840
Web site: www.iworld.com

OFFICERS

Chairman, President, and CEO:
  Alan M. Meckler, age 50, $191,000 pay
SVP Internet Business Development:
  Bill H. Washburn, age 49, $100,100 pay
EVP and CFO: Christopher S. Cardell, age 36
President and COO, Trade Show Group:
  Carl S. Pugh, age 41
Executive Director of Development, iWorld:
  Tristan Louis
VP Administration and Secretary:
  James S. Mulholland III, age 35
Manager Marketing: Matthew Kurtz
Director Technology: Lance Rosen
Auditors: Andersen Worldwide

SELECTED PRODUCTS AND SERVICES

Books
  Official Internet World books (with International Data Group and McGraw-Hill Books International)
Online
  Internet World Forum (on CompuServe)
  iWorld (World Wide Web site)
Publications
  Internet World
  Web Developer
  Web Week
Tradeshows
  Internet World
  VR WORLD + VRML WORLD
  Web Developer

KEY COMPETITORS

CMP Publications	SOFTBANK
Cowles Media	United News & Media
HyperMedia	Upside
International Data Group	VNU
McGraw-Hill	Wired Ventures
Reed Elsevier	Wolff New Media
Sendai Media Group	Ziff-Davis

Meckler limited the service to putting Mecklermedia magazines online and selling advertising.

In 1995 Mecklermedia sold off several more directories, publications (including *VR World*), and trade shows as it continued to narrow its focus to the Internet. That year it launched an Internet book publishing project while iWorld introduced motion video on its Web site. In 1996 the company formed Mecklermedia Internet Consulting to provide Internet business services.

MECKLERMEDIA: THE NUMBERS

Nasdaq symbol (SC): MECK FYE: September 30	Annual Growth	1990	1991	1992	1993[1]	1994	1995
Sales ($ mil.)	43.6%	—	—	4.9	4.4	8.3	14.5
Net income ($ mil.)	—	—	—	0.4	0.1	(2.0)	(1.3)
Income as % of sales	—	—	—	—	—	—	—
Earnings per share ($)	—	—	—	—	—	(0.32)	(0.17)
Stock price – high ($)	—	—	—	—	—	6.50	24.38
Stock price – low ($)	—	—	—	—	—	2.13	2.63
Stock price – close ($)	71.7%	—	—	—	—	3.44	16.00
P/E – high	—	—	—	—	—	—	—
P/E – low	—	—	—	—	—	—	—
Dividends per share ($)	—	—	—	—	—	0.00	0.00
Book value per share ($)	81.1%	—	—	—	—	0.44	2.14
Employees	61.0%	—	—	—	35	49	80

[1] 9-month fiscal year

1995 YEAR-END

Debt ratio: 0.1%
Return on equity: —
Cash (mil.): $19.4
Current ratio: 2.94
Long-term debt (mil.): $0.0
No. of shares (mil.): 8.4
Dividends
　Yield: —
　Payout: —
Market value (mil.): $134.4
Advertising as % of sales: 33.9%

QUARTER ENDED 6/30

	1996	1995
Sales ($ millions)	11.6	5.4
Net Income ($ millions)	0.5	0.1
Earnings Per Share ($)	0.06	0.01
No. of Shares (thou.)	8,420	7,115

9 MONTHS ENDED 6/30

	1996	1995
Sales ($ millions)	24.5	11.6
Net Income ($ millions)	(2.0)	0.7
Earnings Per Share ($)	(0.23)	0.10
No. of Shares (thou.)	8,420	7,115

STOCK PRICE HISTORY: High/Low/Close

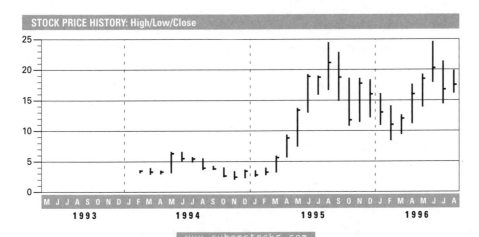

- Should benefit from mobile computing, Internet/intranet growth
- Ricochet is less expensive than any other wireless service
- Use of unlicensed spectrum, cheap repeaters, keeps costs low
- Future ISDN service is possible
- University campuses present a large opportunity
- Expansion to more metros may encourage bundling deals with laptop makers

- Losses continue to accelerate
- Burning cash rapidly and will need more to add metro areas
- Ricochet subscriber base appears to be very small at the present
- Small "cells," limited coverage reduce Ricochet's geographical reach
- Unable to pull off $75 million convertible debenture offering
- PCS is lurking as a competing wireless technology of the future

INTERNET
ACCESS

Metricom, Inc.

Metricom lets Internet and e-mail fiends get their fix without getting wired. Based in Los Gatos, California, Metricom provides 2-way wireless data communications services. It offers the Ricochet wireless Internet-access service to computer users in the San Francisco Bay Area and at several corporate and college campuses (including Austin College [Sherman, Texas], Oregon State University, and the University of California at Santa Cruz). The system works by broadcasting signals back and forth from transmitters mounted on building tops and utility poles to small radio modems connected to subscribers' computers. Metricom also offers wireless control and monitoring services to electric, natural gas, and wastewater utilities under the name UtiliNet. Expenses related to the development, installation, and marketing of the Ricochet system have kept Metricom bouncing around in the red. Microsoft cofounder Paul Allen owns about 14% of the company through Vulcan Ventures.

Network technology trailblazer Paul Baran (who developed a theory of distributed networking that was the basis for the Internet) started Metricom in 1985 to develop an inexpensive radio-based data communications system. Two years later the company adapted its technology for use in the utility industry. Until 1992 Metricom relied primarily on sales to the Southern California Edison electric company while it spent heavily on researching wireless networks. Metricom went public in 1992 and began to broaden the base of its utility customers the next year. Also in 1993 the firm launched the Ricochet wireless data communications service, targeted to users of

METRICOM, INC.
HQ: 980 University Ave.,
　　Los Gatos, CA 95030-2375
Phone: 408-399-8200
Fax: 408-354-1024
Web site: www.metricom.com

OFFICERS

Chairman: Cornelius C. Bond Jr.
President and CEO:
　Robert P. Dilworth, age 54, $393,266 pay
EVP and COO:
　Gary M. Green, age 55, $240,510 pay
EVP; General Manager, Ricochet Division:
　Donald F. Wood, age 41, $212,313 pay
CFO and Secretary:
　William D. Swain, age 55, $159,340 pay
VP Corporate Development:
　Stephens F. Millard, age 58
VP Human Resources: Chris Millard
Auditors: Andersen Worldwide

SELECTED PRODUCTS AND SERVICES

Ricochet (subscriber-based wireless data
　communications service)
UtiliNet (wireless data communications
　equipment for utility providers)

Selected Customers

Austin College (Sherman, Texas)
Hewlett-Packard
Metropolitan Sewer District of Cincinnati
Oregon State University
Pacific Gas & Electric
Southern California Edison
Stanford University
University of California Santa Cruz
University of Oregon
Wisconsin Power & Light

KEY COMPETITORS

Adage
ARDIS
CellNet Data Systems
Ericsson
General Electric
Itron
QUALCOMM
RAM Mobile Data Network

notebook computers and personal digital assistants. By 1995 Ricochet was available in 30 Silicon Valley cities. Metricom began installing the Ricochet system in Seattle the next year and joined with a subsidiary of Potomac Electric Power Company to deploy it in Washington, DC. Also in 1996 Hitachi agreed to preload some of its portable computers with Ricochet software.

METRICOM: THE NUMBERS

Nasdaq symbol: MCOM FYE: December 31	Annual Growth	1990	1991	1992	1993	1994	1995
Sales ($ mil.)	(8.8%)	9.2	10.7	6.4	10.1	21.6	5.8
Net income ($ mil.)	—	(0.6)	(1.3)	(4.5)	(6.1)	(11.7)	(23.5)
Income as % of sales	—	—	—	—	—	—	—
Earnings per share ($)	—	(0.11)	(0.23)	(0.61)	(0.74)	(0.96)	(1.79)
Stock price – high ($)	—	—	—	7.75	28.75	34.00	25.75
Stock price – low ($)	—	—	—	3.75	5.38	11.50	10.25
Stock price – close ($)	28.0%	—	—	6.50	24.00	15.00	13.63
P/E – high	—	—	—	—	—	—	—
P/E – low	—	—	—	—	—	—	—
Dividends per share ($)	—	—	—	0.00	0.00	0.00	0.00
Book value per share ($)	45.4%	—	—	1.97	3.11	7.82	6.05
Employees	49.1%	—	—	—	90	176	200

1995 YEAR-END

Debt ratio: 0.0%
Return on equity: —
Cash (mil.): $45.3
Current ratio: 10.19
Long-term debt (mil.): $0.0
No. of shares (mil.): 13.3
Dividends
  Yield: —
  Payout: —
Market value (mil.): $181.1
R&D as % of sales: 157.3%

QUARTER ENDED 6/30

	1996	1995
Sales ($ millions)	2.6	1.1
Net Income ($ millions)	(8.5)	(5.6)
Earnings Per Share ($)	(0.63)	(0.43)
No. of Shares (thou.)	13,462	13,141

6 MONTHS ENDED 6/30

	1996	1995
Sales ($ millions)	4.3	2.7
Net Income ($ millions)	(15.6)	(10.8)
Earnings Per Share ($)	(1.17)	(0.83)
No. of Shares (thou.)	13,462	13,141

STOCK PRICE HISTORY: High/Low/Close

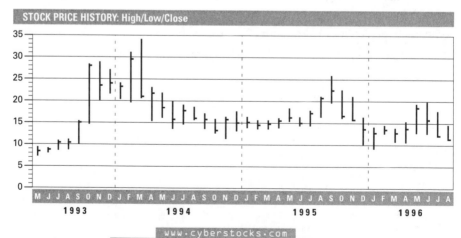

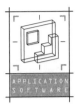 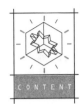

Microsoft Corporation

The world's #1 independent software company, Redmond, Washington-based Microsoft is the 800-pound gorilla of the computer jungle. However, CEO Bill Gates hasn't been able to thump his chest for long because an even bigger but undefinable beast has entered the scene — the Internet. To stave off competition from rivals such as Web software maker Netscape and UNIX workstation manufacturer and Internet software language developer Sun Microsystems, it has developed an Internet-intensive strategy. It has re-aligned its online service, the Microsoft Network, to embrace the Internet and to provide some free information. It has signed deals with other major online services, including America Online and CompuServe, to make Microsoft's Web browser, Internet Explorer, their primary browser. And it is releasing software that allows users to easily develop pages for the Web. Gates owns about 24% of Microsoft.

Microsoft (originally Micro-soft) was founded in 1975 after 19-year-old Gates dropped out of Harvard and teamed with high school friend Paul Allen to sell a version of the programming language BASIC written for the Altair, the first commercial microcomputer. Microsoft's big break came in 1980, when it was chosen by IBM to write the operating system for IBM's new PC. The popularity of IBM's PC gave the software, MS-DOS, instant success because other PC makers wanted to be compatible with IBM. It became the standard PC operating system in the 1980s. Microsoft began to tighten its grip on the market in 1985 when it introduced Windows, al-though it took several years before it replaced MS-DOS as the industry stan-

- Leader in PC operating systems, application software
- Enjoys recurring software upgrade revenues
- New corporate strategy seeks to put Microsoft at the heart of the Internet
- Leveraging operating system dominance to gain Internet market position
- Windows NT takes aim at corporate server market
- Strong cashflow, balance sheet

- Saturation of desktop application and operating systems market could be approaching
- Sales of Windows 95 have been slower than expected
- Justice Department probes into possible anticompetitive practices continue
- Must compete on many fronts to execute new strategy

MICROSOFT CORPORATION

HQ: One Microsoft Way,
Redmond, WA 98052-6399
Phone: 206-882-8080
Fax: 206-883-8101
Web site: www.microsoft.com

OFFICERS

Chairman and CEO:
William H. Gates III, age 39, $415,580 pay

EVP and COO:
Robert J. Herbold, age 53, $740,133 pay

EVP Worldwide Sales and Support:
Steven A. Ballmer, age 39, $411,974 pay

SVP; President, Microsoft Europe:
Bernard P. Vergnes, age 50, $526,445 pay

SVP Law and Corporate Affairs and Secretary:
William H. Neukom, age 53

SVP Consumer Systems:
Craig J. Mundie, age 46

SVP Personal Systems: Brad A. Silverberg

SVP Business Systems:
James E. Allchin, age 44

VP Finance and CFO:
Michael W. Brown, age 49

VP Human Resources and Administration:
Michael R. Murray

Auditors: Deloitte & Touche LLP

SELECTED PRODUCTS AND SERVICES

Desktop Application Software
Microsoft Excel
Microsoft Internet Explorer
Microsoft Office
Microsoft PowerPoint
Microsoft Word

Developer Products
Microsoft Access
Microsoft ActiveX
Microsoft Backoffice

Operating Systems
MS-DOS
Windows NT
Windows 3.11
Microsoft Windows 95
Microsoft Windows for Workgroups

Other
Microsoft Network (MSN)
MSNBC (24-hour cable news channel and Internet site)

KEY COMPETITORS

Adobe	FTP Software	Open Market
America Online	General Magic	Oracle
Apple	Hewlett-Packard	Pearson
Borland	IBM	QUALCOMM
Brøderbund	Informix	Quarterdeck
CompuServe	International	Silicon Graphics
Computer	Wireless	Softkey
Associates	NetManage	Sun
CONNECT	Netscape	Microsystems
Corel	NeXT	Sybase
DEC	Novell	Symantec
Electronic Arts	OneWave	Time Warner

dard. Microsoft went public in 1986. It released its network operating system, Windows NT, in 1993. In 1995 the company released Windows 95, the latest version of its operating system, backed by a torrent of advertising. As part of its Internet strategy, in 1996 Microsoft announced it would integrate its browser into its operating systems and give away its Web server with Windows NT.

MICROSOFT: THE NUMBERS

Nasdaq symbol: MSFT FYE: June 30	Annual Growth	1990	1991	1992	1993	1994	1995
Sales ($ mil.)	38.1%	1,183	1,843	2,759	3,753	4,649	5,937
Net income ($ mil.)	39.1%	279	463	708	953	1,146	1,453
Income as % of sales	—	23.6%	25.1%	25.7%	25.4%	24.7%	24.5%
Earnings per share ($)	34.9%	0.52	0.82	1.21	1.58	1.88	2.32
Stock price – high ($)	—	17.96	37.35	47.50	49.00	65.13	109.25
Stock price – low ($)	—	9.34	16.24	32.75	35.19	39.00	58.25
Stock price – close ($)	39.3%	16.74	37.10	42.69	40.31	61.13	87.75
P/E – high	—	35	46	39	31	35	47
P/E – low	—	18	20	27	22	21	25
Dividends per share ($)	—	0.00	0.00	0.00	0.00	0.00	0.00
Book value per share ($)	38.5%	1.80	2.59	4.03	5.75	7.88	9.18
Employees	25.9%	5,635	8,226	11,542	14,430	15,257	17,801

1995 YEAR-END

Debt ratio: 0.0%
Return on equity: 29.7%
Cash (mil.): $4,750
Current ratio: 4.17
Long-term debt (mil.): $0
No. of shares (mil.): 581
Dividends
  Yield: —
  Payout: —
Market value (mil.): $50,983

QUARTER ENDED 6/30

	1996	1995
Sales ($ millions)	2,255	1,621
Net Income ($ millions)	559	368
Earnings Per Share ($)	0.87	0.58
No. of Shares (thou.)	645,000	581,000

12 MONTHS ENDED 6/30

	1996	1995
Sales ($ millions)	8,671	5,937
Net Income ($ millions)	2,195	1,453
Earnings Per Share ($)	3.43	2.32
No. of Shares (thou.)	645,000	581,000

STOCK PRICE HISTORY: High/Low/Close

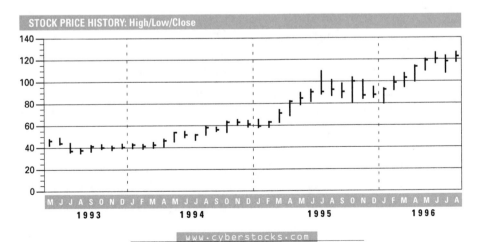

www·cyberstocks·com

- Enjoying rapid consumer and business subscriber growth

- Has been rapidly expanding subscriber base by acquiring smaller ISPs

- Acquisition of PSINet subscribers quadruples base and makes Mindspring a national service

- First half 1996 sales up 743%

- Internet service is hard to differentiate, pricing environment is tough

- AT&T, RBOCs are becoming major competitors

- PSINet subscriber acquisition has created additional financing requirements

- Losses are accelerating and pro forma statements reflecting PSINet purchase are not encouraging

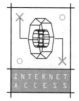

MindSpring Enterprises

The word that springs to mind is offbeat. Atlanta-based regional Internet access provider MindSpring Enterprises, which claims a dog named Henri as its cofounder and honorary chairman, offers Internet access to individual subscribers in 29 cities in Alabama, Florida, Georgia, Kentucky, Maryland, North Carolina, South Carolina, Tennessee, Virginia, and the District of Columbia. MindSpring also offers its subscribers a software package that includes e-mail, file transfer, access to news and chat sessions, and a Web browser. The company moved closer to its goal of becoming the Southeast's leading Internet access provider when troubled online service provider PSINet agreed to transfer its base of 100,000 subscribers to MindSpring. Founder Charles Brewer holds a 20% stake in the company, and telecommunications firm ITC Holding has a 38% stake.

Brewer, who previously served as CEO of fax server software developer AudioFax, started MindSpring in 1994 (an associate says Brewer came up with the name while sipping Samuel Adams beer). MindSpring bought regional subscribers from companies including Montgomery OnLine (Alabama) and Viper Net (Auburn, Alabama) in 1995 and CyberNet (Atlanta) in 1996 to build its customer base, which grew from 4,000 in 1995 to more than 21,500 in 1996.

That year Brewer took MindSpring public and promoted COO Mike McQuary, a former manager with petrochemical company Mobil, to the position of president. The company teamed up with Nustar's Real Estate Xtra!

MINDSPRING ENTERPRISES, INC.
HQ: 1430 W. Peachtree St. NW, Ste. 400,
Atlanta, GA 30309
Phone: 404-815-0770
Fax: 404-815-8805
Web site: www.mindspring.com

OFFICERS

Chairman and CEO:
Charles M. Brewer, age 37, $70,000 pay

President and COO:
Michael S. McQuary, age 36

VP, CFO, Secretary, and Treasurer:
Michael G. Misikoff, age 43

VP Network Operations:
James T. Markle, age 36

VP Marketing: Susan F. Nicholson, age 35

VP Engineering: J. Fredrick Nixon, age 39

**VP Network Engineering and Chief
Technical Officer:**
Robert D. Sanders, age 22

VP Customer Service:
Gregory J. Stromberg, age 43

VP Business Development:
Alan J. Taetle, age 32

Auditors: Andersen Worldwide

SELECTED PRODUCTS AND SERVICES

Internet access
Internet software (offering chat sessions, e-mail, file transfer, network news, and a Web browser)

Dial-up and dedicated access

	1995 Sales	
	$ mil.	% of total
Dial-up access to Internet	1.4	64
Start-up fees	0.6	27
Dedicated access to Internet	0.1	3
Web-hosting agreements	0.1	3
Total	**2.2**	**100**

KEY COMPETITORS

America Online
AT&T
BBN
Bell Atlantic
BellSouth
CompuServe
EarthLink
IBM
IDT
MCI
MFS Communications
Microsoft
NETCOM
Novell
PSINet
Sprint

(an information service developed by online publisher Nustar International and the Real Estate Book) to provide comprehensive real estate information to consumers online). Also in 1996 it agreed to pay $23 million for PSINet's subscriber base, and it got its feet wet in the corporate subscriber arena by forming a business services division to focus on business-to-business sales.

MINDSPRING: THE NUMBERS

Nasdaq symbol: MSPG FYE: December 31	Annual Growth	1990	1991	1992	1993	1994	1995
Sales ($ mil.)	—	—	—	—	—	0.1	2.2
Net income ($ mil.)	—	—	—	—	—	(0.1)	(2.0)
Income as % of sales	—	—	—	—	—	—	—
Employees	—	—	—	—	—	—	101

1995 YEAR-END

Debt ratio: 83.8%
Return on equity: —
Cash (mil.): $0.4
Current ratio: 0.27
Long-term debt (mil.): $0.0
No. of shares (mil.): —
Dividends
  Yield: —
  Payout: —
Market value (mil.): —

QUARTER ENDED 6/30

	1996	1995
Sales ($ millions)	2.5	0.3
Net Income ($ millions)	(1.5)	(0.2)
Earnings Per Share ($)	(0.29)	(0.06)
No. of Shares (thou.)	5,126	2,871

6 MONTHS ENDED 6/30

	1996	1995
Sales ($ millions)	4.3	0.5
Net Income ($ millions)	(2.5)	(0.3)
Earnings Per Share ($)	(0.58)	(0.09)
No. of Shares (thou.)	5,126	2,871

STOCK PRICE HISTORY: High/Low/Close

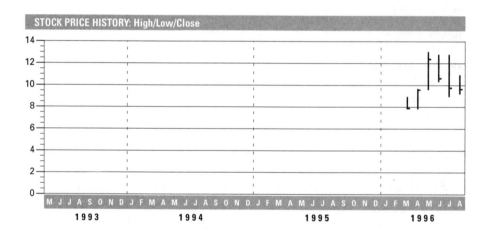

Multimedia Games, Inc.

Let the multimedia games begin! Although hardly Olympic in spirit, Tulsa-based Multimedia Games is the leading operator of electronic-based bingo games for gaming and entertainment businesses. The company has been given permission by the National Indian Gaming Commission to operate MegaMania, its high-stakes bingo game, in over 50 Indian nations. Its other products include MegaBingo, MegaBingo Lite, and MegaCash, which are transmitted to players in bingo halls via a linked network. Individuals can play at home through proxy players (to meet gaming laws) on Indian reservations by accessing the company's Web page (www.betnet.com).

Although televised bingo has been in existence since 1952 (Ronald Reagan was a guest host that year for a Las Vegas operation), TV viewers couldn't participate. With the liberalizing of gaming laws that came with the 1988 Indian Gaming Regulatory Act, entrepreneurs saw opportunities to bring Indian reservation-based gaming to players around the country. Gordon Graves, the founder of Datatrol — which launched the first online lottery system in the US — set up TV Bingo Network in 1991. After some trial projects on Indian reservations, the bingo operation went public in 1993.

The company acquired American Gaming & Entertainment, which operated high-stakes bingo games via closed-circuit television in about 52 bingo halls in Indian reservations, in 1994. That year the company changed its

- Rare online gambling play
- MegaMania high-speed bingo game appears to be doing well
- Linking many bingo players and halls electronically results in large jackpots
- First half sales up 47%

- Thinly traded issue on Nasdaq Small Cap list
- MegaBingo revenues are dwindling
- Financing activities are complex and seemingly continuous
- The financing of equipment to be placed on tribal lands presents special problems
- First half earnings were down

MULTIMEDIA GAMES, INC.
HQ: 7335 S. Lewis Ave., Ste. 302,
Tulsa, OK 74136
Phone: 918-494-0576
Fax: 918-501-0043
Web site: www.betnet.com/info.html

OFFICERS

Chairman and CEO:
Gordon T. Graves, age 58, $46,364 pay

President and COO:
Larry Montgomery, age 57, $108,000 pay

VP: Gordon Sjodin, age 54, $108,000 pay

VP Finance and CFO: Mike Howard

VP: Michael E. Newell, age 44

VP: Gary W. Watkins, age 41

VP Administration and Controller:
Frederick E. Roll, age 52

Auditors: Coopers & Lybrand L.L.P.

SELECTED PRODUCTS AND SERVICES

BetNet (online bingo game)

MegaBingo (closed-circuit electronic bingo game)

MegaBingo Lite (regional version of MegaBingo)

MegaCash (closed-circuit electronic bingo game)

MegaMania (high-stakes electronic bingo game)

	1995 Sales	
	$ mil.	% of total
MegaBingo Gaming revenue	14.8	86
MegaBingo services fee	0.7	4
Intellectual property sales	0.5	3
Project development revenue	0.5	3
Electronic player station sales	0.3	2
Other	0.3	2
Total	**17.1**	**100**

KEY COMPETITORS

American Casino
GTECH
International Game Technology
Mikohn Gaming
NTN Communications
Stuart Entertainment
Video Lottery

name to Multimedia Games. Graves owns 37% of the company.

In 1995 Multimedia teamed up with Cable Video Store, a subsidiary of adult entertainment provider Graff Pay-Per-View to develop new gaming products. Graff owns 23% of the company. The next year Multimedia launched MegaMania, the world's largest high-stakes, high-speed jackpot bingo game.

MULTIMEDIA GAMES: THE NUMBERS

Nasdaq symbol (SC): MGAM FYE: September 30	Annual Growth	1990	1991	1992	1993	1994	1995
Sales ($ mil.)	442.6%	—	0.0	0.0	0.0	1.4	17.1
Net income ($ mil.)	—	—	(0.1)	(0.4)	(0.9)	(1.4)	0.5
Income as % of sales	—	—	—	—	—	—	2.9%
Earnings per share ($)	—	—	(0.13)	(0.55)	(0.89)	(1.13)	0.24
Stock price – high ($)	—	—	—	—	—	3.50	3.50
Stock price – low ($)	—	—	—	—	—	1.00	1.75
Stock price – close ($)	—	—	—	—	—	1.25	2.50
P/E – high	—	—	—	—	—	—	15
P/E – low	—	—	—	—	—	—	7
Dividends per share ($)	—	—	—	—	—	0.00	0.00
Book value per share ($)	—	—	—	—	—	(0.41)	1.15
Employees	—	—	—	—	—	—	57

1995 YEAR-END

Debt ratio: 30.8%
Return on equity: 63.8%
Cash (mil.): $1.5
Current ratio: 1.18
Long-term debt (mil.): $0.8
No. of shares (mil.): 1.8
Dividends
  Yield: —
  Payout: —
Market value (mil.): $4.6

QUARTER ENDED 6/30

	1996	1995
Sales ($ millions)	6.1	4.5
Net Income ($ millions)	0.1	0.2
Earnings Per Share ($)	0.02	0.08
No. of Shares (thou.)	1,840	1,840

9 MONTHS ENDED 6/30

	1996	1995
Sales ($ millions)	15.6	10.6
Net Income ($ millions)	0.2	0.4
Earnings Per Share ($)	0.05	0.22
No. of Shares (thou.)	1,840	1,840

STOCK PRICE HISTORY: High/Low/Close

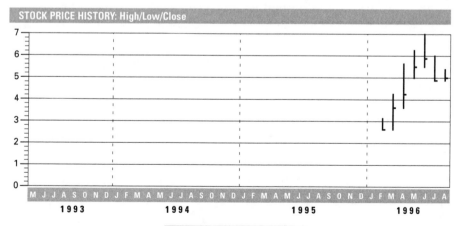

- The leading independent ISP with 500,000 subscribers (7/96)

- Expanding in the more lucrative small-to-medium-sized-business market

- Most telcos seem more focused on voice services for consumers, small business

- Industry may have room for many players, as in the long-distance business

- A potential takeover candidate

- Company has more than $10 per share in cash

- Internet service is hard to differentiate, pricing environment is tough

- AT&T, presumed low-cost operator, is competing with aggressive pricing

- RBOCs are using existing customer relationships to enter the market

- Never made a profit; break-even appears to be a moving target

- Company appears to be burning $1 per share of cash per quarter

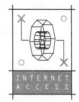

NETCOM On-Line Communication

Like a comet, fast-moving NETCOM is blazing a trail as a leading Internet service provider. The San Jose, California-based company supplies direct Internet access to about 500,000 subscribers, while its NetCruiser web browser software offers a graphical point-and-click format for accessing the Internet's resources, including the World Wide Web and e-mail.

The company was founded in 1988 by Robert Rieger, an information services engineer for Lockheed, who had let other students in his night school class use his equipment to access the Internet. He began charging for the service, using the proceeds to buy more equipment. In 1991 Rieger quit his job at Lockheed, incorporated the business in 1992, mortgaged his house, and relocated from his den to a more commercial site in San Jose.

NETCOM grew, opening more points of presence with data lines leased from Wil-tel and concentrating on California and larger cities in the US. It soon attracted the interest of venture capitalists, who helped finance its expansion. In 1994 NETCOM went public in a well-received IPO, using the more than $22 million in proceeds primarily to finance expansion.

That year the company agreed to allow Auto-Graphics to sell NETCOM access to schools and libraries in the US and Canada. In 1995 David Garrison,

NETCOM ON-LINE COMMUNICATION SERVICES, INC.
HQ: 3031 Tisch Way, 2nd Fl.,
San Jose, CA 95128
Phone: 408-556-3233
Fax: 408-556-3250
Web site: www.netcom.com

OFFICERS

Chairman, President, and CEO:
David W. Garrison, age 40, $263,112 pay

SVP Strategic Partnerships:
Donald P. Hutchison, age 39, $242,938 pay

SVP, CFO, and Secretary:
Clifton T. Weatherford, age 49

SVP Marketing: John E. Zeisler, age 43
SVP Customer Support: Eric V. Goffney, age 42
President, International:
Eric W. Spivey, age 35

VP and Chief Technology Officer:
Rick C. Francis, age 34, $185,948 pay

VP Operations: Robert E. Tomasi, age 44
Manager Human Resources: Irene Meister
Auditors: Ernst & Young LLP

SELECTED PRODUCTS AND SERVICES

Internet connection services
NetCruiser software

KEY COMPETITORS

America Online
AT&T
BBN
BT
CompuServe
EarthLink
IBM
IDT
International Wireless
MCI
MFS Communications
MindSpring
Netscape
Pacific Bell
PSINet
Sprint

formerly of Skytel, took over as president. NETCOM's subscriber growth increased more than 300% that year, but the company posted a $14 million loss due, in part, to costs related to the expansion of its network.

In 1996 founder Rieger left the company. NETCOM also announced plans to provide service in the UK.

NETCOM: THE NUMBERS

Nasdaq symbol: NETC FYE: December 31	Annual Growth	1990	1991	1992[1]	1993	1994	1995
Sales ($ mil.)	407.9%	—	—	0.4	2.4	12.4	52.4
Net income ($ mil.)	—	—	—	0.0	0.2	(0.1)	(14.1)
Income as % of sales	—	—	—	—	0.2%	—	—
Earnings per share ($)	—	—	—	—	—	(0.02)	(1.68)
Stock price – high ($)	—	—	—	—	—	29.25	91.50
Stock price – low ($)	—	—	—	—	—	16.75	19.00
Stock price – close ($)	—	—	—	—	—	28.38	36.00
P/E – high	—	—	—	—	—	—	—
P/E – low	—	—	—	—	—	—	—
Dividends per share ($)	—	—	—	—	—	0.00	0.00
Book value per share ($)	—	—	—	—	—	4.16	16.71
Employees	118.9%	—	—	—	106	153	508

[1] 4-month fiscal year

1995 YEAR-END

Debt ratio: 0.0%
Return on equity: —
Cash (mil.): $146.0
Current ratio: 8.66
Long-term debt (mil.): $0.0
No. of shares (mil.): 11.1
Dividends
  Yield: —
  Payout: —
Market value (mil.): $399.5

QUARTER ENDED 6/30

	1996	1995
Sales ($ millions)	28.0	10.5
Net Income ($ millions)	(12.6)	(2.9)
Earnings Per Share ($)	(1.09)	(0.37)
No. of Shares (thou.)	11,553	8,926

6 MONTHS ENDED 6/30

	1996	1995
Sales ($ millions)	52.1	18.0
Net Income ($ millions)	(19.2)	(4.2)
Earnings Per Share ($)	(1.68)	(0.57)
No. of Shares (thou.)	11,553	8,926

STOCK PRICE HISTORY: High/Low/Close

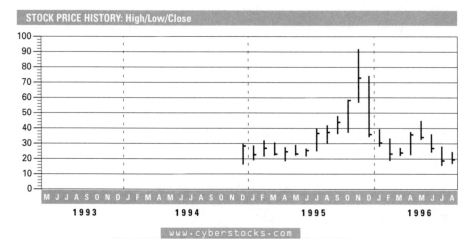

www·cyberstocks·com

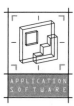

APPLICATION
SOFTWARE

NetManage, Inc.

NetManage is its name, managing the 'net (intra or Inter) is its game. The Cupertino, California-based company's products facilitate communication, information sharing, and collaboration between workgroups. Used by 90% of *FORTUNE* 100 companies, NetManage's products include connectivity software, servers, and development tools. Most are based on universal networking language TCP/IP (NetManage was one of the first to use TCP/IP for Windows). Chameleon, NetManage's flagship family of software products, has the industry's largest number of installations. CEO Zvi Alon owns 24% of the company; investment advisor J&W Seligman & Co. owns 7%.

Alon, an Israeli-born computer entrepreneur, founded NetManage in 1990. (He had been president of Halley Systems, a manufacturer of computer network equipment, before starting NetManage.) The company went public in 1993; on its first day of trading, shares climbed 50%. It has continued to grow as corporations have made the Internet a primary vehicle for conducting business with consumers, business partners, and internal business units. NetManage is building on the success of its TCP/IP products to become a complete intranet provider. To that end the company is entering alliances and licensing agreements with major companies (Microsoft and Apple in 1995; Sun Microsystems and Borland in 1996) and buying intranet-oriented companies such as AGE Logic (connectivity software) and Syzygy Communications (communications software) in 1996.

Also it is introducing new or expanded products and services. New offerings in 1996 included Bobcat (a Chameleon upgrade) and ECCO Workgroup

- Many companies want to buy TCP/IP applications from a single source
- Extending its TCP/IP suite with e-mail, groupware
- Making an international sales push
- Marketing relationships with industry leaders
- Opportunity to sell product upgrades whenever Windows is upgraded
- Gross margins run around 90%

- Many product features are present in common software packages
- Can look forward to tough sledding in Web browser market
- Attempts to build indirect sales will hurt gross margins
- Many users are delaying upgrading to Windows 95
- Flat sales, declining earnings in 1st half of 1996

NETMANAGE

NETMANAGE, INC.
HQ: 10725 N. De Anza Blvd.,
Cupertino, CA 95014
Phone: 408-973-7171
Fax: 408-257-6405
Web site: www.netmanage.com

OFFICERS

Chairman, President, and CEO:
Zvi Alon, age 44, $426,250 pay
SVP Finance, CFO, and Secretary:
Walter D. Amaral, age 44, $220,812 pay
SVP Worldwide Marketing: Carl Peede
SVP Human Resources: Pat Roboostoff
VP Business Development:
Robert Williams, age 41, $182,435 pay
VP Business Development:
Amatzia Ben-Artzi, age 43, $173,250 pay
VP OEM and International Marketing:
Dan Geisler, age 46
Auditors: Andersen Worldwide

SELECTED PRODUCTS AND SERVICES

Chameleon Software Family
Chameleon (basic application suite for Windows, Windows NT, Windows 95, and Mac OS)
ChameleonNFS (with an NFS client and server)
ChameleonNFS/X (X-server bundled with ChameleonNFS)
Internet Chameleon (for Internet access)

Desktop Management and Development Tools
NEWT-SDK (software development kit)
NEWTWatch (desktop management and analysis)
WinSock SDK for Mac OS (ports WinSock-based applications from Windows to the Mac OS platform)

Groupware and Group Collaboration Tools
ECCO (workgroup information manager)
InPerson (video/audio conferencing and shared electronic whiteboard)
IntraNet Server (collaboration platform for workgroups using Windows NT)

Messaging Products
JetMail Client and Server
JetMail Fax Server
Z-Mail (cross-platform e-mail system)

KEY COMPETITORS

Attachmate	Intel	Silicon Graphics
ForeFront	Microsoft	Spyglass
Frontier	Netscape	Sun Microsystems
Technologies	Novell	Trumpet Software
FTP Software	QUALCOMM	Wall Data
IBM	Quarterdeck	

Administrator, which permits the exchange of information between workgroups. The company, which has distributors on every continent except Antarctica, continues to seek growth opportunities in international markets.

NETMANAGE: THE NUMBERS

Nasdaq symbol: NETM FYE: December 31	Annual Growth	1990	1991	1992	1993	1994	1995
Sales ($ mil.)	320.8%	—	0.4	5.0	20.8	61.6	125.4
Net income ($ mil.)	286.4%	—	0.1	0.9	4.8	16.4	22.3
Income as % of sales	—	—	15.5%	17.2%	23.0%	26.6%	17.8%
Earnings per share ($)	158.8%	—	—	0.03	0.17	0.41	0.52
Stock price – high ($)	—	—	—	—	9.19	11.25	34.00
Stock price – low ($)	—	—	—	—	5.75	5.63	13.00
Stock price – close ($)	59.1%	—	—	—	9.19	20.25	23.25
P/E – high	—	—	—	—	54	27	65
P/E – low	—	—	—	—	34	14	25
Dividends per share ($)	—	—	—	—	0.00	0.00	0.00
Book value per share ($)	61.0%	—	—	—	1.20	2.44	3.11
Employees	93.7%	—	—	85	105	355	618

1995 YEAR-END

Debt ratio: 0.0%
Return on equity: 19.7%
Cash (mil.): $57.7
Current ratio: 3.59
Long-term debt (mil.): $0.0
No. of shares (mil.): 41.7
Dividends
  Yield: —
  Payout: —
Market value (mil.): $968.6
R&D as % of sales: 19.0%

QUARTER ENDED 6/30

	1996	1995
Sales ($ millions)	26.8	30.2
Net Income ($ millions)	1.6	6.8
Earnings Per Share ($)	0.04	0.16
No. of Shares (thou.)	42,746	41,789

6 MONTHS ENDED 6/30

	1996	1995
Sales ($ millions)	59.8	56.0
Net Income ($ millions)	6.7	12.5
Earnings Per Share ($)	0.15	0.30
No. of Shares (thou.)	42,746	41,789

STOCK PRICE HISTORY: High/Low/Close

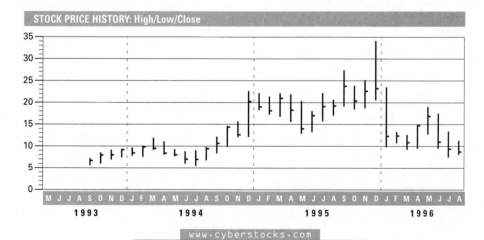

www·cyberstocks·com

- Web-browser market dominance:
  - *Enables Netscape to set (defacto) browser standards
  - *Gives Netscape an advantage in add-in software, publishing tools markets
- Solid track record of creating new products rapidly
- Well-positioned in lucrative corporate intranet and commercial markets
- Server software runs on multiple operating systems
- 1st-half, 1996 revenues up 531%

- Microsoft's Internet strategy targets Netscape's markets
- Microsoft is merging or giving away browsers and servers with its operating systems
- Pricing in the server product line is deteriorating
- Market cap. of $3.5 billion (8/96) vs. 1st-half 1996 revenue of $131 million

Netscape

Netscape Communications, one of the first companies to cast its net of software applications into cyberspace, has hauled in more clients than any of its rivals. The Mountain View, California-based company is the leading developer of software that supports information exchange and commercial transactions over the Internet. Partly because its Navigator software (and its predecessor Mosaic) was distributed free of charge, it has become the dominant browser for the World Wide Web. Other products include Netscape Commerce Server, which provides a secure method of paying for Internet purchases, as well as software products that offer commercial data management, publishing, and electronic shopping services.

Computer wunderkind Marc Andreessen was instrumental in writing Mosaic, an Internet software program developed at the University of Illinois-Champaign. In 1994 he joined James Clark, founder of Silicon Graphics, to start Mosaic Communications, which licensed Mosaic technology from the University. That year the company, facing legal action from the university, became Netscape.

In 1995 Microsoft licensed Mosaic from Spyglass for inclusion in its new Windows 95 operating system and began a major assault on Netscape's turf. A group of media and computer companies, including Hearst Corp. and Times Mirror, acquired an 11% stake in Netscape the same year. In addition, Netscape formed an alliance with Sun Microsystems in which its products would be offered with SunSoft's server software, which holds 50% of the

NETSCAPE

NETSCAPE COMMUNICATIONS CORPORATION

HQ: 501 E. Middlefield Rd.,
Mountain View, CA 94043
Phone: 415-254-1900
Fax: 415-528-4125
Web site: home.netscape.com

OFFICERS

Chairman:
James H. Clark, age 52, $100,000 pay

President and CEO:
James L. Barksdale, age 53, $96,154 pay

VP Sales and Field Operations:
Conway Rulon-Miller, age 45, $447,125 pay

VP Product Development:
Richard M. Schell, age 46, $215,000 pay

VP Product Development:
James C. J. Sha, age 45, $200,000 pay

VP Marketing:
Michael J. Homer, age 38, $175,000 pay

VP Technology: Marc Andreessen, age 24

VP Enterprise Technology:
Eric A. Hahn, age 35

VP and CFO: Peter L. S. Currie, age 39

VP Human Resources: Kandis Malefyt, age 41

Auditors: Ernst & Young LLP

SELECTED PRODUCTS AND SERVICES

Netscape Client Software
Netscape Navigator Gold
Netscape Navigator LAN Edition
Netscape Navigator Personal Edition
Netscape Power Pack

Netscape Server Software
Netscape Catalog Server
Netscape Commerce Server
Netscape Communications Server

Commercial Applications
Netscape Community System
Netscape I-Store
Netscape Merchant System
Netscape Proxy Server
Netscape Publishing System

KEY COMPETITORS

Adobe	Infosafe	Quarterdeck
America Online	Innovex	SoftQuad
Apple	Macromedia	Spyglass
BroadVision	Microsoft	Sun
CompuServe	NetManage	Microsystems
CONNECT	Network	Sybase
DEC	Computing	Symantec
Edify	Novell	Verity
FTP Software	OneWave	VocalTec
Hewlett-Packard	Open Market	
IBM	Oracle	

Internet server market. Netscape went public in 1995 in one of the hottest IPOs of the decade. Clark, the chairman, owns 23.1% of the company.

In an ongoing battle with Microsoft to rule the Internet applications market, in 1996 Netscape agreed to acquire InSoft Inc., a multimedia software concern, and also bought an equity stake in privately held Voxware, a maker of voice-processing software.

NETSCAPE: THE NUMBERS

Nasdaq symbol: NSCP FYE: December 31	Annual Growth	1990	1991	1992	1993	1994[1]	1995
Sales ($ mil.)	—	—	—	—	—	0.7	80.7
Net income ($ mil.)	—	—	—	—	—	(8.5)	(3.4)
Income as % of sales	—	—	—	—	—	—	—
Earnings per share ($)	—	—	—	—	—	(0.25)	(0.05)
Stock price – high ($)	—	—	—	—	—	—	71.33
Stock price – low ($)	—	—	—	—	—	—	22.88
Stock price – close ($)	—	—	—	—	—	—	68.63
P/E – high	—	—	—	—	—	—	—
P/E – low	—	—	—	—	—	—	—
Dividends per share ($)	—	—	—	—	—	—	0.00
Book value per share ($)	—	—	—	—	—	—	2.14
Employees	—	—	—	—	—	102	725

[1] 9-month fiscal year

1995 YEAR-END

Debt ratio: 1.4%
Return on equity: —
Cash (mil.): $148.5
Current ratio: 3.43
Long-term debt (mil.): $1.2
No. of shares (mil.): 81.1
Dividends
  Yield: —
  Payout: —
Market value (mil.): $5,563.0
R&D as % of sales: 30.9%

QUARTER ENDED 6/30

	1996	1995
Sales ($ millions)	75.0	11.9
Net Income ($ millions)	0.9	(1.6)
Earnings Per Share ($)	0.01	(0.03)
No. of Shares (thou.)	84,494	66,322

6 MONTHS ENDED 6/30

	1996	1995
Sales ($ millions)	131.1	16.6
Net Income ($ millions)	4.5	(4.3)
Earnings Per Share ($)	0.05	(0.07)
No. of Shares (thou.)	84,494	66,322

STOCK PRICE HISTORY: High/Low/Close

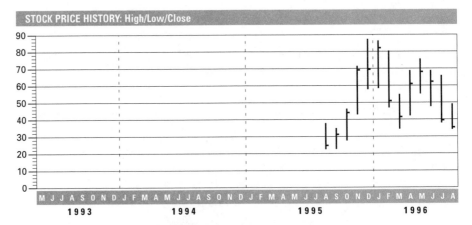

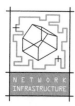

NETWORK
INFRASTRUCTURE

Newbridge Networks

- Market leader in WAN-ATM switches and T1 multiplexers
- Strong overseas presence
- Broad line of WAN and internetworking products
- Focuses on products for telcos, large multinational companies
- The stock's P/E of 19 (8/96) is one of the lowest in the industry

Newbridge Networks is bridging the global communications gap. The Kanata, Ontario-based company makes equipment for both private and public networks transmitting data, images, video, and voice. Most of the company's revenues come from its networking switches and routers and related support services. Newbridge sells its products in more than 75 countries. Its customers include major telecoms AT&T and Cable & Wireless and equipment makers Alcatel Alsthom and Siemens. Founder and CEO Terence Matthews owns 25% of the company.

A cofounder of telecommunications equipment company Mitel, Matthews founded Newbridge Networks (named for the Welsh town where he was born) in 1986. At the time, most networking companies offered proprietary systems that were difficult for global companies to integrate across international phone lines. Matthews focused on designing an open system that could be used on all the world's major telephone systems. The idea was a hit with multinational customers, and sales topped $55 million after just 3 years. Newbridge expanded its customer base to include phone companies and in 1989 went public. To increase its marketing abilities, the company has signed alliances with a number of partners, including Hewlett-Packard and AT&T. In 1994 it signed a deal with MCI, linking its networking products with MCI's voice and data communication services.

Newbridge won several substantial overseas contracts in 1995, including awards from 75 telephone companies in China. That year it acquired con-

- Cisco and Cascade are well-entrenched with switches at US telco sites
- Older time-division multiplexing products dominate Newbridge's sales mix
- Upgrading to its ATM integrated router/switch product is expensive
- ATM's future remains somewhat in doubt

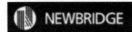

NEWBRIDGE NETWORKS CORPORATION
HQ: 600 March Rd. ,
Kanata, ON, K2K 2E6, Canada
Phone: 613-591-3600
Fax: 613-591-3615
US HQ: 593 Herndon Pkwy.,
Herndon, VA 22070-5241
Phone: 703-834-3600
Fax: 703-471-7080
Web site: www.newbridge.com

OFFICERS

Chairman and CEO:
Terence H. Matthews, age 52, C$148,800 pay

President and COO:
Peter Sommerer, age 46, C$194,372 pay

EVP, North and South America:
F. Michael Pascoe, age 43, C$234,872 pay

EVP, Europe, Middle East, and Africa:
John D. Everard, age 46, C$215,987 pay

EVP Operations:
Bruce W. Rodgers, age 40, C$153,635 pay

EVP Finance and CFO:
Peter D. Charbonneau, age 41

EVP, General Counsel, and Secretary:
James C. Avis, age 45

EVP Research and Development:
Scott W. Marshall, age 41

Director Human Resources:
Michael Gaffney

Auditors: Deloitte & Touche LLP

SELECTED PRODUCTS AND SERVICES

Bridge/routers for large-scale remote LAN access

ATM, frame relay, and packet broadband networking products

MainStreet Data Termination Unit product family

WAN access devices

Network and Services Management Systems
Systems for managing complex telecommunications networks

Synchronous Transfer Network Products
3600 MainStreet Bandwidth Manager networking multiplexers

3645 MainStreet High-capacity Bandwidth Manager networking multiplexers

Vivid Products
ATM internetworking products for campus LANs television)

KEY COMPETITORS

3Com	IPC
Alcatel Alsthom	Lucent
Ascend	NEC
Ascom/Timeplex	Network Equipment
Bay Networks	Technologies
Cascade Communications	Northern Telecom
Cisco Systems	Premisys
DSC Communications	Siemens
FORE Systems	Tellabs
Fujitsu	Unisys
General DataComm	Xylan
IBM	

trolling interests in Advanced Computer Communications, a maker of LAN bridges and routers, and Transistemas S.A., an Argentina-based systems integrator. In 1996 Newbridge and Siemens announced an alliance to develop products for ATM (asynchronous transfer mode) networks. The 2 companies will also market each others' telephone switching products.

NEWBRIDGE: THE NUMBERS

NYSE symbol: NN FYE: April 30	Annual Growth	1991	1992	1993	1994	1995	1996
Sales ($ mil.)	39.2%	129.3	152.1	242.0	399.6	590.4	676.6
Net income ($ mil.)	—	(10.3)	8.2	47.2	114.1	138.9	149.0
Income as % of sales	—	—	5.4%	19.5%	28.6%	23.5%	22.0%
Earnings per share ($)	—	(0.15)	0.12	0.61	1.37	1.64	1.74
Stock price – high ($)[1]	—	7.75	4.84	21.63	73.88	68.75	45.38
Stock price – low ($)[1]	—	1.50	1.56	3.81	19.13	26.50	25.00
Stock price – close ($)[1]	91.0%	1.63	3.81	20.63	54.75	38.25	41.38
P/E – high	—	—	40	36	54	42	26
P/E – low	—	—	13	6	14	16	14
Dividends per share ($)	—	0.00	0.00	0.00	0.00	0.00	0.00
Book value per share ($)	44.2%	1.26	1.31	2.87	4.24	6.05	7.86
Employees	—	—	—	—	2,155	2,955	3,400

[1] Stock prices are for the prior calendar year.

1996 YEAR-END

Debt ratio: 0.3%
Return on equity: 25.7%
Cash (mil.): $334.7
Current ratio: 4.94
Long-term debt (mil.): $0.6
No. of shares (mil.): 84.3
Dividends
  Yield: —
  Payout: —
Market value (mil.): $3,489.5
R&D as % of sales: 10.6%

QUARTER ENDED 7/31

	1996	1995
Sales ($ millions)	208.1	143.4
Net Income ($ millions)	44.2	27.2
Earnings Per Share ($)	0.52	0.33
No. of Shares (thou.)	85,320	82,883

3 MONTHS ENDED 7/31

	1996	1995
Sales ($ millions)	208.1	143.4
Net Income ($ millions)	44.2	27.2
Earnings Per Share ($)	0.52	0.33
No. of Shares (thou.)	85,320	82,883

STOCK PRICE HISTORY: High/Low/Close

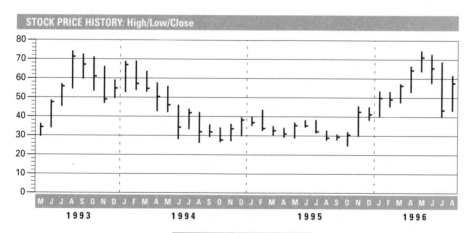

www.cyberstocks.com

- Installed base accounts for more than half of all LANs

- Massive opportunity to upgrade existing installations

- Has regained focus on network operating systems

- Finally embraced open systems, offered customers a migration path to intranets

- UNIX, Windows NT have a big head start in TCP/IP-based applications

- Netware has been difficult to install and administer

- With Microsoft's muscle, Windows NT poses a grave long-term threat to Novell

- Inexplicably late to launch intranet products

- Searching for new CEO

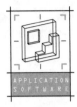

APPLICATION SOFTWARE

Novell, Inc.

Computer networks are everywhere, and more than half of all networks run on Novell software. The Orem, Utah-based company's flagship product is the NetWare network operating system. It also makes GroupWise group-ware products and LAN Workplace and LANalyzer.

With the increasing popularity of the Internet and intranets, rival software developer Microsoft's powerful NT server operating system, and newer networking technologies putting pressure on NetWare sales, Novell is redefining its role in the networking marketplace. It has embraced the Internet, enhancing its software with options that help NetWare customers connect their LANs to the Net. Former Novell CEO Ray Noorda owns 7%; WordPerfect cofounder Alan Ashton owns about 4%.

Novell Data Systems started out in 1980 as a Provo, Utah-based maker of PC peripherals. In 1981 Safeguard Scientifics, a high-tech venture capital firm, bought a majority stake in Novell and 2 years later brought in as CEO turn-around artist Raymond Noorda, who moved the struggling Novell into PC networking. That year, Novell introduced NetWare, the first LAN software based on file server technology. After going public in 1985, Novell began acquiring other companies, including Santa Clara Systems (microcomputer workstations, 1987), Digital Research (PC operating software), and Univel (UNIX products) in 1991, and UNIX Systems Laboratories and object-oriented software tool developer Serius in 1993. Noorda stepped down in 1994 and was succeeded by Robert Frankenberg, an experienced Hewlett-Packard

▧ NOVELL.

NOVELL, INC.
HQ: 1555 N. Technology Way,
   Orem, UT 84057
Phone: 801-222-6000
Fax: 801-222-7077
Web site: www.novell.com

OFFICERS

Chairman:
   John A. Young, age 64

President:
   Joseph A. Marengi, age 42, $552,618 pay

EVP and CFO:
   James R. Tolonen, age 46, $498,529 pay

EVP and COO:
   Mary M. Burnside, age 48, $489,489 pay

**SVP Corporate Research and Development
and Chief Technology Officer:**
   Glen Ricart, age 46

**SVP, General Counsel, and Corporate
Secretary:** David R. Bradford, age 45

SVP Human Resources:
   Jennifer Konecny-Costa

Auditors: Ernst & Young LLP

SELECTED PRODUCTS AND SERVICES

GroupWise (integrated document management,
e-mail, forms, group calendaring, online
conferencing, and scheduling)

LAN Workplace TCP/IP (for connecting PCs to
UNIX systems and the Internet)

LANalyzer (for monitoring, analyzing, and
troubleshooting NetWare networks)

ManageWise (for management of the Novell
environment)

NetWare Connect (for remote access to
NetWare networks)

NetWare 3, NetWare 4 (network operating
systems)

TUXEDO System (for development of distributed
client/server applications)

KEY COMPETITORS

Apple	IBM
Artisoft	Microsoft
Banyan Systems	NCR
Cheyenne Software	NetManage
DEC	Netscape
FTP	Santa Cruz Operation
Hewlett-Packard	Sun Microsystems

---

executive. In 1995 Novell sold its WordPerfect subsidiary (acquired in 1994) to
Corel Corporation and its UnixWare product line to Santa Cruz Operation.

Novell licensed Java, Sun Microsystems's Internet development language, to speed
its development of Internet capabilities for Novell software in 1996. However, dis-
satisfied with Novell's position in the Internet marketplace, the company's board
forced Frankenberg out in August 1996. John Young, a board member and former
head of Hewlett-Packard, was named chairman, and the company began searching
for a new CEO.

NOVELL, INC.: THE NUMBERS

Nasdaq symbol: NOVL FYE: October 31	Annual Growth	1990	1991	1992	1993	1994	1995
Sales ($ mil.)	32.6%	497.5	640.1	933.4	1,122.9	1,998.1	2,041.2
Net income ($ mil.)	29.2%	94.3	162.5	249.0	(35.2)	206.7	338.3
Income as % of sales	—	19.0%	25.4%	26.7%	—	10.3%	16.6%
Earnings per share ($)	21.5%	0.34	0.55	0.81	(0.11)	0.56	0.90
Stock price – high ($)	—	8.50	32.38	33.50	35.25	26.25	23.25
Stock price – low ($)	—	3.44	7.63	22.50	17.00	13.75	13.75
Stock price – close ($)	11.6%	8.25	30.00	28.50	20.75	17.13	14.25
P/E – high	—	25	59	41	—	47	26
P/E – low	—	10	14	28	—	25	15
Dividends per share ($)	—	0.00	0.00	0.00	0.00	0.00	0.00
Book value per share ($)	29.9%	1.41	2.08	3.12	3.23	4.08	5.22
Employees	24.6%	2,419	2,843	3,637	4,335	7,914	7,272

1995 YEAR-END

Debt ratio: 0.0%
Return on equity: 19.8%
Cash (mil.): $1,321.2
Current ratio: 4.18
Long-term debt (mil.): $0.0
No. of shares (mil.): 371.6
Dividends
  Yield: —
  Payout: —
Market value (mil.): $5,294.8

QUARTER ENDED 7/31

	1996	1995
Sales ($ millions)	365.1	537.9
Net Income ($ millions)	58.8	102.0
Earnings Per Share ($)	0.17	0.27
No. of Shares (thou.)	352,129	370,156

9 MONTHS ENDED 7/31

	1996	1995
Sales ($ millions)	991.2	1,560.7
Net Income ($ millions)	67.0	279.4
Earnings Per Share ($)	0.18	0.75
No. of Shares (thou.)	352,129	370,156

STOCK PRICE HISTORY: High/Low/Close

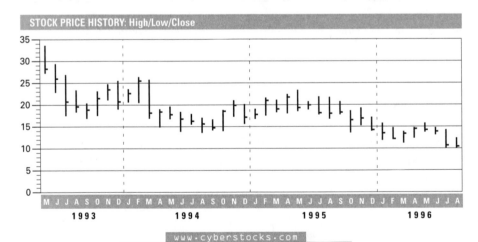

NTN
Communications

- May be only profitable interactive-TV programmer

- Subscription base of bars and restaurants is still growing

- Business is content-focused, technology-independent

- Moving its sports and trivia games to online services and the Internet

- Entering the online horse-race gambling business

- 1st half 1996 sales up 55%, Internet-related sales up 250%

When the game is played on NTN Communications's field, nobody gets left on the bench. Carlsbad, California-based NTN is an industry leader in providing games and other interactive entertainment allowing multiple users to participate simultaneously through TV and online. Its NTN ENTERTAIN-MENT NETWORK, which uses satellite broadcasts combined with PC, telephone, and hand-held keypad technology, reaches more than 3,100 hospitality locations, such as bars, hotel lounges, restaurants, and country clubs. The products are offered via other media including online services (America Online, GEnie, and ImagiNation) and cable systems (GTE mainStreet and Booth Cable). NTN has licensing agreements with professional football, baseball, and hockey leagues to provide competitive play-along programming. Through its IWN joint venture, the company develops online services for the gaming industry. Subsidiary LearnStar, Inc., provides an interactive educational system for schools. CEO Patrick Downs and his brother Daniel, president and COO, together control about 8% of the stock.

In the early 1980s the Downs brothers helped develop QB1 (still one of NTN's top products), an interactive game in which players try to predict the progress of live football broadcasts. They were doing business by 1983, and Alroy Industries was incorporated in 1984, with Patrick as CEO. Alroy went public that year and changed its name to NTN Communications following the acquisition of National Telecommunicator Network in 1985. The company grew by developing QB1 and other proprietary TV programming and distributing these products in income-generating group settings in order to

- Interactive TV is far from reaching most homes

- On the Internet, barriers to competition seem low

- NFL licensing agreement expires in 1997

- New start-up businesses have been unprofitable so far

NTN COMMUNICATIONS, INC.

HQ: 5966 La Place Ct.,
Carlsbad, CA 92008
Phone: 619-438-7400
Fax: 619-438-7470

OFFICERS

Chairman and CEO:
Patrick J. Downs, age 59, $192,044 pay
VC: Alan P. Magerman, age 61
President and COO:
Daniel C. Downs, age 56, $192,044 pay
EVP Systems:
Gerald P. McLaughlin, age 56, $184,333 pay
EVP Marketing: Jerry V. Petrie, age 53
EVP and CFO:
Gerald Sokol Jr., age 33
Chief Administrative Officer:
Ronald E. Hogan, age 57, $150,177 pay
President, IWN, Inc.:
Colleen Anderson, age 45
President, LearnStar, Inc.:
Michael J. Downs, age 62
Director Human Resources:
Genice Eichert
Auditors: KPMG Peat Marwick LLP

SELECTED PRODUCTS AND SERVICES

Business Units
Hospitality Services (interactive TV network for bars, restaurants and other group environments)
International Licensing (provides interactive TV to hospitality sites outside the US)
Home Interactive Services (games and other programming through online and other 3rd-party providers)
LearnStar, Inc. (interactive educational systems for schools)

Game Titles
DiamondBall
PlayBack
QB1
Showdown
Sports IQ

KEY COMPETITORS

3DO	Microsoft
Brøderbund	Multimedia Games
CEL Communications	Producers Entertainment
Edunetics	Spelling Entertainment
Electronic Arts	TCI
IBM	Video Jukebox
Interactive Technologies	Video Lottery
Jostens	

build brand recognition. NTN acquired New World Computing, Inc., a software developer, in 1993 to broaden NTN's game portfolio. It formed educational joint venture LearnStar that year and gambling subsidiary IWN in 1994.

NTN signed deals with America Online in 1995 and CompuServe in 1996 to provide programming to their global base of online subscribers. That year NTN sold New World Computing to entertainment systems company 3DO.

NTN: THE NUMBERS

AMEX symbol: NTN FYE: December 31	Annual Growth	1990	1991	1992[1]	1993	1994	1995
Sales ($ mil.)	40.1%	5.9	5.9	10.7	17.3	24.6	31.8
Net income ($ mil.)	—	(1.9)	(2.4)	(2.2)	(1.3)	0.7	(3.9)
Income as % of sales	—	—	—	—	—	2.9%	—
Earnings per share ($)	—	(0.71)	(0.24)	(0.20)	(0.08)	0.03	(0.19)
Stock price – high ($)	—	5.94	5.94	6.00	11.50	10.25	8.25
Stock price – low ($)	—	0.94	2.75	3.00	4.38	4.31	4.06
Stock price – close ($)	19.1%	1.88	3.13	4.94	10.00	6.00	4.50
P/E – high	—	—	—	—	—	342	—
P/E – low	—	—	—	—	—	144	—
Dividends per share ($)	—	0.00	0.00	0.00	0.00	0.00	0.00
Book value per share ($)	—	(3.44)	0.27	0.56	1.26	1.33	1.49
Employees	23.8%	—	—	145	155	210	275

[1] 4-month fiscal year

1995 YEAR-END

Debt ratio: 5.9%
Return on equity: —
Cash (mil.): $8.1
Current ratio: 3.27
Long-term debt (mil.): $0.0
No. of shares (mil.): 22.5
Dividends
  Yield: —
  Payout: —
Market value (mil.): $101.0
R&D as % of sales: 4.6%

QUARTER ENDED 6/30

	1996	1995
Sales ($ millions)	9.3	6.2
Net Income ($ millions)	2.4	0.1
Earnings Per Share ($)	0.10	0.01
No. of Shares (thou.)	23,848	20,949

6 MONTHS ENDED 6/30

	1996	1995
Sales ($ millions)	16.4	12.0
Net Income ($ millions)	2.6	(1.8)
Earnings Per Share ($)	0.11	(0.09)
No. of Shares (thou.)	23,848	20,949

STOCK PRICE HISTORY: High/Low/Close

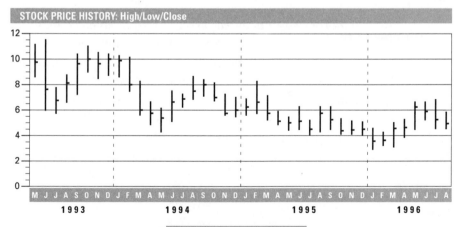

- Claims to be the leader in object databases

- New strategic emphasis on Internet and intranet applications

- Products are well-suited to Web data types, including multimedia

- Appears to have restored profitability through cost cutting

- Relatively new top management

- Market cap near $300 million (8/96) vs. first half 1996 sales of $18.2 million

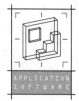

Object Design

A small but aggressive software company with Big Blue at its side can't lose, right? Wrong. Burlington, Massachusetts-based Object Design is the leading supplier of data management systems that use object-oriented programs, a kind of software that breaks computer code into self-contained blocks and can provide easier access to certain types of data. The company has changed its focus to the growing Internet and intranet markets, where it believes its enhanced ObjectStore database management system will function particularly well; its customers in this sector include Southwest Airlines and GTE.

The idea for Object Design came from 7 database engineers, including Thomas Atwood and David Stryker, who met in their respective living rooms during 1988 to talk about starting their own company. Venture capital firms Harvard Management, the Vista Group, and Orient Ventures put up $2.75 million in early financing.

In 1990 the company introduced ObjectStore; early customers included 3 leading CAD engineering firms. Between 1992 and 1994 the list of high-profile customers grew with the addition of AT&T, Intel, and Kodak. IBM paid $27 million for a stake in the company and its product license in 1993 and began selling ObjectStore directly to its customers the next year. After an $10 million loss in 1995, CEO Ken Marshall was ousted. Cofounders Atwood and Stryker also left the company that year. Object Design went public in 1996 and began a restructuring program that included layoffs and

OBJECT DESIGN, INC.
HQ: 25 Mall Rd.,
Burlington, MA 01803
Phone: 617-674-5000
Fax: 617-674-5010
Web site: www.odi.com

OFFICERS

President and CEO:
Robert N. Goldman, age 47, $47,726 pay
EVP and COO:
Justin J. Perreault, age 33, $22,759 pay
CFO: Lacey P. Brandt, age 38
SVP Sales:
Robert J. Potter, age 42, $269,092 pay
VP Product Development:
Gregory A. Baryza, age 49, $114,885 pay
VP Professional Services:
Brian W. Otis, age 37, $164,508 pay
Director Human Resources:
Andrea Johnson
Auditors: Coopers & Lybrand L.L.P.

SELECTED PRODUCTS AND SERVICES

DBconnect (connectivity tool)

Internet Solution Suite (products for building Internet and intranet applications)

ObjectStore (database management system)

ObjectStore Inspector (Graphical browser, editor, and query tool)

ObjectStore OpenAccess (query and reporting interface tool)

ObjectStore Performance Expert (graphical interactive analysis and monitoring tool)

Maintenance and support services

Training and consulting

	1995 Sales	
	$ mil.	% of total
Software	18.7	57
Services	10.9	33
Related-party software & services	3.1	10
Total	**32.7**	**100**

KEY COMPETITORS

Borland	O2 Corp.
Computer Associates	Objectivity
Gemstone	Oracle
IBM	Poet
Informix	Sybase
Microsoft	Versant Object

other cost-cutting measures. The company also restructured its product marketing and introduced Internet Solution Suite, a database management system for the Internet and intranet markets.

OBJECT DESIGN: THE NUMBERS

Nasdaq symbol: ODIS FYE: December 31	Annual Growth	1990	1991	1992	1993	1994	1995
Sales ($ mil.)	69.1%	—	4.0	10.6	24.7	25.5	32.7
Net income ($ mil.)	—	—	(3.9)	(2.3)	0.6	(12.0)	(10.3)
Income as % of sales	—	—	—	—	2.5%	—	—
Employees	—	—	—	—	—	—	204

1995 YEAR-END

Debt ratio: 100.0%
Return on equity: —
Cash (mil.): $4.0
Current ratio: 0.93
Long-term debt (mil.): $0.5
No. of shares (mil.): —
Dividends
  Yield: —
  Payout: —
Market value (mil.): —

QUARTER ENDED 6/30

	1996	1995
Sales ($ millions)	9.2	7.1
Net Income ($ millions)	(0.4)	(4.6)
Earnings Per Share ($)	(0.03)	(0.48)
No. of Shares (thou.)	12,631	9,532

6 MONTHS ENDED 6/30

	1996	1995
Sales ($ millions)	18.2	15.1
Net Income ($ millions)	(0.6)	(6.6)
Earnings Per Share ($)	(0.05)	(0.69)
No. of Shares (thou.)	12,631	9,532

STOCK PRICE HISTORY: High/Low/Close

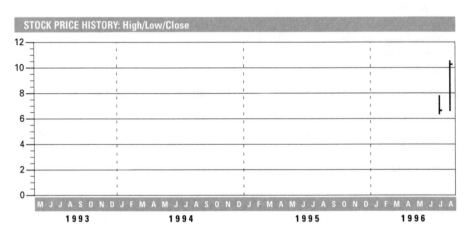

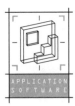

OneWave, Inc.

OneWave is hoping it can hang 10 on the tidal wave-like growth of the World Wide Web. The Watertown, Massachusetts-based company is a leading provider of software for client/server applications that use both the Internet and private intranets. Its OpenScape software family allows businesses to create Web-based departmental networks and links with partners, distributors, and customers. By using the standard Internet protocols, the software allows users to set up cheap, easy-to-use, multi-level networks, so an employee could take an order from a customer, check a distributor's inventory level, and send a request to the shipping department. Founders Sundar Subramaniam and John Donovan (and his family) own around 21% and 25%, respectively. CEO Klaus Besier's owns 7%.

OneWave, originally named Object Power, was started by Donovan (founder of consulting and software development firm Cambridge Technology Group), Subramaniam, and James Nondorf (VP Strategic Alliances) in 1994 as a spinoff from Cambridge Technology to develop and market OpenScape, which was developed by Subramaniam. Object Power changed its name to Business@Web in 1996 and yet again in the same year to OneWave, because the company considered Business@Web too generic to copyright.

To speed the distribution of OpenScape, the company has formed alliances with leading providers of software, hardware, and consulting services, in

- Technology enables older applications to operate over the Internet or intranets

- Market appears to be very receptive

- Among many impressive partnerships:
  * Informix
  * Sterling Commerce
  * Hewlett-Packard
  * PeopleSoft
  * KPMG Peat Marwick

- First half 1996 sales up 446%

- Products could be viewed more as an interim, rather than long-term, solution

- New management team

- Mounting losses

- Market cap of $225 million (8/96) vs first half 1996 sales of $5.5 million

ONEWAVE, INC.

HQ: One Arsenal Marketplace,
Watertown, MA 02172
Phone: 617-923-6500
Fax: 617-923-6565
Web site: www.onewave.com

OFFICERS

Chairman, President, and CEO:
Klaus P. Besier, age 44, $200,000 pay

VP Marketing:
Carolyn LoGalbo, age 45, $225,000 pay

VP Technology:
John Coviello, age 50, $215,000 pay

VP Support Services and Quality:
Joseph Gruttadauria, age 36, $212,000 pay

VP Sales: John Burke, age 36, $200,000 pay

VP Strategic Alliances:
James Nondorf, age 28, $110,000 pay

VP Finance and Treasurer: Eric Sockol, age 35

CFO: Mark Gallagher, age 41, $200,000 pay

General Counsel and Secretary:
Craig Newfield, age 36

Director Product Development:
William Cullen, age 37

Director Human Resources:
David Kimmelman

Auditors: Andersen Worldwide

SELECTED PRODUCTS AND SERVICES

OpenExtensions (point-and-click interface for creating consistent programming components mapped to client/server or other systems)

OpenScape Workbench (object-oriented programming environment)

Visual Component Builder (point-and-click programming language to create presentation components)

Web Engine Client (provides interface for visual components)

	1995 Sales	
	$ mil.	% of total
Consulting & education services	3.9	65
Software license and maintenance	2.2	35
Total	**6.1**	**100**

KEY COMPETITORS

CONNECT
DEC
Dynasty Technologies
Edify
Forte Software
IBM
Microsoft
Netscape
Object Design

Open Market
Oracle
Premenos Technology
Sun Microsystems
Sybase
Versant Object

cluding Hewlett-Packard, NEC, SAP, and Sterling Commerce.

One Wave hired Besier, former CEO of SAP America, a business application software vendor, to run the company in 1996. That year OneWave went public and watched Internet-hungry investors stumble over each other to snap up its stock. Also in 1996 OneWave formed alliances with software leader Microsoft and Informix to develop object linking and Internet software.

ONEWAVE: THE NUMBERS

Nasdaq symbol: OWAV FYE: December 31	Annual Growth	1990	1991	1992	1993	1994	1995
Sales ($ mil.)	—	—	—	—	—	0.0	6.1
Net income ($ mil.)	—	—	—	—	—	(1.2)	(2.7)
Income as % of sales	—	—	—	—	—	—	—
Employees	—	—	—	—	—	—	114

1995 YEAR-END

Debt ratio: 100.0%
Return on equity: —
Cash (mil.): $0.1
Current ratio: 0.56
Long-term debt (mil.): $1.0
No. of shares (mil.): —
Dividends
  Yield: —
  Payout: —
Market value (mil.): —
R&D as % of sales: 52.4%

QUARTER ENDED 6/30

	1996	1995
Sales ($ millions)	3.2	0.6
Net Income ($ millions)	(0.8)	(0.3)
Earnings Per Share ($)	(0.06)	(0.03)
No. of Shares (thou.)	14,758	14,758

6 MONTHS ENDED 6/30

	1996	1995
Sales ($ millions)	5.5	1.0
Net Income ($ millions)	(9.3)	(0.6)
Earnings Per Share ($)	(0.71)	(0.06)
No. of Shares (thou.)	14,758	14,758

STOCK PRICE HISTORY: High/Low/Close

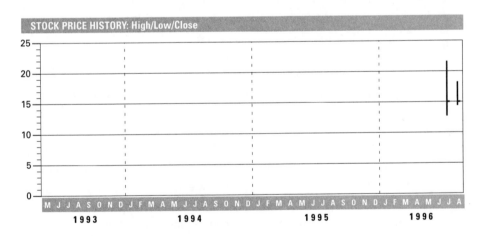

- Focused on high-end of Internet commerce server market

- Products enable centralized, secure Web transaction processing and distributed merchandising

- Key partnerships with Novell, Silicon Graphics, FTP

- Rapidly expanding sales force

- 1st half sales up over 2,700%

- Products are pricy

- Going head-to-head with Netscape, Microsoft, Oracle

- 3 customers, one a stockholder, accounted for 64% of revenue in the 1st half of 1996

- Accelerating losses

- Market cap of $400 million vs. 1st half, 1996 sales of $7.4 million

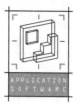

APPLICATION
SOFTWARE

Open Market

The field is still wide open in the race to set the standard for secured payment on the Internet. Who'll win is anybody's guess, but Open Market is making its bid. The Cambridge, Massachusetts-based company makes software that manages transactions over the Internet. Other software products include tools to build Web sites and to create and manage private intranets. It already has a stable of high-profile clients (including First Union bank, Banc One, and financial information publisher Bloomberg) and investors. Some of its largest investors are also clients, including publishers Advance Publications (which owns more than 6% of the company) and Tribune Co. (about 7%). Founders Shikhar Ghosh and David Gifford each own about 13% of the company.

Ghosh, a former Electronic Data Systems executive, and Gifford, an M.I.T. professor, founded Open Market in 1994. Anticipating the growth of the commercial side of the Internet, they began developing a secure method for buying things over the World Wide Web. Starting out with StoreBuilder Web site software, Ghosh and Gifford proposed to develop a product consisting of a client/server system that combined back-office functions like order processing, customer database building, and customer service with a secured link for collecting payment information. Unlike most systems, Open Market planned for ongoing customer accounts authenticated by coded information.

After developing the concept, the company found investors and worked on the products through 1995. Gary Eichorn, an executive with high-tech stalwart Hewlett-Packard, succeeded Ghosh as CEO late that year. In 1996, after

OPEN MARKET, INC.
HQ: 245 First St., Cambridge, MA 02142
Phone: 617-621-9500
Fax: 617-621-1703
Web site: www.openmarket.com

OFFICERS

Chairman:
Shikhar Ghosh, age 38, $140,000 pay
VC and Scientific Officer:
David K. Gifford, age 41
President and CEO: Gary B. Eichorn, age 41
CFO and Secretary: Regina O. Sommer, age 38
Chief Technical Officer:
Lawrence C. Stewart, age 40
VP Service and Operations:
Thomas A. Nephew, age 44
VP Sales: Daniel E. Ross, age 43
VP Corporate Marketing:
Robert C. Weinberger, age 43
VP Engineering: Peter Y. Woon, age 61
VP Human Resources:
Joanne C. Conrad, age 43
Auditors: Andersen Worldwide

SELECTED PRODUCTS AND SERVICES

OM-Axcess (Intranet authentication and
authorization system)
OM-Express (Internet downloading and delayed
viewing software)
OM-Transact (transaction management system)
Store Builder (Web site construction software)

	1995 Sales	
	$ mil.	% of total
Services to Time Warner (deferred payment)	1.4	78
Products	0.4	22
Total	**1.8**	**100**

KEY COMPETITORS

BroadVision
CONNECT
Cylink
IBM
Microsoft
Netscape
Oracle
Virtual Open Network Environment

$38 million in private investments and with its applications hot off the presses, Open Market went public. Early reaction was favorable, despite the products' high cost, and buyers included telecommunications companies British Telecommunications and MCI. Media conglomerate Time Warner, another early investor, began using the system on its Pathfinder service on the Internet. Conde Nast's Traveler Online also uses the system. The company does not foresee posting a profit in the near term, as it expects to use all of its revenues for rapid growth.

OPEN MARKET: THE NUMBERS

Nasdaq symbol: OMKT FYE: December 31	Annual Growth	1990	1991	1992	1993	1994	1995
Sales ($ mil.)	—	—	—	—	—	0.0	1.8
Net income ($ mil.)	—	—	—	—	—	(1.3)	(13.9)
Income as % of sales	—	—	—	—	—	—	—
Employees	—	—	—	—	—	—	257

1995 YEAR-END

Debt ratio: 100.0%
Return on equity: —
Cash (mil.): $3.7
Current ratio: 0.49
Long-term debt (mil.): $0.7
No. of shares (mil.): —
Dividends
  Yield: —
  Payout: —
Market value (mil.): —
R&D as % of sales: 371.9%

QUARTER ENDED 6/30

	1996	1995
Sales ($ millions)	4.7	0.2
Net Income ($ millions)	(6.7)	(2.5)
Earnings Per Share ($)	(0.24)	(0.10)
No. of Shares (thou.)	28,141	22,940

6 MONTHS ENDED 6/30

	1996	1995
Sales ($ millions)	7.4	0.3
Net Income ($ millions)	(13.5)	(3.6)
Earnings Per Share ($)	(0.50)	(0.13)
No. of Shares (thou.)	28,141	22,940

STOCK PRICE HISTORY: High/Low/Close

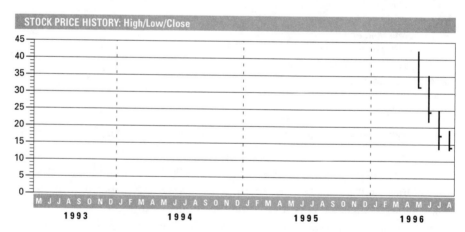

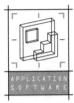
APPLICATION
SOFTWARE

SPECIALIZED
SERVICES

Open Text Corporation

It all started with a battle to index all 22,000 pages of the *Oxford English Dictionary*. Now Waterloo, Ontario-based Open Text Corporation wants to conquer the Internet. The company produces software that enables users to electronically store, search, and distribute large amounts of information. Its primary product, Open Text Index, sorts information on the World Wide Web, indexing every word on a page, rather than a selection of key words. The company also provides stand-alone indexing software, Open Text 5, for custom-designed document management systems. Several big-name firms, including IBM, MCI, and Ford, use Open Text products. Chairman Donald Webster owns about 33% of the company.

Tim Bray, a computer scientist at the University of Waterloo, and 2 of his colleagues began working in 1987 on a system to electronically store and catalog the text in the *Oxford English Dictionary*. When they completed that task in 1989, the idea for Open Text was born. Bray and the others founded the enterprise in 1991. Open Text started out producing text-indexing software for document retrieval, but Bray, finding that market too small, wanted to move on to something more challenging. As the World Wide Web began to take hold in 1994, he put the company to work on developing software that could organize the seemingly endless amount of information on the Web. It released Open Text Index in 1995.

The firm made several acquisitions in 1995 that have substantially expanded its product line, especially in Internet services. These included

OPEN TEXT CORPORATION

HQ: 180 Columbia St. West,
    Waterloo, ON, N2L 3L3, Canada
Phone: 519-888-7111
Fax: 519-888-0677
US HQ: 2201 S. Waukegan Rd.,
    Bannockburn, IL 60015
US Phone: 847-267-9332
US Fax: 847-267-9332
Web site: www.opentext.com

OFFICERS

Chairman: Donald C. Webster, age 65
President and CEO:
  P. Thomas Jenkins, age 36, $140,385 pay
EVP: Michael F. Farrell, age 42, $132,240 pay
President, Odesta: Daniel Cheifetz, age 47
SVP Technology: Timothy W. Bray, age 40
Auditors: KPMG Peat Marwick

SELECTED PRODUCTS AND SERVICES

Internet Anywhere (client-based Internet access tools)

Latitude Web Server (directory tool kit for indexing Web pages)

Livelink (work-flow and document management software for work-group collaboration)

Open Text 5 (indexing and search engine for custom-designed document management systems)

Open Text Index (search engine for indexing Web information)

PC Search (PC search engine, query tool, and viewer; developed from merging its acquired Intunix product with Open Text 5)

	1995 Sales	
	$ mil.	% of total
License	1.8	72
Service	.7	2
Total	**2.5**	**100**

KEY COMPETITORS

America Online	Fulcrum Technologies
CompuServe	Information Dimensions
Dataware	Infoseek
DEC	Lycos
Documentum	Verity
Excalibur Technologies	Yahoo!
Excite!	

Odesta (maker of Livelink, an Internet and Intranet document manager) and Internet Anywhere (a software suite that assists users with Internet access). Although the company is concentrating its efforts on the Internet, it hasn't forgotten its roots. In 1995 it acquired Intunix, an information search product that was combined with Open Text 5 for PC hard drive and CD-ROM searches. The company went public in 1996.

OPEN TEXT: THE NUMBERS

Nasdaq symbol: OTEXF FYE: June 30	Annual Growth	1990	1991	1992	1993	1994	1995
Sales ($ mil.)	88.0%	—	0.2	1.3	1.2	1.6	2.5
Net income ($ mil.)	—	—	(0.3)	0.2	(0.3)	(0.7)	(1.2)
Income as % of sales	—	—	—	15.4%	—	—	—
Employees	—	—	—	—	—	—	113

1995 YEAR-END

Debt ratio: 70.5%
Return on equity: —
Cash (mil.): $0.0
Current ratio: 1.06
Long-term debt (mil.): $0.2
No. of shares (mil.): —
Dividends
　Yield: —
　Payout: —
Market value (mil.): —
R&D as % of sales: 28.6%

QUARTER ENDED 3/31

	1996	1995
Sales ($ millions)	3.3	0.7
Net Income ($ millions)	(2.1)	(0.1)
Earnings Per Share ($)	(0.14)	(0.05)
No. of Shares (thou.)	15,813	2,758

9 MONTHS ENDED 3/31

	1996	1995
Sales ($ millions)	6.2	1.4
Net Income ($ millions)	(27.7)	(1.1)
Earnings Per Share ($)	(2.60)	(0.50)
No. of Shares (thou.)	15,183	2,758

STOCK PRICE HISTORY: High/Low/Close

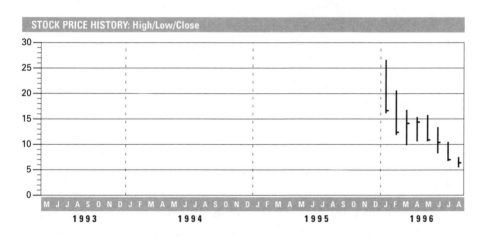

- Holds a strong position in niche market for high-end hubs

- Integrates and sells its hubs with best-selling routers and switches

- Partnership with EDS has resulted in large hub orders

- System integrators (50% of sales) should thrive as network complexity increases

- Knows how to sell to the government

- Single product line results in uneven sales growth

- Resale of 3rd-party products yields lower gross margins

- Depends on EDS for 30% of revenues

- US Government accounts for 10% of revenues

Optical Data Systems, Inc.

Optical Data Systems (ODS) helps computer networks run smarter. The Richardson, Texas-based company makes networking products, including intelligent hubs — a central switching device for a network that also boosts signal strength and monitors network activity. ODS's Infinity series of intelligent hubs, which supports the major networking standards (ATM, Ethernet, FDDI, and token ring), accounts for about 90% of the company's revenues. ODS sells primarily to end users in the aerospace, computer, industrial, and telecommunications markets. Its largest customers — AT&T, systems integrator Electronic Data Systems, and the US government — together account for nearly half of the company's revenues. Cofounder and chairman Ward Paxton and his family own nearly 25% of ODS; cofounder and SVP Joe Head owns 15%.

Paxton and Head, both veterans of Honeywell's optoelectronics division, formed ODS in 1983 to make modems, multiplexers, and fiber-optic data links. The company introduced a nonmodular hub for Ethernet applications in 1987 and 2 years later initiated a program to add token ring and FDDI products to its lineup. ODS unveiled its Infinity series hubs in 1992 and followed with the smaller Micro-Infinity series in 1993. Through alliances with other networking companies, ODS has extended the scope of its products. In 1993 it formed partnerships with FORE Systems for ATM

Optical Data Systems, Inc.

OPTICAL DATA SYSTEMS, INC.

HQ: 1101 E. Arapaho Rd.,
Richardson, TX 75081
Phone: 214-234-6400
Fax: 214-234-1467
Web site: www.ods.com

OFFICERS

Chairman, President, and CEO:
G. Ward Paxton, age 60, $415,400 pay

SVP: T. Joe Head, age 39, $315,742 pay

VP Strategic Business Development:
Eric H. Gore, age 42, $274,686 pay

VP and CFO:
Roger H. Hughes, age 53, $244,704 pay

VP Operations:
Garry L. Hemphill, age 47, $244,704 pay

VP North American Sales:
Joe W. Tucker Jr., age 53, $244,704 pay

Director Administration (HR):
Donna J. Combs, age 47

Auditors: Ernst & Young LLP

SELECTED PRODUCTS AND SERVICES

Infinity intelligent hubs
LAN Vision network management system
Micro-Infinity intelligent hubs

	1995 Sales	
	$ mil.	% of total
Ethernet products	71.4	64
FDDI products	19.2	17
Token ring products	16.2	15
ATM products	3.2	3
Other products & services	1.5	1
Total	**111.5**	**100**

KEY COMPETITORS

3Com
Bay Networks
Boca
Cabletron
Cascade Communications
Cisco Systems
Intel
U.S. Robotics

switches and with Cisco Systems for that company's top-of-the-line router. The next year ODS installed the world's largest ATM backbone (a high-speed connection) for the US Army.

The company expanded into Asia and Latin America in 1995, with offices in Brazil, Japan, Malaysia, and Taiwan. The following year the company opened an office in South Korea and ODS won a subcontract from GTE to provide equipment for the Army's new $259 million network.

ODS: THE NUMBERS

Nasdaq symbol: ODSI FYE: December 31	Annual Growth	1990	1991	1992	1993	1994	1995
Sales ($ mil.)	28.4%	32.0	37.1	49.2	55.9	86.6	111.5
Net income ($ mil.)	51.8%	1.7	1.8	5.0	4.9	8.6	13.7
Income as % of sales	—	5.3%	5.0%	10.2%	8.8%	9.9%	12.3%
Earnings per share ($)	44.2%	0.13	0.14	0.34	0.30	0.52	0.81
Stock price – high ($)	—	—	—	—	—	14.88	43.25
Stock price – low ($)	—	—	—	—	—	5.38	12.75
Stock price – close ($)	—	—	—	—	—	14.56	25.25
P/E – high	—	—	—	—	—	29	53
P/E – low	—	—	—	—	—	10	16
Dividends per share ($)	—	—	—	—	—	0.00	0.00
Book value per share ($)	—	—	—	—	—	2.74	3.63
Employees	18.6%	—	176	—	230	310	348

1995 YEAR-END

Debt ratio:0.0%
Return on equity: 26.8%
Cash (mil.): $25.7
Current ratio: 4.98
Long-term debt (mil.): $0.0
No. of shares (mil.): 16.1
Dividends
  Yield: —
  Payout: —
Market value ($ mil.): $407.8
R&D as % of sales: 7.2%

QUARTER ENDED 6/30

	1996	1995
Sales ($ millions)	31.0	30.9
Net Income ($ millions)	3.6	3.8
Earnings Per Share ($)	0.22	0.23
No. of Shares (thou.)	16,250	16,048

6 MONTHS ENDED 6/30

	1996	1995
Sales ($ millions)	60.5	55.4
Net Income ($ millions)	7.1	6.8
Earnings Per Share ($)	0.42	0.41
No. of Shares (thou.)	16,250	16,048

STOCK PRICE HISTORY: High/Low/Close

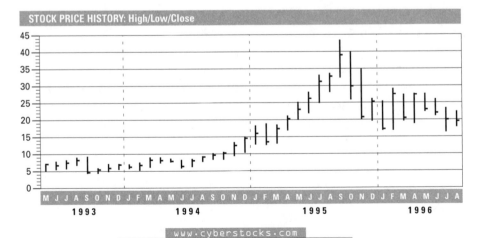

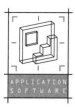

APPLICATION
SOFTWARE

Oracle Corporation

Oracle can claim to be the prophet of profit. As the world's #1 vendor of relational database software, the Redwood City, California-based company has already made a fortune telling corporate computers how to gather information — companies in 90 countries employ Oracle's client/server applications. Now the company is looking for ways to help customers get that information on the Internet. Oracle CEO Lawrence Ellison is forecasting a role for the company in interactive television and electronic commerce. He has also been a leading proponent of network computers (NCs), low-cost ($500) terminals that provide Internet access. Oracle does not plan to sell the terminals but rather the software to run them. The company also has joined telecom superstar MCI and Rupert Murdoch's News Corp. in a joint venture to develop an online information service. Ellison, one of software-dom's richest executives, owns over 23% of Oracle and a majority interest in nCUBE, a maker of massively parallel computers.

Software programmers Ellison, Robert Miner, and Edward Oates founded Oracle in 1977 to create a relational database management system for mini-computers according to theoretical specifications published by IBM. One of Oracle's early advantages was its ability to tailor its products to run on many brands of computers of all sizes — from PCs to mainframes. Oracle

- Leading independent client/server database software developer

- Superbly positioned to profit from Internet and intranet growth

- Strategy of selling large companies integrated business applications is working

- The first inexpensive network computers running Oracle's "NC" operating system may ship soon

- Support revenues accounted for 21% of sales in fiscal 1996

- Rival Sybase has hit the skids

- May encounter new competition in Internet/intranet-related markets

- Microsoft, with control of Windows NT, is a long-term threat in the server market

- P/E over 40 (8/96)

ORACLE®

ORACLE CORPORATION
HQ: 500 Oracle Pkwy.,
Redwood City, CA 94065
Phone: 415-506-7000
Fax: 415-506-7200
Web site: www.oracle.com

OFFICERS

Chairman, President, and CEO:
Lawrence J. Ellison, age 50, $3,343,090 pay
EVP; President, Worldwide Operations:
Raymond J. Lane, age 48, $2,127,434 pay
EVP and CFO:
Jeffrey O. Henley, age 50, $1,519,582 pay
EVP Product Division:
Dirk A. Kabcenell, age 43, $1,055,378 pay
**SVP, General Counsel, and Corporate
Secretary:** Raymond L. Ocampo Jr., age 42
SVP Human Resources: Phillip E. Wilson
Auditors: Andersen Worldwide

SELECTED PRODUCTS AND SERVICES
Application Development and Access Tools
Designer/2000
Developer/2000
Discover/2000
End-User Applications
Oracle Financial
Oracle Government Financials
Oracle Human Resources
Oracle Manufacturing
Server Technology
DBMS (RELATIONAL database)

KEY COMPETITORS

Baan	IBM
BMC Software	Microsoft
Cognos	Novell
Computer Associates	Object Design
CONNECT	PeopleSoft, Inc.
DEC	SAP
Dun & Bradstreet	Software AG
Forte Software	Sybase
Gupta	System Software
Hyperion Software	Associates
Informix	

went public in 1986 and started making inroads into government circles. The company soon added software, including financial management, graphics, and human-resource management programs.

In 1992 Oracle launched Oracle7, a network database featuring simplified information access. The company unveiled Personal Oracle7 in 1995, a desktop version of the business database software. The next year Oracle paid $100 million in cash for Information Resources, including the Express family of online analysis tools. Also in 1996 Oracle got the support of Sun Microsystems, IBM, Apple, and Netscape for technical standards for NC software.

ORACLE: THE NUMBERS

Nasdaq symbol: ORCL FYE: May 31	Annual Growth	1991	1992	1993	1994	1995	1996[1]
Sales ($ mil.)	32.7%	1,027.9	1,178.5	1,502.8	2,001.1	2,966.9	4,223.3
Net income ($ mil.)	—	(12.4)	61.5	141.7	283.7	441.5	603.3
Income as % of sales	—	—	5.2%	9.4%	14.2%	14.9%	14.3%
Earnings per share ($)	—	(0.02)	0.10	0.22	0.43	0.67	0.90
Stock price – high ($)	—	3.69	6.36	16.78	20.67	32.50	40.38
Stock price – low ($)	—	1.22	2.67	5.92	11.67	17.78	26.33
Stock price – close ($)	65.1%	3.22	6.31	12.78	19.61	28.25	39.44
P/E – high	—	—	64	76	48	49	45
P/E – low	—	—	27	27	27	27	29
Dividends per share ($)	—	0.00	0.00	0.00	0.00	0.00	0.00
Book value per share ($)	50.9%	0.56	0.69	0.83	1.15	1.86	4.38
Employees	25.4%	7,466	8,160	9,247	12,058	16,882	23,113

[1] Stock prices through June 30.

1996 YEAR-END

Debt ratio: 0.2%
Return on equity: 29.6%
Cash (mil.): $841
Current ratio: 1.57
Long-term debt (mil.): $1
No. of shares (mil.): 656
Dividends
    Yield: —
    Payout: —
Market value (mil.): $25,864

QUARTER ENDED 5/31

	1996	1995
Sales ($ millions)	1,464.1	1,017.9
Net Income ($ millions)	266.3	181.7
Earnings Per Share ($)	0.40	0.27
No. of Shares (thou.)	655,826	649,711

12 MONTHS ENDED 5/31

	1996	1995
Sales ($ millions)	4,223.3	2,966.9
Net Income ($ millions)	603.3	441.5
Earnings Per Share ($)	0.90	0.67
No. of Shares (thou.)	655,826	649,711

STOCK PRICE HISTORY: High/Low/Close

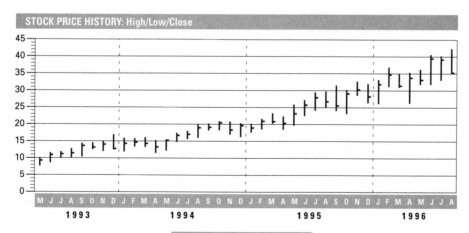

www.cyberstocks.com

- Tightly focused on electronic retrieval of medical information

- Enjoys tremendous market share in major medical institutions

- Delivers information via a broad range of electronic media, including the Internet

- Data distributed is "need-to-know" information

- Internet, as a channel, vastly increases accessible market, enables "pay-as-you-go" service

- Technology is being applied to other specialized markets

- Service is expensive

- Content is not proprietary, theoretically leaving door open to competition

- At present, much of its content is bibliographic, not full text

- Flat earnings

SPECIALIZED
SERVICES

Ovid Technologies

Ovid has metamorphosed medical research. Formerly known as CDP Technologies, the company changed its name in 1995 to reflect its dominant product line, the Ovid database technology. Ovid's software allows physicians, librarians, students, and other researchers to search about 80 databases of biomedical and scientific literature via both the company's online service and the World Wide Web. Most of its customers, including about 2/3 of the major medical centers in the US and Canada, pay an annual subscription fee to access its databases. Founder and CEO Mark Nelson owns 71% of the company. Chairman Martin Kahn owns 8%.

Nelson began writing search programs for a small consulting firm in the early 1980s. He launched Online Research Systems in 1985 and spent the next 3 years writing a search program to access the National Library of Medicine's Medline database, released on CD-ROM in 1988. To satisfy increasing demand for multiple users, the company released its PlusNet networking products in 1989. PlusNet offered the same search software as its CD-ROM products, but up to 24 people could use it simultaneously.

The company introduced the Ovid user interface in 1993 as a common way to access all of the company's products and services. In 1994 CDP Technologies (as it had become known — short for CD Plus Technologies) entered the online market, acquiring BRS Online, one of the original online database services, from MacMillan Communications. That year the company went public. In 1995, the year it took its present name, Ovid released

O V I D

OVID TECHNOLOGIES, INC.
HQ: 333 Seventh Ave.,
   New York, NY 10001
Phone: 212-563-3006
Fax: 212-563-3784
Web site: www.ovid.com

OFFICERS

Chairman: Martin F. Kahn
President and CEO:
   Mark L. Nelson, age 38, $150,000 pay
COO: Deborah M. Hull, age 51, $150,000 pay
CFO: Jerry P. McAuliffe, age 32
VP Worldwide Sales:
   Carleen E. Nelson, age 32
Manager Human Resources: Beatriz Abreu
Auditors: Coopers & Lybrand LLP

SELECTED PRODUCTS AND SERVICES

Internet
   Ovid Online
   Ovid Web Gateway
   Ovid Z39.50 Windows Client
Local Areal Network
   Integrated Library System
   Local Ovid UNIX Server
   Ovid VT-100 Client
   Ovid Z39.50 Windows Client

	1995 Sales	
	$ mil.	% of total
Database subscriptions & software	27.2	93
Maintenance & other	2.1	7
Total	**29.3**	**100**

KEY COMPETITORS

Access Health	OneSource
CompuServe	Primark
Dataware Technologies	Prodigy
Excalibur Technologies	Reed Elsevier
Fulcrum Technologies	Telescan
Healtheon	Verity
Infonautics	

the Core Biomedical Collection, making the full text of 15 respected biomedical journals available online.

In 1996 the company released the Ovid Web Gateway to allow users to access Ovid software over the Web. Ovid plans to increase its presence in the worldwide academic, scientific, and biomedical markets, and it recently opened new sales offices in Paris and Bonn and expanded its global sales staff.

OVID TECHNOLOGIES: THE NUMBERS

Nasdaq symbol: OVID FYE: December 31	Annual Growth	1990	1991	1992	1993	1994	1995
Sales ($ mil.)	44.6%	—	—	9.7	11.1	22.2	29.3
Net income ($ mil.)	102.7%	—	—	0.3	0.5	1.1	2.5
Income as % of sales	—	—	—	2.7%	4.8%	5.0%	8.4%
Earnings per share ($)	97.2%	—	—	—	0.09	0.17	0.35
Stock price – high ($)	—	—	—	—	—	11.00	14.50
Stock price – low ($)	—	—	—	—	—	5.75	6.75
Stock price – close ($)	—	—	—	—	—	8.75	7.25
P/E – high	—	—	—	—	—	65	41
P/E – low	—	—	—	—	—	34	19
Dividends per share ($)	—	—	—	—	—	0.00	0.00
Book value per share ($)	—	—	—	—	—	1.44	1.96
Employees	30.3%	—	—	—	99	143	168

1995 YEAR-END

Debt ratio: 0.0%
Return on equity: 26.0%
Cash (mil.): $5.4
Current ratio: 1.66
Long-term debt (mil.): $0.0
No. of shares (mil.): 5.7
Dividends
  Yield: —
  Payout: —
Market value (mil.): $41.3

QUARTER ENDED 6/30

	1996	1995
Sales ($ millions)	8.7	7.0
Net Income ($ millions)	0.7	0.6
Earnings Per Share ($)	0.10	0.09
No. of Shares (thou.)	5,745	5,535

6 MONTHS ENDED 6/30

	1996	1995
Sales ($ millions)	16.0	13.7
Net Income ($ millions)	0.9	1.0
Earnings Per Share ($)	0.13	0.13
No. of Shares (thou.)	5,745	5,535

STOCK PRICE HISTORY: High/Low/Close

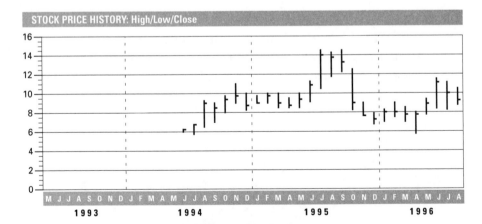

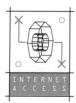

OzEmail Limited

Serving more than 82,000 customers, OzEmail is the largest Internet service provider in Australia and New Zealand. The Sydney, Australia-based company serves 70% of the Australian market (all the state capitals and several regional centers) and major markets in New Zealand. The company's network includes 16 points of presence (POPs) in Australia and 6 in New Zealand. Although Australia has a population of only 18 million, it is estimated that its citizens are second only to the US in per capita use of the Internet and that 30% of its homes have personal computers. The company faces stiff competition in the Internet market from such Australian telecoms as Telstra and Optus Network Ltd. as well as from international providers MCI and BT.

OzEmail was founded in 1994 by Sean Howard. Howard had started *Australia Personal Computer*, a PC magazine, in 1980. He subsequently sold a majority stake in the magazine to publisher Australian Consolidated Press Ltd. in 1984, forming the Computer Publications Pty Ltd. partnership, for which Howard served as managing director until 1992. Between 1992 and 1994 Howard ran an electronic mail business before establishing OzEmail as an Internet service provider in 1994.

The company completed its launch strategy in 1995 by establishing 16 POPs across Australia. That year OzEmail formed 80%-owned subsidiary Voyager New Zealand Ltd. to provide local call Internet access across New Zealand. In 1996 OzEmail expanded its business in Australia, launching *Australian NetGuide Magazine* and Australian NetGuide Online, and setting up an ISDN division for its enterprise customers. The company went public

- #1 ISP in Australia and New Zealand
- Contracted to provide Internet access to every government school in New South Wales
- Eyeing Asia for expansion opportunities
- Has started addressing the business market
- Profitable, unlike US-based ISPs
- First half 1996 sales up 185%

- Network expansion is hurting earnings
- Still small by US standards
- Competitive pressures make price reductions likely
- Entangled in lawsuit brought by Trumpet Software

OZEMAIL LIMITED

HQ: MDIS House, 39 Herbert St., St.
Leonards, 2065 Sydney, Australia
Phone: +61-2-391-0400
Web site: www.ozemail.com.au

OFFICERS

Chairman: Malcolm B. Turnbull, age 41
CEO: Sean Howard, age 36
President and COO: David Spence, age 44
CFO: John Worton, age 35
VP Sales: Gerard Kohne, age 37
VP Marketing: Michael Komoroski, age 37
VP Technical Services: Andrew Kent, age 34
VP Customer Support Services:
Lavell Baylor, age 33

Corporate Sales Manager:
Stephen Standish, age 35

Controller: Anna Cvetkovska, age 29
Network Services Manager:
David Hayhoe, age 23

Company Secretary: Michael Hughes
Auditors: Price Waterhouse LLP

SELECTED PRODUCTS AND SERVICES

Class C license registration
Commercial Web site hosting
Dial-up ISDN connections
Domain name registration
Free technical support
Instant mail
Internet security
List servers
Local call access
Permanent 28,800-bps modem connections
Permanent IP address
Permanent ISDN access
SMTP and UUCP e-mail gateways
Virtual Web servers
World Wide Web access and site leasing
World Wide Web page design and development

KEY COMPETITORS

AAP Telecommuni-cations	Microplex
Access One	Microsoft
Ausnet	New Zealand Telecom
BT	Novell
Connect.com	Optus Network
IBM	Telstra
MCI	

that year. CEO Howard holds 34% of the company; chairman Malcolm Turnbull and director Trevor Kennedy each own a 17% stake.

OzEmail is planning to establish its leadership in Asia/Pacific markets as well as in Australasia. In 1996 it set up a joint venture to apply for Internet service provider licenses in India. The company is also eyeing similar expansion in Indonesia and Malaysia.

OZEMAIL: THE NUMBERS

Nasdaq symbol: OZEMY FYE: December 31	Annual Growth	1990	1991	1992	1993	1994	1995
Sales ($ mil.)	—	—	—	—	—	0.5	6.6
Net income ($ mil.)	—	—	—	—	—	0.0	0.3
Income as % of sales	—	—	—	—	—	2.6%	4.5%
Employees	—	—	—	—	—	—	134

1995 YEAR-END

Debt ratio: 24.8%
Return on equity: 52.2%
Cash (mil.): $0.0
Current ratio: 0.64
Long-term debt (mil.): $0.4
No. of shares (mil.): —
Dividends
  Yield: —
  Payout: —
Market value (mil.): —

QUARTER ENDED 6/30

	1996	1995
Sales ($ millions)	5.1	1.6
Net Income ($ millions)	0.6	0.4
Earnings Per Share ($)	0.07	0.05
No. of Shares (thou.)	8,620	7,440

6 MONTHS ENDING 6/30

	1996	1995
Sales ($ millions)	8.3	2.6
Net Income ($ millions)	(0.0)	0.6
Earnings Per Share ($)	(0.01)	0.08
No. of Shares (thou.)	8,620	7,440

STOCK PRICE HISTORY: High/Low/Close

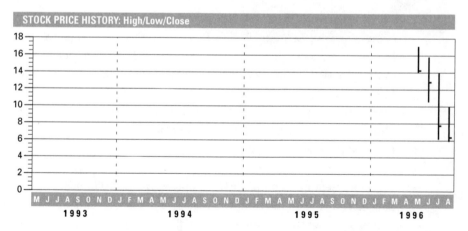

- A leading provider of bulk quote feeds to financial institutions and online publishers

- Entering wireless quote business in partnership with Wireless Financial

- Has popular Web site, provides quotes to MSN

- Blamed 2nd quarter 1996 loss on expenses incurred for its Internet activities

- Appears to have lost contract to provide quotes to America Online

- Competes with industry heavies including ADP, Reuters

- Recent turnover in executive offices

- Spotty track record

SPECIALIZED
SERVICES

PC Quote, Inc.

PC Quote is among the leading suppliers of financial market data to commercial and individual customers. The secret to its ability to capture such big-league partners as Charles Schwab and Microsoft is its HyperFeed transmission system. Hyperfeed allows PC Quote to supply its data instantaneously via satellite rather than over phone lines. Additionally, unlike that of many competitors PC Quote's data can be manipulated by clients' systems instead of being confined to a rigid format. Chairman Louis Morgan owns 5.5% of the company.

On-Line Response, PC Quote's predecessor, built the world's first real-time option analysis system in 1975. In 1980 the company incorporated with Morgan as president. It became PC Quote in 1983 and went public the following year. The company garnered a clientele of banks and financial institutions and received a cash infusion from investor and ally Bridge Information Systems (now Global Financial Services). However, it remained unprofitable because of high product-development costs. The company introduced HyperFeed in 1989.

PC Quote crept into profitability, but operating costs ballooned as it expanded and in 1994 the company began a cost-cutting campaign. This initiative, along with new contracts (including one in 1995 to provide data for Microsoft Network), caused profits to quintuple in 1995. That year Global

PC QUOTE, INC.

PC QUOTE, INC.
HQ: 300 S. Wacker Dr., Ste. 300,
Chicago, IL 60606
Phone: 312-913-2800
Fax: 312-913-2900
Web site: www.pcquote.com

OFFICERS

Chairman, CEO, and Treasurer:
Louis J. Morgan, age 59, $241,896 pay

President and COO: Howard C. Meltzer
CFO: Richard F. Chappetto, age 46, $174,298 pay
SVP Systems Development:
Michael J. Kreutzjans, $135,696 pay

VP Sales and Marketing:
Jerry M. Traver, $145,619 pay

VP Operations and Client Support:
James M. Yates

Corporate Secretary (HR): Darlene Czaja
Auditors: McGladrey & Pullen, LLP

SELECTED PRODUCTS AND SERVICES

HyperFeed (digital data transmission product)

MarketSmart (consumer Internet quote service)

PC QUOTE (real-time stock and commodity trading data software for DOS, OS2, and Windows)

PriceWare (asset pricing service)

QuoteLan (for networks)

QuoteWare (data interfaces with user systems)

Stock Mania (joint venture Internet service with Corel Corp.)

	1995 Sales	
	$ mil.	% of total
Services	9.5	71
Services to Global Financial Services	3.9	29
Total	**13.4**	**100**

KEY COMPETITORS

ADP	Knight-Ridder
Bloomberg	Quote.com
Checkfree	Reuters
Data Broadcasting	SunRiver
Dow Jones	Telescan
Global Financial	

sold its interest to Physicians Insurance Co. of Ohio, which now owns about 29% of PC Quote.

In 1996 PC Quote diversified by charging for advertising on its Web site, which receives more than 1.5 million hits per day.

PC QUOTE: THE NUMBERS

AMEX symbol: PQT FYE: December 31	Annual Growth	1990	1991	1992	1993	1994	1995
Sales ($ mil.)	6.0%	10.0	10.2	11.0	12.2	12.9	13.4
Net income ($ mil.)	—	(1.4)	(0.5)	0.1	0.2	0.3	1.5
Income as % of sales	—	—	—	0.9%	1.6%	2.5%	11.3%
Earnings per share ($)	—	(0.21)	(0.08)	0.01	0.03	0.04	0.21
Stock price – high ($)	—	2.38	1.06	1.75	3.75	3.13	27.50
Stock price – low ($)	—	0.81	0.63	0.63	0.75	1.00	1.06
Stock price – close ($)	81.3%	0.81	0.63	0.69	2.13	1.50	15.88
P/E – high	—	—	—	175	125	78	131
P/E – low	—	—	—	63	25	25	5
Dividends per share ($)	—	0.00	0.00	0.00	0.00	0.00	0.00
Book value per share ($)	6.5%	0.67	0.60	0.61	0.64	0.69	0.92
Employees	(1.7%)	85	68	68	79	76	78

1995 YEAR-END

Debt ratio: 12.2%
Return on equity: 26.4%
Cash (mil.): $1.0
Current ratio: 0.83
Long-term debt (mil.): $0.2
No. of shares (mil.): 7.2
Dividends
  Yield: —
  Payout: —
Market value (mil.): $114.1
R&D as % of sales: 4.2%

QUARTER ENDED 6/30

	1996	1995
Sales ($ millions)	4.4	3.2
Net Income ($ millions)	(0.3)	0.4
Earnings Per Share ($)	(0.04)	0.06
No. of Shares (thou.)	7,266	6,992

6 MONTHS ENDED 6/30

	1996	1995
Sales ($ millions)	8.4	6.4
Net Income ($ millions)	0.0	0.7
Earnings Per Share ($)	0.00	0.10
No. of Shares (thou.)	7,266	6,992

STOCK PRICE HISTORY: High/Low/Close

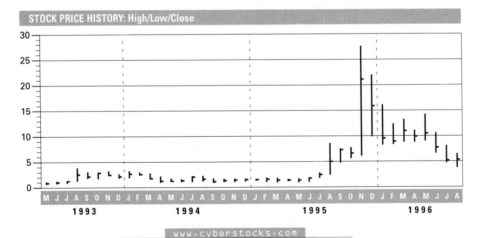

APPLICATION
SOFTWARE

Premenos Technology

Company founder Lew Jenkins had a premonition that Premenos Technology could make money in electronic commerce. Concord, California-based Premenos produces software to increase the speed and decrease the cost of business transactions and communications through Electronic Data Interchange (EDI). The company's EDI/400, used by IBM's AS/400 midrange computer, performs such functions as ordering and invoicing. Premenos also has developed a version that works on UNIX-based computers. More than 3,000 businesses worldwide use the company's EDI translation software. Premenos is expanding its servers to the Internet, providing low-cost EDI to companies previously unable to affort it. The firm's Templar software lets businesses conduct secure and verifiable electronic commerce transactions over the Internet.

Jenkins and 2 partners founded Apparel Computer Systems in 1978. The software company pioneered the use of electronic commerce in the textile industry, installing about 400 of its EDI systems nationwide. In 1987 Jenkins founded Premenos and began developing software for IBM's System/36 and System/38 computers, quickly becoming the most widely used EDI translator for IBM midrange computers. When IBM launched the AS/400 in 1988, Premenos already had an EDI translator for the new system. In 1991 Premenos released its UNIX-based system EDI/e. The company

- Was first company to begin integrating EDI with the Internet
- Internet technology makes EDI transactions less expensive
- Don Valley acquisition to adds EDI products for smaller companies

- Small player in an industry dominated by GE, IBM, Sterling Commerce
- Acquisition costs pushed the company into the red in the 2nd quarter, 1996

Premenos

PREMENOS TECHNOLOGY CORP.
HQ: 1000 Burnett Ave., 2nd Fl.,
  Concord, CA 94520
Phone: 510-602-2000
Fax: 510-602-2024
Web site: www.premenos.com

OFFICERS

Chairman: Lew Jenkins, age 48, $281,250 pay
VC and Secretary:
  David Hildes, age 45
President and CEO:
  Daniel M. Federman, age 61, $225,000 pay
SVP Worldwide Sales and Customer Support:
  Robert M. Davis, age 37, $242,893 pay
SVP Development and Product Management:
  Robert E. Schneider, age 38, $152,885 pay
VP Finance and Administration:
  H. Ward Wolff, age 47, $142,000 pay
Auditors: Coopers & Lybrand L.L.P.

SELECTED PRODUCTS AND SERVICES

EDI/400 (software for translation and communications that supports major EDI standards)

EDI/e for UNIX (EDI software for UNIX)

QMAIL (AS/400 E-mail solution)

Templar (provides software and services for the secure transmission of EDI documents over the Internet)

	1995 Sales	
	$ mil.	% of total
Software license	17.8	70
Services	7.7	30
Total	**25.5**	**100**

KEY COMPETITORS

CONNECT
Elcom International
General Electric
Harbinger
IBM
Sterling Commerce

---

introduced QMAIL in 1992, the first open systems e-mail product designed for the AS/400. Premenos continues to introduce new electronic commerce products and services. In 1995, the year it went public, the company launched Templar, a Web-accessible electronic commerce system. Jenkins owns 48% of Premenos.

The company signed an agreement in 1996 to acquire Don Valley Technology, maker of the PowerDox electronic commerce platform. The purchase gives Premenos a tool to serve the growing market for small businesses using electronic commerce.

PREMENOS: THE NUMBERS

Nasdaq symbol: PRMO FYE: December 31	Annual Growth	1990	1991	1992	1993	1994	1995
Sales ($ mil.)	43.0%	—	6.1	10.4	13.1	20.0	25.5
Net income ($ mil.)	—	—	(0.3)	(0.1)	0.1	1.8	1.5
Income as % of sales	—	—	—	—	1.1%	9.1%	5.9%
Earnings per share ($)	—	—	(0.03)	(0.01)	0.03	0.28	0.16
Stock price – high ($)	—	—	—	—	—	—	47.00
Stock price – low ($)	—	—	—	—	—	—	24.00
Stock price – close ($)	—	—	—	—	—	—	26.38
P/E – high	—	—	—	—	—	—	294
P/E – low	—	—	—	—	—	—	150
Dividends per share ($)	—	—	—	—	—	—	0.00
Book value per share ($)	—	—	—	—	—	—	6.23
Employees	—	—	—	—	—	173	193

1995 YEAR-END

Debt ratio: 2.2%
Return on equity: 2.3%
Cash (mil.): $63.2
Current ratio: 6.58
Long-term debt (mil.): $0.8
No. of shares (mil.): 10.5
Dividends
  Yield: —
  Payout: —
Market value (mil.): $278.0

QUARTER ENDED 6/30

	1996	1995
Sales ($ millions)	8.0	5.9
Net Income ($ millions)	(1.6)	0.2
Earnings Per Share ($)	(0.15)	0.02
No. of Shares (thou.)	10,542	5,852

6 MONTHS ENDED 6/30

	1996	1995
Sales ($ millions)	14.6	10.3
Net Income ($ millions)	(1.3)	(0.1)
Earnings Per Share ($)	(0.12)	(0.02)
No. of Shares (thou.)	10,542	5,852

STOCK PRICE HISTORY: High/Low/Close

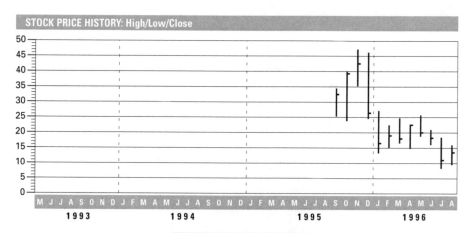

- An industry leader in integrated access products for telcos

- Products offer telcos, ISPs flexibility, cost savings in providing telecomm services

- Products help reduce strain on telco equipment from increasing Internet traffic

- Strategic partners include ATT Paradyne, DSC, Alcatel, Motorola, and FORE

- ATT owns a small stake

- 1996 revenue up 139%, EPS up 256%

- ATT Paradyne, DSC Communications, Motorola account for 72% of sales

- ATT Paradyne orders have been choppy, ATT wants to sell Paradyne

- Stock trades at a P/E of 57 (8/96) and a market cap of $1 billion

NETWORK
INFRASTRUCTURE

Premisys
Communications

Premisys Communications wants to make sure your wireless telephone can communicate with your pager. The Fremont, California-based company provides integrated access equipment for telecommunications services providers. Its core product is the Integrated Multiple Access Communications Server (IMACS), a hardware-and-software system that works with a telephone company's equipment to allow customers access to services operating on a variety of platforms, including asynchronous transfer mode (ATM), Centrex, integrated services digital network (ISDN), and plain old telephone service. Among the company's customers are long-distance carriers (AT&T, Sprint), competitive-access carriers (Cox Fibernet, Time Warner), and wireless operators (American Paging, AT&T's McCaw Cellular, GTE Mobilnet). The firm's largest reseller is AT&T's Paradyne subsidiary, which controls 5.8% of the company's stock and accounted for 45% of its 1995 revenues.

Premisys was founded in 1990 by Raymond Lin and Russian emigré brothers Boris and Marcus Auerbuch. Lin and Boris Auerbuch had been executives at telecommunications equipment maker Telco Systems. The trio formed Premisys to provide telecommunications equipment that could be installed on a customer's premises (thus the company's name). Its Singapore-based affiliate, Premisys Communications Pte Ltd, was formed that same year. Premisys pioneered integrated access equipment and

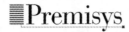

PREMISYS COMMUNICATIONS, INC.
HQ: 48664 Milmont Dr.,
 Fremont, CA 94538
Phone: 510-353-7600
Fax: 510-353-7601
Web site: www.premisys.com

OFFICERS

President and CEO:
 Raymond C. Lin, age 41, $262,976 pay
SVP Sales and Marketing:
 William J.Smith, age 61, $209,183 pay
SVP Finance and Administration, CFO, and Secretary:
 Riley R. Willcox, age 55, $207,578 pay
SVP Engineering and CTO:
 Boris J. Auerbuch, age 49, $192,398 pay
VP Sales:
 Owen Frances, age 54, $176,104 pay
VP Technology: Marcus J. Auerbuch, age 54
Director Human Resources: Ann Mazzini
Auditors: Price Waterhouse LLP

SELECTED PRODUCTS AND SERVICES

 BRX (preconfigured IMACS product for the small office/home office and Internet access market)
 IMACS family (hardware platform, integrated hardware/software modules, and optional network management software)

Distribution Partners
 ADC Telecommunications
 Alcatel Network Systems
 Alcatel SEL AG
 AT&T Paradyne
 DSC Communications
 Harris Corporation/Farinon Division
 Motorola
 Telematics

KEY COMPETITORS

Ascend
Ascom Group
Digital Link
General Datacom
NEC
Newbridge Networks
Nokia
Tellabs

shipped its first IMACS products in fiscal 1992. The company formed a joint development and distribution agreement with AT&T Paradyne in 1993.

The firm went public in 1995. Also in 1995 Fore Systems and Premisys formed a strategic partnership to develop products for the transmission of voice and video traffic and legacy data (i.e., data originated on an older system) over ATM networks. That same year the company also added ECI Telecom as a reseller.

News that AT&T would auction off its Paradyne unit caused Premisys to scrap a secondary stock offering in late 1995, leaving questions about the future role of the company's biggest reseller.

PREMISYS: THE NUMBERS

Nasdaq symbol: PRMS FYE: June 30	Annual Growth	1990	1991	1992	1993	1994	1995
Sales ($ mil.)	—	—	0.0	0.6	3.5	17.2	30.9
Net income ($ mil.)	—	—	(1.1)	(2.5)	(3.7)	0.9	4.0
Income as % of sales	—	—	—	—	—	5.2%	12.8%
Earnings per share ($)	—	—	—	—	—	0.05	0.18
Stock price – high ($)	—	—	—	—	—	—	57.25
Stock price – low ($)	—	—	—	—	—	—	15.75
Stock price – close ($)	—	—	—	—	—	—	56.00
P/E – high	—	—	—	—	—	—	159
P/E – low	—	—	—	—	—	—	44
Dividends per share ($)	—	—	—	—	—	—	0.00
Book value per share ($)	—	—	—	—	—	—	4.01
Employees	69.6%	—	—	24	38	88	117

1995 YEAR-END

Debt ratio: 0.4%
Return on equity: 8.7%
Cash (mil.): $43.0
Current ratio: 9.27
Long-term debt (mil.): $0.1
No. of shares (mil.): 11.7
Dividends
  Yield: —
  Payout: —
Market value (mil.): $656.1
R&D as % of sales: 14.7%

QUARTER ENDED 6/30

	1996	1995
Sales ($ millions)	22.5	10.5
Net Income ($ millions)	5.0	1.8
Earnings Per Share ($)	0.19	0.07
No. of Shares (thou.)	26,659	23,432

12 MONTHS ENDED 6/30

	1996	1995
Sales ($ millions)	73.9	30.9
Net Income ($ millions)	16.8	4.0
Earnings Per Share ($)	0.64	0.18
No. of Shares (thou.)	26,659	23,432

STOCK PRICE HISTORY: High/Low/Close

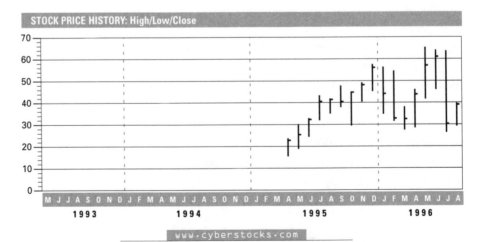

www.cyberstocks.com

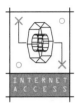

INTERNET
ACCESS

PSINet, Inc.

With some regions of cyberspace growing a bit crowded, PSINet is limiting its role as an Internet service provider (ISP) for individual consumers. Finding it hard to compete with AT&T's entry into the consumer Internet market, Herndon, Virginia-based PSINet is refocusing on corporate customers and more sophisticated individual users. The company provides services ranging from consumer dial-up access to high-speed dedicated leased line attachments in the US, Canada, the UK, and Japan. Founders William Schrader and Martin Schoffstall own about 14% and 6% of the company, respectively.

Former executives with data networking services company NYSERNet, Schrader and Schoffstall founded Performance Systems International (PSI) in 1989 and began providing Internet access to organizations the next year. PSI offered its first service for individual users in 1991 through a system called PSILink. In 1992 the company introduced InterFrame, a continuous, high-speed Internet connection for corporate LANs.

As the Internet market heated up, PSI teamed up with Boston's Continental Cablevision in 1994 to introduce the first commercial Internet access over a cable TV network. The company also debuted InterRamp to provide direct, unrestricted access to the Internet. In 1995 PSI acquired the Pipeline Network, a New York-based Internet access provider catering to less sophisticated computer users. The company went public and changed its name to

- Sold off its retail Internet service business, cutting losses

- Focusing on less-cutthroat corporate, wholesale-consumer markets

- Can offer small ISPs a national backbone, full line of services

- Corporate customer base tripled in size in the 12 months ended 6/30

- Potential takeover target

- Remains unprofitable; breakeven is not imminent

- Cash burn is troublesome in light of the capital-intensity of the business

- Most ISPs and telcos are actively pursuing the corporate market

- Stock sells for 5-1/2 times trailing 12-month sales (8/96)

PSINET, INC.

HQ: 510 Huntmar Park Dr.,
Herndon, VA 22070
Phone: 703-904-4100
Fax: 703-904-4200
Web site: www.psi.net

OFFICERS

Chairman, President, and CEO:
William L. Schrader, age 44, $214,618 pay
EVP, COO, and Acting CFO:
Harold Wills, age 54
VP International Operations, General Counsel, and Secretary:
David N. Kunkel, age 53, $183,361 pay
VP Sales:
Stephen A. Schoffstall, age 29, $149,236 pay
VP Network Operations:
Mitchell Levinn, age 36, $111,864 pay
VP Finance and Treasurer:
Daniel P. Cunningham, age 41
VP Marketing, Corporate Services:
Bruce M. Ley, age 44
VP Marketing, Consumer Services:
Kurt D. Baumann, age 36
VP Individual Customer Support:
Mary Ann Carolan, age 35
VP Human Resources: David Mann, age 55
Auditors: Price Waterhouse LLP

SELECTED PRODUCTS AND SERVICES

Consumer Services
PipelinePro (formerly InterRamp; direct, unrestricted Internet access for more sophisticated users)
Corporate Services
InterFrame (continuous LAN connection to the Internet)

InterMAN (full-time dedicated connection to the Internet for high-bandwidth needs, such as Web servers)

Internet Warehouse (listing of software and hardware that can be purchased through PSINet)

InterPPP (entry-level dedicated Internet connection for small companies)

LAN On-Demand (dial-up LAN connection to Internet for organizations)

PSINet Security Services Inc. (Internet security programs)

PSIWeb (Web hosting service)

UUPSI (basic dial-up Internet access for organizations)

KEY COMPETITORS

America Online	MFS Communications
Ameritech	NETCOM
AT&T	NYNEX
BBN	Pacific Telesys
Bell Atlantic	SBC Communications
BellSouth	Sprint
Compuserve	U S West
MCI	

PSINet that year. PSINet ran up a loss of $53 million in 1995 due to its expansion strategy and writedowns. In a move away from the entry-level consumer market, PSINet announced in 1996 that it would sell a subscriber base of about 100,000 customers and a support center to MindSpring Enterprises of Atlanta for $23 million.

PSINET: THE NUMBERS

Nasdaq symbol: PSIX FYE: December 31	Annual Growth	1990	1991	1992	1993	1994	1995
Sales ($ mil.)	64.6%	3.2	4.7	6.4	8.7	15.2	38.7
Net income ($ mil.)	—	(0.3)	0.2	0.4	(1.9)	(5.3)	(53.2)
Income as % of sales	—	—	5.0%	6.7%	—	—	—
Earnings per share ($)	—	—	—	—	—	(0.26)	(1.78)
Stock price – high ($)	—	—	—	—	—	—	29.00
Stock price – low ($)	—	—	—	—	—	—	12.00
Stock price – close ($)	—	—	—	—	—	—	22.88
P/E – high	—	—	—	—	—	—	—
P/E – low	—	—	—	—	—	—	—
Dividends per share ($)	—	—	—	—	—	—	0.00
Book value per share ($)	—	—	—	—	—	—	3.78
Employees	135.8%	—	—	48	85	129	629

1995 YEAR-END

Debt ratio: 22.2%
Return on equity: —
Cash (mil.): $102.7
Current ratio: 3.56
Long-term debt (mil.): $24.1
No. of shares (mil.): 37.9
Dividends
  Yield: —
  Payout: —
Market value (mil.): $867.5

QUARTER ENDED 6/30

	1996	1995
Sales ($ millions)	22.6	7.7
Net Income ($ millions)	(10.9)	(7.1)
Earnings Per Share ($)	(0.28)	(0.23)
No. of Shares (thou.)	39,931	32,422

6 MONTHS ENDED 6/30

	1996	1995
Sales ($ millions)	39.8	13.6
Net Income ($ millions)	(25.8)	(10.3)
Earnings Per Share ($)	(0.67)	(0.36)
No. of Shares (thou.)	39,931	32,422

STOCK PRICE HISTORY: High/Low/Close

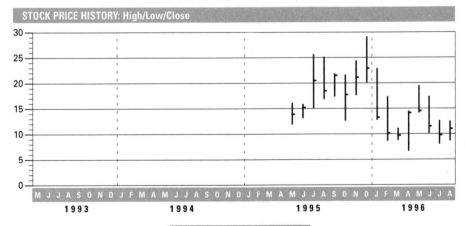

1993 1994 1995 1996

- Demand for wireless voice and data communications continues to grow rapidly
- CDMA promises to be superior to competitive technologies for wireless data transmission
- Wireless technology is atttractive to developing countries with poor telecommunications infrastructures
- CDMA royalties could become a significant revenue source
- Eudora is the world's #1 Internet-based e-mail application
- 9-month sales up 100% of fiscal 1996

- Will CDMA ever live up to expectations?
- Much of the rest of the world appears to be committed to GSM, a rival technology
- Motorola and Lucent are entering the CDMA handset market
- Operating margins have turned negative depite sales growth
- Eudora accounts for a miniscule proportion of revenue
- P/E over 120 (8/96)

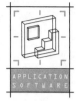

APPLICATION SOFTWARE

QUALCOMM Inc.

QUALCOMM has made a quantum leap. The San Diego-based company's Code Division Multiple Access (CDMA) technology has become the new standard for mobile communications. CDMA gives cellular users a cleaner signal at lower cost than the previous standard, Time Division Multiple Access (TDMA). The firm's CDMA products — digital cellular phones and infrastructure equipment — now have an edge in cellular, personal communication services (PCS), and wireless local loop (WLL) systems. QUALCOMM also makes Eudora, the #1 e-mail software, which has an estimated 10 million users.

QUALCOMM is the world's largest satellite-based mobile communications company. Its OmniTRACS, a 2-way satellite messaging and position-tracking system, is used mostly in the transportation industry. In a joint venture with Loral Corp. and others, the company is developing Globalstar, a system of 48 low-orbiting satellites that will offer telecommunication services in nearly every populated area of the world. Chairman Irwin Jacobs controls approximately 4.6% of the company's shares.

Jacobs and Andrew Viterbi met in 1959 at an academic conference. In 1968, the 2 professors started Linkabit, a digital signal processing equipment company, which reached $130 million in sales by 1980 and was acquired by M/A-COM. Irwin and Jacobs stayed on until 1985, then left to start QUALCOMM. The company initially provided contract research and development services. It introduced OmniTRACS in the US in 1988 and unveiled

QUALCOMM INCORPORATED
HQ: 6455 Lusk Blvd.,
San Diego, CA 92121-2779
Phone: 619-587-1121
Fax: 619-658-2501
Web site: www.qualcomm.com

OFFICERS

Chairman and CEO:
Irwin Mark Jacobs, age 62, $640,992 pay
President:
Harvey P. White, age 61, $447,462 pay
VC and Chief Technical Officer:
Andrew J. Viterbi, age 60, $376,032 pay
COO: Richard Sulpizio, age 45, $333,486 pay
VP and CFO:
Anthony S. Thornley, age 49, $296,962 pay
President, Communications Systems Division:
Gerald L. Beckwith, age 47
VP Human Resources: Daniel L. Sullivan
Auditors: Price Waterhouse LLP

SELECTED PRODUCTS AND SERVICES

Electronic Cinema (system for digitizing and compressing 35mm film for electronic delivery to cinemas, under development)

Eudora (electronic mail software)

Globalstar (7.9%, satellite-based digital telecommunications system, joint venture development with Loral and other companies)

Infrastructure products (CDMA cellular, PCS, and WLL products, including base transceiver station and base station controller equipment)

OmniTRACS (satellite-based, 2-way mobile communications and tracking system)

QuSAT (ultrasmall aperture satellite terminal for transaction-based data applications and voice communications, under development)

Subscriber products (digital phones)

KEY COMPETITORS

Alcatel Alsthom	Mitsubishi
American Mobile Satellite	Motorola
AT&T	Nokia
BellSouth	Norstan
California Microwave	Northern Telecom
DSC Communications	Oki
Ericsson	Rockwell
Harris Corp.	SBC Communications
Lucent	Sprint

CDMA technology in 1989, the same year the telecommunications industry selected TDMA as the new standard for cellular systems.

In 1994 QUALCOMM and Sony entered a joint venture to develop digital cellular telephone equipment. In 1996 the joint venture won 2 orders worth about $850 million to supply new digital wireless phones.

By late 1995, 10 of the 14 largest cellular providers and 2 of the largest bidders in the FCC's recent auction for PCS licenses said they would use CDMA technology.

QUALCOMM: THE NUMBERS

Nasdaq symbol: QCOM FYE: September 26	Annual Growth	1990	1991	1992	1993	1994	1995
Sales ($ mil.)	52.7%	46.5	90.3	107.5	168.7	271.6	386.6
Net income ($ mil.)	—	(17.1)	(8.4)	(4.1)	12.6	15.2	30.2
Income as % of sales	—	—	—	—	7.5%	5.6%	7.8%
Earnings per share ($)	—	(0.58)	(0.27)	(0.10)	0.25	0.28	0.52
Stock price – high ($)	—	—	12.50	14.63	43.38	33.75	54.75
Stock price – low ($)	—	—	8.38	6.25	11.25	15.00	20.50
Stock price – close ($)	36.5%	—	12.38	12.13	26.50	24.00	43.00
P/E – high	—	—	—	—	174	121	105
P/E – low	—	—	—	—	45	54	39
Dividends per share ($)	—	—	0.00	0.00	0.00	0.00	0.00
Book value per share ($)	218.6%	—	0.12	1.65	4.71	5.09	12.36
Employees	50.4%	—	619	845	1,262	1,900	3,167

1995 YEAR-END

Debt ratio: 4.1%
Return on equity: 5.7%
Cash (mil.): $567.0
Current ratio: 6.71
Long-term debt (mil.): $33.5
No. of shares (mil.): 64.7
Dividends
  Yield: —
  Payout: —
Market value (mil.): $2,781.8
R&D as % of sales: 20.7%

QUARTER ENDED 6/30

	1996	1995
Sales ($ millions)	234.9	99.5
Net Income ($ millions)	1.5	7.3
Earnings Per Share ($)	0.02	0.13
No. of Shares (thou.)	70,738	55,750

9 MONTHS ENDED 6/30

	1996	1995
Sales ($ millions)	530.7	265.1
Net Income ($ millions)	13.1	19.3
Earnings Per Share ($)	0.19	0.35
No. of Shares (thou.)	70,738	55,750

STOCK PRICE HISTORY: High/Low/Close

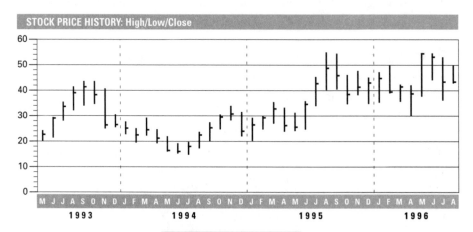

www.cyberstocks.com

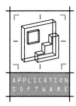

Quarterdeck Corporation

By seizing other ships, Quarterdeck has not only avoided a watery grave, but launched a new flotilla. The California-based firm develops, markets, and supports Internet, telecommunications, and utility software. Quarterdeck has been feverishly acquiring companies, products, and services to broaden its offerings. Investors Warren White and Michael Siewruk own about 7% and 6% of the firm's shares, respectively.

Quarterdeck Office Systems was founded in a garage (yes, really) in 1982 by Therese Myers and Gary Pope to develop software to enhance a PC's performance. Although Microsoft was its main rival, Quarterdeck was also dependent on the software giant. In fact, when Windows 3.0 was released, Quarterdeck experienced a surge in sales because its memory management products worked better than their Windows counterparts. The company went public in 1991.

Sales of its QEMM memory manager software continued to be strong through the early 1990s, but when Microsoft began improving Windows' memory management software, Quarterdeck's sales plummeted. The head of a consulting firm, King Lee, took over from Myers in a 1994 shake-up. In 1995 Gaston Bastiaens, a former general manager at Apple Computer, replaced Lee as president and CEO. That year the company changed its name to Quarterdeck Corp.

Quarterdeck turned to Internet users for a new revenue source. The firm

- Well-known brand names include HiJaak, QEMM, PROCOMM, WebCompass
- Gains direct marketing channel with VertiSoft acquisition
- Plans upgrade of its major products in 4th quarter 1996
- Has initiated cost-cutting program

- Historically, appears to have substituted opportunism for strategy
- Looking for a new CEO
- Windows utility and Internet collaboration software markets are crowded
- Sales of most recently acquired products have been disappointing
- 2nd quarter 1996 sales plunged 43%
- Market cap of $250 million (8/96)

QUARTERDECK CORPORATION
HQ: 13160 Mindanao Way,
Marina del Rey, CA 90292-9705
Phone: 310-309-3700
Fax: 310-309-4218
Web site: www.qdeck.com

OFFICERS

Chairman: Frank W. T. LaHaye, age 66
Temporary Office of the President:
King R. Lee and Anatoly Tikhman
SVP Worldwide Sales:
James D. Moise, age 40, $334,069 pay
**SVP and General Manager Internet
Services:**
Stephen W. Tropp, age 40, $217,736 pay
(prior to promotion)
SVP and CFO: Frank R. Greico
VP Strategic Business Development and CTO:
Robert D. Kutnick, age 38
Director Human Resources:
Teresa Hammond
Auditors: KPMG Peat Marwick LLP

SELECTED PRODUCTS AND SERVICES

Internet
IWare Connect
Quarterdeck WebAuthor
Quarterdeck WebServer
WebCompass
Memory Management and Utilities
CleanSweep 95
MagnaRAM 2
Quarterdeck Expanded Memory Manager
(QEMM 8)
**Telecommunications and Collaborative
Computing**
eXpertise
Larry Magid's Essential Internet
Quarterdeck InternetSuite
Quarterdeck Mosaic
WebTalk

KEY COMPETITORS

Adobe	Microsoft
Apple	NetManage
Asymetrix	Netscape
Compuserve	Novell
ForeFront	SoftQuad
Frontier Technologies	Symantec
FTP	
IBM	
ichat	

formed alliances with several major Internet service providers in 1995. Quarterdeck also acquired Internet software developers Internetware (Internet software for Novell networks), Prospero Systems Research (Internet chat software), and StarNine Technologies (Internet server and e-mail software). The firm also created an Internet services unit for customers seeking to conduct online commerce.

Continuing its Internet-related acquisitions in 1996, Quarterdeck announced it would buy Datastorm Technologies (communications software), Future Labs Inc. (document-sharing products), and Vertisoft Systems (utility software, direct-mail marketing). Bastiaens resigned unexpectedly in September 1996 to pursue other interests.

QUARTERDECK: THE NUMBERS

Nasdaq symbol: QDEK FYE: September 30	Annual Growth	1990	1991	1992	1993	1994	1995
Sales ($ mil.)	21.9%	26.3	48.0	55.0	44.9	26.8	70.7
Net income ($ mil.)	(8.2%)	6.3	12.0	9.1	1.2	(21.2)	4.1
Income as % of sales	—	23.8%	25.0%	16.6%	2.8%	—	5.8%
Earnings per share ($)	(14.0%)	0.34	0.63	0.45	0.06	(1.06)	0.16
Stock price – high ($)	—	—	23.75	26.63	4.50	4.13	39.50
Stock price – low ($)	—	—	11.50	3.63	1.94	1.88	2.75
Stock price – close ($)	4.3%	—	23.25	4.13	2.19	3.13	27.50
P/E – high	—	—	38	59	75	—	34
P/E – low	—	—	18	8	32	—	17
Dividends per share ($)	—	—	0.00	0.00	0.00	0.00	0.00
Book value per share ($)	(7.4%)	—	1.92	2.43	2.46	1.40	1.41
Employees	43.0%	89	190	302	291	198	532

1995 YEAR-END

Debt ratio: 0.5%
Return on equity: 13.1%
Cash (mil.): $23.1
Current ratio: 2.18
Long-term debt (mil.): $0.1
No. of shares (mil.): 20.0
Dividends
  Yield: —
  Payout: —
Market value (mil.): $550.3
R&D as % of sales: 12.0%

QUARTER ENDED 6/30

	1996	1995
Sales ($ millions)	16.0	17.2
Net Income ($ millions)	(22.9)	0.0
Earnings Per Share ($)	(0.73)	0.00
No. of Shares (thou.)	32,414	23,743

9 MONTHS ENDED 6/30

	1996	1995
Sales ($ millions)	105.7	47.8
Net Income ($ millions)	(19.4)	4.6
Earnings Per Share ($)	(0.62)	0.19
No. of Shares (thou.)	32,414	23,743

STOCK PRICE HISTORY: High/Low/Close

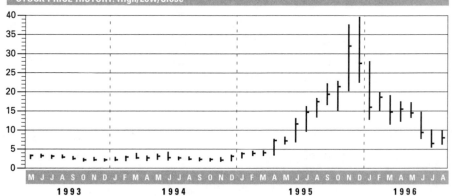

1993 1994 1995 1996

- Sales of its Windows NT products are taking off

- Highly respected by industry leaders

- Expanding its reseller channel rapidly

- Became profitable in 2nd quarter 1996

- 1st half 1996 sales up 324%

- 2nd quarter earnings would have been negative without interest on IPO cash

- Software developers are embedding security functions in their products

NETWORK
INFRASTRUCTURE

Raptor Systems

Raptor's talons are out to protect databases and networks from computer predators. A leader in firewall security management software and services, Waltham, Massachusetts-based Raptor's primary product is the Eagle family of modular software, which provides companies with network security for Internet, workgroup, mobile computing, and remote office domains and can be used individually or as part of an integrated network security management system. Raptor sells to large companies and OEM business developers worldwide through a direct-sales force. It has also established a network of VARs to serve small to medium-sized businesses.

The company was founded in 1992 by David Pensak, a DuPont veteran who was a corporate advisor for that company's computing technology group and a research advisor in the areas of expert systems, artificial intelligence, automated analysis, and interactive graphics. The firm's first Eagle product, launched in 1992, was an active security firewall for local area networks (LANs).

Raptor moved its corporate headquarters to Waltham from Wilmington, Delaware, in 1994 and raised capital from Boston-based Greylock Management and Minneapolis-based Norwest Equity Partners to support its expansion. Greylock Equity owns 35% of Raptor, Norwest Equity 15.5%, and Pensak 9%.

Raptor's strategy is to provide modular software that can provide security for all aspects of a company's operations — unprotected files on PCs or

RAPTOR SYSTEMS, INC.
HQ: 69 Hickory Dr., Waltham, MA 02154
Phone: 617-487-7700
Fax: 617-487-6755
Web site: www.raptor.com

OFFICERS

Chairman and CEO:
Robert A. Steinkrauss, age 44, $112,382 pay
President and COO:
Shaun McConnon, age 51, $133,672 pay
Chief Technology Advisor:
David A. Pensak, age 47
SVP Engineering and Chief Technical Officer:
Alan Kirby, age 43, $109,889 pay
VP Business Development:
Jimmy W. Charlton, age 36, $170,234 pay
VP International Sales, Europe:
Jack F. Hembrough, age 46, $102,933 pay
VP Marketing: Michael L. Grandinetti, age 35
VP, Treasurer, and Controller:
Robert H. Fincke, age 50
VP Technical Services: Lance Urbas
Auditors: Coopers & Lybrand L.L.P.

SELECTED PRODUCTS AND SERVICES

Eagle firewall (Internet security)
EagleLAN/EagleDesk (workgroup security)
EagleMobile (mobile PC security)
EagleNetwatch (integrated network security)
EagleRemote (remote site security)

KEY COMPETITORS

America Online
Ascend
Check Point Software
Cylink
Microsoft
Milkyway Networks
Morningstar Technologies
Network Systems
Secure
Security Dynamics
Sun Microsystems
Trusted Information
Virtual Open Network Environment

within servers as well as databases at branch offices, divisions, and remote offices and information exchanged on the Internet.

Raptor in 1995 introduced EagleNomad (now called EagleMobile), a product that provides mobile PC users with secure access to both public and private networks. The company went public in 1996. That year Raptor teamed up with Internet Security Systems to create software that allows managers to get a 3-D visualization of their network security and automatically test the configuration of the firewalls.

RAPTOR SYSTEMS: THE NUMBERS

Nasdaq symbol: RAPT FYE: December 31	Annual Growth	1990	1991	1992	1993	1994	1995
Sales ($ mil.)	179.3%	—	—	—	0.5	0.2	3.9
Net income ($ mil.)	—	—	—	—	(0.2)	(2.0)	(2.7)
Income as % of sales	—	—	—	—	—	—	—
Employees	—	—	—	—	—	—	58

1995 YEAR-END

Debt ratio: 100.0%
Return on equity: —
Cash (mil.): $1.9
Current ratio: 1.34
Long-term debt (mil.): $0.3
No. of shares (mil.): —
Dividends
 Yield: —
 Payout: —
Market value (mil.): —
R&D as % of sales: 35.0%

QUARTER ENDED 6/30

	1996	1995
Sales ($ millions)	2.9	0.7
Net Income ($ millions)	0.2	(0.6)
Earnings Per Share ($)	0.01	(0.08)
No. of Shares (thou.)	12,556	7,048

6 MONTHS ENDED 6/30

	1996	1995
Sales ($ millions)	5.0	1.1
Net Income ($ millions)	(0.3)	(1.0)
Earnings Per Share ($)	(0.03)	(0.14)
No. of Shares (thou.)	12,556	7,048

STOCK PRICE HISTORY: High/Low/Close

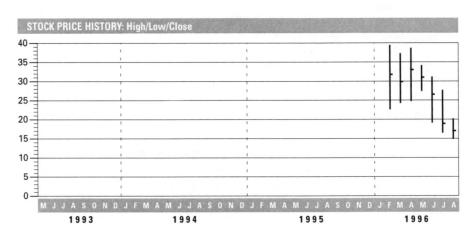

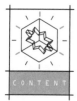 

CONTENT SPECIALIZED SERVICES

Reuters Holdings PLC

- Global electronic publisher of news and financial data in text, graphic, and video formats

- Owns huge historical databases

- Benefits from increasingly international outlook of financial institutions and investors

- Online securities-trading systems will likely continue to replace older, less automated systems

- Leading online-news provider; invested in customers Infoseek, Yahoo!, Sportsline USA

Reuters has good writers. But the London-based financial press agency's edge lies in transmitting financial data, news photos, and text to media outlets and the world's financial capitals faster than its competitors. The company relays news and financial information to 327,000 computer terminals in 154 nations. It provides data feeds to financial markets and software to analyze bonds, currencies, futures, options, and stocks. As a news agency, the company delivers graphics, sound, still pictures, television images, and text, to broadcasters, newspaper publishers, online content providers, and Web sites around the world. Reuters is controlled by the Reuters Founders Share Co., Ltd., set up by the companies that bought into Reuters as a trust in the 1940s.

In 1851, as the first English Channel cable was laid, former bookseller Paul Julius Reuter began telegraphing stock quotes between Paris and London and selling them to financial institutions. Coverage expanded to agricultural information and then general news, and the company grew with the British Empire. The company changed its name to Reuters Ltd. in 1916. During the 1950s Reuters experienced problems as the Empire broke up, contending with the often restrictive press rules of the new governments.

Moving into electronic media, Reuters gained non-US rights to Ultronic Systems Corporation's electronic stock reporting system, Stockmaster, in 1964. In 1973, after currency exchange rates began to float, the press agency launched its Monitor electronic marketplace, which kept track of

- Financial services industry continues to consolidate, lowering customer count

- Reuters has become accustomed to premium pricing for its financial services

- Quotron apparently remains unprofitable

- P/E near 30 (8/96)

Reuters NewMedia

REUTERS HOLDINGS PLC

HQ: 85 Fleet St., London, EC4P 4AJ, UK
Phone: +44-171-250-1122
Fax: +44-171-510-5896
US HQ: Reuters America Inc., 1700
Broadway, New York, NY 10019
US Phone: 212-603-3300
US Fax: 212-247-0346
Web site: www.reutersnm.com

OFFICERS

Chairman:
Sir Christopher A. Hogg, age 59, £75,000 pay
CEO: Peter J. D. Job, age 54, £650,000 pay
Director Finance:
Robert O. "Rob" Rowley, age 46, £408,000 pay
Editor-in-Chief:
Mark W. Wood, age 43, £343,000 pay
Director Marketing and Technical Policy:
David G. Ure, age 48, £440,000 pay
Director Personnel and Quality Programmes:
Patrick A. V. Mannix, age 53
Secretary: Simon A. Yeancken
President, Reuters America:
Andre Villeneuve, age 51
Auditors: Price Waterhouse LLP

SELECTED PRODUCTS AND SERVICES

Information
2000 Series (data feeds to financial markets and software tools to analyze data)
Teknekron (data management software for subscribers)
Triarch (data management software for subscribers)

Transaction
Dealing 2000-1 (transaction service)
GLOBEX (after-hours future exchange)
Instinet (electronic brokering service)

Media
Graphics
Online services
Television
Textual information

KEY COMPETITORS

ADP	Dow Jones	New York Times
Agence France-Press	Global Financial Information	Quick Corp.
AMEX	Knight-Ridder	Telekurs A.G.
Associated Press	M.A.I.D	Telescan
Bloomberg	McGraw-Hill	Time Warner
Bowne	Minex	Times Mirror
Citicorp	Misys	Tribune
CSK	Nasdaq	UPI
Data Broadcasting	News Corp.	
	NYSE	

the foreign exchange market. Reuters went public in 1984. Since then the company has acquired numerous online services including the real-time news and stock quote vendor, Quotron, in 1993. Reuters acquired Reality Technologies in 1994, which developed Reuters Money Network.

The following year Reuters teamed up with satellite TV programmer British Sky Broadcasting (BSkyB) to increase the news quality of BSkyB's Sky News Channel. The media group launched Business Briefing for Macintosh, a business information service for users of the Apple computers, in 1996.

REUTERS: THE NUMBERS

Nasdaq symbol: RTRSY FYE: December 31	Annual Growth	1990	1991	1992	1993	1994	1995
Sales ($ mil.)	9.7%	2,642.2	2,743.6	2,374.0	2,772.6	3,613.5	4,118.4
Net income ($ mil.)	9.9%	399.7	429.5	386.5	442.4	543.1	641.5
Income as % of sales	—	15.1%	15.7%	15.1%	16.0%	15.0%	15.3%
Earnings per share ($)	10.7%	1.44	1.54	1.41	1.38	1.02	2.39
Stock price – high ($)	—	35.56	29.06	34.56	42.56	48.38	58.88
Stock price – low ($)	—	16.06	17.88	17.88	27.69	38.94	36.38
Stock price – close ($)	22.2%	20.25	28.88	31.88	39.50	43.88	55.13
P/E – high	—	25	19	25	27	47	25
P/E – low	—	11	12	19	17	38	15
Dividends per share ($)	22.7%	0.41	0.45	0.54	0.61	0.66	1.14
Book value per share ($)	7.7%	3.68	4.63	4.49	3.47	14.72	5.33
Employees	6.0%	10,731	10,450	10,393	11,306	12,718	14,348

1995 YEAR-END

Debt ratio: 21.2%
Return on equity: 50.4%
Cash (mil.): $819.7
Current ratio: 1.39
Long-term debt (mil.): $209.2
No. of shares (mil.): 279.5
Dividends
  Yield: 2.1%
  Payout: 47.6%
Market value (mil.): $15,407.4

3 MONTHS ENDED 6/30

	1996	1995
Sales ($ millions)	1,107.1	1,001.9
Net Income ($ millions)	—	—
Earnings Per Share ($)	—	—
No. of Shares (thou.)	—	—

6 MONTHS ENDED 6/30

	1996	1995
Sales ($ millions)	2,232.8	2,066.1
Net Income ($ millions)	366.4	314.3
Earnings Per Share ($)	1.36	1.18
No. of Shares (thou.)	269,500	267,300

STOCK PRICE HISTORY: High/Low/Close

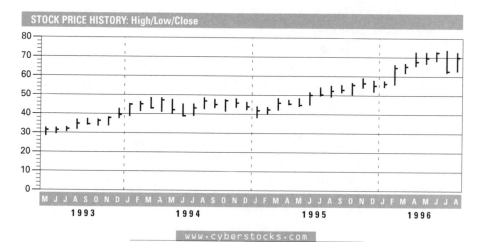

www.cyberstocks.com

- Pure Internet/intranet security play
- Border Networks acquisition

  * adds low-priced products, international presence

  * appears to have made it the #2 firewall company

- Other recent purchases broadened network security product line
- Firewalled "Internet Challenge" site has never been successfully hacked
- 1st half 1996 sales up 57.2%

- Unprofitable in 1995, 1st half of 1996
- Low-margin government contracts accounted for 70% of 1st half 1996 sales
- The company may be overextended, simultaneously attempting to

  * establish sales channels and aggressively expand in the commercial marketplace

  * enter several new security market segments

  * integrate acquired companies and product lines

  * return to profitability

NETWORK INFRASTRUCTURE

Secure Computing

Secure Computing is both this company's name and its aim. The Roseville, Minnesota-based company doesn't have a lock on the highly competitive network security software market, but it is one of its key players. Secure Computing products protect an organization's computer network from unauthorized users. Its flagship product is Sidewinder, which creates an entry barrier, or firewall, around a computer network. In the event of an attempt at unauthorized entry, Sidewinder blocks the intrusion, alerts the system administrator, and traces the origin of the attack. Other software includes LOCKguard, a secure network server product, and LOCKout, an authentication product that allows companies to set up workers offsite while maintaining secure data.

The company was formed in 1989 as a spinoff of Honeywell's network security operations, which at that time were developing technologies for the National Security Agency and other US government bodies. It launched its first commercial products in 1993 and its Sidewinder software in 1994. Led by Motorola veteran Kermit Beseke, CEO since 1992, the company went public in 1995. Investment groups Grotech Capital and Corporate Venture Partners own 27% and 22% of the company, respectively.

Faced with a consolidating market, Beseke is pursuing a two-pronged strategy to keep Secure Computing at the forefront of the industry: product expansion and international distribution. It has invested heavily in developing intrawall, secure client, and Web screening products. With its

Secure Computing Corporation

SECURE COMPUTING CORPORATION
HQ: 2675 Long Lake Rd.,
     Roseville, MN 55113
Phone: 612-628-2700
Fax: 612-628-2701
Web site: www.sctc.com

OFFICERS

President and CEO:
   Kermit M. Beseke, age 52, $281,771 pay
VP Internetworked Products:
   Gene C. Leonard, age 44, $121,170 pay
VP Sales and Marketing:
   Joe R. Anzures, age 44
Controller:
   Dean W. Nordahl, age 53, $110,677 pay
CFO and Treasurer: Timothy P. McGurran
Corporate Secretary: James E. Nicholson
Public and Investor Relations Manager:
   Julie Herubin
Auditors: Ernst & Young LLP

SELECTED PRODUCTS AND SERVICES

LOCKguard (secure network server product)
LOCKout (authentication product)
Sidewinder (Internet firewall product)
Consultation
Product support
Security alert (hacker monitoring and updates)
Training programs

	1995 Sales	
	$ mil.	% of total
Government contracts	14.8	72
Products & services	5.9	28
Total	**20.7**	**100**

KEY COMPETITORS

America Online	Morningstar Technologies
Ascend	Raptor Systems
Check Point Software	Security Dynamics
Cylink	Sun Microsystems
Information Resource	Trusted Information
Engineering	Virtual Open Network
Milkyway Networks	Environment

1996 acquisition of rival Border Network Technologies, the company picked up that company's well-established distribution system. Also in 1996, the company acquired Webster Network Strategies, the maker of WebTrack Internet monitoring and filtering software, which allows organizations to control employee and student access to the World Wide Web.

SECURE: THE NUMBERS

Nasdaq symbol: SCUR FYE: December 31	Annual Growth	1990	1991	1992	1993	1994	1995
Sales ($ mil.)	29.9%	5.6	4.0	5.3	9.4	15.2	20.7
Net income ($ mil.)	—	(0.6)	(1.4)	(1.1)	1.1	1.5	(1.0)
Income as % of sales	—	—	—	—	11.3%	9.8%	—
Earnings per share ($)	—	—	—	—	0.00	0.43	(0.20)
Stock price – high ($)	—	—	—	—	—	—	64.50
Stock price – low ($)	—	—	—	—	—	—	39.50
Stock price – close ($)	—	—	—	—	—	—	56.00
P/E – high	—	—	—	—	—	—	—
P/E – low	—	—	—	—	—	—	—
Dividends per share ($)	—	—	—	—	—	—	0.00
Book value per share ($)	—	—	—	—	—	—	5.77
Employees	—	—	—	—	—	—	276

1995 YEAR-END

Debt ratio: 0.0%
Return on equity: —
Cash (mil.): $32.6
Current ratio: 9.54
Long-term debt (mil.): $0.0
No. of shares (mil.): 6.5
Dividends
  Yield: —
  Payout: —
Market value (mil.): $362.9
R&D as % of sales: 17.8%

QUARTER ENDED 6/30

	1996	1995
Sales ($ millions)	6.1	4.0
Net Income ($ millions)	(9.0)	(1.1)
Earnings Per Share ($)	(1.35)	(0.28)
No. of Shares (thou.)	6,772	5,870

6 MONTHS ENDED 6/30

	1996	1995
Sales ($ millions)	13.4	8.5
Net Income ($ millions)	(9.2)	(1.0)
Earnings Per Share ($)	(1.39)	(0.27)
No. of Shares (thou.)	6,772	5,870

STOCK PRICE HISTORY: High/Low/Close

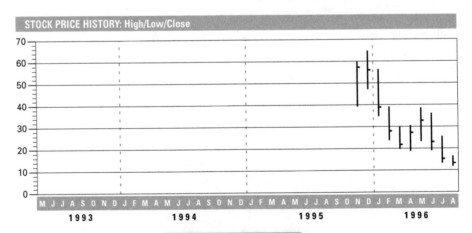

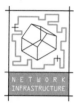

NETWORK
INFRASTRUCTURE

Security Dynamics

Computer hackers beware: Security Dynamics Technologies is on the job. The Cambridge, Massachusetts-based company provides software and hardware security products for computers and networks. Its primary product, SecurID Tokens, prevents unauthorized access by requiring the user to enter a PIN number along with a random access code displayed on a hand-held card or token. Display codes, which are changed every 60 seconds, are then transmitted along with the PIN to a control module that manages user access.

The company, which is the market leader in smart card security systems, has acquired encryption software developer RSA Data Security. A leading provider of security products for Internet software developers, RSA licenses tool kits to Microsoft, Netscape, and others, and it manufactures RSA Secure, an end-user encryption system. Jim Bidzos, former president of RSA and current EVP at Security Dynamics, owns 17.5% of the company.

Security Dynamics was started in 1984 by Kenneth Weiss, inventor of the SecurID technology. At first, the company was primarily a research and development firm, but it moved into production of SecurID tokens and access control module (ACM) hardware in 1986. The company introduced its ACM software for mainframes and minicomputers in 1988 and its ACM

- The leader in the rapidly growing network security market

- RSA acquisition combines leader in encryption with leader in authentication

- Token ID card installations generate recurring service and upgrade revenue

- Has marketing agreements with top software and network equipment vendors

- Holds an important patent on time-synchronization-based security technology

- 1st half 1996 sales up 82%, EPS up 81%

- Software developers are adding encryption, other security functions to their programs

- The market may abandon tokens in favor of digital-signature software

- Token ID cards are produced in China, exposing investors to political risk

- RSA's principal encryption patent expires on September 20, 2000

- The US severely restricts exports of encryption software

- P/E exceeds 120 (8/96)

SECURITY DYNAMICS

SECURITY DYNAMICS TECHNOLOGIES, INC.
HQ: 20 Crosby Drive
Bedford, MA 01730
Phone: 617-687-7000
Fax: 617-687-7010
Web site: www.securid.com

OFFICERS

Chairman, President, and CEO:
Charles R. Stuckey Jr., age 53, $473,434 pay

EVP, Treasurer, and CFO:
Arthur W. Coviello Jr., age 42

EVP; President and CEO, RSA Data Security:
James Bidzos

VP Sales, The Americas:
Robert W. Fine, age 53, $272,973 pay

VP Marketing:
James M. Geary, age 39, $187,681 pay

VP Operations:
Linda E. Saris, age 43, $139,719 pay

Director Human Resources: Vivian Vitale
Auditors: Deloitte & Touche LLP

SELECTED PRODUCTS AND SERVICES

SECURID TOKENS (part of dual code used with ACM systems)

SecurID Card (credit-card sized with LCD)

SecurID PINPAD Card (credit-card sized with keypad)

SecurID Key Fob (token for keychain)

ACE/SERVER (security software for client/server networks)

ACCESS CONTROL MODULE (software for host-based production)

DEC Open VMS/VAX and Alpha environments

IBM/MVS mainframne

CRAY/UNICOS supercomputers

ACCESS CONTROL MODULE (hardware for host-based systems)

ACM/1600 HS (for 16 RS/232 ports)

ACM/400 HS (for mid-sized computer environments)

ACM/100 HS (for small systems or limited user environments)

KEY COMPETITORS

Cylink	Northern Telecom
Digital Pathway	Rainbow Technologies
Information Resource	Secure Computing
Leemah Datacom	Schlumberger
Lucent	Virtual Open Network
Machines Bull	

software for intranets in 1991. It suffered a setback in 1992 when it had to recall approximately 13,000 SecurID tokens due to programming errors.

Security Dynamics has benefited from the increasing number of LANs and WANs, and attributes its success to the growing number of users with access to corporate intranets and confidential data. The company's purchase of RSA was part of its strategy to improve its position in the growing Internet and electronic commerce markets by tapping into RSA's Internet-focused customer base.

SECURITY DYNAMICS: THE NUMBERS

Nasdaq symbol: SDTI FYE: December 31	Annual Growth	1990	1991	1992	1993	1994	1995
Sales ($ mil.)	44.7%	5.3	6.1	8.9	12.1	17.6	33.6
Net income ($ mil.)	80.8%	0.3	0.5	1.2	1.7	2.3	5.8
Income as % of sales	—	6.2%	7.6%	13.6%	13.8%	13.2%	17.2%
Earnings per share ($)	55.6%	—	—	—	0.19	0.25	0.46
Stock price – high ($)	—	—	—	—	—	10.13	58.25
Stock price – low ($)	—	—	—	—	—	7.00	8.81
Stock price – close ($)	—	—	—	—	—	9.31	54.50
P/E – high	—	—	—	—	—	41	127
P/E – low	—	—	—	—	—	28	19
Dividends per share ($)	—	—	—	—	—	0.00	0.00
Book value per share ($)	—	—	—	—	—	2.59	7.06
Employees	—	—	—	—	—	94	162

1995 YEAR-END

Debt ratio: 0.0%
Return on equity: 9.4%
Cash (mil.): $89.5
Current ratio: 15.06
Long-term debt (mil.): $0.0
No. of shares (mil.): 13.5
Dividends
 Yield: —
 Payout: —
Market value (mil.): $733.2
R&D as % of sales: 12.0%

QUARTER ENDED 6/30

	1996	1995
Sales ($ millions)	14.1	8.2
Net Income ($ millions)	2.9	1.5
Earnings Per Share ($)	0.20	0.12
No. of Shares (thou.)	14,435	11,862

6 MONTHS ENDED 6/30

	1996	1995
Sales ($ millions)	26.2	14.4
Net Income ($ millions)	5.4	2.6
Earnings Per Share ($)	0.38	0.21
No. of Shares (thou.)	14,435	11,862

STOCK PRICE HISTORY: High/Low/Close

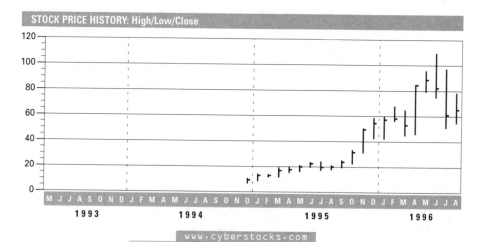

M J J A S O N D J F M A M J J A S O N D J F M A M J J A S O N D J F M A M J J A
1993   1994   1995   1996

www·cyberstocks·com

- Tightly focused on the remote-access market

- A leader in remote access server market

- Spider acquisition gives greater international presence

- In Airsoft, gets a WAN-caching technology for cutting phone costs

- Has begun licensing its client software to OEMs

- 1st half 1996 sales up 243%, earnings per share up 130%

- Competes with companies with broader networking equipment product lines

- Integrating UK-based Spider with Shiva could pose problems

- P/E of about 75 times consensus 1996 EPS forecast (7/96)

NETWORK INFRASTRUCTURE

Shiva Corporation

Shiva is helping office workers find new lives as telecommuters. With 24% of the market, Bedford, Massachusetts-based Shiva is the leading provider of remote-access hardware and software — products that let computer users at home or on the road connect to office computers via telephone lines. Founders Daniel Schwinn and Frank Slaughter own about 8% and 6% of the company, respectively.

MIT graduates Schwinn and Slaughter founded Shiva in 1985. They chose the name (after a type of laser) because it didn't sound too "techie," only later discovering it was the name of the many-armed Hindu god of destruction and rebirth.

In the beginning the company concentrated on making communication products for AppleTalk networks. In 1987 Shiva introduced NetModem, the first dial-in remote-access product for the Macintosh. The company began a shift toward multi-platform, remote-access products in the early 1990s. It licensed the FastPath router from Novell in 1990 and introduced the NetModem/E in 1991 and the LanRover/L in 1992.

Shiva grew rapidly, thanks to its innovative technology and the growing popularity of the "virtual" office. However, the company had trouble managing its growth and expansion beyond Apple products. In 1993 it hired Frank Ingari, VP of marketing at Lotus Development, as CEO to help guide its rapid expansion. Shiva went public in 1994 in one of the most successful

SHIVA CORPORATION
HQ: 28 Crosby Dr., Bedford, MA 01730
Phone: 617-270-8300
Fax: 617-270-8599
Web site: www.shiva.com

OFFICERS

Chairman, President, and CEO:
Frank A. Ingari, age 46, $577,200 pay

SVP Worldwide Sales and Marketing:
Steven J. Benson, age 37, $350,760 pay

SVP Finance and Administration, CFO, and Treasurer:
Cynthia M. Deysher, age 38, $245,000 pay

SVP Research and Development:
Guy A. Daniello, age 51

VP Sales North and South America:
Maria A. Cirino, age 32, $252,363 pay

VP Operations; General Manager, Edinburgh:
Dennis R. Chateauneuf, age 42, $213,666 pay

VP Human Resources: Jane Callanan, age 39
Auditors: Price Waterhouse LLP

SELECTED PRODUCTS AND SERVICES

LanRover family (remote-access communications servers)

NetModem (communications server for small offices and workgroups)

ShivaIntegrator (remote-access system for ISDN networks)

ShivaPort (communications server for Ethernet networks)

	1995 Sales	
	$ mil.	% of total
Remote-access products	83.1	71
Other communications products	24.0	20
Services	10.6	9
Total	**117.7**	**100**

KEY COMPETITORS

3Com
Ascend Communications
Bay Networks
Cisco Systems
Gandalf
GlobalVillage
U.S. Robotics
Zoom

IPOs of the year. The firm entered a new market in 1995 when it acquired UK-based Spider Systems, a maker of telephone switching devices that allow phone companies to route calls onto the Internet. Costs associated with the Spider acquisition left Shiva with a loss for the year. Shiva bought AirSoft, a California-based developer of remote-access software, the following year.

SHIVA: THE NUMBERS

Nasdaq symbol: SHVA FYE: December 31	Annual Growth	1990	1991	1992	1993	1994	1995
Sales ($ mil.)	48.7%	16.2	28.0	23.5	29.5	41.6	117.7
Net income ($ mil.)	—	1.2	(1.0)	(4.7)	0.2	2.7	(2.9)
Income as % of sales	—	7.4%	—	—	0.7%	6.4%	—
Earnings per share ($)	—	—	—	—	0.02	0.14	(0.11)
Stock price – high ($)	—	—	—	—	—	21.50	38.75
Stock price – low ($)	—	—	—	—	—	13.25	13.50
Stock price – close ($)	—	—	—	—	—	19.94	36.38
P/E – high	—	—	—	—	—	154	—
P/E – low	—	—	—	—	—	95	—
Dividends per share ($)	—	—	—	—	—	0.00	0.00
Book value per share ($)	—	—	—	—	—	1.78	4.49
Employees	39.6%	—	128	123	146	172	486

1995 YEAR-END

Debt ratio: 0.9%
Return on equity: —
Cash (mil.): $101.5
Current ratio: 5.23
Long-term debt (mil.): $0.5
No. of shares (mil.): 27.3
Dividends
  Yield: —
  Payout: —
Market value (mil.): $992.0
R&D as % of sales: 11.6%

QUARTER ENDED 6/30

	1996	1995
Sales ($ millions)	51.5	15.7
Net Income ($ millions)	5.0	1.6
Earnings Per Share ($)	0.16	0.07
No. of Shares (thou.)	28,493	20,464

6 MONTHS ENDED 6/30

	1996	1995
Sales ($ millions)	94.8	28.8
Net Income ($ millions)	9.3	2.9
Earnings Per Share ($)	0.30	0.13
No. of Shares (thou.)	28,493	20,464

STOCK PRICE HISTORY: High/Low/Close

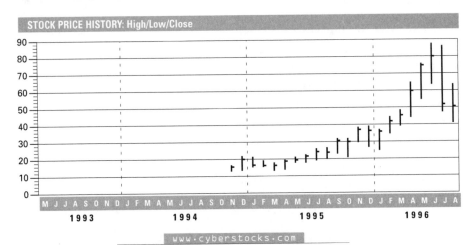

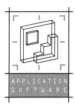

APPLICATION
SOFTWARE

SoftQuad
International

- Focused on editors for text markup languages
- Upgradable "Lite" version of HoTMetaL HTML (Web) editor is widely distributed
- Has achieved significant retail distribution
- Has begun European expansion
- Sales up 129% in first half 1996

Softquad International makes it easier to publish everything from resumes to annual reports online. The Toronto-based company offers point-and-click HTML and SGML publishing tools for the World Wide Web and in-tranets. It also offers consulting services for intranet planning for corporate clientele. HTML (Hypertext Markup Language) is a subset of SGML (Standard Generalized Markup Language), the standard for formatting and organizing text electronically. Originally designed to simplify the typeset-ting process, SGML is used to organize large amounts of text on CD-ROM or online databases. HTML allows users to publish documents on the World Wide Web and provide links to other sites across a broad range of platforms.

- Has numerous competitors, including Netscape and Microsoft, in the HTML editor market
- Netscape and Microsoft have de facto control over HTML specifications
- Remains unprofitable

The company has its roots in the 25-year-old Coach House Press, a Canadian experimental literary publishing house. David Slocombe and Yuri Rubinsky took the technology they were developing at Coach House — software to make SGML a basis for international document information sys-tems — and founded Softquad Inc. in 1984. After failing to find a market for its initial software, the company began developing a product based on the new SGML standard in 1987. The new package, Author/Editor, was the first commercial application to support SGML and quickly became Softquad's primary source of revenue.

Canadian investment firm Hatco Capital acquired an 81% interest in Softquad in 1992, renamed itself Softquad International, and went public on the Vancouver Stock Exchange. In 1993 the company announced plans

SOFTQUAD INTERNATIONAL

HQ: 56 Aberfoyle Crescent, 5th Fl.,
Toronto, Ontario M8X 2W4, Canada
Phone: 416-239-4801
Fax: 416-239-7105
US HQ: 100 Park Ave., 16th Floor
New York, NY 10017
US Phone: 212-880-6430
US Fax: 212-880-6421
Web site: www.softquad.com

OFFICERS

Chairman, President and CEO:
David J. Gurney, age 39

COO: Michael Cooperman, age 44

EVP, Softquad Inc.: William Clark, age 56

VP and CFO: Selwyn Wener, age 45

VP Professional and Consulting Services, Softquad Inc.:
Roberto Drassinower, age 32

Secretary: Frank Ruffolo, age 37

Director International Sales, Softquad Inc.:
Stephen Downie, age 43

Director Marketing, Softquad Inc.:
Linda Hazzan, age 30

Manager Human Resources: Janis Haydar
Auditors: Deloitte and Touche LLP

SELECTED PRODUCTS AND SERVICES

Network Monitoring Software
SmartAlert

Publishing and Browsing Software for the Internet and intranets
HoTMetaL
MetalWorks
Panorama

SGML Authoring and Publishing Tools
Author/Editor
Explorer
RulesBuilder
Sculptor
SGML Enabler for QuarkXPress

Subsidiaries:
Carolian Systems Corporation
SoftQuad Deutschland
SoftQuad Inc.
SoftQuad (UK) Ltd.

KEY COMPETITORS

Accent Software	Microsoft
Adobe	Nesbitt Software
America Online	Netscape
Electronic Book	Quarterdeck
Technologies	Sausage Software
Internet Software	
Technologies	

to acquire Carolian Systems, a maker of network monitoring software, and it named Carolian head David Gurney CEO of SoftQuad. In 1994 it launched HoTMetaL, which allows users to create and edit HTML documents for the Web. Softquad Inc. became a wholly owned subsidiary in 1996.

The company continues to introduce localized products for the European and Asian markets. It opened sales offices in the UK and Germany, and began trading on the Nasdaq in 1996. That year cofounder and president Rubinsky died; Gurney took over the position of president.

SOFTQUAD: THE NUMBERS

Nasdaq symbol: SWEBF FYE: December 31	Annual Growth	1990	1991	1992	1993	1994	1995
Sales ($ mil.)	57.4%	0.6	1.2	0.5	1.7	2.8	5.8
Net income ($ mil.)	—	(1.7)	(1.1)	(0.8)	(1.4)	(2.4)	(3.1)
Income as % of sales	—	—	—	—	—	—	—
Employees	—	—	—	—	—	—	105

1995 YEAR-END

Debt ratio: 0.0%
Return on equity: —
Cash (mil.): $1.9
Current ratio: 3.16
Long-term debt (mil.): $0.0
No. of shares (mil.): —
Dividends
  Yield: —
  Payout: —
Market value (mil.): —
R&D as % of sales: 25.1%

QUARTER ENDED 6/30

	1996	1995
Sales ($ millions)	3.2	1.1
Net Income ($ millions)	(3.6)	(0.2)
Earnings Per Share ($)	(0.34)	(0.02)
No. of Shares (thou.)	8,500	8,500

6 MONTHS ENDED 6/30

	1996	1995
Sales ($ millions)	5.4	2.2
Net Income ($ millions)	(7.4)	(0.4)
Earnings Per Share ($)	(0.74)	(0.03)
No. of Shares (thou.)	8,500	8,500

STOCK PRICE HISTORY: High/Low/Close

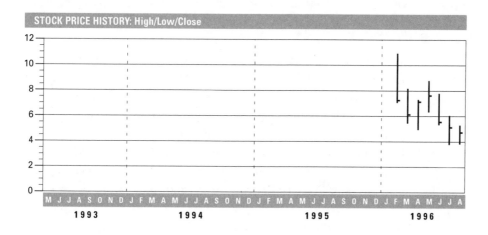

- Profitable and a pure play in Web software

- Component sales strategy makes company "the arms dealer for the Holy War" for Web browser market

- Adding new Web software components through acquisitions

- Microsoft is a browser software customer

- Revenue for first 9 months of fiscal 1996 up 100%, earnings per share up 111%

- Free browsers, integration of Web software in operating systems could hurt non-Microsoft sales

- Microsoft may eventually switch from customer to competitor

- P/E over 60 (8/96)

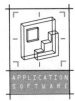

APPLICATION SOFTWARE

Spyglass, Inc.

Spyglass is inviting customers to take a closer look at its technology. The Naperville, Illinois-based company makes software that allows users to access and view the World Wide Web. Its Spyglass Client Web Technology Kit gives developers a set of software building blocks that can be used to add Web functionality to PCs, TVs, cellular phones, and other devices. Spyglass licenses its Internet technology to other companies to embed in their products (Microsoft, for instance, uses Mosaic, Spyglass's primary Web access and viewing software, in its Internet Explorer Web browser). Spyglass licenses Mosaic software to more than 72 OEMs for use in 170 products. The company also makes a World Wide Web software server.

Spyglass was started in 1990 by University of Illinois graduate Tim Krauskopf and others to commercialize the university's in-house technology. Krauskopf recruited software executive Doug Colbeth in 1991 to raise venture capital for the fledgling company. The university chose the company as a partner for commercializing Mosaic (it beat out Mosaic Communications, now known as Netscape) in 1994. Spyglass licensed a commercial version of the program for use in products by such industry giants as IBM, AT&T, DEC, CompuServe, and NEC.

In 1995 Spyglass released the upgraded version 2.1 of Spyglass Mosaic, which provides secure checking and credit card transactions over the Internet. The company sold its visual data analysis software and announced that it would expand its marketing efforts in Europe and Asia. Also that year Microsoft put Spyglass Mosaic features into its Windows 95 operating

SPYGLASS, INC.
HQ: Naperville Corporate Ctr.,
  1230 E. Diehl Rd., Ste. 304,
  Naperville, IL 60563
Phone: 708-505-1010
Fax: 708-505-4944
Web site: www.spyglass.com

OFFICERS

President and CEO:
  Douglas P. Colbeth, age 40, $187,900 pay
EVP Business Development:
  Michael F. Tyrrell, age 36, $293,200 pay
Treasurer, Controller, and Secretary:
  Thomas S. Lewicki, age 41, $93,000 pay
VP Research and Development and Chief Technical Officer:
  Tim Krauskopf, age 32, $150,300 pay
VP Sales: Thomas E. Banahan, age 37
VP Finance: Gary Vilchick
VP Human Resources: Lee Nelson
Auditors: Price Waterhouse LLP

SELECTED PRODUCTS AND SERVICES

Spyglass Client Web Technology Kit
  (multiplatform software components for
  viewing content on the World Wide Web)
Spyglass Mosaic (software for viewing content
  on the World Wide Web)
Spyglass Server (World Wide Web database
  management software)

Selected Licensing Partners

Adobe Systems	IBM
Alis Technologies	Ipswitch
Arcland	Luckman Interactive
AT&T Global	MicrosoftNEC
Information	Oracle
Systems	O'Reilly & Associates
BBN	PSINet
Broderbund	Quarterdeck
CompuServe	Spry
Corel	TGV Software
DEC	Ventana
Firefox	White Pine
FTP Software	WRQ
Fujitsu	

KEY COMPETITORS

Frontier Technology
IBM
NetManage
Netscape
Novell
Sun Microsystems

system. Spyglass went public in 1995. Krauskopf owns 6% of the company. The following year the company agreed to acquire text formatting software firm Stonehand, Surfwatch Software (whose product allows users to filter out the Internet's naughty bits), and OS Technologies Corp., a company that licenses World Wide Web conferencing technologies.

SPYGLASS: THE NUMBERS

Nasdaq symbol: SPYG FYE: September 30	Annual Growth	1990	1991	1992	1993	1994	1995
Sales ($ mil.)	153.2%	0.1	0.6	0.9	1.4	3.6	10.4
Net income ($ mil.)	—	(0.3)	(0.8)	(0.6)	(0.6)	1.1	2.0
Income as % of sales	—	—	—	—	—	29.6%	19.2%
Earnings per share ($)	—	—	(0.32)	(0.26)	(0.23)	0.16	0.23
Stock price – high ($)	—	—	—	—	—	—	61.00
Stock price – low ($)	—	—	—	—	—	—	13.25
Stock price – close ($)	—	—	—	—	—	—	57.00
P/E – high	—	—	—	—	—	—	265
P/E – low	—	—	—	—	—	—	58
Dividends per share ($)	—	—	—	—	—	—	0.00
Book value per share ($)	—	—	—	—	—	—	3.51
Employees	128.3%	—	—	—	14	54	73

1995 YEAR-END

Debt ratio: 0.0%
Return on equity: 5.8%
Cash (mil.): $34.3
Current ratio: 11.07
Long-term debt (mil.): $0.0
No. of shares (mil.): 10.6
Dividends
  Yield: —
  Payout: —
Market value (mil.): $605.3
R&D as % of sales: 19.4%

QUARTER ENDED 6/30

	1996	1995
Sales ($ millions)	6.0	3.2
Net Income ($ millions)	0.9	0.3
Earnings Per Share ($)	0.07	0.03
No. of Shares (thou.)	11,699	8,729

9 MONTHS ENDED 6/30

	1996	1995
Sales ($ millions)	15.8	7.9
Net Income ($ millions)	2.5	0.8
Earnings Per Share ($)	0.19	0.09
No. of Shares (thou.)	11,699	8,729

STOCK PRICE HISTORY: High/Low/Close

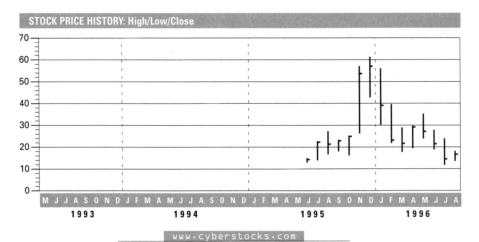

M J J A S O N D J F M A M J J A S O N D J F M A M J J A S O N D J F M A M J J A
1993   1994   1995   1996

www·cyberstocks·com

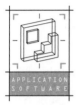
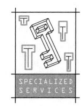

Sterling Commerce, Inc.

Electronic commerce is money in the bank for Sterling Commerce. The Dallas-based company offers electronic commerce software and network services (including automated business-to-business communication, e-mail, electronic funds transfer, and catalog services) to 17,000 customers world-wide in industries such as banking, transportation, health care, retail, and telecommunications. The company's electronic payment software (Vector) is used by 99 of the 100 largest US banks; 85% of all US banks using financial electronic data interchange (EDI) use Vector products. Sterling Commerce's other product offerings include software for automated file transfer (Connect, #1 in market share) and messaging management and EDI translation software (Gentran).

Sterling Commerce was originally the electronic commerce unit of Sterling Software (provider of systems management, application development, and reengineering software products). The 1990s marked the expansion of the unit bolstered by Sterling Software's key acquisitions: National Systems (provider of banking EDI products) in 1992; Systems Center, Inc. (data communications and systems software) in 1993; and American Business Computer (UNIX-based EDI products) in 1994.

Sterling Software spun off the unit in 1995 and created Sterling Commerce as a wholly owned subsidiary. The same year Sterling Commerce bought MAXXUS, Inc., expanding its banking customer base and product portfolio to include products and services for small and mid-sized financial institu-

- A global leader in EDI, electronic commerce over LANs and WANs

- Has begun selling products for EDI, electronic commerce over the Internet

- Customers include the US Treasury Department, 99 of top 100 banks

- Has just begun to tap international markets

- Support fees, service fees, and royalties account for most of revenue

- Excellent track record

- Just under half of revenue still related to the sales of mainframe products

- May encounter increased competition from players in lower end of Web commerce market

- P/E over 45 (8/96)

STERLING COMMERCE, INC.
HQ: 8080 N. Central Expwy., Ste. 1100,
Dallas, TX 75206
Phone: 214-891-8680
Fax: 214-739-0535
Web site: www.stercomm.com

OFFICERS

Chairman and CEO:
Sterling L. Williams, age 52, $1,200,000 pay
President and COO:
Warner C. Blow, age 58, $621,610 pay
EVP, CFO, Secretary, and General Counsel:
Jeannette P. Meier, age 48, $480,000 pay
EVP: Phillip A. Moore, age 53, $370,000 pay
SVP; President, Banking Systems Group:
William W. Hymes, age 59
SVP; President, Network Services Group:
Paul L. H. Olson, age 45
SVP; President, Communications Software Group:
Stephen R. Perkins, age 52
SVP; President, Interchange Software Group:
J. Brad Sharp, age 38
Auditors: Ernst & Young LLP

SELECTED PRODUCTS AND SERVICES

Commerce (value-added network services)
Connect (file transfer and communications management software)
Gentran (message handling and EDI translation software)
Vector (financial EDI and bank automation software)

	1995 Sales	
	$ mil.	% of total
Services	74.1	36
Products	71.6	35
Product support	46.2	23
Royalties from affiliated companies	11.7	6
Total	**203.6**	**100**

KEY COMPETITORS

CheckFree
CONNECT
CyberCash
DigiCash
Elcom International
General Electric
Harbinger
IBM
Intuit
Microsoft
Premenos Technology

tions. Sterling Commerce went public in 1996 with Sterling Software retaining an 82% stake. Later that year the parent announced plans to distribute its remaining stake to its shareholders. Also in 1996 the company agreed with Online Resources & Communications Corp. to resell Online's electronic banking and bill paying service to financial institutions nationwide, complementing Sterling Commerce's cash management product line.

STERLING COMMERCE: THE NUMBERS

NYSE symbol: SE FYE: September 30	Annual Growth	1990	1991	1992	1993	1994	1995
Sales ($ mil.)	30.1%	—	71.0	88.9	117.8	155.9	203.6
Net income ($ mil.)	51.7%	—	8.1	9.0	15.2	27.8	42.9
Income as % of sales	—	—	11.4%	10.1%	12.9%	17.8%	21.1%
Employees	—	—	—	—	—	—	1,009

1995 YEAR-END

Debt ratio: 0.0%
Return on equity: 37.4%
Cash (mil.): $0.4
Current ratio: 1.07
Long-term debt (mil.): $0.0
No. of shares (mil.): —
Dividends
  Yield: —
  Payout: —
Market value (mil.): —
R&D as % of sales: 7.3%

QUARTER ENDED 6/30

	1996	1995
Sales ($ millions)	69.2	51.6
Net Income ($ millions)	14.8	10.9
Earnings Per Share ($)	0.19	0.15
No. of Shares (thou.)	75,000	73,200

9 MONTHS ENDED 6/30

	1996	1995
Sales ($ millions)	187.5	143.0
Net Income ($ millions)	40.3	29.2
Earnings Per Share ($)	0.54	0.40
No. of Shares (thou.)	75,000	73,200

STOCK PRICE HISTORY: High/Low/Close

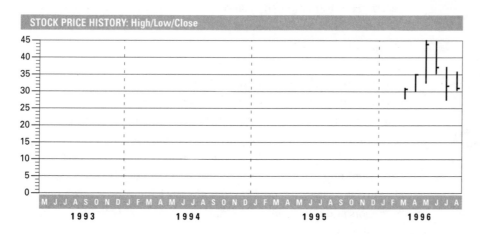

- Leader in Unix-based workstations and Internet servers

- Well-positioned to continue to benefit from growth in intranet/Internet applications

- Making a move on the high end of the enterprise networking market

- Java programming language may become a fixture in network computing

- Microsoft's Windows NT increasingly threatens UNIX as a server platform

- Computers based on Intel chips threaten to take share from UNIX workstations

- UNIX is not very easy to use

- New push into big company market will meet stiff resistance from Hewlett-Packard, IBM

- Unclear if Java will generate big profits

- Microsoft is pushing ActiveX as Java competitor

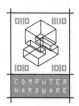
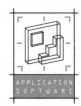

COMPUTER HARDWARE

APPLICATION SOFTWARE

Sun Microsystems

Heliocentricism is alive and well at Sun Microsystems. The Mountain View, California-based company is a leading maker of UNIX-based computer systems and Internet software. Sun's servers run more than 1/3 of the networks that make up the Internet. The company's Java programming language, a platform-independent, software tool, allows easy transmission of programs from servers to computers and enables Internet publishers to add such applications as animation and real-time video to their Web sites. Sun also produces workstations, microprocessors, and software used to create and manage local networks.

Andreas Bechtolsheim, Scott McNealy, William Joy, and Vinod Khosla founded Sun Microsystems in 1982 to make workstations that could share data using the UNIX operating system. The company's equipment was designed to network easily with the hardware and software of other vendors. Sun zoomed to more than $500 million in sales in just 5 years. The company went public in 1986 and the next year signed with AT&T to develop an enhanced UNIX operating system. In 1993 Sun moved into microprocessors and other computer chips in an effort to become a one-stop technology shop.

Sun unveiled the Hot Java browser and the Java programming language in 1995. It also introduced Internet products for the x86 platform (Internet

SUN MICROSYSTEMS, INC.
HQ: 2550 Garcia Ave.,
Mountain View, CA 94043-1100
Phone: 415-960-1300
Fax: 415-969-9131
Web site: www.sun.com

OFFICERS

Chairman, President, and CEO:
Scott G. McNealy, age 40, $3,000,000 pay

President, Sun Microsystems Computer Co.:
Edward J. Zander, age 48, $900,000 pay

VP Worldwide Field Operations, Sun Microsystems Computer Co.:
Joseph P. Roebuck, age 59, $781,648 pay

VP Corporate Planning and Development and Chief Information Officer:
William J. Raduchel, age 49, $699,769 pay

VP and CFO: Michael E. Lehman, age 45
VP Human Resources:
Kenneth M. Alvares, age 51

President, SunService:
Lawrence W. Hambly, age 49, $702,618 pay

President, SunExpress:
Dorothy A. Terrell, age 50

President, SunSoft: Janpieter T. Scheerder, 46
President, SPARC Technology Business:
Chester J. Silvestri, age 46

Auditors: Ernst & Young LLP

SELECTED PRODUCTS AND SERVICES

Operating Companies
SPARC Technology Business (SPARC microprocessors)
Sun Microsystems Computer Co. (SPARC workstations and servers)
SunExpress, Inc. (distribution of software, accessories, and 3rd-party products)
SunService (UNIX service and support)
SunSoft, Inc. (develops and markets Solaris, a UNIX operating system, and other software)
JavaSoft (develops and markets the Java programming language)

Workstations
SPARCstations
SPARC Xterminal 1

KEY COMPETITORS

AMD	Intergraph
Apple	Microsoft
Ceridian	Motorola
Compaq	NCR
Data General	Novell
DEC	Siemens
Hewlett-Packard	Silicon Graphics
Hitachi	Tandem
IBM	Unisys
Intel	Wang

Gateway) and for PCs (SolarNet). In 1996, the 4 creators of Java left Sun to form a networking products company called Marimba. Also, that year, Sun and Motorola created an alliance to develop high-speed Internet access systems for home PCs; and Apple, IBM, and Microsoft added their names to those supporting Java as a programming standard.

SUN MICROSYSTEMS: THE NUMBERS

Nasdaq symbol: SUNW FYE: June 30	Annual Growth	1990	1991	1992	1993	1994	1995
Sales ($ mil.)	19.1%	2,466.2	3,221.3	3,588.9	4,308.6	4,689.9	5,901.9
Net income ($ mil.)	26.2%	111.2	190.3	173.3	156.7	195.8	355.8
Income as % of sales	—	4.5%	5.9%	4.8%	3.6%	4.2%	6.0%
Earnings per share ($)	24.3%	0.61	0.93	0.86	0.75	1.01	1.81
Stock price – high ($)	—	18.56	19.31	18.06	20.50	18.81	51.44
Stock price – low ($)	—	7.50	10.38	11.25	10.56	9.13	14.94
Stock price – close ($)	33.7%	10.69	14.19	16.81	14.56	17.75	45.63
P/E – high	—	30	21	21	27	19	28
P/E – low	—	12	11	13	14	9	8
Dividends per share ($)	—	0.00	0.00	0.00	0.00	0.00	0.00
Book value per share ($)	16.6%	5.00	6.29	7.43	8.04	8.67	10.77
Employees	4.7%	11,500	12,480	12,800	13,253	13,282	14,498

1995 YEAR-END

Debt ratio: 7.8%
Return on equity: 19.0%
Cash (mil.): $1,228.0
Current ratio: 2.20
Long-term debt (mil.): $91.2
No. of shares (mil.): 197.0
Dividends
  Yield: —
  Payout: —
Market value (mil.): $8,900.4

QUARTER ENDED 6/30

	1996	1995
Sales ($ millions)	2,018.1	1,648.1
Net Income ($ millions)	122.3	128.2
Earnings Per Share ($)	0.62	0.63
No. of Shares (thou.)	197,419	197,028

12 MONTHS ENDED 6/30

	1996	1995
Sales ($ millions)	7,094.8	5,901.9
Net Income ($ millions)	476.4	355.8
Earnings Per Share ($)	2.42	1.81
No. of Shares (thou.)	197,419	197,028

STOCK PRICE HISTORY: High/Low/Close

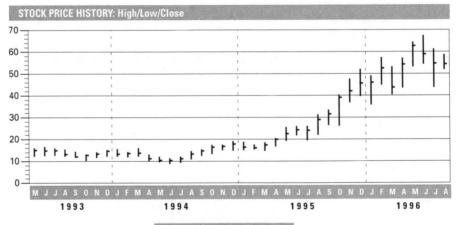

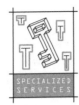

CONTENT   SPECIALIZED SERVICES

Telescan, Inc.

Telescan lets you conduct important business online — from managing your investments to golfing with your business contacts. The Houston-based company's online services help investors access financial news and information, while its Computer Sports Network serves up golf and baseball games. Telescan provides online services in conjunction with other companies and organizations such as the American Institute of Architects and the Editor and Publisher Company. Its online database serves universities, corporations, and the US government. Microsoft cofounder Paul Allen's Vulcan Ventures owns 15% of the company. Telescan cofounder and CEO David Brown owns 9%.

While working on his doctorate in biochemical engineering, Richard Carlin created a computer program to track his investments. With seed money from Brown, a former NASA engineer who helped design landing gear for the lunar module, the pair founded Telescan in 1983. They introduced their first product, Telescan Analyzer investment software, in 1986 and debuted an online golf game in 1987. The company added a portfolio manager in 1990 and a mutual fund search product in 1992. Telescan began trading on Nasdaq in 1993.

In 1995 Telescan developed several 3rd-party online services, including those for *Adweek* and *Billboard* magazines. It also created TIPnet, a World Wide Web investor "supersite" linking information on major international stock markets. That year Telescan introduced its Sunflower development

TELESCAN, INC.
HQ: 10550 Richmond Ave., Ste. 250,
Houston, TX 77042
Phone: 713-588-9700
Fax: 713-588-9797
Web site: www.telescan.com

OFFICERS
Chairman and CEO:
David L. Brown, age 55, $107,625 pay
VC and SVP: Richard K. Carlin, age 40
EVP and Acting COO: Luiz V. Alvim, age 65
SVP: Roger C. Wadsworth, age 48
SVP: Scott L. Brown
CFO: Karen R. Fohn, age 35
Director Human Resources:
Brigette Dewhurst
Auditors: Hein + Associates LLP

SELECTED PRODUCTS AND SERVIES
Computer Sports Network
General Manager (simulated baseball game)
Links Tour (computer golf tournaments)
Knowledge Express Data Systems (KEDS, online database serving the US government, universities, and corporations)
Telescan Financial
Options Search (custom options search)
QuoteLink (link with other financial service software)
Telescan Analyzer (financial database access and analysis)
Telescan Esearch (investment screening based on earnings estimates)
Telescan Gateway (online library)
Telescan Mutual Fund Search (mutual fund screening program)
Telescan Portfolio Manager (investment management program)
Telescan Prosearch (investment selection tool)
TIPnet (financial Web site)
Wall Street City (financial Web supersite)

KEY COMPETITORS
America Online	Global Financial	Prodigy
Bloomberg	Information	Quote.Com
CompuServe	Knight-Ridder	Reuters
Data	M.A.I.D.	Thomson Corp.
Broadcasting	Microsoft	
Dow Jones	PC Quote	

tool, user-friendly software that allows small organizations to set up their own on-line services.

The company launched Wall Street City, a Web site for individual investors, in 1996. It also announced an alliance with Internet access provider NETCOM whereby NETCOM will offer access to TIPnet and include promotional information about Telescan with its NetCruiser disks.

TELESCAN: THE NUMBERS

Nasdaq symbol (SC): TSCN FYE: December 31	Annual Growth	1990	1991	1992	1993	1994	1995
Sales ($ mil.)	41.1%	2.5	3.0	4.2	6.9	10.5	14.0
Net income ($ mil.)	—	(0.3)	(0.6)	(0.3)	0.0	(2.6)	(1.2)
Income as % of sales	—	—	—	—	0.0%	—	—
Earnings per share ($)	—	(0.70)	(0.11)	(0.05)	0.00	(0.28)	(0.12)
Stock price – high ($)	—	—	—	2.25	10.50	9.63	9.50
Stock price – low ($)	—	—	—	1.75	1.75	3.75	4.00
Stock price – close ($)	59.6%	—	—	2.00	9.13	4.38	8.13
P/E – high	—	—	—	—	—	—	—
P/E – low	—	—	—	—	—	—	—
Dividends per share ($)	—	—	0.00	0.00	0.00	0.00	0.00
Book value per share ($)	44.3%	—	0.18	0.49	0.91	0.63	0.78
Employees	39.0%	—	—	57	95	142	153

1995 YEAR-END

Debt ratio: 9.2%
Return on equity: —
Cash (mil.): $1.8
Current ratio: 2.05
Long-term debt (mil.): $0.5
No. of shares (mil.): 10.2
Dividends
  Yield: 0.0%
  Payout: —
Market value (mil.): $83.2
R&D as % of sales: 11.4%

QUARTER ENDED 6/30

	1996	1995
Sales ($ millions)	3.2	3.6
Net Income ($ millions)	(0.9)	0.1
Earnings Per Share ($)	(0.09)	0.01
No. of Shares (thou.)	10,605	9,555

6 MONTHS ENDED 6/30

	1996	1995
Sales ($ millions)	6.7	6.7
Net Income ($ millions)	(1.5)	(0.2)
Earnings Per Share ($)	(0.14)	(0.02)
No. of Shares (thou.)	10,605	9,555

STOCK PRICE HISTORY: High/Low/Close

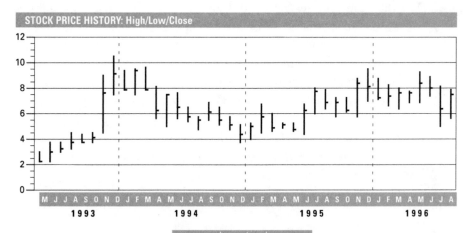

www·cyberstocks·com

- Increased digital traffic over telephone and cable networks is a favorable condition
- Deregulation of telecommunications has created new customers
- Has a strong relationship with Ericsson
- Wireless products business is expanding rapidly
- Solid track record

- Significant sales of cable products have not yet materialized
- Analog product sales are withering
- More of a telecommunications play than an Internet play

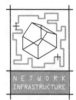

NETWORK INFRASTRUCTURE

Tellabs, Inc.

You can bet your telephone that Tellabs was in favor of the Telecommunications Act of 1996. Headquartered in Lisle, Illinois, the company makes equipment used to transmit data, video, and voice signals over wireline networks. Its CABLESPAN transport system allows cable TV operators to send telephone signals over their existing coaxial and fiber optic cables, a business that is set for expansion under the regulatory freedom afforded by the new federal law.

Tellabs (shortened from Telecommunications Laboratories) was founded in 1975 by CEO Michael Birck, VP Charles Cooney, and several others. Birck, a former Bell Labs employee, developed an echo suppressor on the company's homemade workbench. Increased use of satellites for phone transmission created a market for the product. Tellabs went public in 1980. Birck owns about 11% of Tellabs stock.

The creation of the regional Bell companies and several new long-distance services in the mid-1980s created a surge of new competitors; Tellabs sales rose but profits fell. The company boosted R&D spending and refocused on high-end products. In 1987 a $10 million contract from Sprint for digital echo cancellers helped revive Tellabs, which began marketing to overseas telecommunications services and making acquisitions, including Delta Communications (Ireland, 1987). Tellabs in 1991 introduced its TITAN digital cross-connect products for routing and switching voice and data transmissions at very high speeds. Two years later it acquired Martis Oy, a

TELLABS, INC.
HQ: 4951 Indiana Ave., Lisle, IL 60532
Phone: 708-969-8800
Fax: 708-512-8202
Web site: www.tellabs.com

OFFICERS

President and CEO:
Michael J. Birck, age 58, $491,354 pay

EVP; President, Tellabs Operations, Inc.:
Brian J. Jackman, age 55, $344,808 pay

EVP, CFO, and Treasurer; President, Tellabs International, Inc.:
Peter A. Guglielmi, age 54, $334,808 pay

VP Sales and Service, Tellabs Operations, Inc.:
Charles C. Cooney, age 55, $223,922 pay

VP and General Manager Network Access Systems Division, Tellabs Operations, Inc.:
Jon C. Grimes, age 49, $215,269 pay

Secretary; VP, General Counsel, and Secretary, Tellabs Operations, Inc.:
Carol Coghlan Gavin, age 40

Director Human Resources: Dan Stolle
Auditors: Grant Thornton LLP

SELECTED PRODUCTS AND SERVICES

Digital cross-connect systems (TITAN; cross-connect systems and network management platforms)

Managed digital networks (CROSSNET and Martis DXX; multiplexers, packet switches, and network management systems)

Network access systems (CABLESPAN and EXPRESSPAN; products for digital signal processing, special services, and local access)

	1995 Sales % of total
Digital cross-connect systems	49
Managed digital networks	28
Digital signaling products	15
Special services products	5
Other	3
Total	**100**

KEY COMPETITORS

ADC Telecommunications
ADTRAN
Ascend Communications
Aydin
Coherent Communications
Ditech
DSC Communications
General DataComm
Motorola
Network Equipment

Technologies
Newbridge Networks
Nokia Group
Northern Telecom
PairGain
Premisys
Scientific-Atlanta
Siemens
Timeplex

Finnish manufacturer of multiplexers (which allow multiple signals to travel over a single circuit). Tellabs continued its global expansion in 1994 with contracts from phone providers in Namibia and Singapore. It also introduced an asynchronous transfer mode (ATM) switch and CABLESPAN, a system for sending phone signals over cable TV lines.

The company formed a marketing alliance with Swedish telecommunications equipment giant Ericsson in 1995. In 1996 Tellabs purchased wireless network systems manufacturer Steinbrecher Corp. for about $76 million.

TELLABS: THE NUMBERS

Nasdaq symbol: TLAB FYE: December 31	Annual Growth	1990	1991	1992	1993	1994	1995
Sales ($ mil.)	24.7%	211.0	212.8	258.6	320.5	494.2	635.2
Net income ($ mil.)	70.2%	8.1	6.6	16.9	30.5	72.4	115.6
Income as % of sales	—	3.8%	3.1%	6.5%	9.5%	14.6%	18.2%
Earnings per share ($)	62.9%	0.11	0.09	0.20	0.35	0.80	1.26
Stock price – high ($)	—	2.52	3.67	4.40	13.59	28.00	52.75
Stock price – low ($)	—	1.40	2.04	2.63	3.17	10.94	23.50
Stock price – close ($)	71.4%	2.50	3.61	4.13	11.81	27.88	37.00
P/E – high	—	23	41	22	39	35	42
P/E – low	—	13	23	13	9	14	19
Dividends per share ($)	—	0.00	0.00	0.00	0.00	0.00	0.00
Book value per share ($)	23.5%	1.70	1.80	2.01	2.41	3.35	4.88
Employees	5.8%	2,127	2,094	2,000	2,370	2,585	2,814

1995 YEAR-END

Debt ratio: 0.7%
Return on equity: 31.8%
Cash (mil.): $162.2
Current ratio: 3.72
Long-term debt (mil.): $2.9
No. of shares (mil.): 88.8
Dividends
  Yield: —
  Payout: —
Market value (mil.): $3,285.5
R&D as % of sales: 12.9%

QUARTER ENDED 6/30

	1996	1995
Sales ($ millions)	189.5	159.9
Net Income ($ millions)	(18.7)	27.1
Earnings Per Share ($)	(0.20)	0.30
No. of Shares (thou.)	89,064	88,420

6 MONTHS ENDED 6/30

	1996	1995
Sales ($ millions)	361.7	302.2
Net Income ($ millions)	12.4	50.1
Earnings Per Share ($)	0.14	0.55
No. of Shares (thou.)	89,064	88,420

STOCK PRICE HISTORY: High/Low/Close

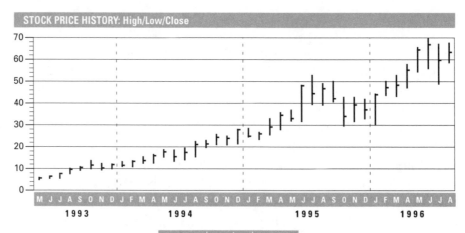

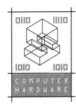

NETWORK INFRASTRUCTURE

COMPUTER HARDWARE

U.S. Robotics Corporation

U.S. Robotics is counting on a digital future. The Skokie, Illinois-based company designs and manufactures the hardware that makes it possible for computers to communicate with each other, whether over a phone line (analog modems), in an office (local area network [LAN] cards and hubs), or from outside the office (remote access servers).

U.S. Robotics is the leading supplier of these products. The firm's new Courier I-Modem fuses 2 technologies: it has an analog modem that can be used on regular phone lines and an adapter that allows the device to connect directly with the much faster ISDN digital feed provided (at a premium) by regional telephone companies. Some analysts expect that market to grow more than 60% per year. The company has also broadened its product line with acquisitions.

In 1975 CEO Casey Cowell, a University of Chicago economics graduate, teamed up with fellow Chicago graduates Paul Collard (who later left the firm) and Steve Muka (who died in 1985) to go into the budding computer field. U.S. Robotics (named after a company in Isaac Asimov's "I, Robot") first produced an acoustic coupler that connected computers over phone lines via the handsets. In 1976 an FCC ruling allowed non-AT&T products to be plugged into phone lines, freeing the company to move into modems. It grew quickly, first as a distributor and after 1988 as a manufac-

- In-house manufacturing and DSP technology usually enable USR to be first to market with new products and a low-cost, high-volume manufacturer
- Gross margins are much higher than the rest of the industry
- Aggressively expanding internationally
- Beginning "Communications by U.S. Robotics" co-branding campaign with OEMs
- In first 9 months of fiscal 1996 revenues up 129%, EPS up 143%

- Faces tough price competition in modem market
- Analog modems may have reached maximum speed
- In-house manufacturing strategy could backfire if modem demand drops

US Robotics

U.S. ROBOTICS CORPORATION
HQ: 8100 N. McCormick Blvd.,
   Skokie, IL 60076-2999
Phone: 847-982-5010
Fax: 847-933-5551
Web site: www.usr.com

OFFICERS

Chairman, President, and CEO:
   Casey G. Cowell, age 43, $2,799,000 pay
EVP and COO:
   John McCartney, age 43, $1,739,400 pay (prior to promotion)
EVP Strategy and Corporate Development:
   Jonathan N. Zakin, age 46, $1,739,400 pay
**SVP and General Manager
Corporate/Systems:**
   Ross W. Manire, age 44, $1,449,500 pay
VP Finance and CFO: Mark Remissong, age 43
VP Human Resources: Elizabeth S. Ryan
Auditors: Grant Thornton LLP

SELECTED PRODUCTS AND SERVICES

ConferenceLink Conference Speakerphones
Courier I-Modems with ISDN/V.34 (modems that offer ISDN and analog capabilities)
Megahertz PC Card Ethernet Adapters (PCMCIA cards to connect laptops to LANs)
Megahertz PC Card Modems (PCMCIA card modems)
Palm Computing software (for handheld computers)
Sportster Faxmodems (PC modems with a transmission speed up to 28.8 kpbs)
Total Control Enterprise Network Hubs

KEY COMPETITORS

3Com	Digi International	Multi-Tech
ADTRAN	General	Oki Electric
Apex Data	DataComm	PairGain
Apple	Global Village	Proteon
Asante	GVC Technologies	Shiva
Ascend	Hayes	Standard
Communications	Microcomputer	Microsystems
Bay Networks	IBM	System
Boca Research	Intel	Connection
Cincinnati	Microcom	Tandem
Microwave	Microdyne	Xircom
DATA RACE	Motorola	Zoom Telephonics

turer. U.S. Robotics went public in 1991, and it has been riding the streaking Internet growth curve by providing ever faster, lower-priced modems for PCs. In 1994 it expanded its LAN product line. The company introduced its first ISDN products in 1995 and acquired Megahertz (credit card-sized modems, LAN adapter cards), ISDN Systems (LAN connection devices), and Palm Computing (handheld computer software). In 1996 the company acquired Amber Wave Systems, opening a door to the Ethernet switching market.

U.S. ROBOTICS: THE NUMBERS

Nasdaq symbol: USRX FYE: Sunday nearest Sept. 30	Annual Growth	1990	1991	1992	1993	1994	1995
Sales ($ mil.)	73.6%	56.4	78.8	112.4	189.2	378.7	889.3
Net income ($ mil.)	69.6%	4.7	7.3	10.9	17.0	26.4	66.0
Income as % of sales	—	8.4%	9.3%	9.7%	9.0%	7.0%	7.4%
Earnings per share ($)	48.0%	0.11	0.20	0.25	0.35	0.52	0.78
Stock price – high ($)	—	—	4.19	6.06	8.81	11.50	55.25
Stock price – low ($)	—	—	3.06	3.34	4.25	6.00	9.81
Stock price – close ($)	82.0%	—	4.00	5.13	8.66	10.81	43.88
P/E – high	—	—	21	24	25	22	71
P/E – low	—	—	16	13	12	12	13
Dividends per share ($)	—	—	0.00	0.00	0.00	0.00	0.00
Book value per share ($)	63.1%	—	0.71	1.56	2.34	2.99	5.03
Employees	60.3%	316	402	479	755	1,451	3,347

1995 YEAR-END

Debt ratio: 13.4%
Return on equity: 23.3%
Cash (mil.): $232.8
Current ratio: 3.21
Long-term debt (mil.): $65.7
No. of shares (mil.): 84.4
Dividends
  Yield: —
  Payout: —
Market value (mil.): $3,702.5
R&D as % of sales: 5.9%

QUARTER ENDED 6/30

	1996	1995
Sales ($ millions)	546.8	237.3
Net Income ($ millions)	63.3	24.9
Earnings Per Share ($)	0.66	0.30
No. of Shares (thou.)	96,613	81,916

9 MONTHS ENDED 6/30

	1996	1995
Sales ($ millions)	1,366.1	595.9
Net Income ($ millions)	156.5	31.7
Earnings Per Share ($)	1.65	0.40
No. of Shares (thou.)	96,613	81,916

STOCK PRICE HISTORY: High/Low/Close

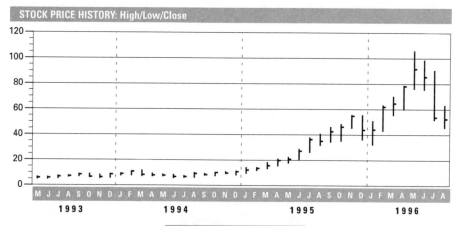

www.cyberstocks.com

- Dominates in-store credit card payment systems market

- New Internet payment system works with existing credit card systems

- Point-Of-Sale software to be included in Microsoft's new Merchant System

- Integrating its technology with Netscape's and Oracle's electronic commerce products

- Smart-card systems offer potential for additional growth

- With 75% of the US retail market, merchant card systems may experience slower growth

- Currently, Internet-related revenue is insignificant

SPECIALIZED
SERVICES

VeriFone, Inc.

Someday you may hear VeriFone users admonish their children: "Don't you understand, plastic doesn't grow on trees." Headquartered in Redwood City, California, VeriFone is a leading worldwide provider (with 75% of the US market) of electronic payment systems, which process information encoded on plastic cards to transfer funds from people's accounts. Customers include banks, convenience stores, credit card services, health care providers, restaurants, and retail stores. In addition, Verifone recently began exploring methods to allow secure commercial transactions over the Internet.

William Melton (now a company director) founded the company in 1981 to focus on electronic mail systems that kept employees on the road in touch with their offices. By 1984 VeriFone had diversified into transaction automation systems, introducing ZON, the first low-cost electronic credit card and check verification terminal. This product gave the company its competitive edge. The business evolved away from hardware toward software-driven systems that connect computers, printers, operating systems, and terminals. VeriFone went public in 1990. The next year it released the Gemstone family of transaction systems, which incorporate point-of-service tasks with other functions, such as inventory control and price checks. In 1992 it introduced an electronic cash register that verifies checks and accepts credit and debit card payments. Two years later VeriFone established regional offices in Japan, Hong Kong, China, and Canada. In 1995 the com-

VERIFONE, INC.
HQ: 3 Lagoon Dr., Ste. 400,
Redwood City, CA 94065-1561
Phone: 415-591-6500
Fax: 415-598-5504
Web site: www.verifone.com

OFFICERS

Chairman, President, and CEO:
Hatim A. Tyabji, age 51, $692,764 pay
EVP: John Hinds, age 59, $403,305 pay
EVP Development and Manufacturing:
James A. Palmer, age 59, $321,575 pay
SVP, General Counsel, and Secretary:
William G. Barmeier, age 42
SVP Finance and Administration and CFO:
Joseph M. Zaelit, age 50
VP Human Resources:
Katherine B. Beall, age 38
Auditors: Ernst & Young LLP

SELECTED PRODUCTS AND SERVICES

System Components
Card readers/writers
Management software
PIN pads
Printers
Transaction terminals

Other Products
Omnihost 2 (transaction switching and authorization system)
VeriTalk (monitoring and tracking software)

	1995 Sales	
	$ mil.	% of total
High-functionality terminals	164.9	43
Printers & PIN pads	122.7	32
Fully integrated systems	27.4	7
Basic terminals	15.9	4
Other	56.1	14
Total	**387.0**	**100**

KEY COMPETITORS

American Express
Checkfree
CyberCash
Deluxe
DigiCash
Equifax
First Data
First USA Paymentech
IBM
National Data
Total Systems
Virtual Open Network

pany purchased electronic commerce concern Enterprise Integration Technologies and labor management firm TimeCorp Systems.

In 1996 VeriFone opened a subsidiary in Sandton-Johannesburg to address growing market demand throughout the African continent. That year VeriFone created its Internet Commerce Division and teamed with Netscape to develop a system to securely transfer funds over the Internet. The system would allow cyber-shoppers to make credit card purchases on the World Wide Web without fear of having their card numbers appropriated by a computer hacker.

VERIFONE: THE NUMBERS

NYSE symbol: VFI FYE: December 31	Annual Growth	1990	1991	1992	1993	1994	1995
Sales ($ mil.)	20.1%	155.0	187.9	226.1	258.9	309.1	387.0
Net income ($ mil.)	21.6%	12.2	18.7	24.0	21.5	27.7	32.5
Income as % of sales	—	7.8%	10.0%	10.6%	8.3%	9.0%	8.4%
Earnings per share ($)	19.1%	0.55	0.82	1.02	0.90	1.18	1.32
Stock price – high ($)	—	26.00	21.75	27.75	30.00	24.25	31.38
Stock price – low ($)	—	5.75	8.50	16.50	16.00	14.50	19.75
Stock price – close ($)	26.0%	9.00	18.13	20.25	19.25	22.25	28.63
P/E – high	—	47	27	27	33	21	24
P/E – low	—	10	10	16	18	12	15
Dividends per share ($)	—	0.00	0.00	0.00	0.00	0.00	0.00
Book value per share ($)	13.9%	5.53	6.37	7.48	8.21	9.17	10.62
Employees	18.2%	1,042	1,385	1,562	1,750	1,932	2,400

1995 YEAR-END

Debt ratio: 4.6%
Return on equity: 13.5%
Cash (mil.): $82.8
Current ratio: 3.66
Long-term debt (mil.): $2.2
No. of shares (mil.): 24.9
Dividends
  Yield: —
  Payout: —
Market value (mil.): $713.1
R&D as % of sales: 11.6%
Advertising as % of sales: —

QUARTER ENDED 6/30

	1996	1995
Sales ($ millions)	125.0	92.8
Net Income ($ millions)	11.2	8.8
Earnings Per Share ($)	0.43	0.38
No. of Shares (thou.)	25,205	22,840

6 MONTHS ENDED 6/30

	1996	1995
Sales ($ millions)	227.9	170.3
Net Income ($ millions)	18.0	13.9
Earnings Per Share ($)	0.69	0.60
No. of Shares (thou.)	25,205	22,840

STOCK PRICE HISTORY: High/Low/Close

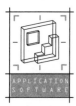

APPLICATION SOFTWARE

Verity, Inc.

The topic of conversation at Verity is the company's 2-word strategy: "Topic Everywhere." Mountain View, California-based Verity makes Topic software to search for and retrieve textual information stored in such locations as computer networks and the Internet. To help it really be "everywhere," the company is signing up a legion of licensees and partners in the software and publishing industries to embed Verity's search technology in their products or to bundle Topic with their products. CEO Philippe Courtot owns 8% of the company; Olympic Venture Partners owns about 7%.

Verity got its start when Michael Pliner, cofounder and former CEO of networking company Sytek, joined the board of Advanced Decision Systems (ADS) and found a primitive text-retrieval program there. Recognizing its potential, he recommended it be rewritten so topic-based queries could be posed to a host database. He then convinced ADS to spin off the technology. With venture capital he put together, Pliner founded Verity (which means "truth") with John Lehman and Clifford Reid in 1988. Topic was introduced later that year. But Verity's focus on selling expensive software to a few large customers was not profitable.

In 1993, the company hired turnaround artist Philippe Courtot as CEO. His first act was to drastically cut prices, hoping to appeal to ordinary computer users. He increased R&D spending to more than 30% of sales and began a program to embed the company's search engine in as many 3rd-party applications as possible, seeking to make it the industry standard. The company,

- Appears to be the leader in client/server search and retrieval market

- Switch to high-volume, low-price business model appears to be paying off

- Personal agents can search many kinds of documents including HTML, SGML, .pdf, TIFF

- Important partners include AT&T, Netscape, Adobe

- Customer list is growing rapidly

- Fiscal 1996 sales up 93%

- Rival Fulcrum is developing browser-specific software for Netscape and Microsoft products

- Market cap of $250 million vs. $30.7 million in fiscal 1996 sales

VERITY, INC.
HQ: 894 Ross Dr., Sunnyvale, CA 94089
Phone: 415-960-7600
Fax: 415-541-1600
Web site: www.verity.com

OFFICERS

Chairman, President, and CEO:
Philippe F. Courtot, age 51, $222,402 pay

VP, CFO, and Secretary:
Donald C. McCauley, age 43, $145,779 pay

VP Marketing:
Susan P. Barsamian, age 36, $151,541 pay

VP Sales and Marketing:
Anthony J. Bettencourt, age 34

VP Research and Development:
Christopher Helgeson, age 39

Director Corporate Communications:
Marguerite Padovani

Manager Human Resources: Rima Touma
Auditors: Coopers & Lybrand L.L.P.

SELECTED PRODUCTS AND SERVICES

Topic Developer's Toolkit (software development for embedding Topic engine in other applications)

Topic Client (retrieval software for searching and filtering information)

Topic Enterprise Server (enterprise data access across major platforms, formats, and locations)

Topic CD Publisher (integrated system for searching CD-ROM and Web servers)

Topic Internet Server (Topic-indexed information publishing and searching across the Internet)

Topic Newswire Access (news wire feeds added to Topic databases)

Topic Agent Server (static and dynamic information source monitoring and automatic delivery)

SELECTED PARTNERS AND VENDORS

Adobe	IBM	Reuters
Attachmate	Informix	*San Jose*
Cisco Systems	Infoseek	*Mercury News*
	MCI	SoftQuad
CondeNet	Microsoft	Sybase
Dow Jones	NetManage	Tandem Computer
Hewlett-Packard	Netscape	*Time*
Hitachi	The News Corp.	
	Quarterdeck	

KEY COMPETITORS

America Online	Fulcrum Technologies
Dataware Technologies	General Magic
Excalibur Technologies	Information Dimensions
Folio	Open Text

which went public in 1995, has yet to have a profitable year. Verity entered into almost 2 dozen alliances in 1996, including deals with software makers Informix and Sybase, who will include text search functions in their database software designed for the World Wide Web. Also in 1996, the company bought UK groupware developer InSite Computer Technology.

VERITY: THE NUMBERS

Nasdaq symbol: VRTY FYE: May 31	Annual Growth	1991	1992	1993	1994	1995	1996[1]
Sales ($ mil.)	16.8%	—	—	19.3	16.6	15.9	30.7
Net income ($ mil.)	—	—	—	(1.0)	(5.1)	(5.8)	(0.3)
Income as % of sales	—	—	—	—	—	—	—
Earnings per share ($)	—	—	—	(1.09)	(2.67)	(2.18)	(0.12)
Stock price – high ($)	—	—	—	—	—	57.50	55.00
Stock price – low ($)	—	—	—	—	—	14.25	23.56
Stock price – close ($)	—	—	—	—	—	44.25	28.75
P/E – high	—	—	—	—	—	—	—
P/E – low	—	—	—	—	—	—	—
Dividends per share ($)	—	—	—	—	—	0.00	0.00
Book value per share ($)	—	—	—	—	—	—	4.92
Employees	—	—	—	—	—	173	216

[1] Stock prices through June 30.

1996 YEAR-END

Debt ratio: 2.0%
Return on equity: —
Cash (mil.): $43.4
Current ratio: 5.75
Long-term debt (mil.): $0.6
No. of shares (mil.): 10.7
Dividends
  Yield: —
  Payout: —
Market value (mil.): $308.6
R&D as % of sales: 27.7%

QUARTER ENDED 5/31

	1996	1995
Sales ($ millions)	10.0	4.2
Net Income ($ millions)	0.4	(1.8)
Earnings Per Share ($)	0.03	(0.58)
No. of Shares (thou.)	11,395	1,581

12 MONTHS ENDED 5/31

	1996	1995
Sales ($ millions)	30.7	15.9
Net Income ($ millions)	(0.3)	(5.8)
Earnings Per Share ($)	(0.12)	(2.18)
No. of Shares (thou.)	11,395	1,581

STOCK PRICE HISTORY: High/Low/Close

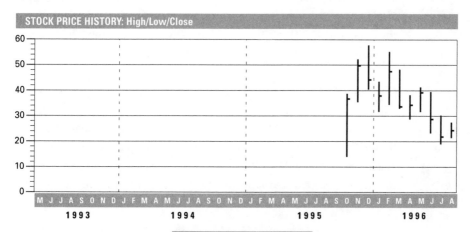

1993   1994   1995   1996

- V-ONE is a network security play

- V-ONE's SmartGate is well-suited to electronic commerce security applications

- SmartGate works with most existing TCP/IP networks and software

- Customers include the NSA, the US Navy, and VISA International

- 1st half 1996 sales up 544%

- V-ONE is a new, small player in the crowded network security market

- Share price of $10 in SEC registration statement values V-ONE at 110 times 1995 sales

- Losses are accelerating as the company expands

- Government and government contractors account for a "substantial" proportion of sales

- V-ONE is still building its distribution channels

NETWORK INFRASTRUCTURE

Virtual Open Network Environment

"Safety first" is spelled V-ONE. Rockville, Maryland-based Virtual Open Network Environment (V-ONE) is a leading provider of security-oriented technology products. These include the SmartWorld campus card (for ID, security, library privileges, food and vending, telephone calls, and access to academic and financial records), Wallet Technology (for secure transactions over the Internet), and SmartWall (for protection of corporate and government networks).

The company is a pioneer in smart card and firewall technology. The smart card resembles a credit card but has a microprocessor chip that can store data and process encryption algorithms; V-ONE has the only smart card-based network security system available off-the-shelf. A firewall controls access between 2 networks or between a network and the outside world; V-ONE's SmartWall is used by US military and intelligence agencies and *FORTUNE* 100 corporations. Founder and CEO James Chen owns 58% of the company; Hai Hua Cheng, majority owner of Scientek (which invested in V-ONE), owns 16%.

Chen founded V-ONE in 1993 to help organizations maintain security while using open networks. Late the next year the company introduced its first products: SmartCAT card-reading software and SmartWall (a combination of SmartCAT and firewall technologies). The SmartGATE client/server system was launched in 1995 to ensure data exchange and safe transactions in industries such as banking, financial trading, health care, insurance, and

VIRTUAL OPEN NETWORK ENVIRONMENT CORPORATION

HQ: 1803 Research Blvd., Ste. 305, Rockville, MD 20850
Phone: 301-838-8900
Fax: 301-838-8909
Web site: www.v-one.com

OFFICERS

President and CEO:
James F. Chen, age 45, $18,000 pay

Chief Scientist: Marcus J. Ranum, age 33
SVP Engineering: Jieh-Shan Wang, age 41
VP Indirect Channels:
Robert W. Rybicki, age 51

VP Technology: Frederick J. Hitt, age 52
VP Business Development:
William C. Wilson, age 41

VP Direct Sales: Barnaby M. Page, age 32
Treasurer and Acting CFO:
Chansothi Um, age 27

Secretary: Charles C. Chen, age 41
Manager Personnel: Dan Davis
Auditors: Coopers & Lybrand L.L.P.

SELECTED PRODUCTS AND SERVICES

NetChart (online stock performance analysis)

Online Registration (client/server token for access)

SmartCAT (smart card client software)

SmartGATE (client/server security)

SmartWall (firewall defense)

Wallet Technology (secured payment transactions)

KEY COMPETITORS

America Online	Network Systems
Checkpoint Systems	Open Market
Cylink	Raptor Systems
DEC	Secure
Harris Corp.	Security Dynamics
IBM	Sun Microsystems
Milkyway Networks	Trusted Information
Morningstar Technologies	Systems
Netscape	

publishing. Also that year the company hired Marcus Ranum (considered the "father of the commercial firewall") as chief scientist.

In addition to augmenting and integrating its product lines with existing network security systems, V-ONE is developing alliances. Such alliances include deals with Web software maker Spyglass, information management pioneer General Electric Information Services, and database management applications maker Oracle.

In 1996 V-ONE was chosen by the National Security Agency to develop network protection for its Defense Messaging System. The company, which has not yet made a profit, filed in 1996 to go public.

VIRTUAL OPEN: THE NUMBERS

FYE: December 31	Annual Growth	1990	1991	1992	1993	1994	1995
Sales ($ mil.)	231.7%	—	—	—	0.1	0.1	1.1
Net income ($ mil.)	—	—	—	—	0.0	(0.4)	(1.0)
Income as % of sales	—	—	—	—	—	—	—
Employees	—	—	—	—	—	—	52

1995 YEAR-END

Debt ratio: 100.0%
Return on equity: —
Cash (mil.): $1.3
Current ratio: 0.92
Long-term debt (mil.): $0.1
No. of shares (mil.): —
Dividends
  Yield: —
  Payout: —
Market value (mil.): —
R&D as % of sales: 25.2%

QUARTER ENDED 6/30

	1996	1995
Sales ($ millions)	1.4	0.2
Net Income ($ millions)	(2.0)	(0.2)
Earnings Per Share ($)	(0.22)	(0.03)
No. of Shares (thou.)	9,582	8,595

6 MONTHS ENDED 6/30

	1996	1995
Sales ($ millions)	2.4	0.4
Net Income ($ millions)	(2.9)	(0.4)
Earnings Per Share ($)	(0.31)	(0.05)
No. of Shares (thou.)	9,582	8,595

www·cyberstocks·com

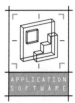

APPLICATION
SOFTWARE

VocalTec Ltd.

You can say "Shalom" to someone in Jerusalem for the price of an Internet connection. Israel-based VocalTec — which has its US head office in Northvale, New Jersey — is the #1 supplier of software that enables voice communications over the Internet, with 80% of the market. Its core product, Internet Phone, allows 2 Internet users to conduct a real-time conversation using their PCs without paying long distance charges, which has the phone companies a little uncomfortable. VocalTec's other products include Internet Conference, which enables users in remote locations to edit and create documents or images on their computer screens in real time over the Internet, and Internet Wave (I-Wave), which allows users to broadcast shows, lectures, and music in a high-quality audio format to Internet users worldwide.

Israeli army engineers Alon Cohen and Lior Haramaty met in 1988 and worked on one of the first text-to-speech systems that produced human-sounding speech, developed for the visually impaired under contract from the Israeli Ministry of Defense. They founded VocalTec in 1989. That year the company also developed the SpeechBoard 1001, one of the first digital soundboards for IBM PC compatibles. After bringing in entrepreneur Elon Ganor, the company added new products. In 1993 it released CAT (Compact Audio Technology), a peripheral device (connected through a PC's printer port) that provides audio recording and playback capabilities.

VocalTec released Internet Phone in 1995, the first software sold for users of PCs to transmit voice calls over the Internet. Motorola led a stampede of

- Pioneer and global leader in low-cost Internet telephony
- Has achieved broad distribution through retail, OEM, and Internet-direct channels
- New products enable PCs to call telephones as well as other PCs
- Business market remains largely untapped
- 1st half 1996 sales up 283%

- Has never been profitable
- Competes with many large and small companies, including Netscape, IBM
- The Internet is not friendly to time-sensitive applications such as voice communications
- Industry agreement on standards could commoditize Internet telephony products

VOCALTEC LTD.
HQ: One Maskit St.,
　　Herzliya, 46733, Israel
Phone: +972-9-562-121
Fax: +972-9-561-867
US HQ: 85 Industrial Pkwy.,
　　Northvale, NJ 07647
US Phone: 201-768-9400
US Fax: 201-768-8893
Web site: www.vocaltec.com

OFFICERS

Chairman and CEO: Elon A. Ganor, age 45
COO: Amil Tal, age 47
CFO and Secretary: Yahal Zilka, age 38
Chief Technology Officer: Alan Cohen, age 33
VP Technical Marketing:
　Lior Haramaty, age 29
VP Marketing: Daniel Nissan, age 29
VP International Sales:
　Ohad Finkelstein, age 35
Auditors: Andersen Worldwide

SELECTED PRODUCTS AND SERVICES

Internet Conference (enables users in remote locations to edit and create documents or images in real time over the Internet and corporate networks)

Internet Conference Professional (allows users to simultaneously edit, debate, and save changes to documents from within the applications that created them)

Internet Phone (voice communications product for PC users on the Internet)

Internet Phone Release for the MacOS (allows Macintosh and Windows Internet Phone users to talk to one another)

Internet Wave (I-Wave; gives organizations and individuals a way to broadcast shows, lectures, music, and more in a high-quality audio format to Internet users worldwide)

KEY COMPETITORS

AT&T	Intel	Progressive
Apple	Microsoft	Network
Camelot	Netscape	Quarterdeck
ForeFront	Northern	VDO Net
IBM	Telecom	Voxware
IDT		White Pine

high-tech manufacturers in signing license agreements with VocalTec to bundle Internet Phone with their products.

Haramaty and Cohen each own 7.7% of the company, which went public in 1996; an investment fund controlled by CEO Ganor and COO Ami Tal owns 15.6%. That year VocalTec teamed up with voice processing firm Dialogic to develop Internet Phone Telephony Gateway. This system, which is aimed at businesses that ring up large telephone bills calling offices outside the US, will enable people without access to a PC to make voice calls over the Internet via a telephone.

VOCALTEC: THE NUMBERS

Nasdaq symbol: VOCLF FYE: December 31	Annual Growth	1990	1991	1992	1993	1994	1995
Sales ($ mil.)	123.6%	—	0.1	0.1	0.3	0.4	2.5
Net income ($ mil.)	—	—	0.0	(0.1)	(0.6)	(1.4)	(1.4)
Income as % of sales	—	—	17.6%	—	—	—	—
Employees	—	—	—	—	—	—	47

1995 YEAR-END

Debt ratio: 100.0%
Return on equity: —
Cash (mil.): $2.1
Current ratio: 1.86
Long-term debt (mil.): $0.4
No. of shares (mil.): —
Dividends
　Yield: —
　Payout: —
Market value (mil.): —

QUARTER ENDED 6/30

	1996	1995
Sales ($ millions)	1.8	0.5
Net Income ($ millions)	(2.2)	(0.2)
Earnings Per Share ($)	(0.25)	(0.04)
No. of Shares (thou.)	8,613	6,015

6 MONTHS ENDED 6/30

	1996	1995
Sales ($ millions)	3.1	0.8
Net Income ($ millions)	(2.8)	(0.5)
Earnings Per Share ($)	(0.35)	(0.07)
No. of Shares (thou.)	8,613	6,015

STOCK PRICE HISTORY: High/Low/Close

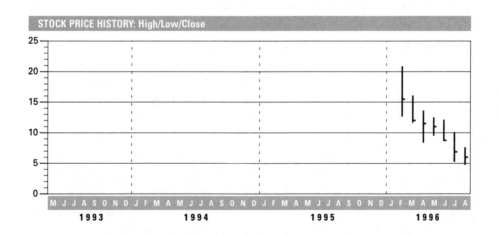

- Unquestioned leader in magazines covering the "digital revolution"

- Impressive subscription growth, great demographics

- Strong brand name

- Expanding into book publishing under the HardWired imprint

- First quarter 1996 revenues up 77%

- Mounting losses

- Postponed IPO when the market balked at a $415 million valuation

- Market usually assigns relatively low P/Es to magazine publishers

- Web-based HotWired appears to be losing more than $1 million per month

CONTENT

Wired Ventures, Inc.

When the world you're covering spins faster than a stock analyst's head at the mention of the word "Internet," you have got to be a little unconventional. San Francisco-based Wired Ventures has made a name for itself by chronicling the ever-changing, ever-growing online community. Reflecting the cyberculture it follows, the company's flagship magazine, *Wired*, offers irreverent but technologically savvy articles and a splashy graphic style that owes more to the fast-paced world of point-and-click than the traditional magazine layout. The company also offers an online version of its cyber-chronicle, HotWired, on the World Wide Web.

Wired Ventures is trying to expand its brand into other media, including books and television. To raise the cash for the move the company filed to go public in May 1996, hoping to take advantage of Wall Street's white hot interest in cyber-related stocks. The IPO valued the company at around $415 million. Following the offering, cofounders Louis Rossetto and Jane Metcalfe would own about 16% and 15%, respectively, and media holding company Advance Publications would own 11%.

Metcalfe and Rossetto attempted to publish a tech-culture magazine, *Electric Pencil*, in Europe in the 1980s, but the venture failed. They brought their idea to the US and recruited MIT Media Lab founder Nicholas Negroponte as a financial backer and eventual contributor. The magazine's first issue hit newsstands in 1993. By January 1994 it had over 110,000 paid subscribers, and in March of that year upscale magazine publisher Conde Nast bought a

WIRED VENTURES, INC.
HQ: 520 Third St., 4th Fl.,
San Francisco, CA 94107-1815
Phone: 415-222-6200
Fax: 415-222-6209
Web site: www.hotwired.com

OFFICERS

CEO; Editor and Publisher, *Wired*; Editor-in-Chief, HotWired:
Louis Rossetto, age 46, $88,558 pay

President:
Jane Metcalfe, age 34, $88,558 pay

CFO and Secretary:
Jeffrey Simon, age 34, $110,000 pay

VP Interactive:
Andrew Anker, age 32, $140,369 pay

VP Corporate and Business Development:
Rex O. Ishibashi, age 32, $110,000 pay

VP and Chief Technology Officer:
Jacquard W. Guenon

VP Operations: Todd Sotkiewicz

SELECTED PRODUCTS AND SERVICES

***Wired* Selected Features**
"Deductible Junkets" (information technology conferences)
"Electric Word" (technology news)
"Fetish" (product news)
"Geek Page" (changing technology news)
"Net Surf" (online directory)

Hotwired Selected Features
Cocktail (lounge culture)
Dreamjobs (career opportunities)
Pop (art, literature & music)
Webmonkey (browser enhancements)

Selected Hardwired Books
Digerati: Encounters with the Cyber Elite, by John Brockman
Wired Style: Principles of English Usage in the Digital Age, by the editors of *Wired*

KEY COMPETITORS

CMP Publications	Lycos	Upside Publishing
C|NET	McGraw-Hill	Verity
Excite	Mecklermedia	Wolff New Media
Hypermedia	Open Text	Yahoo!
InfoSeek International Data Group	Sendai Media Group	Ziff-Davis
	Simon & Schuster	

17% stake in the company. The magazine had a circulation of 240,000 for the US edition and another 30,000 for the UK edition by 1995.

Wired's online sister, HotWired, which features shorter info-bites and pieces not available in the magazine, debuted in 1994, receiving more than 100,000 connections and 4,000 subscribers its first day, growing to 235,000 subscribers the next year. HotWired is supported by advertisers — including IBM, Apple, and MCI — that pay approximately $15,000 per month. In 1996, HotWired unveiled Hotbot, a search engine that combs the complete text of all documents on the Web.

WIRED: THE NUMBERS

FYE: December 31	Annual Growth	1990	1991	1992	1993	1994	1995
Sales ($ mil.)	195.4%	—	—	—	2.9	9.2	25.3
Net income ($ mil.)	—	—	—	—	(1.0)	(3.5)	(6.5)
Income as % of sales	—	—	—	—	—	—	—
Employees	—	—	—	—	—	—	284

1995 YEAR-END

Debt ratio: 100.0%
Return on equity: —
Cash (mil.): $7.2
Current ratio: 0.9
Long-term debt (mil.): $1.2
No. of shares (mil.): —
Dividends
  Yield: —
  Payout: —
Market value (mil.): —

QUARTER ENDED 3/31

	1996	1995
Sales ($ millions)	7.6	4.3
Net Income ($ millions)	(3.4)	(2.4)
Earnings Per Share ($)	—	—
No. of Shares (thou.)	—	—

3 MONTHS ENDED 3/31

	1996	1995
Sales ($ millions)	7.6	4.3
Net Income ($ millions)	(3.4)	(2.4)
Earnings Per Share ($)	—	—
No. of Shares (thou.)	—	—

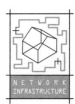 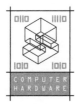

NETWORK INFRASTRUCTURE   COMPUTER HARDWARE

Xircom, Inc.

Xircom is a leading manufacturer of advanced networking products that connect portable PCs to LANs. The Thousand Oaks, California-based company's products include external and wireless LAN adapters and network interface cards (NICs). Cofounders Kirk Mathews and Dirk Gates each owns 10.3% of Xircom.

Mathews (former chairman of Pertron, a controls maker) and Gates (then a 27-year-old computer wunderkind and Pertron employee) founded Xircom in 1988. The company was formed out of an idea for connecting portable computers to networks via the parallel port. Gates's fellow students in his (uncompleted) MBA course helped him design the company, and within a year of the firm's launch, Xircom (named after "Kirk" and "Dirk" and "communications") was shipping products in volume. Xircom had 300 external LAN adapters made and sold them all at its first trade show.

The company has grown by catering to 2 growth areas: portable PCs and LANs. By connecting the 2, Xircom allows portable PC users to leave the office and still be able to plug into their company's local-area network. With competition heating up, Xircom continues to develop new products. In 1993 Xircom launched Netwave, a cordless LAN connectivity product that can support 20 mobile PC users within a 150-foot radius. After technical delays the product received FCC clearance in 1994. Also in 1994 the

- A leader in laptop NICs and modems
- Laptop NIC market has been forecast to grow at 70% annually through 2000
- Positioned to benefit from growth in Fast Ethernet
- Gross margin appears to have stabilized
- Has brought manufacturing in-house, lowered expense levels
- Has returned to profitability

- Quarter-to-quarter sales performance has been erratic
- Competition is intensifying in laptop NICs
- Change in pricing strategy has lowered gross margins substantially
- Appears to be losing market share in NICs
- Sales of new remote access products remain low

Xircom

XIRCOM, INC.
HQ: 2300 Corporate Center Dr.,
Thousand Oaks, CA 91320-1420
Phone: 805-376-9300
Fax: 805-376-9311
Web site: www.xircom.com

OFFICERS

Chairman: J. Kirk Mathews, age 52
President and CEO:
Dirk I. Gates, age 33, $312,449 pay
EVP; General Manager, Wireless Products:
Kenneth J. Biba, age 44, $228,965 pay
VP Worldwide Sales:
Russell J. Dopson, $241,864 pay
VP Finance and Administration and CFO:
Jerry N. Ulrich, age 40, $228,965 pay
VP Operations:
Robert W. "Sam" Bass, age 48, $212,746 pay
VP Corporate Communications and Marketing:
Thomas V. Brown, age 52
Director Human Resources: Ken Bauer
Auditors: Ernst & Young LLP

SELECTED PRODUCTS AND SERVICES

Selected Products
CreditCard LAN adapter (PCMCIA card adapter)
Ethernet+Modem (LAN adapter and high-speed modem)
Netwave (cordless LAN adapter)
Pocket LAN adapter (parallel-port LAN adapter)

	1995 Sales
	% of total
PC card LAN adapters	59
Ethernet+Modem products	23
Other	18
Total	**100**

KEY COMPETITORS

3Com
Artisoft
AsantA
AT&T GIS
Compaq
IBM
Madge
Microdyne
Motorola
National Semiconductor
NEC
Olicom USA
Shiva
Standard Microsystems
Texas Instruments
Toshiba

company's Ethernet+Modem, which provides mobile networking and fax capabilities, was introduced.

In 1995 Xircom formed strategic alliances with BellSouth and NEC. In mid-1995 Xircom acquired Primary Rate Inc. (PRI), a developer of products based on the integrated services digital network (ISDN) standard for data transmission. Charges related to that acquisition as well as lower margins on its PC card products pushed the company into the loss column in fiscal 1995.

In 1996 the company opened a plant in Panang, Malaysia.

XIRCOM: THE NUMBERS

Nasdaq symbol: XIRC FYE: September 30	Annual Growth	1990	1991	1992	1993	1994	1995
Sales ($ mil.)	65.5%	10.2	26.3	59.1	82.2	131.6	126.6
Net income ($ mil.)	—	1.2	2.5	6.1	9.7	15.9	(58.8)
Income as % of sales	—	12.0%	9.5%	10.3%	11.8%	12.1%	—
Earnings per share ($)	—	0.11	0.19	0.41	0.59	0.95	(3.44)
Stock price – high ($)	—	—	—	22.00	19.50	28.25	19.00
Stock price – low ($)	—	—	—	7.00	7.25	12.75	8.88
Stock price – close ($)	10.2%	—	—	9.25	17.00	17.75	12.38
P/E – high	—	—	—	54	33	30	—
P/E – low	—	—	—	17	12	13	—
Dividends per share ($)	—	—	—	0.00	0.00	0.00	0.00
Book value per share ($)	(6.3%)	—	—	3.42	3.99	5.10	2.81
Employees	118.7%	10	69	154	193	300	500

1995 YEAR-END

Debt ratio: 3.0%
Return on equity: —
Cash (mil.): $13.7
Current ratio: 1.82
Long-term debt (mil.): $0.8
No. of shares (mil.): 18.9
Dividends
 Yield: —
 Payout: —
Market value (mil.): $234.3
R&D as % of sales: 10.9%

QUARTER ENDED 6/30

	1996	1995
Sales ($ millions)	52.2	16.5
Net Income ($ millions)	2.5	(48.8)
Earnings Per Share ($)	0.13	(2.87)
No. of Shares (thou.)	19,562	17,018

9 MONTHS ENDED 6/30

	1996	1995
Sales ($ millions)	135.2	96.6
Net Income ($ millions)	3.1	(41.7)
Earnings Per Share ($)	0.16	(2.53)
No. of Shares (thou.)	19,562	17,018

STOCK PRICE HISTORY: High/Low/Close

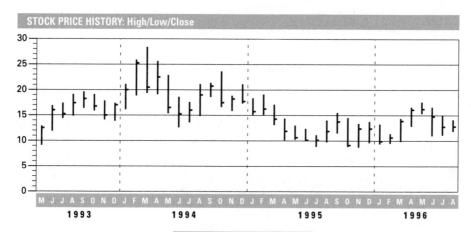

www·cyberstocks·com

- Pure Internet growth play

- Offers both directory and word search services

- Very strong and extensible brand name

- Targeted listings and advertising possible

- New alliance with AltaVista

- Adding content to differentiate service

- "Chief Yahoos" are aged 27 and 29

- Market cap of $500 million (8/96) vs. 1st half sales of $5 million.

- Several well-funded competitors

- Relatively low technical barriers to entry into market

- Unproven advertising-based business model

- Browser companies can influence traffic flow

- "Chief Yahoos" are aged 27 and 29

SPECIALIZED SERVICES

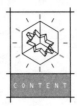

CONTENT

Yahoo! Inc.

In *Gulliver's Travels,* Yahoos were a dirty and backward people. Now they're trying to clean up on the Internet. Sunnyvale, California-based Yahoo! is one of the premier services for getting around the World Wide Web. Its free navigational guide is featured on several online networks and leading Web sites, including CompuServe, the Microsoft Network, and Pacific Bell Internet. Among companies providing content to Yahoo! are Ziff-Davis Publishing, Reuters New Media, and Rogers Communications. Yahoo! advertisers, including American Express, Discovery Channel Online, and Samsung, account for about 90% of its sales. Despite its meager revenues and minimal operating history, the company's estimated valuation at the time of its 1996 IPO was a staggering $300 million. The company went public in April 1996, offering 2.6 million shares (about 10%) at $13 per share. Investors screamed "Yahoo!" as the stock price rose to a high of $43 during its first day of trading and closed at $33, up 154% (2 months later the price had fallen to about $20). Following the offering, investment firm Sequoia Capital owned 21% of the company, and founders David Filo (whose title is Chief Yahoo and acting VP of engineering and operations) and Jerry Yang (who also has the Chief Yahoo title) each owned 19.5%. Other shareholders included Reuters New Media and SOFTBANK.

While graduate students at Stanford, Filo and Yang developed the Yahoo! (an acronym for "Yet Another Hierarchical Officious Oracle") search engine to compile a list of their favorite Internet sites. They set up their own Web index site in 1994, and it was soon being accessed by thousands of web surfers each day. Marc Andreessen, who had written the original Mosaic web browser and cofounded Netscape Communications, and Randy Adams,

YAHOO! INC.
HQ: 635 Vaqueros Ave.,
  Sunnyvale, CA 94086
Phone: 408-328-3300
Fax: 408-328-3301
Web site: www.yahoo.com

OFFICERS

President and CEO:
  Timothy Koogle, age 44, $68,750 pay

Chief Yahoo: Jerry Yang, age 27

Chief Yahoo and Acting VP Engineering and Operations:
  David Filo, age 29

SVP Business Operations:
  Jeff Mallett, age 31

SVP Finance and Administration and CFO:
  Gary Valenzuela, age 39

Auditors: Price Waterhouse LLP

SELECTED PRODUCTS AND SERVICES

Search Catagories
  Arts
  Business and Economy
  Computers and Internet
  Education
  Entertainment
  Government
  Health
  News
  Recreation
  Reference
  Regional
  Science
  Social Science
  Society and Culture

KEY COMPETITORS

America Online	Individual	Open Text
Compuserve	Infonautics	Wired Ventures
DEC	InfoSeek	Wolff New
Excite	Lycos	Media

president of the Internet Shopping Network, stepped in to help Filo and Yang commercialize the service. Yahoo! moved to corporate offices and hired Timothy Koogle, the former head of Intermec, a maker of data collection and data communications products, as president and CEO. Meanwhile, the company continued to add Web sites to its index — as many as 1,000 a day. In late 1995 Yahoo! and Ziff-Davis announced that they would codevelop products for delivery online, on CD-ROM, and in print.

By that time it was being accessed by about one million users a day. Yahoo! continues to expand its services, with Yahooligans!, an Internet navigation guide for children ages 8-14; Yahoo! Canada; Yahoo! Japan; and Yahoo! Internet Life, an online and print magazine that resulted from its Ziff-Davis partnership.

YAHOO!: THE NUMBERS

Nasdaq symbol: YHOO FYE: December 31	Annual Growth	1990	1991	1992	1993	1994	1995[1]
Sales ($ mil.)	—	—	—	—	—	—	1.4
Net income ($ mil.)	—	—	—	—	—	—	(0.6)
Income as % of sales	—	—	—	—	—	—	—
Employees	—	—	—	—	—	—	39

[1] 10-month fiscal year

1995 YEAR-END

Debt ratio: —
Return on equity: —
Cash (mil.): $5.3
Current ratio: 8.14
Long-term debt (mil.): $0.1
No. of shares (mil.): —
Dividends
 Yield: —
 Payout: —
Market value (mil.): —
R&D as % of sales: 17.8%
Advertising as % of sales: 9.2%

QUARTER ENDED 6/30

	1996	1995
Sales ($ millions)	3.3	0.0
Net Income ($ millions)	(1.4)	(0.4)
Earnings Per Share ($)	(0.05)	(0.02)
No. of Shares (thou.)	26,262	10,253

6 MONTHS ENDED 6/30

	1996	1995
Sales ($ millions)	5.0	0.0
Net Income ($ millions)	(1.3)	(0.4)
Earnings Per Share ($)	(0.06)	(0.02)
No. of Shares (thou.)	26,262	10,253

STOCK PRICE HISTORY: High/Low/Close

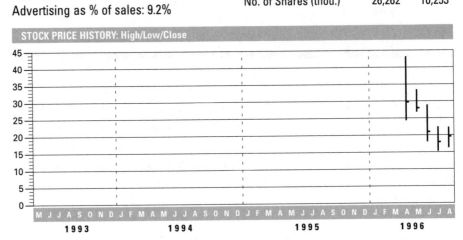

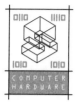
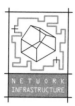

COMPUTER HARDWARE

NETWORK INFRASTRUCTURE

Zoom Telephonics,Inc.

Modem maker Zoom wants you to be able to talk and share data at the same time. The Boston-based company makes PC communications devices such as its ComStar Speakerphone/FaxModem, which can simultaneously send and receive voice and data over one phone line. Zoom is building its international sales and targeting OEMs amid the rising communications expectations of PC users around the world. Founders Frank Manning and Peter Kramer own about about 10% and 7% of the company, respectively. Pat Manning owns about 6%.

Manning and Kramer started Zoom in 1977 to sell speed dialers that Manning had designed while he was a student at MIT. The company marketed the dialers to customers of MCI and Sprint, who needed to dial a long string of numbers to access their long-distance services. In 1985 regulators eliminated the need for a long-distance access code; Zoom's sales plummeted, but they rebounded when the company changed gears and concentrated on making and selling modems.

Unable to find enough financing in the US, in 1988 Zoom went public on the Vancouver Stock Exchange. The company withdrew at the end of 1991, when it began trading on Nasdaq.

In 1993 Zoom began selling a modem that integrated voice processing and

- Is attempting to establish higher-margin business product lines
- Has entered the remote access market with Tribe acquisition
- Demand for modem and remote access products continues to boom
- Has achieved a very low cost structure
- European sales are strong

- Gross margins under pressure from:
  * Modem price cutting
  * Shift in sales mix toward OEM accounts (28% of sales in 2nd quarter 1996)
- Sales growth through retail channels appears to be slowing
- 5 customers accounted for 40% of sales in 1995

ZOOM TELEPHONICS, INC.
HQ: 207 South St., Boston, MA 02111
Phone: 617-423-1072
Fax: 617-338-5015
Web site: www.zoomtel.com

OFFICERS

Chairman, President, and CEO:
Frank B. Manning, age 47, $88,750 pay

EVP: Peter R. Kramer, age 44
VP Finance and CFO: Steven T. Shedd, age 43
VP Operations: Deena M. Randall, age 42
VP Engineering: Dana Whitney, age 33
VP Sales and Marketing:
Terry J. Manning, age 44

VP Strategic Business Development:
Eugene Chang, age 42

Chief Accounting Officer:
Stephen P. Golden, age 38

Director Human Resources: Marty Levin
Auditors: KPMG Peat Marwick LLP

SELECTED PRODUCTS AND SERVICES

External Fax/Modems
Zoom/FaxModem V.34X (28.8 kbps, Internet software)

Internal Fax/Modems
Internet Complete 28.8 (28.8 kbps, Internet software, Internet extras)

Zoom/ComStar 28.8 (28.8 kbps, Caller ID, full-duplex speakerphone, Internet software, Plug & Play)

Zoom/ComStar V.34 (33.6 kbps, digital answering machine, full-duplex speakerphone, simultaneous voice and data, speed dialer, voice mail, and VoiceView, which allows a quick switch between voice and data mode)

PCMCIA
Zoom PCMCIA V.34C (28.8 Kbps, Internet software)

KEY COMPETITORS

Active Voice	Global Village	NCR
Apex Data	GVC	Oki
Boca Research	Technologies	Racal Electronics
Brooktrout	Hayes	System
Technology	Microcomputer	Connection
DATA RACE	Motorola	U.S. Robotics
Diamond	Multi-Tech	
Multimedia	Systems	

fax technology; it entered the fast-growing PCMCIA (also known as PC card) modem market in 1994.

The next year the company introduced HotScan as a feature on its new Zoom/Voice FaxModem, enabling a fax machine to be used as a computer scanner. In 1996 the company entered the remote access market via its acquisition of Tribe Computer Works.

ZOOM TELEPHONICS: THE NUMBERS

Nasdaq symbol: ZOOM FYE: December 31	Annual Growth	1990	1991	1992	1993	1994	1995
Sales ($ mil.)	49.5%	13.0	25.6	41.9	55.2	68.2	97.0
Net income ($ mil.)	32.4%	1.5	2.3	3.6	3.8	2.8	6.1
Income as % of sales	—	11.5%	9.0%	8.6%	6.9%	4.1%	6.3%
Earnings per share ($)	29.4%	0.27	0.40	0.62	0.63	0.47	0.98
Stock price – high ($)	—	3.00	16.25	18.25	20.00	14.25	20.75
Stock price – low ($)	—	2.00	3.13	9.63	9.75	5.88	6.75
Stock price – close ($)	45.8%	3.00	15.75	17.25	11.25	7.88	19.75
P/E – high	—	11	41	29	32	30	21
P/E – low	—	7	8	16	15	13	7
Dividends per share ($)	—	0.00	0.00	0.00	0.00	0.00	0.00
Book value per share ($)	52.1%	0.54	1.02	1.94	2.70	3.21	4.40
Employees	38.6%	49	75	97	110	165	251

1995 YEAR-END

Debt ratio: 8.4%
Return on equity: 26.0%
Cash (mil.): $0.2
Current ratio: 2.08
Long-term debt (mil.): $0.0
No. of shares (mil.): 6.0
Dividends
  Yield: —
  Payout: —
Market value (mil.): $122.5
R&D as % of sales: 1.9%

QUARTER ENDED 6/30

	1996	1995
Sales ($ millions)	21.1	17.1
Net Income ($ millions)	0.3	1.1
Earnings Per Share ($)	0.04	0.18
No. of Shares (thou.)	7,260	6,015

6 MONTHS ENDED 6/30

	1996	1995
Sales ($ millions)	54.4	37.5
Net Income ($ millions)	2.5	2.2
Earnings Per Share ($)	0.36	0.37
No. of Shares (thou.)	7,260	6,015

STOCK PRICE HISTORY: High/Low/Close

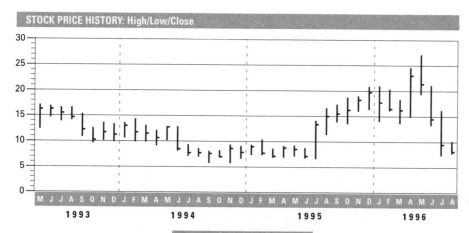

www·cyberstocks·com

Cyberstocks

VI. INDEX

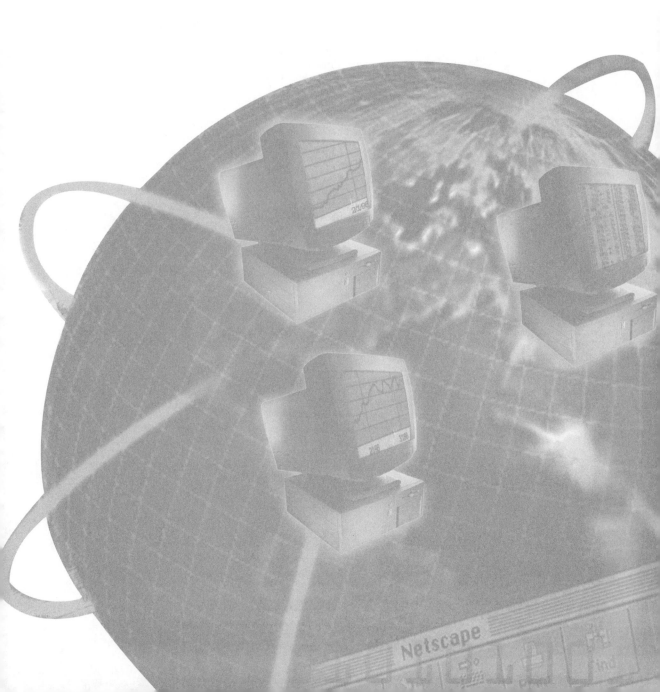

Index

Index

Index

Index